Income Distribution Theory

Income Distribution Theory

Family, Social Values, and Work Incentives

Tsuneo Ishikawa

UNIVERSITY OF TOKYO PRESS

Printed in Japan

ISBN 4-13-047066-3

ISBN 0-8600-8528-7

Contents

Foreword

Tsuneo Ishikawa was professor of economics at University of Tokyo when he died in 1998 at the age of 51. The loss of a brilliant economist and dedicated teacher at such a young age has been devastating for us. His untimely death is all the more regrettable, for had he lived, he would have contributed more significantly to both research and teaching. His contributions to the field of income distribution, labor, and savings were numerous and important. To honor his life and work, we have collected his papers in this memorial volume. It is our sincere wish that they will be read by many readers throughout the world.

Ishikawa was born in 1947 and completed his undergraduate education in economics at University of Tokyo. The influence of his father, a professor of economics at Hitotsubashi University, was strong in young Ishikawa's choice of major. He continued his postgraduate studies in the United States for two reasons. One was the student movement of the late 1960s, which disrupted classes and research at University of Tokyo. The other important reason was that he had lived in the United States during his childhood and wished to return to the country of which he had fond memories.

From 1969, he attended Johns Hopkins University and in 1972 obtained his Ph.D. He then taught at Harvard University as assistant professor for three years. At Johns Hopkins he came under the strong influence of Jurg Niehans and at Harvard of Kenneth Arrow.

In 1975, he returned to Japan to take a position at University of Tokyo and in 1988 was promoted as professor. There, he met two teachers and colleagues who were to be influential in his intellectual development: Ryutaro Komiya and Hirofumi Uzawa.

Ishikawa's research was published in English in such recognized journals as *Review of Economic Studies*, *Journal of Political Economy*, and *Quarterly Journal of Economics*. These were important theoretical papers based on his Ph.D. thesis, an indication of the high quality of his thesis.

After returning to Japan, he developed an interest in empirical studies and began publishing not only in theoretical but in empirical fields by applying large-scale individual data. We believe that he sought to put his theoretical ideas to test and see whether they could be supported empirically by data. Although he never described himself as an econometrician, the quality of his empirical analyses was such that he attracted the attention of many contemporary economists of the Japanese economy.

The papers collected in this volume reflect Ishikawa's thoughts on the economy as well as on society in general because it was his belief that humanistic considerations were important in any scientific work. We cherish the memory of Ishikawa's genial and sincere personality and hope that readers will benefit not only from his contributions to the field but also his humanistic attitude toward society.

Publication of this volume was supported by the Ishikawa Memorial Fund. We are grateful to Katsuhito Iwai and Masahiro Okuno who initiated the fund. Needless to say, all contributors to the fund are its principal executors. Asami Tokuda, Hiromi Hara, Mamiko Ishiwara, and Ryo Kambayashi assisted in various ways to the publication of this book. Nina Raj and Takuya Kuroda of University of Tokyo Press were helpful in editing and producing this book. Their assistance is gratefully acknowledged.

Yuji GENDA
Konosuke ODAKA
December 2000 Toshiaki TACHIBANAKI

I. Human Investment, Education, and Learning

1. Conceptualization of Learning by Doing: A Note on Paul David's "Learning by Doing and ... the Ante-Bellum United States Cotton Textile Industry"

The application of the notion of learning by doing to account for the measured input efficiency growth of an aggregation of production units admittedly creates worrisome ambiguities about exactly what was being "learned," how, and by whom.
—Paul A. David (1970: 562)

1. Introduction

In a recent article, Professor David (1970) has reexamined Taussig's classic discussion of the effectiveness of tariff protection of the ante-bellum cotton textile industry. His query can be restated as follows: granting Taussig's description that the U.S. cotton industry had reached its technological frontier and thus "graduated" from its infancy by 1824, was there any ground left for justification of its continued tariff protection? Professor David followed the familiar theoretical discourse pertaining to the existence of externalities in production—as caused by economies of scale that are external to each firm, or learning by doing, which provides inappropriable benefits to others—as an excuse for protection. His econometric findings, on the one hand, turned against the presence of economies of scale, but, on the other hand, confirmed the presence of learning by doing. The adoption of cumulated time of firms' operations rather than cumulated output of firms as the appropriate measure of learning led him to conclude that blanket subsidization through tariffs was redundant and that protection could have been provided effectively by the much cheaper method of establishing pilot firms.

Originally published in *The Journal of Economic History* 33, no. 4 (December 1973): 851–60.

Apart from the reliability of his statistical results, which will be taken for granted in the following discussion,[1] there are two major issues to be examined. The first is the validity of his choice of cumulated time of firms' operations as the measure of learning; the second is the cogency of his case for pilot firms relative to that for tariff protection. While I do not find Professor David's choice to be satisfactorily grounded, I shall leave my comments on this issue to a footnote,[2] and, in the main text, concentrate on the second issue. Specifically, I shall argue that his pilot firms case rests upon a particular but rather ambiguous conceptualization of learning by doing, and a clearer conception of learning-by-doing processes may provide cases for which tariff protection may be justified on second-best grounds.[3] Finally, that a certain type of learning by doing might, in fact, have enhanced the productivity of the cotton textile industry significantly during the period concerned is suggested as a hypothesis to be further examined.

2. Conceptualization of Learning by Doing

Let us start by reflecting over the meaning of the production function of integrated textile firms, which Professor David postulates in his study (1970: 540):[4]

$$X = A(G, \tau)\, F(K, L, M). \qquad (1)$$

There are two assumptions in this model. First, within the existing framework of technical and managerial knowledge, a textile output (X) is produced by three basic inputs, capital services (K), labor services (L), and purchased materials (mainly raw cotton) (M), and that the value of the production function (1) represents the volume of output for given levels of inputs with technical and organizational optimization being achieved, i.e., with the firm producing on the efficient production frontier. Second, development of technical and managerial knowledge either by the learning-by-doing factor (G) or by some exogenous factors (τ) augments the efficiency of all inputs uniformly at the rate $A(G, \tau)$. The learning-by-doing component of $A(G, \tau)$ may reflect various types of knowledge obtained through experience. However, as the following quotation shows,

> Where the learning process involves experimental determination of optimum plant layouts, or work organization, or operating speeds and machinery maintenance schedules, or similar best-practice information that can be introduced rather straightforwardly elsewhere—perhaps by managers, superintendents, and foremen initially trained in the "pilot" establishments—the effect

> upon industry-wide level of productivity deriving from the growth of cumulated output in those few leading establishments is likely to be very potent. (David, 1970: 537)

the content of learning by doing as conceptualized by Professor David consists mostly of technical and managerial know-how which, rather than being internalized within firms,[5] spills over to other firms largely through the movement of "technical-managerial cadre."[6]

There are two aspects of what Professor David refers to as learning by doing. The first pertains to discoveries of new technical and managerial know-how (a "factor of production" implicit in the production function [1][7]), which generate a new and the foremost technological frontier for the whole industry. This process of discovering seems to be the primary role of the putative pilot firms. Let us supply the symbol N to represent some index of technical-managerial know-how, and furthermore designate the process of achieving a new technological frontier through the discovery of new know-how (N) as *Process N*. The second pertains to the transmission of new technical and managerial know-how acquired within a production unit to other production units in the industry rather than discovery of new know-how itself. This aspect is clearly suggested by the following quotation:

> Now there is ample reason to expect precisely such redundancies if much of the commercial and technical knowledge gained by pioneer enterprises were placed at the disposal of new entrants, or by the ability of entrants to simply mimic observable business procedures established by the pioneers, without immediately grasping the underlying rationale. (David, 1970: 586)

These two aspects of learning—discovery and transmission—however, are not clearly distinguished by Professor David. The confusion is most apparent in his discussion of the learning units. In his study, firms and not mills are regarded as unit learning entities: "it should be evident that in a long-run context, where physical facilities as well as production personnel may be changed, it is the firm rather than the mill that must be regarded as the relevant 'learning entity.'" (David, 1970: 562–63) Professor David's contention in this statement may be justified if our main interest lies in the *transmission* of new information. However, if we are interested in the *discovery* of new information, mills and even individual production processes within each mill may also become the *relevant* units of discovery, especially for those types of know-how related to the operations of mills. The failure to distinguish these two aspects provides one important source of ambiguity in Professor David's whole discussion.[8]

Now we have come to the main argument of this paper. So long as acquired know-how is transferable either through movement of personnel, instruction, or imitation, repetitive discoveries (and, in this specific sense, repetitive learning) of the same knowledge become indeed redundant, as Professor David suggests in the above quotation (1970: 586).[9] Encouragement of repetitive learning by means of tariffs then becomes grossly ineffective and the appropriate public policy is to clear away any obstacles to the smooth transmission of information within the industry. However, this very point which Professor David presents as the primary ground for the case for pilot firms does not in itself support its case, nor does he provide persuasive evidence and rationales as to why confinement of learning processes to a few leading firms is enough to bring out all potentially significant discoveries. Two criticisms are in order.

First, apart from deliberate research activities, discovery of new knowledge by managers and technicians seems to originate in the occasions in which technicians and managers perceive certain circumstances of production activities as problematical, and then make efforts themselves to solve the problem thus raised.[10] As mentioned above, some discoveries related to the know-how of production processes and the organization of mills may be effected on a mill level, while others related to the organization of a firm as a whole may be discovered only at the firm level. Since (a) the occurrence of circumstances which, if perceived, may potentially lead to innovation, (b) attention by technicians and managers—(a) and (b) constitute preconditions for a new discovery—and (c) discovery of solutions are all highly (if not purely) probabilistic matters, we naturally expect that the larger the magnitude of production experience (as, for instance, measured by current or cumulated output) and the number of learning units (plants and firms), the greater the number of new discoveries likely to result.[11] Moreover, since technical change in reality does not necessarily proceed in a continuous manner, there is no particular reason why new knowledge should not come out of "average practice" firms.[12] Under these circumstances, there still remains room for tariff protection as an effective means of enhancing discovery of new technical and managerial know-how.

Second, although Professor David has confined the contents of learning by doing principally to technical and managerial know-how, another type of learning by doing which gives external benefits to others is conceivable—discoveries of major or minor improvements in spinning and weaving machines. Just as in the case of technical and managerial know-how, it seems plausible to suppose that there exists a certain probability distribution for the discovery of new machine designs associated with production activities of each plant or firm and that it is independent of or positively correlated with those for other plants or firms. Let us designate this case as *Process K*.[13] This process may arise through two sources: (A) learning in textile machine shops within each plant—the process of *producing* capital goods; and (B) suggestions from experience in the spinning and weaving shops within each plant—the process of *using* capital goods[14] (because machine shops and spinning and weaving shops are integrated[15]). It can then be argued that stimulation of textile goods production and setting up new textile plants by means of tariff protection encourage discoveries of improvements in machinery not only directly through the *Process K-B*, but also indirectly through the joint functioning of the price mechanism (contrary to Professor David's contention)[16] and the *Process K-A*. Thus, to conclude, under the conditions that (i) the probability of obtaining new information is positively related to the production experience as measured by current or cumulated output of production units, (ii) occurrence of discoveries is not confined to leading establishments, and (iii) the new information obtained can be easily transmitted to other production units, the *Processes K-A* and *K-B* as well as the *Process N* provide grounds for the justification of tariff protection as an effective means to increase the opportunities through which discovery of new information is made.[17]

3. Hypothetical Explanation of Productivity Growth

Above, I have discussed the learning processes through which technological progress is achieved and the conditions under which tariff protection may possibly be justified. In order to answer whether or not the actual circumstances of the antebellum New England cotton textile industry satisfied those conditions[18] and whether or not the processes suggested above were really relevant to them, a detailed but interesting historical study seems to be required. At this point, I shall merely add a few remarks concerning the possible relevance of the above processes in explaining the steady growth of labor productivity observed in this industry.

The New England cotton textile industry during the period concerned exhibited the following features: (a) As compared with the revolutionary changes in the technological and organization structure resulting from the introduction of power looms preceding this period, technical change was characteristically less dramatic; however, textile machinery underwent innumerable improvements.[19] (b) The composition of machine operatives underwent a dramatic change from the relatively well-cultured young women recruited from rural farms to largely illiterate immigrant operatives.[20]

First, rather than treating the improvements in textile machinery as exogenously given, as supposed by Professor David (1970: 553), it seems more appropriate to attribute them to the working of the forces of learning by doing, specifically our *Processes K-A* and *K-B*. Second, as noted by Gibb and McGouldrick, the improvements in machinery may have been influenced by the efforts to adjust to the changes in the character of skilled as well as unskilled workers,[21] and such circumstances may be interpreted as belonging to our *Processes K-B* and *N*. Thus the steadily increasing labor productivity during this period as reported by Davis and Stettler and McGouldrick[22] may be explained largely by the possibility that new technical and managerial know-how and improvements in machinery as developed by our *Processes K-A*, *K-B*, and *N* acted to augment the efficiency of laborers in a disembodied form,[23] thereby offsetting any direct loss in efficiency as caused by the change in labor composition.[24] The continued tariff protection may have been helpful in stimulating the processes noted here. This is a hypothesis whose validation requires further study.

In view of all these considerations, Professor David's study, carefully done as it is, seems to fail in exhausting the full implications of learning by doing, and his pilot firms case does not stand on firm ground. The vindication of the Taussigian free trade position pertaining to the case of the antebellum cotton textile industry is still far from complete.

NOTES

This paper is an outgrowth of my study in Professor Paul Uselding's seminar in American Economic History at Johns Hopkins University. My hearty thanks are due to him, for had it not been for his helpful comments and encouragement this paper would never have materialized. I am also very grateful to Professors Stanley Engerman, Nathan Rosenberg, and an anonymous referee for their valuable comments and criticisms on the earlier versions of this paper.

1. For further econometric discussion of Professor David's paper, see Jeffrey G. Williamson (1972) and Paul A. David (1972). The thrust of my argument, however, is not affected by either of those papers.

2. Confronted by the almost equal statistical performance of the two alternative hypotheses of learning by doing, the cumulated output and the cumulated time hypotheses, Professor David bases his choice of the latter on the following two major considerations (David, 1970: 573–85). (i) In consideration of relatively strong imperfections (oligopsony) in the labor market, the real wages paid are expected to be less than the marginal physical product; thus the wage share should be less than the estimated output elasticity coefficient for labor. However, Zevin's finding that the two are almost identical for his sample firm (i.e., Blackstone Company) (around 0.41) under the cumulated output hypothesis implies a rejection of the cumulated output hypothesis. On the contrary, the estimated value of the output elasticity coefficient for labor under the cumulated time hypothesis is consis-

tent with this "exploitation" interpretation. Furthermore, the estimated labor elasticity coefficients for the two different sets of sample data under the cumulated time hypothesis are "very close" (à la Professor David) to each other (0.66 and 0.59), which is *as it should be*, since constant returns to scale are observed statistically and the Blackstone Company and other sample firms are similar in character. (ii) While the estimated magnitude of the learning coefficient under the cumulated time hypothesis is reasonable—doubling of experience gives about 20 percent increase in productivity—the estimated magnitude of that under the cumulated output hypothesis is far smaller than the figure above suggested by past studies.

The following comments seem pertinent to Professor David's argument. First, we must admit the fact that there is no unanimity in the literature with regard to the existence of monopsony elements. (For instance, Paul M. McGouldrick argues that there may have been rather strong competitiveness in the labor market: see McGouldrick [1968: 34–38]). Even if we assume the existence of the monopsony elements, however, his argument that the similarity of the estimated elasticity coefficients for labor between the two sample bodies is another piece of strong evidence for the cumulated time hypothesis to be seriously qualified. In fact, the very test which Professor David reports in footnote 73 (1970: 573)—to the effect that the output elasticity coefficients for labor for the two samples are not identical statistically—indicates that the two sample bodies do not come from the same population. His interpretation of this "inconvenient" result (idem, 1970: 573), namely, the attribution of the cause of this difference to the shift in the sampling intervals of the two sets of data, is not correct, for both statistical models assume that each time series consists of stochastically independent sample points; otherwise, his argument concerning the similarity of the estimated elasticity coefficients itself loses its meaning. (For a criticism of this assumption, see footnote 12 below.) Professor David's second argument ([ii] above) is no more cogent than the first. This is because the particular magnitudes of learning coefficients observed for a particular industry during a particular period have nothing to do with those observed in others.

In view of the points discussed above, Professor David's choice of the cumulated time hypothesis over the cumulated output hypothesis is not persuasive. On the other hand, the study of Professor Williamson (1972) also fails to provide cogent grounds for his choice of the cumulated output hypothesis. We are thus left with the two production models with the productivity growth largely explained by the two learning indexes whose correlation coefficient is 0.999 (David, 1970: 574n76).

3. The notion of second best used here concurs with Professor David's usage on page 528, which refers to the discussion of optimal intervention against domestic distortions. Cf. Jagdish Bhagwati and V.K. Ramaswami (1963); Harry G. Johnson (1965). These authors have noted that in the presence of domestic distortions tariff policy may not be the optimal mode of intervention; but it may nonetheless help to rectify the distortion partially if not completely. In this very sense, I use the word *second best*, and I shall thus discuss the effectiveness of the tariff policy in this weak sense only.

4. As will be discussed further below, Professor David regards firms and not mills (plants) as unit learning entities. Thus the production function (1) is defined at the firm level basically, although in the empirical part he applies it to the aggregation of firms.

5. In the case where know-how is specific to a firm, no justifiable grounds for protection exist so long as (a) accumulation of specific knowledge is the only learning-by-doing effect, (b) firms can correctly foresee such effects, and (c) the capital market is perfect (David, 1970: 529–30). For further theoretical discussion of this case, see Sherwin Rosen (1972). For the historical relevance of "perfection" in the capital market, see David (1970: 535).

6. Later (see the quotation from David, 1970: 586 below) Professor David adds imitation as another means of transmission. There is the following rather subtle point to note: Discovery of new knowledge is made by technical-managerial cadre, but the information thus acquired is *embodied* in the production routines and institutional arrangements of firms and mills. This implies, first, that know-how, once embodied in firms and mills, will remain in place even if the technicians or managers who discovered or introduced it originally might leave the firms or mills in question; in other words, they

cannot appropriate material ownership rights to this new information. Contrast this case with the case of ordinary workers in which skill leaves the firms with the departure of workers. Thus, insofar as transmission of information is concerned, technicians and managers function only as *mediators* (or more appropriately *catalyzers*) of the transmission process. This point, however, does not preclude the possibility that managers and technicians are remunerated for the knowledge they transmit and are also charged the cost of learning and training. In such cases no externalities are involved, and the logic of David (1970: 530n17) applies. The main source of externality, however, as we shall indicate below, lies in the *production* of new information. Another implication is that the information thus acquired is susceptible to *imitation* by others. The preceding interpretation makes his assumption of *irreversibility* of "learning" consistent with his notion that know-how is carried around by technicians and managers among the firms. And indeed, if there is no permanent obstacle to the transmission of knowledge and also if there is no further discovery of new knowledge, then the level of know-how (N) of each firm which survives in the industry will after a certain time lag be equalized perfectly.

7. In this connection Professor David's terms "average practice" and "best practice," seemingly following the usage of Anne P. Gross (1953: esp. 402–20), are by no means clearly defined concepts. Here we interpret the distinction between them to reflect differences in the amount and content of technical and managerial know-how, assuming that the forementioned technicians and organizers' optimization procedures—the process to reach the efficient frontier—is achieved sufficiently rapidly so that what we are comparing are, in fact, the positions of two efficient frontiers.

8. I am grateful to Professor Stanley Engerman for questioning whether we should regard the *pilot firm* or the *pilot plant* as the relevant unit of learning. The consideration of this question led me to the point raised here.

9. "There is no gain in acquiring the same information twice," in Kenneth J. Arrow (1969: 30).

10. For a closely related discussion, see Adam Smith, *The Wealth of Nations* (1880), Book I: 10–11.

11. Thus, so far as discovery of new information is concerned, the cumulated output measure of firms or mills seems to have much more relevance than the cumulated time measure. The passage of Zevin as quoted by Professor David (1970: 543) also fails to provide a sufficiently cogent argument for the relevance of the cumulated time measure. Zevin's logic (in the last sentence of the quoted passage) applies mostly to the transmission process of already acquired information but not to the discovery of new information itself.

12. Professor David (1970: 562) writes:

> "And if, as therefore seems most probable, efficiency gains largely reflected changes in best-practice methods that spread rapidly among this collection of mills, it is also reasonable to think that a substantial number of those improvements derived from the experience being acquired by these leading firms, rather than from 'learning' that was taking place elsewhere in a less progressive segment of the industry."

He gives no substantial evidence for his assertion. Confirmation of his statement requires detailed historical studies concerning the relationship between innovative capacities of firms or plants and the measure of "leadingness," such as the size of a firm or that of a plant. For some evidence to the effect that innovations do not necessarily come from leading firms, see George S. Gibb (1950: 14, 40, 76–77, 192), especially pp. 76–77 where he concludes:

> "Between 1825 and 1845, American textile machinery was immeasurably improved. Many inventions or adaptations of great value and universal application were made. The strange fact about these inventions is, however, that few of them originated in Lowell, in this period the greatest textile-manufacturing center in the country."

and:

"The fact remains that in this period many new machines equal or superior to those developed earlier at Waltham were being built by machine shops outside Lowell—and even outside New England."

Even if, contrary to Gibb's remark, it generally turns out that the probability distribution of discovery of new information per experience unit is favorably biased for the more advanced firms, this mere fact does not imply that the "average-practice" firms need not be protected unless the latter's probability distribution is close to nil. Moreover, the same fact by no means discredits the innovative efficiency of multi-plant operations.

Somewhat related to the preceding argument is Professor David's proposition: "... the acquisition of further experience in the industry through multiplication of the number of similarly situated firms proved less effective in reducing costs than an equivalent rate of addition in the years of experience of a small cadre of pioneer, or 'pilot enterprise.'" (David, 1970: 585–86) His proposed evidence to the effect that the learning coefficient for a single Blackstone firm is larger than that for a six-firms aggregate, even though possible aggregation bias is taken into account (ibid.: 586–91), seems superficial and also logically unsatisfactory. (Here I shall grant, for the sake of argument, the relevance of the cumulated time hypothesis—note that in the case of the cumulated output hypothesis, there is little difference between the estimated learning coefficients for two sample bodies. See ibid.: 565, Table 3.) This is because the two sample bodies can hardly be regarded as isolated from each other, and, hence, the two "learning" processes cannot be regarded as independent of each other. In fact, it is conceivable that the Blackstone firm might have required the experience of the six firms as an essential step in acquiring new knowledge. In such a case comparison of two learning coefficients on the assumption that the two are based on independent experiments cannot be justified.

13. In general we may suppose that the production function is given by

$$X = F^{\circ}([K], [L], [M], N; \tau) \qquad (2)$$

where [K], [L], [M] represent various vintages of capital, labor and material, and where N and τ represent the level of know-how and the exogenous technical progress factor. We can then suppose learning by doing generates embodied technical changes in labor and material, say, *Processes L* and *M*, as well as in capital goods, *Process K*, as suggested in the text.

However, first, the changes in the quality of materials are conditioned largely by factors outside textile mills and therefore we may leave the *Process M* outside the scope of the present consideration. Second, before the arrival of immigrant workers the character of labor force (especially in Massachusetts mills) was temporary, and in a way, the industry was constantly engaged in the training of newcomers. For instance, Caroline F. Ware (1931: 13) summarily states: "The result was a large body of unskilled labor continually drifting into mills, forming a stream of fresh, vigorous country workers rather than a permanent worker class." See also ibid.: 64–65, 224–26; Nathan Appleton (1858: 15); and Samuel Batchelder (1863: 89). Therefore, the skills, if any, acquired and embodied in laborers did not remain permanently within the industry. Furthermore, although the revolutionary change in the labor composition did establish a permanent work force (Ware, 1931: 228–30), the generally unskilled nature of the operatives' work leads us to surmise that the *Process L*, if not totally irrelevant, was not very significant. These are the reasons why we concentrate our attention on the *Process K*.

We also note at this point that the fact that the two forms of technical progress—embodied and disembodied—are impossible to distinguish empirically (because the total productivity index and the price index of investment goods which is supposed to reflect the quality of new capital goods are in dual relationship) so that either one can be transformed into the other—Jorgenson's theorem—and, therefore, the two production functions (1) and (2) are empirically not distinguishable. This is not relevant since we are here concerned only with the conceptualization of technical change. Cf. Dale W. Jorgenson (1966).

14. Professor David (1970) does not see this possibility of direct linkage between the two sectors in his discussion on pp. 532–34.

15. David, 1970: 534. There also was a development of independent textile machinery shops such as Saco-Lowell machinery works and these specialized shops gradually dominated the machinery field. See Gibb, 1950: 21–22.

16. In his discussion of the "price effects" and the "income effects" of tariffs on machinery production, Professor David seems to forget that the demand for machines should be regarded as a *derived demand*. Thus when the tariff raises the price of textile products, the direct effect is to raise the rental price of machines, resulting in expansion of machine production—contrary to Professor David's assertion. Note that this picture is not affected by the fact that the firms concerned built their machinery in their own machine shops.

17. The conditions raised here are a part—albeit an important part—of the necessary conditions for the justification of tariffs. Full justification further requires, on the one hand, that the *real cost* of discovery through learning is not significantly large (cf. Robert Baldwin [1969]), and, on the other hand, that the textile industry during the period concerned deserves more protection than other industries—a broader question than the ones dealt with in this note. Our discussion so far assumes implicitly that there exists no significant distortion as caused by the similar learning-by-doing effect or other factors in any other part of the economy. On this point see David (1970: 531) and the literature referred to in his footnote 99. I am again indebted to Professor Engerman for stressing this point.

18. For some suggestive remarks as to condition (ii), see footnote 12 above. Somewhat related to condition (i) is the study made by Schmookler about the relationship between the magnitude of production and that of invention in the railroad industry. See Jacob Schmookler (1967: chs. IV–VI). Schmookler provides as alternative or, more appropriately, a complementary explanation to ours, namely that inventions are conditioned by inventors' consideration of profitability as reflected in the size of the market or output, to the observed positive correlation between these two variables.

Condition (iii) may be regarded as having been satisfied. Among all categories of workers especially machine workers wandered among firms in order to accumulate experience and obtain the best remunerative opportunity. This tendency was strong enough that it is recorded, for instance, that Lowell mills attempted to make a reciprocal arrangement to issue a "discharge certificate," conditioning members not to employ workers without certificate, which was issued to those employees who left the mills for reasons deemed "fair and adequate" by the former employers. It is also recorded, however, that this system apparently did not work well (Gibb, 1950: 88). See also Ware, 1931: 207–8, and David, 1970: 537–38.

19. Gibb (1950: 173) writes: "Before 1830 the incidence of revolutionary inventions was particularly high. After this time progress was less spectacular and, with important exceptions such as the self-acting mule and the ring spinning frame, manifested itself in the form of innumerable improvements of existing machine types. The cumulative effect of these improvements over the next two decades, however, was probably as profound as that produced by the sweeping changes of Paul Moody's day.... These innovations and improvements were the work not of scientists but of practical mechanics, working by trial-and-error methods."

See also L.E. Davis and H.L. Stettler (1966: 230), whose passage is quoted by David (1970: 527).

20. For the process and implications of this change, see Stephan Thernstrom (1964: ch. 1) and Ware, (1931: 109, 228–35).

21. Gibb notes "the recalcitrant attitude of certain groups of foreign skilled laborers" as an important stimulant to the introduction of automatic textile machinery (1950: 173). McGouldrick, on the other hand, suggests the following explanation to his finding that the period 1839–55 exhibited an increase in the capital/labor ratio: that is, in order to maintain work efficiency in the face of less qualified immigrant workers, various processes had to be broken down into simpler components that required more capital goods per man than before (McGouldrick, 1968: 39).

22. See Davis and Stettler (1966) and the comment made by McGouldrick (1966: 240).

23. This possibility is in fact incorporated as an assumption into various economic growth models with embodied technical change. E.g., Kenneth J. Arrow (1962) and Robert M. Solow (1962).

24. Ware records the report of an experiment performed by a manufacturer of the time showing very high work efficiency of women machine operatives who are recruited from the country farms. Ware, 1931: 201; see also p. 232.

REFERENCES

Appleton, Nathan. 1858. Introduction of the Power Loom and Origin of Lowell. Lowell, Mass.

Arrow, Kenneth J. 1962. The economic implications of learning by doing. Review of Economic Studies 29 (June): 155–73.

———. 1969. Classificatory notes on the production and transmission of technological knowledge. American Economic Review, Papers and Proceedings 59 (May): 29–33.

Baldwin, Robert. 1969. The case against infant-industry tariff protection. Journal of Political Economy 77 (May/June): 295–305.

Batchelder, Samuel. 1863. Introduction and Early Progress of the Cotton Manufactures in the United States. Boston: Little, Brown and Co.

Bhagwati, Jagdish, and V.K. Ramaswami. 1963. Domestic distortions, tariffs, and the theory of optimal subsidy. Journal of Political Economy 71 (Feb.): 44–50.

David, Paul A. 1970. Learning by doing and tariff protection: A reconsideration of the case of ante-bellum United States cotton textile industry. Journal of Economic History 30 (Sept.): 521–601.

———. 1972. The use and abuse of prior information in econometric history. Journal of Economic History 32 (Sept.): 706–27.

Davis, L.E., and H.L. Stettler. 1966. The New England textile industry, 1825–60: Trends and fluctuations. In Output, Employment and Productivity in the United States after 1800. Studies in Income and Wealth Series, vol. 30, National Bureau of Economic Research.

Gibb, George S. 1950. The Saco-Lowell Shops, Textile Machinery Building in New England 1813–1949. Cambridge, Mass.: Harvard University Press.

Gross, Anne P. 1953. The technological structure of the cotton textile industry. In Studies in the Structure of the American Economy, Wassily Leontief, 360–420. New York: Oxford University Press.

Johnson, Harry G. 1965. Optimal trade intervention in the presence of domestic distortions. In Trade, Growth and Balance of Payments, Robert Baldwin et al. Amsterdam: North Holland.

Jorgenson, Dale W. 1966. The embodiment hypothesis. Journal of Political Economy 74 (Feb.): 1–17.

McGouldrick, Paul 1966. Comment. In Output, Employment and Productivity in the United States after 1800, p. 240. Studies in Income and Wealth Series, vol. 30, National Bureau of Economic Research.

———. 1968. New England Textiles in the Nineteenth Century: Profits and Investment. Cambridge, Mass.: Harvard University Press.

Rosen, Sherwin. 1972. Learning by experience as joint production. Quarterly Journal of Economics 86 (Aug.): 366–82.

Schmookler, Jacob. 1967. Invention and Economic Growth. Cambridge, Mass.: Harvard University Press.

Smith, Adam. 1880. The Wealth of Nations. 2nd ed. Oxford: Clarendon Press.

Solow, Robert M. 1962. Substitution and fixed proportions in the theory of capital. Review of Economic Studies 29 (June): 207–18.

Thernstrom, Stephan. 1964. Poverty and Progress. Cambridge, Mass.: Harvard University Press.

Ware, Caroline F. 1931. The Early New England Cotton Manufactures. Boston and New York: Houghton Mifflin Co.

Williamson, Jeffrey G. 1972. Embodiment, disembodiment, learning by doing, and return to scale in nineteenth century cotton textiles. Journal of Economic History 32 (Sept.): 691–705.

2. A Note on the Optimal Spacing Properties in a Simple Jevonian Model of Educational Investment

In the frequently used simplified model of educational investment behavior that originates from Jevons's vintage capital model,[1] it is implicitly assumed that education is taken consecutively from the moment of an individual's economic birth. The main purpose of this note is to show that there are inherent optimal spacing properties within the surface structure of the simplified model; namely, even if we allow education to be taken in any intermittent manner, the optimum education program, under certain conditions, coincides with that of the basic model. This result links directly with the similar properties observed in the technically more sophisticated models of educational investment[2] and thus provides a rationalization for the use of such a simplified model.[3]

1. The Basic Model

Consider an individual who is economically born at age 0 and dies at age L. During the first J years (where J $[0 < J \leqq L]$ is given exogenously), he is endowed with an opportunity to invest his time resource in education, which increases his earning capacity. We assume that the individual can allocate his time between work and education only in a discrete manner; that is, during the period he takes education, he devotes his whole time available to education, and during the rest of his life he devotes his time wholly to work. We then assume that there exists a simple functional relationship between the annual wage earnings w, and the number of years of education taken E, $w = w(E)$, which will be referred to as the earnings capacity schedule. We assume that this

Originally published in *The Quarterly Journal of Economics* 89 (Nov. 1975): 633–42.

function is twice continuously differentiable and that[4]

$$w'(E) > 0, w''(E) < 0 \quad \text{for } 0 \leqq E < \infty, \text{ and } w'(0) = \infty. \tag{1}$$

Finally, we assume that there exists a perfect capital market and that the market rate of interest is expected to remain constant at the level r.

It is a familiar result that the optimal length of education for an individual who regards education purely as an investment opportunity and thus maximizes the present value of the future earnings stream,[5]

$$V(E;L) = \int_E^L w(E) \cdot e^{-rt}\, dt = \frac{w(E)}{r} \cdot (e^{-rE} - e^{-rL}) \tag{2}$$

is given by $\min\{E^*(L), J\}$, where $E^*(L)$ is defined by

$$\frac{w'(E^*(L))}{w(E^*(L))} = \frac{r \cdot e^{-rE^*(L)}}{e^{-rE^*(L)} - e^{-rL}}. \tag{3}$$

As a comparative static property we note that[6]

$$\frac{\partial E^*(L)}{\partial L} > 0, \quad \frac{\partial (L - E^*(L))}{\partial L} > 0. \tag{4}$$

2. The Extended Model

The above discussion has been based on an implicit assumption that education is taken consecutively from the moment of economic birth. A priori there is no justification for such an assumption. However, we shall show that, under certain conditions, the above conclusion holds true even within the framework where an individual can take education in any intermittent manner.

Consider now the case where an individual can take any finite number of intermissions in schooling during which he works and earns on the basis of an already acquired level of attributes in the education process. First, we assume that the annual wage earnings depend only on the total number of years of schooling and, specifically, not on whether or not schooling is taken consecutively. Therefore, the earnings capacity schedule continues to hold with a reinterpretation of E as the sum of the years of schooling already taken. Second, we assume that the educational investment is sufficiently productive so that the discounted value of annual wage earnings after the education of maximum feasible length, J $(0 < J \leqq L)$, is taken is larger than the annual wage earnings that are to be obtained if no education is ever taken at all, i.e.,

$$w(J) \cdot e^{-rJ} > w(0). \tag{5}$$

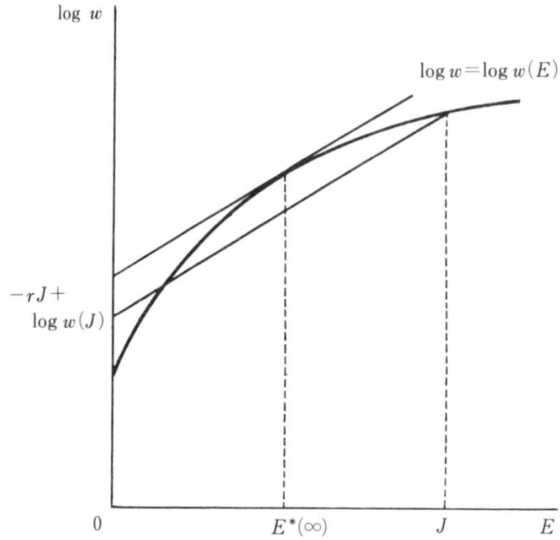

Figure 1

The characterization of the optimal education program under these assumptions (to be referred to hereinafter as the extended model) proceeds in two steps: first, we shall discuss the optimal spacing of education and earning, given the total length of education; second, we shall determine the optimal total length of education itself.

The answer to the optimal spacing problem turns out to depend crucially upon whether or not the total length of education E exceeds the value $E^*(\infty)$ defined (See Fig. 1.) by

$$\frac{w'(E^*(\infty))}{w(E^*(\infty))} = r. \tag{6}$$

This value $E^*(\infty)$ represents the length of education that would be taken within the framework of the basic model if the length of life span L were infinite and if $E^*(\infty) \leqq J$. From (4) it is greater than $E^*(L)$. Then we observe the following:

PROPOSITION 1. *For a given total length of education E such that $E \leqq J$ and $E \leqq E^*(\infty)$, the optimal spacing of education and earning is achieved if education is taken consecutively from the moment of economic birth, i.e., without any delay or intermissions.*

A proof of this proposition is given as follows. Suppose that the interval $[0, J]$ (in which education can be pursued) is partitioned into any finite number of intervals, say $[0, x_1], [x_1, x_2], \ldots, [x_i, x_{i+1}], \ldots,$

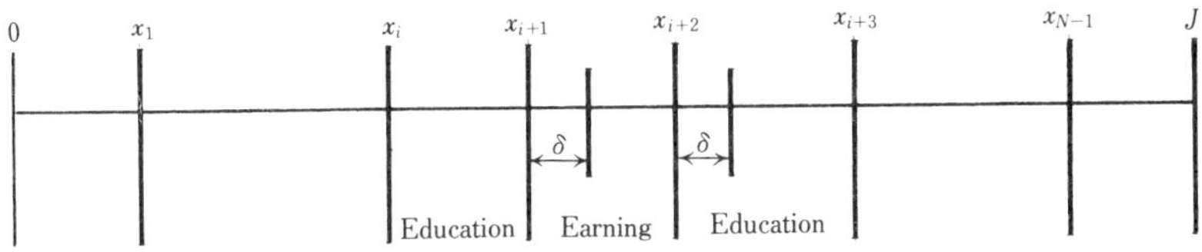

Figure 2

$[x_{N-1}, J]$, where each education interval is followed by an earning interval, and vice versa. (It does not matter which occupies the first interval $[0, x_1]$ and the last interval $[x_{N-1}, J]$.) Then consider any education interval, say $[x_i, x_{i+1}]$, which is followed by an earning interval $[x_{i+1}, x_{i+2}]$ and another education interval $[x_{i+2}, x_{i+3}]$. Take a small amount δ of schooling years from this last interval $[x_{i+2}, x_{i+3}]$ and add it to the interval $[x_i, x_{i+1}]$. (See Fig. 2.)

If we compare the present value of the earnings stream for the original $(i+2)$nd interval $[x_{i+1}, x_{i+2}]$ and that for the modified $(i+2)$nd interval $[x_{i+1}+\delta, x_{i+2}+\delta]$, then the former is expressed by

$$v_0 = \int_{x_{i+1}}^{x_{i+2}} w(E' + E_{i+1}) \cdot e^{-rt}\, dt$$
$$= \frac{w(E' + E_{i+1})}{r} \cdot (e^{-rx_{i+1}} - e^{-rx_{i+2}}); \tag{7}$$

whereas the latter is expressed by

$$v_\delta = \int_{x_{i+1}+\delta}^{x_{i+2}+\delta} w(E' + E_{i+1} + \delta) \cdot e^{-rt}\, dt$$
$$= \frac{w(E' + E_{i+1} + \delta)}{r} \cdot e^{-r\delta} \cdot (e^{-rx_{i+1}} - e^{-rx_{i+2}}), \tag{8}$$

where E' is the total length of education taken before the $(i+1)$st interval $[x_i, x_{i+1}]$, and where E_{i+1} is the length of education during the $(i+1)$st interval, i.e., $E_{i+1} = x_{i+1} - x_i$. Since no other part of the original education program is affected, the individual will gain through this reshuffle if v_δ is greater than v_0 in (7). Under our "productiveness" assumption (5), this condition is replaced by

$$w(E' + E_{i+1}) \cdot e^{-r(E'+E_{i+1})} < w(E' + E_{i+1} + \delta) \cdot e^{-r(E'+E_{i+1}+\delta)}. \tag{9}$$

However, since it is clear from Figure 1 that the function

$$w(\xi) \cdot e^{-r\xi}$$

is monotonically increasing with respect to ξ for

$$0 \leqq \xi \leqq E^*(\infty),$$

and since, by our assumption and by our construction,

$$E' + E_{i+1} < E' + E_{i+1} + \delta < E \leqq E^*(\infty),$$

we observe that the inequality (9) is always satisfied. Moreover, the difference $v_\delta - v_0$ is monotonically increasing with respect to δ. Hence, the individual can gain more, the more schooling of the $(i+3)$rd interval he shifts back to the $(i+2)$nd interval. This reshuffle can proceed further for all other intervals always with some gain in the present value of the earnings stream, until finally the individual finds his E years of education wholly concentrated in the interval $[0, E]$, i.e., no delay or intermissions will actually be made.

This completes the proof of Proposition 1. One of the consequences of this proposition is that, if the critical value $E^*(\infty)$ happens to be greater than J, then the optimal education program within the extended model coincides with that of the basic model. However, there is no a priori reason why $E^*(\infty) \geqq J$ holds. We are thus forced to consider the optimal education program for the general case where J may be greater than the critical level $E^*(\infty)$. By assuming that $J > E^*(\infty)$, let us next consider the optimal spacing problem when the given total length of education E exceeds the critical level $E^*(\infty)$. We observe the following:

PROPOSITION 2. *For a given total length of education E such that* $E^*(\infty) < E \leqq J$, *the optimal spacing of education and earning is achieved if the education is taken in two disjoint intervals,* $[0, E^*(\infty)]$ *and* $[J - (E - E^*(\infty)), J]$.

The proposition amounts to saying that an individual should take as much education as possible during the first period of life marked off by $E^*(\infty)$, and leave the remainder of education till the latest period that is possible, $[J - (E - E^*(\infty)), J]$. It can be proved by resorting to the proof of the previous proposition.

Let us start from an arbitrary partition of the interval $[0, J]$. We first note that the individual will gain by reshuffling any education interval to an earlier stage of his life as long as the condition (9) holds. This forward reshuffling of education intervals may continue until the individual exhausts the interval $[0, E^*(\infty)]$, at which point the inequality (9) ceases to hold. Thus, there will be no delay in the start of education, and education will be taken consecutively in the whole interval $[0, E^*(\infty)]$. The problem that remains is how to space the remainder of education for the interval $[E^*(\infty), J]$. We then note that, since the inequality sign in (9) is reversed for this interval (see Fig. 1), exactly the opposite situation to the case of the interval $[0, E^*(\infty)]$ occurs: namely, the individual will gain by reshuffling the education intervals within $[E^*(\infty), J]$ backward. This backward reshuffle may continue until he finds the remainder of education wholly concentrated in the interval $[J-(E-E^*(\infty)), J]$ (without any intermissions). This completes the proof of Proposition 2.

The above two propositions complete the characterization of the optimal spacing problem. Let us now turn to the question of the optimal length of education per se. We know from Proposition 1 and the discussion of the basic model that the maximum of the present value of the future earnings stream for the range of total length of education such that $0 < E \leqq E^*(\infty)$ is achieved by the education program that takes $\min\{E^*(L), J\}$ years of schooling consecutively from the moment of economic birth. As we have already remarked, if $J \leqq E^*(\infty)$, then this program becomes the optimum. The question remains for the case where $J > E^*(\infty)$. It is to be noted then that this program will still be the overall optimum if its present value of the future earnings stream is not surpassed by the maximum present value of the program whose total length of education exceeds $E^*(\infty)$. Let us see that this, in fact, is the case under the present assumptions.

Let us assume that $J > E^*(\infty)$, and consider an optimally spaced education program (by Proposition 2) with its total length of education E satisfying $J \geqq E > E^*(\infty)$. Its present value, to be denoted by $\Omega(E)$, (defined for $J \geqq E \geqq E^*[\infty])$ is expressed by

$$\Omega(E) = \frac{1}{r}\{w(E^*(\infty)) \cdot e^{-rE^*(\infty)} \cdot (1 - e^{-r(J-E)}) + w(E) \cdot (e^{-rJ} - e^{-rL})\}. \tag{10}$$

We can then show that $\Omega(E)$ is monotonically decreasing with respect to E over the range $J \geqq E \geqq E^*(\infty)$. In fact, by noting the definition of $E^*(\infty)$ in (6), we have

$$\left.\frac{d\Omega(E)}{dE}\right|_{E=E^*(\infty)} = -\frac{w'(E^*(\infty))}{r} \cdot e^{-rL} < 0. \tag{11}$$

Moreover, for all E such that $J \geqq E \geqq E^*(\infty)$,

$$\frac{d^2\Omega(E)}{dE^2} = -r \cdot w(E^*(\infty)) \cdot e^{-rE^*(\infty)} + \frac{w''(E)}{r} \cdot (e^{-rJ} - e^{-rL}) < 0. \tag{12}$$

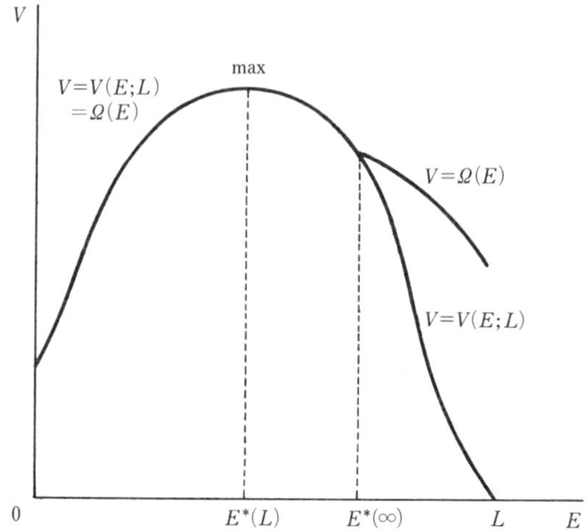

Figure 3

Hence, by using (11) and (12), we have

$$\frac{d\Omega(E)}{dE} < 0 \quad \text{for all } E \text{ such that } J \geqq E \geqq E^*(\infty), \tag{13}$$

proving the statement made above. Therefore, (13) implies that $\Omega(E)$ takes its maximum value at $E = E^*(\infty)$, and, moreover, the maximum value $\Omega(E^*(\infty))$ coincides with the present value of the education program with its length $E^*(\infty)$ within the basic model, i.e.,

$$\Omega(E^*(\infty)) = V(E^*(\infty); L). \tag{14}$$

In view of the results (13), (14), and Propositions 1 and 2, we can draw the graphs of the present value of the future earnings stream within the extended and the basic models. It can readily be seen from Figure 3 that $E = E^*(L)$ or J, whichever is the smaller, i.e., $\min\{E^*(L), J\}$, gives the overall optimum length of education. We have thus arrived at the main proposition of this note:

PROPOSITION 3. *The optimal education within the basic model and that within the extended model coincide; that is, the education process will start immediately after an individual's economic birth and will extend for* $E^*(L)$ *years or* J *years, whichever is the smaller (i.e.,* $\min\{E^*(L), J\}$ *years).*

Thus, as long as education is viewed solely as an object of investment, the optimal education program derived for the basic model continues to hold even if we allow any delay in the start of education and any intermissions in the educational process. This characteristic links with the results of Ben-Porath, Oniki, and Sheshinski (who allow continuous allocation of time between work and education at each moment of time) to the effect that there may, and in some cases, in fact, does occur a complete specialization toward education during the earlier phase of individual's lifetime.[7]

3. Concluding Remarks

In the above, we have seen that the simple Jevonian model of educational investment has the optimal spacing property implicit under its surface structure. We also note, however, that if there exists a sufficiently strong consumption element with respect to the level of education itself, so that the optimum feasible length of education exceeds the critical level $E^*(\infty)$, then the advantage of taking education intermittently actually becomes effective.

In order to substantiate the statement just made, let us consider the effects of the consumption element of education a little more carefully. We shall assume that an individual's utility at each period depends upon the level of education as well as that of consumption, so that the individual's problem is given by

$$\text{maximize} \int_0^L u(c_t, E_t) \cdot e^{-\gamma t}\, dt, \quad (u_c > 0, u_E > 0)$$

subject to $\int_0^L c_t \cdot e^{-rt}\, dt =$ the present value of the earnings stream, where c_t and E_t are the level of consumption and the level of education already attained at the moment t. It is clear that, as far as the consumption aspect of education is concerned, any given total length of education should be concentrated in the beginning. This is because, the earlier the education is taken, the more time the individual is left with to enjoy it; moreover, (although this factor is not essential) the presence of discounting future utilities ($\gamma > 0$) gives an additional incentive to do so. If we combine this consideration with our Propositions 1 and 2, we observe that, as long as the consumption element of education is relatively weak, so that the total length of education does not exceed $E^*(\infty)$, the schooling should be taken consecutively from the moment of economic birth; however, if the consumption element is strong enough so that the total length of education E exceeds the level $E^*(\infty)$, then the first $E^*(\infty)$ years should be devoted to education (as in Proposition 2), and the remaining $(E - E^*[\infty])$ years should be allocated in such a way that the force, coming from the consumption aspect, to take the remaining education as early as possible, is balanced with the force, coming from the investment aspect, to take the remaining education as late as possible (as in Proposition 2). Thus, the remaining education will generally be taken in an intermittent manner, with a clear advantage over the case where no intermission is allowed.[8]

Our discussion is based on the fundamental assumption that the acquired level of attributes through education depends only on the total number of years of schooling, and, specifically, not on the way schooling is taken. Obviously, this is a strong assumption. For instance, a change in one's engagement from work to schooling might require some period of psychological adjustment. In such a case, the earnings capacity schedule must take account of the cost of transition explicitly, and therefore becomes no longer independent of the spacing of education. However, this would provide a clear incentive to take education consecutively, and our main result holds a fortiori.

NOTES

This note is mostly derived from chapter two of the author's doctoral dissertation, "The Dynamics of Wealth Accumulation and Education Under Different Family Institutions as Determinants of the Size Distribution of Income," Ph.D. thesis, Johns Hopkins University, 1972. The author is very grateful to Professors Peter Newman, Jürg Niehans, and Richard Musgrave for their valuable comments and suggestions. I am particularly indebted to Professor Newman, whose mathematical suggestion, giving me the essential part of the general proof of Proposition 1, strengthened the proofs contained in my original draft.

1. W.S. Jevons (1871). The use of such a simplified model is made, for instance, by J. Mincer (1958).
2. Y. Ben-Porath (1967); E. Sheshinski (1968); H. Oniki (1970).
3. For a detailed analysis of the mechanism of transmission of wealth, incorporating the model of educational investment discussed in this note, and its implications on the distribution of income, see T. Ishikawa (1975).
4. The factors that underlie this schedule are discussed in Ishikawa (1975). For the sake of simplicity, we ignore uncertainty, learning, obsolescence, and on-the-job training effects. However, the incorporation of certain (e.g., exponential) learning by doing or obsolescence factors can be made in a straightforward manner.
5. The graph of the present value of the future earnings stream for a given L, $V(E;L)$ can be shown to have a shape as depicted in Figure 3. First, we note that $V(L;L)=0$. Second, consider the second derivative of V with respect to E:

$$\frac{\partial^2 V}{\partial E^2} = \frac{1}{r} \cdot \{w'' \cdot (e^{-rE} - e^{-rL}) - 2r \cdot w' \cdot e^{-rE} + r^2 \cdot w \cdot e^{-rE}\}. \tag{N.1}$$

The sign of (N.1) is, in general, ambiguous. Nevertheless, it is easy to see by inserting (3) in (N.1) that it is negative at the critical point where the first-order condition (3) is satisfied. Moreover, using (1), we see that

$$\left.\frac{\partial V}{\partial E}\right|_{E=0} = \infty > 0; \quad \left.\frac{\partial V}{\partial E}\right|_{E=L} = -w(L) \cdot e^{-rL} < 0. \tag{N.2}$$

Therefore, by the continuity property of $\partial V/\partial E$ with respect to E; there exists a unique local maximum. By (N.2) this local maximum point lies in the interior of the interval $[0, L]$.

6. By differentiating (3), we obtain

$$\frac{dE^*(L)}{dL} = \frac{r \cdot w'^* \cdot e^{-rL}}{2 \cdot r \cdot w'^* \cdot e^{-rE^*(L)} - r^2 \cdot w^* \cdot e^{-rE^*(L)} - w''^* \cdot (e^{-rE^*(L)} - e^{-rL})},$$

where $w^* = w(E^*(L))$, $w'^* = w'(E^*(L))$, and $w''^* = w''(E^*(L))$. Since the denominator is positive, we have $dE^*(L)/dL > 0$. Also, by inserting (3) into the formula, we immediately see that $dE^*(L)/dL < 1$.

7. See Sheshinski (1968: 47); Oniki (1970: 11); and Ben-Porath (1967: 358) (this gives a good economic account of the problem).

8. If we let the feasible number of intermissions N tend to ∞, then the problem becomes that of finding the optimal "density" in which education is taken over the interval $[E^*(\infty), J]$ and, in the limit, becomes mathematically equivalent to the optimal control problems that apply to the continuous time allocation problems. I am indebted to Professor Musgrave for the emphasis on the empirical relevance of the consumption aspect of education, which led me to the further consideration made here.

References

Ben-Porath, Y. 1967. The production of human capital and the life cycle of earnings. Journal of Political Economy 75 (Aug.): 352–65.

Ishikawa, Tsuneo. 1975. Family structures and family values in the theory of income distribution. Journal of Political Economy 83, 5: 987–1008. Reprinted in this volume.

Jevons, W.S. 1871. The Theory of Political Economy. London: Macmillan.

Mincer, J. 1958. Investment in human capital and personal income distribution. Journal of Political Economy 66 (Aug.): 281–302.

Oniki, H. 1970. On deriving the individual's demand function for educational investment. Discussion Paper 154 (Dec.). Harvard Institute of Economic Research.

Sheshinski, E. 1968. On the individual's lifetime allocation between education and work. Metroeconomica 20 (Jan.): 42–49.

3. On the Two Conceptualizations of Human Investment

1. Introduction

The notion of human investment as a source of worker productivity is by now quite familiar. In fact, quantitative studies on the sources of economic growth have repeatedly shown the importance of the improvement of labor quality as a major component of the residual factor initially termed "technical progress" (Denison [1967], Jorgenson-Griliches [1967]). An accounting framework that has appeared to deal with the phenomenon is the human capital theory (as developed by Schultz [1971], Becker [1964], and Mincer [1974]). This theory holds that an increase in worker productivity can be accounted for as a result of a rational calculus on the part of individuals as to the cost and the benefit of resources put into the process of acquiring knowledge and skills. Among the costs considered are those of real material input directly into the process and the opportunity cost of time spent by individuals on education and training. The opportunity cost refers to the income that the individuals would have earned had they actually spent the time otherwise doing work. Parallel to the cost at an individual level is a social cost in the form of sacrifices in the current output. Numerous studies have been conducted to measure the rate of return on the cost of investment thus defined (Hanoch [1967], Griliches [1977, 1979]).

Such an accounting framework has from the start been subject to a particular kind of criticism as Becker himself described (1964: 45–47). The criticism runs as follows. Considering the fact that learning by doing involves no sacrifice of actual production, it is a phenomenon

Originally published in Discussion Paper Series, Research Institute for the Japanese Economy, Faculty of Economics, University of Tokyo, 1993.

that is outside the realm of the human capital theory, and so long as such a kind of skill formation is prevalent the argument that a rationally conducted investment decision on the part of individuals lies behind any productivity increase on their part is nothing more than an exaggeration. Becker provided two counterarguments to the above criticism.

First, in reality there always exists a job with virtually no room for learning by doing, and that individuals face a choice between taking a flat earnings profile of such a job and taking a seniority wage profile that reflects the presence of learning by doing. When the latter alternative is chosen, it can be construed to involve a sacrifice of current income, whose cost can then be identified as investment.

Second, the situation that a flat wage profile is superseded by a wage profile of a job accompanying learning by doing can formally be understood as a special case of an infinite rate of return on human investment whereby some finite amount of benefit (productivity increase) results from zero costs. Becker, however, goes on to state that the case of an infinite rate of return largely results either from the lack of effort on the part of researchers not searching enough for alternative job opportunities or else from the lack of effort on the part of firm managers not pursuing the profit opportunities strictly enough, and therefore such a case cannot be regarded as important.

In opposition to such counterarguments, Blaug (1976: 837) has reiterated that, in reality, there can never be any job without learning by doing so that many facets remain where productivity increases cannot be accounted for by means of costs and returns. (This point has been repeated in a somewhat weaker form by Psacharopoulos and Layard [1979: 489–90].) It seems that the above criticism also contains an irritation over the rather ad hoc manner in which human capital theorists extend the notion of opportunity costs. In fact, the opportunity costs that are considered to be generated alongside learning by doing are qualitatively clearly different from the opportunity costs associated with the input of time resources, and it seems that the assumptions and the mechanism of generating the former category of opportunity costs must be made explicit. A more fundamental criticism yet seems to be directed to the fact that the productivity-enhancing effect of learning by doing is not evaluated for its own sake. The evaluation depends critically on what other job opportunities are present, which is quite an external affair as far as the job that generates learning by doing is concerned. However, because of the lack of an alternative theoretical framework to understand the problem at hand, Blaug's criticism immaturely switched to the question of empirical validity, thus leaving the main thrust of the criticism unarticulated.

The purpose of this paper is twofold; first, to reconstruct Becker's argument in a unified framework and thereby to clarify the interpretation, and second, present an alternative accounting system of human investment such that any productivity-enhancing learning activity (including, of course, learning by doing) is evaluated for its own sake within the system defining investment. The basis for the alternative explanation lies in the concept of user costs along the tradition of Marshall and Keynes. More specifically, a worker facing a learning opportunity is regarded as a producer who is managing his or her earnings capacity, in particular, as to how it is utilized, maintained, and improved. The new framework is shown to lead to the same behavioral rules on the part of the workers as those of the original human capital theory (which will be called the "opportunity cost approach") and yet it has a much more general applicability in understanding the phenomenon of human investment, for instance, the case involving unemployment. This paper thus provides one way by which the Becker-Blaug controversy is resolved.

This paper consists of five sections. In Section 2, which follows, a general framework of analysis is specified. Section 3 clarifies the concept of the opportunity cost in the human capital theory. Section 4 develops the alternative explanation (to be called the "user cost" approach), which constitutes the core of this paper. Section 5 compares the notions of investment in the two approaches and points out the limitations of the opportunity cost concept. It concludes by suggesting other possible issues that the user cost approach is well equipped to handle.

2. The Framework of Analysis

Suppose the economic ability of individuals is heterogeneous and is distributed continously over a closed interval $[0, 1]$. Each individual lives for two periods. By allocating some of his or her own time resources for training or learning in period 1, an individual can alter the economic ability in period 2. Call the initial ability position, given as an endownment, x, and the ability position in period 2, x'. The production in this economy is supposed to proceed by combining two types of labor, hereinafter called job A and job B. It is assumed that job A is most conformable with the ability position O, while job B is most conformable with the ability position 1.[1] The efficiency in performing each job is supposed to decline monotonically as the ability position moves away from the most conformable position. Thus writing the work efficiency of an individual with the ability position x at job A as $k_A(x)$ and that at job B as $k_B(x)$, the foregoing assumptions imply

$$\begin{aligned} &k_A'(x) < 0, \quad k_A(x) > 0, \quad k_A(0) = 1 \\ &k_B'(x) > 0, \quad k_B(x) > 0, \quad k_B(1) = 1 \end{aligned} \tag{1}$$

where the last condition in each row is a form of normalization for the efficiency indices.

Suppose that the two jobs are also different in that job B has a learning opportunity while job A has none. The learning opportunity of job B is characterized by the fact that by spending a portion λ $(0 \leqslant \lambda \leqslant 1)$ of the total (potential) working hours on on-the-job training the ability in the next period is increased by the rate $g(\lambda; x)$. In other words,

$$x' = (1 + g(\lambda; x))x \tag{2}$$

where

$$g(0; x) \geqslant 0 \quad g_\lambda \geqslant 0 \quad g_{\lambda\lambda} \leqslant 0. \tag{3}$$

Individuals are supposed to be able to carry their acquired ability freely across different firms.

Labor, output, and capital markets in the economy are all assumed to be perfect and competitive, and furthermore, the economy is assumed to be in a long-run steady state where the same market prices are maintained over periods. Such a world can easily be constructed by supposing an overlapping generations model whereby each generation maintains the same structure of time preference. For our present purpose, however, it suffices to remain solely within the confines of a subjective equilibrium of a single generation under exogenously given market prices.[2]

In the following we shall denote the rate of interest by r, the wage rate (in terms of output) of job A at its most conformable ability position $(x = 0)$ by w_A, and similarly the wage rate of job B at its most comformable ability position $(x = 1)$ by w_B. The individual with the ability position x (hereinafter simply called "ability x") receives $w_A k_A(x)$ for (a necessarily) full-time work at job A while the same individual receives $w_B k_B(x)$ for full-time work at job B. If the individual taking job B chooses to allocate λ of the time for learning, it means that $\lambda w_B k_B(x)$ of wage is foregone in period 1. For simplicity's sake, no additional fee is supposed to be charged by employers to workers for offering a learning opportunity.

What we later focus on as a particular case of the learning opportunity is that of learning by doing. Because learning proceeds in the very process of performing a job, no sacrifice of time, and hence earnings, is involved. In this case,

$$g(0; x) > 0, \quad g_\lambda(\lambda; x) = 0 \tag{4}$$

and

$$x' = (1 + g(0; x))x. \tag{5}$$

(4) is readily seen to be a special case of the general conditions (3) imposed on (2).

We shall distinguish the alternative case of on-the-job training from the case of learning by doing by specifying the conditions (3) as

$$g(0; x) = 0, \quad g_\lambda(\lambda; x) > 0, \quad g_{\lambda\lambda}(\lambda; x) < 0. \tag{6}$$

Finally, without loss of generality, the distribution of population over the ability interval [0, 1] is assumed to be uniform for each generation. The uniformity is merely a convenient assumption to facilitate a geometric discussion wherever possible.

3. The Opportunity Cost Approach to the Definition of Human Investment and Income Accounting

Under a perfect capital market, the rational employment behavior of an individual with an initial endowment ability x is characterized by the maximization of the present value of the earnings stream over the two periods. When the individual takes job A, the present value becomes

$$V_A(x) = w_A k_A(x) + \frac{\max\{w_A k_A(x), w_B k_B(x)\}}{1 + r}, \tag{7}$$

whereas if he takes job B, the present value becomes

$$V_B(x) = (1 - \lambda) w_B k_B(x) + \frac{\max\{w_B k_B(x'), w_A k_A(x')\}}{1 + r}, \tag{8}$$

where x' is defined, in general, by (2). Because the individual can freely choose his job in the beginning of each period given his ability position at that time, the problem becomes that of dynamic programming over two periods. The solution is shown to be achieved, however, even when one forgets that an individual can switch jobs in period 2. Namely, the current choice of job is effected by comparing the two present values, the value of $V_A(x)$ on the supposition that job A is continued in period 2 (hereinafter denoted by $V_{AA}(x)$), on the one hand, and the maximized value of $V_B(x)$ with respect to λ on the supposition that job B is continued in period 2 (hereinafter denoted by $V_{BB}^*(x)$), on the other. The optimum level of λ in the latter alternative is denoted by λ^* (note that $\lambda^* = 0$ in the case of learning by doing). A formal proof is given in the Appendix.

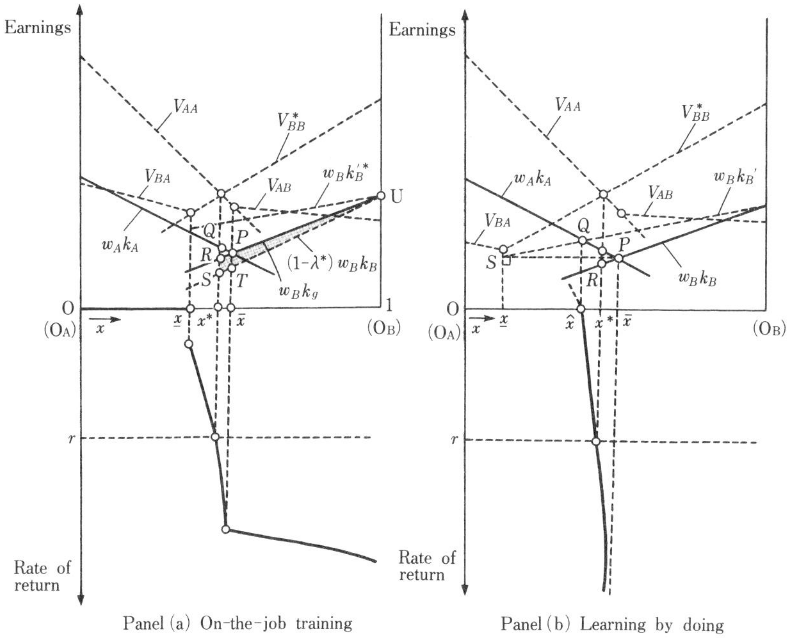

Figure 1. The notion of investment in the opportunity cost approach

The situation can be explained in terms of Panels (a) and (b) of Figure 1. Panel (a) represents the case of on-the-job training while Panel (b) represents the case of learning by doing. The horizontal axis expresses the spectrum of economic ability x. In the upper quadrant, the solid and broken half-lines emanating from the vertical axis at $x = 0$ express the graphs of $w_A k_A(x)$ and $V_{AA}(x)$, respectively. Several graphs also emanate from the vertical axis at $x = 1$. Thus, for Panel (a), the graphs of the earnings in period 1 with the intensity of learning optimally chosen $(1 - \lambda^*)w_B k_B(x)$, the earnings in each period with no learning at all $w_B k_B(x)$, the earnings in period 2 as a result of learning $w_B k_B(x') = w_B k_B(\{1 + g(\lambda^*; x)\}x)$, and the present value of the earnings stream with learning $V_{BB}^*(x)$ are drawn as $(1 - \lambda^*)w_B k_B$, $w_B k_B$, $w_B k_B'^*$ and V_{BB}^*, respectively. Similarly, for Panel (b), the graphs of $w_B k_B(x)$, the earnings in period 2 as a result of learning by doing $w_B k_B(x') = w_B k_B(\{1 + g(0; x)\}x)$, and the present value of the earnings stream with learning by doing are respectively drawn as $w_B k_B$, $w_B k_B'$ and V_{BB}^*. In either case, the intersection of the two graphs V_{AA} and V_{BB}^*, henceforth denoted as x^*, facilitates the borderline of choosing job A (to the left of x^*) and job B (to the right of x^*). x^* is clearly located to the left of $\bar{x}$, defined as the intersection of the graphs $w_A k_A$ and $w_B k_B$, which in turn, expresses the borderline of choice according to the principle of static comparative advantage. Although irrelevant to the ultimate choice itself, it is important for our later discussion to understand how the rational behavior to maximize $V_A(x)$ and $V_B(x)$ is formed given the choice of a particular job in period 1. Suppose that an individual with an arbitrarily given x has taken job A in period 1. Because no learning occurs in this job, the individual's ability remains the same in period 2. Therefore the rule of job choice in period 2 to maximize $V_A(x)$ is simply given by

$$\text{Choose}\begin{cases}\text{job } A \text{ for } x \in [0, \bar{x}] \\ \text{job } B \text{ for } x \in (\bar{x}, 1].\end{cases}$$

While the maximized value of $V_A(x)$ is identical with $V_{AA}(x)$ for $x \in [0, \bar{x}]$ it takes a different value for $x \in (\bar{x}, 1]$. It is denoted as $V_{AB}(x)$ and is represented by the graph V_{AB} in Figure 1.

What happens if the individual takes job B in period 1? First, in the case of learning by doing, it is obvious that the choice of the job in period 2 depends on whether or not the ability position in period 2 exceeds the critical value $\bar{x}$. That is, job B is chosen if it exceeds $\bar{x}$, and job A is taken otherwise.

As a matter of fact, the initial ability position, which is transformed to $\bar{x}$ after learning, is determined at $\underline{x}$, which corresponds to the intersection point S of the line parallel with the horizontal axis that emanates from P (which, in turn, is the intersection of the curves $w_A k_A$ and $w_B k_B$) and the curve $w_B k_B'$.

In the case of on-the-job training, the circumstance is a little complicated due to the variability of λ. As shown rigorously in the Appendix, however, the individuals with the initial ability x sufficiently close to 0 had better not obtain any learning at all and switch to job A in period 2. Writing the value of $V_B(x)$ for such a behavior as $V_{BA}(x)$, the criterion of job choice for period 2 is facilitated by comparing the value of $V_{BA}(x)$ and $V_{BB}^*(x)$. The borderline of choice is determined by the intersection of the curves $V_{BA}(x)$ and $V_{BB}^*(x)$ and will be denoted by $\underline{x}$. Combining these considerations, the rule of job choice for period 2, which maximizes $V_B(x)$, is summarized by

$$\text{Choose}\begin{cases}\text{job } A \text{ for } x \in [0, \underline{x}] \\ \text{job } B \text{ for } x \in (\underline{x}, 1]\end{cases}$$

where $\underline{x}$ is defined previously. It is then obvious from Figure 1 that the graphs of the optimized $V_A(x)$ and $V_B(x)$ are piecewise broken lines but that such a feature does not affect the individual's choice in period 1 at all, and moreover, that the individual will continue to take the same job once the choice is made in period 1. The two critical values $\underline{x}$ and $\bar{x}$ will be seen to play an important role in the following discussion.

The preceding discussion must all be quite familiar. Our main issue is the manner in which the cost of investment is comprehended. The tradition of the human capital school as represented by Schultz and Becker takes the position of perceiving the earnings foregone in period 1 in comparison with the maximum earnings that would have been obtained as the cost of investment. Thus, in the case of on-the-job training (Panel [a] of Figure 1) the investment cost becomes the direct opportunity cost (foregone earnings) of learning $\lambda^* w_B k_B(x)$ with the addition of $w_A(x) - w_B(x)$ in the range of x, where job A brings about a higher pay than job B, i.e., $x \in [x^*, \bar{x}]$. Consequently, the economy-wide human investment cost is expressed (using the assumption of a uniform distribution of ability) by the area of the shaded form QPUTSR. In the case of learning by doing, however, no learning cost is required, and the sole component of the investment cost becomes the foregone earnings $w_A(x) - w_B(x)$, again, for $x \in [x^*, \bar{x}]$. The economy-wide human investment cost is then expressed by the area of the triangle QPR in Panel (b).

The returns on human investment, on the other hand, are defined as the difference between the level of earnings in period 2 after learning $w_B k_B(x')$ and the level of the maximum earnings in the same period without any learning. For both cases (a) and (b), the latter value is $w_A k_A(x)$ for $[\bar{x}, 1]$. The ratio of returns over cost minus 1 has been referred to as the (internal) rate of return on human investment and has long been the object of empirical measurement. The graph of the rate of return is drawn in the lower quadrants of Panels (a) and (b).

Panel (a) shows that in the case of on-the-job training the graph first coincides with the horizontal axis for $x \in [0, \underline{x}]$ and then rises above zero and increases for the remaining range $x \in [\underline{x}, 1]$. Panel (b), on the other hand, shows that the rate of return becomes negative for $x \in [0, \hat{x}]$, where $\hat{x}$ corresponds to the intersection of the curves $w_A k_A$ and $w_B k_B'$ (neccesarily $\underline{x} < \hat{x} < x^*$). For $x \in [\hat{x}, \bar{x}]$ it rises monotonically and becomes asymptotic to the vertical line $x = \bar{x}$.

For both cases (a) and (b), it is easily confirmed that the rate of return becomes equal to that at the critical value x^*. Between the two cases there is a qualitative difference in that for $x \in [\bar{x}, 1]$ the rate of return takes a finite value for case (a) while it is infinite for case (b).

So much for a reconstruction of the discussion by Schultz, Becker, and others. No matter whether it is on-the job training or learning by doing, the notions of cost and returns of investment can be defined in terms of a unified set of accounting principles. The sole discrepancy with Becker's argument quoted in the introduction is that in the case of learning by doing there exists a non-negligible portion of the population for whom the investment cost is zero and the rate of return is infinite. The point we would like to raise, however, is that the logical coherence of a framework itself does not imply that it is the sole possible framework that is logically coherent. Also to answer whether it is a desirable framework or not requires an entirely different criterion. In the next section, we shall propose an alternative conceptualization of human investment.

4. The Notion of Human Investment as a Negative User Cost

An alternative approach to understanding human investment is to not identify it directly with the opportunity cost that arises when an individual's productive capacity is put to alternative uses, but to identify it with the user cost that arises depending on whether the productive capacity is put to actual use or not in the job at hand. It will be shown that from such a viewpoint a logically coherent accounting of investment and income is derived, which gives the correct criterion for investment.

The notion of user costs emphasized in Keynes's *General Theory* is rendered somewhat of a side show in the subsequent development of the macroeconomic theory as well as the microeconomics of investment. It will be helpful to begin by reviewing the concept as discussed by Keynes (1936: 53–55).

The user cost is originally conceived as a notion to take account of the depreciation in capital equipment values associated with the activity of production. Suppose that a firm's capital equipment, after a period of utilizing it in production and simultaneously making new outlays to maintain and improve the equipment optimally, has the value (i.e., the present value of earnings due in future) G. The cost of outlays made on equipment is denoted by A_1. Suppose also that the value of capital equipment becomes G' when it is not put to actual use (i.e., remains idle) during the period. This value implicitly incorporates the result of any possible activity to maintain and improve the equipment that is desirable even though the equipment itself remains idle during the period in question. The outlay thus made is denoted by B'. A_1 and B' can be regarded as investment expenditures in a narrow sense as much as they involve expenditures of real resources (including time). Both $G - A_1$ and $G' - B'$ express the value of capital equipment after the outlays on maintenance and improvement activities are adjusted for, and the difference between the two expressions is attributed to whether or not the capital equipment is put to actual use in the current period. The difference $(G' - B') - (G - A_1)$ is defined as the user cost and it will be denoted by U. Together with other factor outlays, this cost constitutes a part of the current (prime) cost of the firm. The investment of the firm is then defined as the total outlay on capital equipment minus the user cost, $A_1 - U$. In the customary terminology, A_1 is the gross investment, while $A_1 - U$ is the net investment. Futhermore, the income of the firm is defined as the value of output (denoted by A) minus the user cost, $A - U$. The capital equipment referred to above may, in fact, include the stocks of materials, goods in process, and finished products.[3] The most conspicuous characteristic of this definition is that the capital equipment of the firm is not necessarily perfectly employed. And this indeed seems to be the reason why the concept of user costs has not been treated adequately in the subsequent theoretical literature. In the neo-classical theory, the normal feature of the world is that all capital equipment is perfectly utilized except for temporary disturbances or economic obsolescences.[4] Here we take up the notion of user costs from an altogether different viewpoint.

The foregoing definitions can be applied analogously to the case of an individual by regarding him or her to be a producer employing his or her own economic ability as capital and putting it to use in alternative job opportunities. Discussion follows separately for each type of learning.

THE CASE OF LEARNING BY DOING

In this case, the amount of resources spent for improving one's own economic ability (A_1 and B') is identically zero. The user cost is calculated for each job as the difference between the present value of the future earnings capacity in the event that the individual actually works and that in the event that the individual takes the job but does not actually work during the period in question. In the present two-period fomulation, the present value of the future earnings capacity reduces to that of the maximum earnings obtainable, given the ability possessed by the individual at the end of the first period.

Look at Panel (b) of Figure 1. When an individual with ability x chooses job A in period 1, the user cost is zero, and moreover, this fact is independent of the initial ability position. This is because the earnings capacity of period 2 does not change, no matter whether the individual actually works or not in the job taken. (It is $w_A k_A(x)$ for $x \in [0, \bar{x}]$ and $w_B k_B(x)$ for $x \in [\bar{x}, 1]$, both evaluated in current value terms.)

On the other hand, the user cost associated with the choice of job B in period 1 varies depending on the initial ability position x. First, in the case of $x \in [0, \underline{x}]$, the effect of learning by doing, which becomes effective when one actually performs the job, is to reduce the efficiency of work at job A in period 2, and yet $w_A k_A(x') > w_B k_B(x')$ holds so that the earnings capacity for period 2 is $w_A k_A(x')$. If the individual does not actually work in period 1, the detrimental effect of learning by doing is avoided, and therefore, the earnings capacity for period 2 remains at the level $w_A k_A(x)$. The current user cost in this case becomes $(w_A k_A(x) - w_A k_A(x'))/(1+r)$, which is positive.

Second, in the case of $x \in [\underline{x}, \bar{x}]$ it is easily seen that the earnings capacity for period 2 is $w_B k_B(x')$ when one actually works, while it becomes $w_A k_A(x)$ when one does not work, again reflecting the fact that learning by doing is inactive when the job is not performed. Hence the user cost becomes $(w_A k_A(x) - w_B k_B(x'))/(1+r)$. Its value is seen to turn from positive to negative at some intermediate value denoted by $\hat{x}$.

Third, in the remaining case of $x \in [\bar{x}, 1]$ the user cost turns out to be $(w_B k_B(x) - w_B k_B(x'))/(1+r)$. It is uniformly negative in the specified range of x.

All the preceding considerations are summarized in the column representing the user cost under the heading of learning by doing in Table 1. In the table are also written the gross income of period 1 and the net income defined as the former subtracted by the user cost. This net income is identical with Keynes's definition of income. An individual worker is then considered to choose his or her job in period 1 by comparing the level of net income obtained by each job. As a consequence, job A is clearly taken by individuals with $x \in [0, \underline{x}]$ while job B is taken by individuals with $x \in [\bar{x}, 1]$. In the intermediate range of $x \in [\underline{x}, \bar{x}]$, the proposed rule becomes

$$w_A k_A(x) \gtreqless w_B k_B(x) + \frac{w_B k_B(x') - w_A k_A(x)}{1+r} \Leftrightarrow \begin{array}{l}\text{choose job } A\\ \text{indifferent}\\ \text{choose job } B\end{array}$$

It is immediately seen, however, that this criterion is equivalent to the maximization of the present value of the earnings stream, or the comparison of $V_{AA}(x)$ and $V^*_{BB}(x)$, as discussed previously.[5] The critical value governing the choice of job is, again, x^*, and we are left with a new approach that generates identical behavioral rules with the opportunity cost approach.

THE CASE OF ON-THE-JOB TRAINING

A similar discussion can be made for the case of on-the-job training. The only difference with the case of learning by doing is the presence of an outlay of resources made on improving one's economic ability (A_1 in Keynes's terminology) when one chooses and actually performs job B. By the very nature of on-the-job training, learning occurs only when one actually performs the job, and this, in turn, implies that the outlay

Table 1. Income Accounting in the User Cost Approach

Case	Job	Gross income	On-the-job training: User cost	On-the-job training: Net income	Learning by doing: User cost	Learning by doing: Net income
$0 \leqq x \leqq \underline{x}$	A	$w_A k_A(x)$	$\frac{w_A k_A(x) - w_A k_A(x)}{1+r} = 0$	$w_A k_A(x)$	$\frac{w_A k_A(x) - w_A k_A(x)}{1+r} = 0$	$w_A k_A(x)$
	B	$w_B k_B(x)$	$\frac{w_A k_A(x) - w_A k_A(x)}{1+r} = 0$	$w_B k_B(x)$	$\frac{w_A k_A(x) - w_A k_A(x')}{1+r} > 0$	$w_B k_B(x) - \frac{w_A k_A(x) - w_A k_A(x')}{1+r}$
$\underline{x} \leqq x \leqq \bar{x}$	A	$w_A k_A(x)$	$\frac{w_A k_A(x) - w_A k_A(x)}{1+r} = 0$	$w_A k_A(x)$	$\frac{w_A k_A(x) - w_A k_A(x)}{1+r} = 0$	$w_A k_A(x)$
	B	$w_B k_B(x)$	$\lambda^* w_B k_B(x) + \frac{w_A k_A(x) - w_B k_B(x'^*)}{1+r}$	$(1-\lambda^*) w_B k_B(x) + \frac{w_B k_B(x'^*) - w_A k_A(x)}{1+r}$	$\frac{w_A k_A(x) - w_B k_B(x')}{1+r} \gtreqqless 0 \Leftrightarrow x \lesseqqgtr \hat{x}$	$w_B k_B(x) + \frac{w_B k_B(x') - w_A k_A(x)}{1+r}$
$\bar{x} \leqq x \leqq 1$	A	$w_A k_A(x)$	$\frac{w_B k_B(x) - w_B k_B(x)}{1+r} = 0$	$w_A k_A(x)$	$\frac{w_B k_B(x) - w_B k_B(x)}{1+r} = 0$	$w_A k_A(x)$
	B	$w_B k_B(x)$	$\lambda^* w_B k_B(x) + \frac{w_B k_B(x) - w_B k_B(x'^*)}{1+r}$	$(1-\lambda^*) w_B k_B(x) + \frac{w_B k_B(x'^*) - w_B k_B(x)}{1+r}$	$\frac{w_B k_B(x) - w_B k_B(x')}{1+r} < 0$	$w_B k_B(x) + \frac{w_B k_B(x') - w_B k_B(x)}{1+r}$

of resources is not made when one remains idle in the job. Thus gross income as introduced in Table 1 is now interpreted as the revenue in period 1 that can be obtained when the ability then available is utilized fully, i.e., $\lambda = 0$. The outlays for improvement in ability are now identified as a part of the user cost. The user cost is then subtracted from the gross income to arrive at net income.

The user cost for the case of job A is identically (i.e., for all x) zero, just as in the case of learning by doing. In calculating the user cost for job B, it is helpful to divide the range of x into two intervals, $[0, \bar{x}]$ and $[\bar{x}, 1]$. First, we take up the case of $x \in [0, \bar{x}]$. In this case, the earnings capacity in period 2 when job B is actually performed with an arbitrarily specified intensity of learning λ is $\max\{w_A k_A(x'), w_B k_B(x')\}$, where x' is given by (2), whereas that when job B is not actually performed becomes $w_A k_A(x)$. Hence the user cost is expressed by

$$U = \lambda w_B k_B(x) + \frac{\{w_A k_A(x) - \max[w_A k_A(x'), w_B k_B(x')]\}}{1+r}, \qquad (9)$$

where $\lambda w_B k_B(x)$ is the outlay of time resources actually made for the management of economic ability. The net income (or Keynes's income) Y then becomes

$$Y = (1-\lambda) w_B k_B(x) - \frac{\{w_A k_A(x) - \max[w_A k_A(x'), w_B k_B(x')]\}}{1+r}. \qquad (10)$$

By comparing (10) with (8), (10) can be rewritten as

$$Y = V_B(x) - \frac{w_A k_A(x)}{1+r}. \qquad (11)$$

Note that for any given x the second term in (11) is a constant. Therefore, the maximization of Y given the choice of job B reduces to that of maximizing $V_B(x)$ with respect to λ. In the previous section, we have already derived the answer to the problem at hand. Namely, for $x \in [0, \underline{x}]$ the optimum λ is 0, the job to be taken in period 2 is A, and the maximized value of $V_B(x)$ is $V_{BA}(x)$, whereas for $x \in [\underline{x}, \bar{x}]$, the optimum λ is λ^*, the job to be taken in period 2 is B, and the maximized value of $V_B(x)$ is $V_{BB}^*(x)$.

The case of $x \in [\bar{x}, 1]$ can be analyzed in the same manner, and we only give the results in Table 1. The expressions of the user cost and the net income in Table 1 (under the heading of on-the-job training) refer to the optimized values with respect to the intensity of learning λ.

The rule of job choice in our new setting is, again, that of choosing the job that gives a higher net income. Just as in the case of learning by doing, the result is easily seen to be exactly the same as that derived in

Table 2. The Amount of Realized Investment

	On-the-job training		Learning by doing	
	Opportunity cost approach	User cost approach	Opportunity cost approach	User cost approach
$0 \leqq x \leqq x^*$	0	0	0	0
$x^* \leqq x \leqq \bar{x}$	$w_A(x) - w_B(x) + \lambda^* w_B k_B(x)$	$\dfrac{w_B k_B(x'^*) - w_A k_A(x)}{1+r}$	$w_A(x) - w_B(x)$	$\dfrac{w_B k_B(x') - w_A k_A(x)}{1+r}$
$\bar{x} \leqq x \leqq 1$	$\lambda^* w_B k_B(x)$	$\dfrac{w_B k_B(x'^*) - w_B k_B(x)}{1+r}$	0	$\dfrac{w_B k_B(x') - w_B k_B(x)}{1+r}$

the previous section. In particular, the comparison of net income for $x \in [\underline{x}, \bar{x}]$ reduces to that of $V_{AA}(x)$ and $V_{BB}^*(x)$.

In the framework of this section, the amount of investment is defined, as previously mentioned, as the external outlay (A_1) subtracted by the user cost (U). By taking note of the fact that in the range of x, where job B is taken $A_1 = 0$ in the case of learning by doing while $A_1 = \lambda^* w_B k_B(x)$ in the case of on-the-job training, the level of investment can easily be calculated using the expressions in Table 1. The results are given in Table 2, where they are also contrasted with the investment figures defined by the opportunity cost approach.

Table 2 shows that both approaches naturally assign the same zero investment level for the range of x where job A is chosen, but the two figures become wide apart for the range of x where job B is taken, that is, when human investment is actually made. A further discussion of this point is made in the next section.[6]

5. Conclusion: The Significance of the User Cost Approach

We have confirmed above that both the opportunity cost approach and the user cost approach result in exactly the same criterion of human investment as well as job choice. The prominent difference between the two approaches lies in the manner in which the cost of human investment is comprehended, and, in particular, in the manner in which the cost is placed in national income accounting.

The notion of investment according to the opportunity cost approach represents the magnitude of current sacrifice in national income as compared with its maximum possible level. The user cost approach, on the other hand, regards the present value of an increase in the future earnings capacity achieved during the current period as investment. Simultaneously, the corresponding amount is considered to be added to the value of national income. In either approach, the national income accounting system is made consistent in that it satisfies the basic accounting constraint that national income less investment is the maximum possible consumption. One sees investment from the viewpoint of resources put into the process, while the other sees investment from the viewpoint of its effect.

The significance of perceiving investment from the viewpoint of resource input is intuitively clear. There are two qualifications, however, to such an approach.

First, the size of calculated resource inputs is not necessarily a correct indicator of the magnitude of actual accumulation of human capital. A typical example is the case of learning by doing. Suppose in addition to the circumstance depicted by Panel (b) of Figure 1 that learning by doing also occurs in job *A*. In this case, individuals with ability $x \in [x^*, \bar{x}]$ would now choose job *A* and that the static "distortion" in the resource allocation previously existing in period 1 is thereby reduced. Indeed, when the extent of learning by doing for job *A* increases to become identical with that for job *B*, the "distortion" becomes zero, in which case the sacrifice in terms of current national income in period 1 is none. In this process, the accumulation of human capital is enhanced, while the amount of investment measured in terms of the opportunity cost declines. Hence Becker's argument that even in the case of learning by doing an increase in productivity (the earnings capacity) can entirely be attributed to human investment measured in opportunity cost terms (once an infinite rate of return is allowed for) is not a valid one. Although less pathodological there is a room for the same criticism to hold for the case of on-the-job training, in particular, when the opportunity cost other than the time resource cost ($w_A[x] - w_B[x]$ for $x \in [x^*, \bar{x}]$ or the area of $\triangle PQR$ in Panel [a] of Figure 1) is relatively large in magnitude.

Second, and perhaps more fundamentally, the calculation of resource input for human investment is based on the presumption that resources are always perfectly utilized. In a world where workers are not necessarily fully employed (or, to be more precise, where there exists room for some workers to be involuntarily unemployed), the definition of investment cost in the sense of a maximally possible sacrifice in the current output loses its meaning. And, moreover, recent development in the theory of the labor market has shown that there are several grounds upon which involuntary unemployment may continue to exist even in the long run.

The user cost approach, however, turns out to avoid these two criticisms successfully. An expanded accumulation of human capital is registered as a corresponding increase in the amount of investment.

Such a property is quite natural in view of the standpoint of measuring the magnitude of investment from its effect. What is more important may be the second point. Because the user cost of each job is calculated on the basis of a comparison between the situation in which an individual actually works and that in which the individual does not work (or is unemployed), our approach can rightly be regarded as already taking account of the possibility of unemployment. Thus if an individual with ability x becomes unemployed involuntarily it means that the user cost both for job A and job B is zero, and it will be correspondingly excluded in the process of aggregation. Our definition would also provide a useful analytical framework for considering the detrimental effect of unemployment on human resources (e.g., Hargreaves-Heap [1980]). Indeed, the definition of human investment introduced in this paper not only resolves the controversy surrounding the treatment of learning by doing in the human capital calculus but also provides a theoretical ground for properly measuring the long-run effect of unemployment. A further extension of the analysis along the lines suggested here will be left for future study.

Appendix

We provide here a mathematical proof of the statement made in the text concerning the individual's behavior on investment and choice of job in period 2 given the choice of job B in period 1.

For an arbitrarily given x, let

$$\hat{\lambda} = \inf\{\lambda \in [0, 1] \mid w_B k_B(x') \geqslant w_A k_A(x'), \quad x' = (1 + g(\lambda; x))x\}$$

be defined and let it be denoted as $\hat{\lambda}(x)$. It is obvious that $\hat{\lambda}(x) = 0$ for $x \in [\bar{x}, 1]$. For $x \in [0, \bar{x}]$, on the other hand, $\hat{\lambda}(x)$ turns out to be the value of λ such that x' just equals $\bar{x}$. It necessarily takes a positive value. It then follows that

$$V_B(x) = \begin{cases} (1-\lambda)w_B k_B(x) + \dfrac{w_B k_B(x')}{1+r} & \text{for } \lambda \geqslant \hat{\lambda}(x) & \text{(i)} \\[2ex] (1-\lambda)w_B k_B(x) + \dfrac{w_A k_A(x')}{1+r} & \text{for } \lambda < \hat{\lambda}(x). & \text{(ii)} \end{cases}$$

Let us draw the relationship between $V_B(x)$ and λ graphically, keeping x fixed at a given level. Expression (i) for the domain $\lambda \geqslant \hat{\lambda}(x)$ takes a local maximum at $\lambda = \lambda^*$ provided that $\lambda^* \geqslant \hat{\lambda}(x)$ while it becomes monotonically decreasing with respect to λ throughout the interval $[\hat{\lambda}(x), 1]$, provided that $\lambda^* < \hat{\lambda}(x)$. On the other hand, expression (ii) for the domain $\lambda < \hat{\lambda}(x)$ is monotonically decreasing with respect to

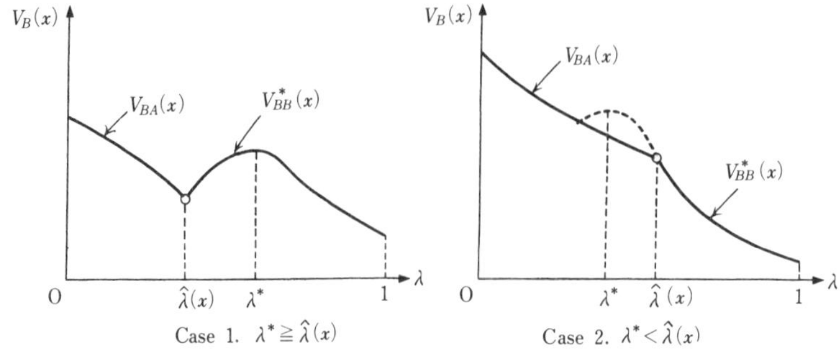

Figure A-1. The relationship between $V_B(x)$ and λ

λ throughout the interval $\lambda \in [0, \hat{\lambda}(x)]$. These properties are summarized in Figure A-1.

In Case 1 of Figure A-1, the value of λ that maximizes $V_B(x)$ is one of two local maximum points, $\lambda = 0$ or $\lambda = \lambda^*$. The problem then exactly matches with the comparison of $V_{BA}(x)$ and $V^*_{BB}(x)$ discussed in the main text. In Case 2 of Figure A-1, the value of λ that maximizes $V_B(x)$ is obviously 0.

With these preparations, we are now ready to discuss the optimal individual behavior for the respective ranges of x.

1. $x \in [0, \underline{x}]$.

In this range of x, both Case 1 and Case 2 referred to above may occur. However, since by definition $V_{BA}(x) \geqslant V^*_{BB}(x)$ (equality holds only for $x = \underline{x}$), the optimal λ is zero irrespective of the relative size of λ^* and $\hat{\lambda}(x)$, and the optimal choice of job in period 2 is to move to job A.

2. $x \in [\underline{x}, \bar{x}]$.

For this range of x, $V^*_{BB}(x) \geqslant V_{BA}(x)$ (again the equality holds only when $x = \underline{x}$). Hence the inequality

$$\begin{aligned}(1-\lambda^*)w_B k_B(x) &+ \frac{w_B k_B((1+r(\lambda^*;x))x)}{1+r} \\ &\geqslant w_B k_B(x) + \frac{w_A k_A(x)}{1+r} \\ &> w_B k_B(x) + \frac{w_A k_A((1+g(\lambda^*;x))x)}{1+r}\end{aligned}$$

holds. This immediately implies

$$\frac{w_A k_A((1+g(\lambda^*;x))x) - w_B k_B((1+g(\lambda^*;x))x)}{1+r} < -\lambda^* w_B k_B(x),$$

which, in turn, implies $\lambda^* > \hat{\lambda}(x)$. Thus Case 1 applies. We already know that in Case 1 the maximum value of $V_B(x)$ is attained by $V_{BB}^*(x)$ or $V_{BA}(x)$, whichever is larger, while the above inequality implies that $V_{BB}^*(x)$ dominates $V_{BA}(x)$. Hence, it is optimal for an individual to choose the intensity λ^* for training and also to remain at job B in period 2.

3. $x \in [\bar{x}, 1]$.

For this range of x, we have already started that $\hat{\lambda}(x) = 0$. Case 1 thus holds and furthermore, $V_{BB}^*(x) > V_{BA}(x)$. Hence the optimal behavior is identical with that for $x \in [\underline{x}, \bar{x}]$. (Q.E.D.)

NOTES

1. Alternatively one can suppose that job B is also conformable with the ability position O. So long as the efficiency curves $k_A(x)$ and $k_B(x)$ are not identical (which is effectively the same thing as saying that jobs A and B are different), the following analysis is not affected. The basic reason behind this is that an individual's choice of a job is always governed by the common principle of comparative advantage (which is well explicated by Rosen [1978]).

2. In principle, the relative wage between the two jobs (w_A/w_B) as well as the rate of interest (r) all change as a result of changes in the individual behavior. However, such "market experiments" have nothing directly to do with the logical substance of this paper. The changes in the relative market prices in nonsteady state situations are also an altogether different issue from the present one.

3. An example would be helpful in understanding the notions discussed in the text. The example chosen below refers to the case of a firm managing its inventory of materials used in production. Suppose that a firm spends \$4,000 for wages of employees and \$3,000 for material input in order to obtain a revenue of \$10,000 on its product. Suppose also that from the viewpoint of lubricating the production flows and meeting uncertain contingencies, it is optimal for the firm to maintain a stock of \$5,000 worth of materials at the beginning of every production period. In this case, $G' = G = \$5{,}000$, $B' = 0$ and $A_1 = \$3{,}000$. The user cost U becomes $U = (G' - B') - (G - A_1) = \$3{,}000$. The (net) income to the firm is the gross income (revenue) A minus the user cost U, which is \$3,000 – \$3,000, or zero.

4. As an exception, there are theories that maintain that firms strategically choose to hold excess capacities in order to deter new entry of rival firms (e.g., Spence [1977]).

5. As a matter of fact, the choice of no work (i.e., voluntary unemployment) is never made in the present model, for that would give that zero income is lower than the income of either job. Needless to say, such a choice may actually be made when a sufficiently high consumption value is attached to leisure. Also there is the possibility of involuntary unemployment. This last problem is discussed in the next section.

6. The analysis of the preceding two sections can easily be extended to the cases of more than two job opportunities and more than two periods. As an example of the more-than-two-jobs case, consider job C, which is most conformable with the ability position 1/2. In this case, the opportunity cost of taking a particular job is calculated on the basis of a comparison with the most directly competitive job. The most fundamental assumption of the entire analysis is that the job opportunities are given exogeneously and that the rents accruing to individuals with an ability close to the most conformable position of some job do not die out even in the face of market competition.

References

Becker, G.S. 1964. Human Capital: A Theoretical and Empirical Analysis, with Special Reference to Education. New York: Columbia University Press (Second edition, 1975).

Blaug, M. 1976. The empirical status of human capital theory: A slightly jaudiced survey. Journal of Economic Literature 14, 3 (Sept.): 827–55.

Denison, E. 1967. Why Growth Rates Differ: Postwar Experience in Nine Western Countries. Washington, D.C.: The Brooking Institution.

Griliches, Z. 1977. Estimating the returns of schooling: Some econometric problems. Econometrica 45, 1 (Jan.): 1–22.

———. 1979. Sibling models and data in economics: Beginning of a survey. Journal of Political Economy 87, 5 (Part 2) (Oct.): S37–S64.

Hanoch, G. 1967. An economic analysis of earnings and schooling. Journal of Human Resources 2, 3: 310–29.

Hargreaves-Heap, S.P. 1980. Choosing the wrong natural rate, accelerating inflation or decelerating unemployment and growth. Economic Journal 90 (Sept.): 611–20.

Jorgenson, D.W., and Z. Griliches. 1967. The explanation of productivity change. Review of Economic Studies 34: 249–83.

Keynes, J.M. 1936. The General Theory of Employment, Interest and Money. London: Macmillan.

Mincer, J. 1974. Schooling, Experience and Earnings. New York: Columbia University Press.

Psacharopoulos, G., and R. Layard. 1979. Human capital and earnings: British evidence and a critique. Review of Economic Studies 46: 485–503.

Rosen, S. 1978. Substitution and the division of labour. Economica 45: 235–50.

Schultz, T. 1971. Investment in Human Capital: The Role of Education and Research. New York: Free Press.

Spence, M. 1977. Entry, capacity, investment and oligopolistic pricing. Bell Journal of Economics 8, 2 (Autumn): 534–44.

4. Elite Schools, High-tech Jobs, and Economic Welfare

1. Introduction

The past two decades have witnessed a significant increase of educational attainment in most developed countries.[1] According to a recent survey on universities by the *Economist*, the biggest single change in higher education has been "massification," the increase both in the number of students going to college and in the percentage of university graduates to the population at theoretical age of graduation.

Educational attainment and human capital accumulation are often viewed as keys to economic performance and growth, and adequate skills are considered a critical factor in the development of new ideas and designs.[2] While educational attainment is clearly important, the quality of education also matters.[3]

In many countries, the majority of students go to ordinary universities and a selected minority is creamed off to a limited number of elite schools. The United States, for example, "has moved farther than most countries toward a system of mass higher education, and yet its 50 or so great research universities probably achieve higher academic standards than before" (*The Economist*, 1997). Other examples include France and Japan. In France, the best students go to the Grandes Ecoles and in Japan they strive to enter the University of Tokyo and other top colleges. These examples apply to college education, but the division of schools into ordinary and elite institutions extends to less than tertiary education.

While the relationship between educational attainment and economic performance has attracted the attention of economists, the question

Coauthored with Giorgio Brunello. Originally published in *Journal of Public Economies* 72 (1999): 395–419.

whether the size of the elite school sector matters for economic performance and welfare has often been overlooked. Our approach to this issue can be briefly summarized as follows. Consider a schooling system that includes both ordinary and elite schools. Compared to ordinary schools, elite schools are more selective and provide better education. Since access to elite schools is limited and regulated by tough entry standards, individuals try to meet these standards by investing in academic skills. Examples of these skills include the basics of reading, mathematics, and science and problem-solving skills. If the accumulation of academic skills and training are complements, the presence of an elite school sector affects both training costs and the relative advantage of adopting complex and highly productive technologies. Changes in the size of this sector modify the number of available slots in elite schools, thereby affecting both individual investment in academic skills and the number of high-tech jobs.

We argue that a satisfactory answer to the question raised in this paper requires that we focus not only on the schooling system but also on its interactions with the industrial structure and the labor market. Depending on the underlying parameters, we show that these interactions can produce multiple locally stable equilibria.[4]

In one equilibrium (*S*-equilibrium), the presence of an elite school sector induces individuals to invest in the accumulation of academic skills. The availability of these skills in the market and the complementarity between education and training facilitates the adoption of complex technologies, which require substantial training costs. Firms that use these technologies pay high wages and attract graduates from the best schools. Other firms, which operate in a secondary labor market, use simple technologies and pay the reservation wage. The expected gain from access into a good school stimulates investment in academic skills.

In another equilibrium (*M*-equilibrium), elite schools do not induce individuals to accumulate more than the minimum stock of academic skills. The limited accumulation of these skills makes the adoption of complex technologies relatively less profitable. Labor turnover is important and labor market experience matters more than school quality in the reduction of training costs faced by firms.

Since the share of high wage and high-productivity firms is higher in the *S*-equilibrium, a shift from the *M*- to the *S*-equilibrium yields a higher average output per head and higher average wages. Starting from the *M*-equilibrium, however, educational reforms that change the size of the elite school sector in a marginal way are unlikely to induce such a shift, and the government can increase both average output and average wages only if it succeeds in changing the hiring policies of firms using complex technologies from reliance upon experienced labor to recruitment of new school graduates from the best schools.

Hence, educational policy must be coordinated with a policy that induces firms to hire from the best schools. Since firms are willing to hire from the best schools only when individual investment in academic skills is high, a coordinated increase in individual investment in academic skills is crucial to push the economy from the M- to the S-equilibrium. This regime switch also increases economic welfare if the profit gains made by firms as a whole are sufficient to compensate the eventual losses made by workers both because of the lower labor market turnover and because of the higher cost of investment in education.

The material in this paper is organized as follows. Section 2 introduces the model and Section 3 is devoted to the discussion of government policy. Conclusions follow.

2. The Model

SET-UP

Consider an economy populated by a given large number of individuals and firms. Each firm employs a single worker. In each period of time, a fraction s of employed workers quits the labor market forever and is replaced by an equal inflow of new workers. If the total number of firms is normalized to one, total outflows and total inflows are both equal to s. For a single firm, new hires can be either new entrants or workers who quit other firms. For the economy as a whole, however, new hires must necessarily come from new entrants.

New entrants differ only in the level of education acquired before entering the labor market. Education is provided free of charge by schools run by the government. The schooling system is composed of ordinary and elite schools. The smaller the size of the elite-school sector, the harder the access into the sector. Elite schools select individuals by adopting tough entry standards. Those who do not pass these standards get into ordinary schools. Access to elite schools requires costly effort in the development of academic skills (such as the ability to solve mathematical problems and language skills) by individuals who are identical both in their innate ability and in their perceived disutility of effort.[5]

Let $[\mu \in \mu_0, 1]$ denote the effort spent by an individual to develop academic skills. There is a one-to-one relationship between effort spent and accumulated skills. Hence, μ denotes also the stock of academic skills. Maximum feasible effort is normalized to one and minimum effort, μ_0, can be produced without cost. A higher μ increases the probability of passing the entry standard and getting into elite schools.

Firms can choose between two technologies, H (high tech) and L (low tech). While individuals do not differ in their innate ability, firms differ in their underlying managerial ability, α, which is assumed to be distributed uniformly in the population of firms as follows

$$\int_{\alpha_{\min}}^{\alpha_{\max}} \frac{1}{\alpha_{\max} - \alpha_{\min}} \, d\alpha \equiv \int_{\alpha_{\min}}^{\alpha_{\max}} f(\alpha) \, d\alpha = 1 \tag{1}$$

where $\alpha_{\max} > 1 > \alpha_{\min}$ and $\alpha = 1$ is the managerial ability associated to the standard firm.

The H-technology has the following features: first, output per head is equal to ϕy, with $\phi > 1$. Second, jobs require that new hires be trained at a cost. Skills are firm-specific, and training is fully paid by firms. Let τ be the cost borne by the standard firm. If the hired employee is a new labor market entrant who has just graduated from an elite school, her formal education and investment in the development of academic skills interact well with the requirements of this technology, thereby enhancing her trainability. Hence, her training cost is reduced at the rate $1 - \beta_g \mu$, with $0 < \beta_g < 1$. On the other hand, if the hired employee is from an ordinary school, the training cost is simply τ (for the standard firm).[6]

An alternative to hiring new school graduates is to hire experienced workers, who have already undertaken some training in low-tech firms. While skills are firm-specific and cannot be fully transferred from firm to firm, labor market experience is useful in that it reduces training costs in the H-technology at the rate λ, with $0 < \lambda \leq 1$.[7] Thus both education in elite schools and labor market experience are productive in this model because they reduce the training costs borne by firms choosing the H-technology.[8]

In the L-technology, both training costs and output per head, y, are lower than in the H-technology. Compared to the H-technology, schooling and investment μ are assumed to be ineffective in the reduction of training costs in this type of technology. Hence, firms choosing the L-technology are simply indifferent among graduates coming from different types of school.

Intuitively, it is useful to think of the H-technology as a complex environment that yields higher output but is more difficult to manage. Higher complexity requires adequate skills. These skills are provided to employees by firms and are more easily acquired by individuals with better (and more) education, prior to that being dissipated in work life. Hence, better education reduces training costs borne by firms adopting this technology. On the other hand, firms adopting the L-technology have a simpler and less productive environment that requires simpler skills. The cost of acquiring these skills, also provided by the hiring firm, depends neither on the quality nor on the quantity of education.

In the rest of this paper, we specialize the model further by assuming that training costs in the L-technology are zero. This assumption preserves the key difference in training costs between the two technologies and has the merit of simplifying the algebra considerably.[9] We also assume that $\lambda\tau > 0$ and $(1 - \beta_g)\tau > 0$.[10] These additional assumptions on parameters λ and β_g imply that either academic skills accumulated in the education process or experience in the labor market can reduce training costs faced by H-technology firms but cannot make training in that technology cheaper than training in the L-technology.

Abler managers are more likely to attract hires from elite schools and to manage and properly organize the complexity of the H-technology, which requires higher training costs. On the other hand, the simpler L-technology is more likely to be chosen by less able managers. Managerial ability affects on-the-job training costs in the L-technology as follows:

$$\frac{\tau}{\alpha_i} < \frac{\tau}{\alpha_j} \quad \text{iff } \alpha_i > \alpha_j.$$

Hence, firms endowed with higher managerial ability face lower training costs.

In this model, individuals invest in education, and firms select the appropriate technology. Each agent is assumed to play a Nash noncooperative game and select the optimal action by taking the action of all other agents as given. Thus each individual chooses μ by taking both the action of other individuals and the allocation of firms to technologies as given. This is equivalent to assuming that individuals are too small compared to the size of the market to internalize the effect of their individual choice of μ on the allocation of firms. On the other hand, each firm chooses the most suitable technology by taking both the choice of other firms and the decision of individuals as given. Hence, each firm is also too small relative to the size of the market to explicitly take into account the impact of its choice of the appropriate technology on the educational choice of individuals. These features of the game played by each agent imply the presence both of spillovers and of strategic complementarities. As a consequence, there could be multiple equilibria.[11]

To solve for the steady state decentralized Nash equilibrium, we start from the optimal allocation of firms to technologies when the individual choice of μ is given.[12] Firms in this frictionless economy live forever and immediately fill vacant jobs created by separations with new hires. Product prices are constant and equal to 1. Define with J the asset value of lifetime profits from a filled job and with R the asset value from a vacant job. In the steady state, the following relation must hold:

$$J_i = \frac{\xi_i + sR_i + (1-s)J_i}{1+r} \tag{2}$$

where i indicates the firm, r is the real rate of interest, and ξ are current operating profits gross of training costs. Since vacant jobs are immediately filled and training costs are fully borne by firms, it must be that

$$R_i = J_i - \frac{\tau_i}{\alpha_i}$$

where $\tau_i = 0$ if the L-technology is chosen. Substituting this relationship into equation (2), we get that $rJ_i = \xi_i - s(\tau_i/\alpha_i) \equiv \pi_i$ and we can simply focus hereafter on current operating profits net of expected training costs, π_i.

Let H be the number of firms that choose the H-technology, with S firms hiring new graduates from elite schools and $M = H - S$ firms hiring experienced workers from other firms. In what follows, we shall adopt the convention of identifying a firm adopting the H-technology as a high-tech firm. Firms adopting the L-technology are identified instead as low-tech firms. The high-tech firm is further labeled as a S (school only)-firm if it hires a new school graduate from elite schools and as a M (market only)-firm if it hires an experienced worker from the market.

WAGE DETERMINATION

In the steady state and with individual utility linear in income, the return from employment in a high-tech firm is

$$rE_H = w_H - sE_H \tag{3}$$

where E_H is the asset value of a job in a high-tech firm, w_H is the wage, and we assume that the return from leaving the labor market is zero. Notice that firm-specific training costs are similar to turnover costs and constitute a match specific economic rent that is shared by the parties.[13] Since training costs paid by high-tech firms are strictly positive, it is reasonable to characterize wage determination in these firms as the outcome of a bargain between the parties.

Suppose that high-tech firms invest in training employees before fixing the wage w_H.[14] After training costs have been sunk, there is a hold-up problem and employees can bargain for a higher wage as a result of the investment. Following Malcomson (1997), define $\bar{w}$ and $\bar{\pi}$ as the default payoffs that the parties receive while they continue to bargain. Suppose also that employees do not take up a temporary job and firms do not hire other employees temporarily during the process of negotiation.[15] The total gain from reaching an agreement once the investment in training has been made turns out to be $\phi y - \bar{w} - \bar{\pi}$, because sunk costs are bygones. If the relative bargaining power of employees is equal to $\eta \in [0, 1]$, the bargained wage is

$$w_H = \bar{w} + \eta[\phi y - \bar{w} - \eta\bar{\pi}]. \tag{4}$$

Normalizing both default payoffs to zero, we obtain

$$w_H = \eta\phi y \tag{5}$$

and the wage paid by high-tech firms is simply a share of output ϕy.

Low-tech firms face no training costs. With no match specific rents to share, we assume that workers in these firms are paid a wage w_L equal to b, the exogenous reservation wage. Hence

$$w_L = b. \tag{6}$$

In the steady state, the reservation wage b, which depends on the value of leisure in consumption units, varies with the level of per-capita consumption. Since per-capita consumption is closely related to output per head, we assume that b is proportional to output per head in the low-tech sector.[16] Hence, $b = \delta y$, where $\delta < 1$. A simplifying assumption that facilitates the algebra with no qualitative consequences on the ensuing discussion is that $\eta = \delta$, which implies that $w_H = \phi\delta y = \phi b$. A consequence of this assumption is that the wage differential between high- and low-tech firms is equal to the productivity differential, thus reflecting the difference in the ability to pay of the two types of firms.[17] Notice that, with $b = \delta y$ and zero training costs, low-tech firms are always profitable. Hence, there are enough jobs in this economy to absorb individuals not employed in the high-tech sector and unemployment is zero.[18]

Since wages in high-tech firms are higher than wages in low-tech firms, endogenous quits can only occur from the latter to the former. Let q be the quit rate. With nonzero quits, the steady-state return from working in a low-tech firm is

$$rE_L = b + q[E_H - E_L] - sE_L, \tag{7}$$

where E_L is the asset value of a job in a low-tech firm. When the wage differential between high- and low-tech firms is positive, the question is whether workers employed by low-tech firms can underbid workers in high-tech firms. The answer is that underbidding is not possible if workers cannot commit to work at a wage lower than w_H and to not renegotiate pay once the training cost has been sunk by firms. With no commitment, the presence of economic rents generated by training costs will induce any worker in a high-tech firm to bargain with the firm and bid the wage up to w_H. With wages equal to w_H, an important implication of the foregoing discussion is that high-tech firms that hire school graduates (S-firms) never select unexperienced individuals from ordinary schools, who are more costly to train than both experienced workers and graduates from elite schools.

HIRING POLICIES

In the steady state, profits depend on the selection of the technology. In particular, the current operating profit net of training costs (hereafter, simply "profit") for firm i selecting the H-technology is defined as

$$\pi_{si} = \phi y - w_H - \frac{s\tau(1-\beta_g\mu)}{\alpha_i} = \phi y(1-\delta) - \frac{s\tau(1-\beta_g\mu)}{\alpha_i} \tag{8}$$

if it chooses to hire a new graduate from an elite school, and

$$\pi_{mi} = \phi y - w_H - \frac{s\tau\lambda}{\alpha_i} = \phi y(1-\delta) - \frac{s\tau\lambda}{\alpha_i} \tag{9}$$

if it chooses to hire an experienced worker from the labor market. In the former case, we are assuming that firms that want to hire from elite schools can always find suitable candidates. Notice that the profit π_{si} is a positive function of μ, the investment in academic skills. This is the source of positive spillovers in the H-technology.

Let L be the number of low-tech firms. Clearly, $L = 1 - H$. Let Q be the total number of quits. Since only M-firms hire experienced workers from the market to replace sM separations, in the steady-state equilibrium it must be that $Q = sM$, and the endogenous quit rate q is given by

$$q = \frac{sM}{1-H}. \tag{10}$$

Since training is costless in the L-technology, the profit earned by firm i if it chooses it is

$$\pi_{li} = y - b = y(1-\delta). \tag{11}$$

The allocation of firms to the available technologies depends on relative profits. Recalling that each firm chooses the most adequate technology by taking the decision of other firms as given, equations (8) and (9) clearly suggest that, independently of the value of α, high-tech firms prefer to hire new graduates rather than experienced workers if

$$\mu \geq \frac{1-\lambda}{\beta_g} \equiv \underline{\mu}, \tag{12}$$

that is, if, for a given μ, the degree of positive interaction between academic skills and the H-technology, which depends on the quality of the education provided by elite schools, is high (β_g is high), and/or if previous labor market experience is of little use for training in the H-technology (λ is high). To put it differently, high-tech firms adopt the S (school only)-hiring policy when investment μ exceeds a certain critical level, $\underline{\mu}$.

If condition equation (12) holds and there are enough graduates from elite schools to fill existing vacancies, *all* high-tech firms hire exclusively from elite schools. With no hirings of experienced workers, there can be neither endogenous quits nor M-firms in the optimal allocation. We call this situation the unconstrained S-regime, where $S = H$ and $M = 0$. When there are not enough graduates from elite schools, however, some high-tech firms are forced to hire experienced workers to fill their vacancies and the S-regime is constrained.

If condition equation (12) does not hold, then all high-tech firms hire experienced workers from the market. Endogenous quits are nonzero and there are only M-firms. This is called the M-regime, where $M = H$ and $S = 0$. We shall consider both regimes in turn.

THE UNCONSTRAINED S-REGIME

In this regime, high-tech firms hire only from schools, and the endogenous quit rate q is equal to zero. Hence, the separation rate in this regime is given by s for each type of firm. The allocation of firms to technologies H and L can be characterized as follows. Our assumptions ensure that

$$\frac{\partial}{\partial \alpha}\pi_s > \frac{\partial}{\partial \alpha}\pi_l = 0. \tag{13}$$

It is also reasonable to assume that

$$[\pi_s - \pi_l] < 0 \quad \text{when } \alpha = \alpha_{\min} \tag{14}$$

so that the marginal firm, which is endowed with the lowest level of managerial ability, prefers the L- to the H-technology. The allocation of firms between the two technologies depends on the condition

$$[\pi_s - \pi_l] \lesseqgtr 0,$$

that is, the H-technology is chosen by firm i if

$$\alpha_i \geq \frac{s[\tau(1-\beta_g\mu)]}{y(\phi-1)(1-\delta)} = \alpha_S. \tag{15}$$

In this case, the equilibrium share of firms that choose the H-technology is

$$\int_{\alpha_s}^{\alpha_{\max}} f(\alpha)\, d\alpha = H, \tag{16}$$

and the share of low-tech firms is $L = 1 - H$.

Using definition equation (1), H is seen to be related to α_S by

$$\alpha_S = \alpha_{\max} - H(\alpha_{\max} - \alpha_{\min}). \tag{17}$$

Equations (15) and (17) imply that

$$\frac{\partial H}{\partial \mu} > 0, \quad \frac{\partial^2 H}{\partial \mu^2} = 0 \tag{18}$$

so that the optimal number of firms selecting the H-technology in the unconstrained S-regime is a linear and increasing function of the investment in academic skills μ.

The foregoing discussion can be geometrically summarized in the (μ, α) plane as in Figure 1. Since α is bounded by $\alpha_{\max}$ from above and by $\alpha_{\min}$ from below, and also μ is bounded by 1 from above and by μ_0 from below, our consideration is restricted to the rectangular domain defined by these boundaries. Furthermore, this rectangular domain is separated into two segments by a vertical line at $\mu = \underline{\mu}$ defined by equation (12). The unconstrained S-regime occurs on the right-hand side and the M-regime on the left-hand side of this vertical line. We

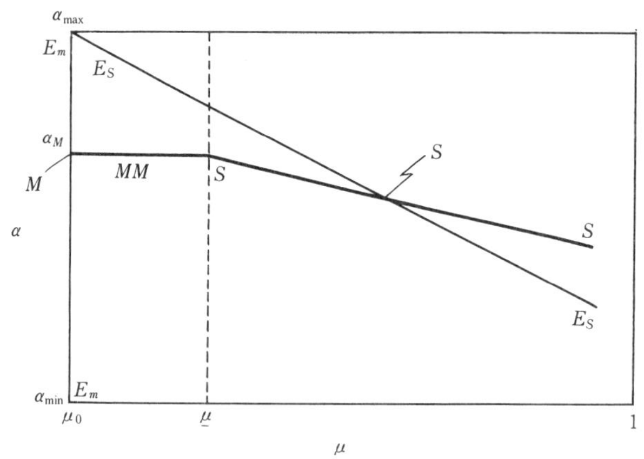

Figure 1

have drawn the downward sloping $\alpha_S = \alpha_S(\mu)$ line specified in equation (15) in the right-hand side and, for later reference, we shall call this line the SS line. For any given level of μ, say $\mu = \mu'$, the selection of technology by a firm is represented by the location of its managerial ability α along the vertical line $\mu = \mu'$. The relative size of the low-tech and the high-tech sectors can then be measured by the relative length of the vertical line segments as dissected by the SS line.

Next, consider the educational investment of individuals. The optimal allocation of firms to technologies implies that new school graduates are hired either by high-tech firms at the wage w_H or by low-tech firms at the wage b. In the steady-state equilibrium, individuals going through the schooling system take these possible outcomes into account in their selection of investment in academic skills, μ.

A constant labor force requires that s individuals graduate from school and enter the labor market in each period of time. As discussed above, schooling systems can vary in the relative size of the elite-school sector. Let Φ be the number of slots available in elite schools, with $\Phi < s$. Among individuals graduating from school and entering the labor market, $\Phi = s\Theta$ are graduates from elite schools and $s - \Phi = s(1-\Theta)$ are graduates from ordinary schools, where $\Theta \in [0, 1]$ is the percentage of graduates from elite schools. The lower Θ, the smaller the size of the elite-school sector and the lower the number of graduates from elite schools, $s\Theta$. In this paper, we assume that Θ is chosen by the government, which can determine the importance of the elite-school sector by setting the number of available slots in elite schools.

In the unconstrained S-regime, high-tech firms can find enough graduates from elite schools to fill their vacancies at the wage w_H. Hence, the following condition holds

$$\Theta \geq H, \tag{19}$$

and the probability that a graduate from an elite school will find a job in the high-tech sector is equal to (H/Θ), because of random selection.[19] In this case, the net return that an individual can expect from access to an elite school is

$$EU_G = \frac{H}{\Theta} E_H + \left(1 - \frac{H}{\Theta}\right) E_L - \Omega(\mu - \mu_0), \tag{20}$$

where $\Omega(\mu - \mu_0)$ is the cost of investment in education with the following properties

$$\Omega(0) = 0, \quad \Omega' \lesseqgtr 0 \text{ as } \mu \lesseqgtr \mu_0, \quad \Omega'' > 0, \tag{21}$$

$(1 - H/\Theta)$ is the probability of finding a job in a low-tech firm, and μ_0

is the minimum level of investment in academic skills, which yields zero investment costs. Moreover, E_H and E_L are defined by equations (3) and (7) with q equal to zero (no endogenous quits).

The expected net return from entry into an ordinary school is

$$EU_B = E_L - \Omega(\mu - \mu_0). \tag{22}$$

With homogeneous individuals, we model entry into elite schools as the outcome of a tournament over an entry standard. Given a standard of performance σ^*, individuals who perform at least up to the standard get into elite schools, while those who perform less than the standard go to ordinary schools. Since participants are homogeneous, they end up investing the same amount μ.[20]

More in detail, define the probability of passing the standard as $\text{Prob}\{\sigma \geq \sigma^*\}$ and let individual performance in the schooling race be measured as

$$\sigma = \mu + \varepsilon \tag{23}$$

where ε is luck, which varies according to a standard normal distribution G. Individuals choose μ to maximize expected utility

$$EU = \text{Prob}\{\sigma \geq \sigma^*\}EU_G + \text{Prob}\{\sigma < \sigma^*\}EU_B. \tag{24}$$

Notice that the individual payoff given by equation (24) is an increasing function of H, the number of high-tech firms. Hence, there are positive spillovers in the interaction among firms and individuals, as it happens in equation (8).

By substituting equations (20) and (22) into equation (24), the first order condition of this maximization problem is

$$g(\sigma^* - \mu)\left[\frac{H(\phi - 1)\delta y}{\Theta(r + s)}\right] = \Omega'(\mu - \mu_0) \tag{25}$$

where g is the normal density function and each individual sets μ by taking both H and Θ as given. Ex-post, the probability of entering an elite school must equal the proportion of available seats. Hence,

$$1 - G(\sigma^* - \mu) = \Theta, \tag{26}$$

where G is the distribution function, and we have used the fact that homogeneous individuals set the same value of μ.[21] Since individual effort in equation (25) is increasing in the number of high-tech firms, there are strategic complementarities in the strategies pursued by individuals and firms.

The comparative static properties of the choice of μ by each individual is summarized by the following lemma:

LEMMA 1. *In the unconstrained S-regime individual investment in academic skills* μ *increases either* (i) *as the number of high-tech firms increases, or* (ii) *as the size of the elite school sector is reduced.*

PROOF. First define $Z = ((\phi - 1)\delta y/(r+s))$. Noting that μ and σ^* are simultaneously determined by equations (25) and (26), we totally differentiate the system to obtain:

$$\begin{pmatrix} -\dfrac{LZ}{\Theta}g' - \Omega'' & \dfrac{LZ}{\Theta}g' \\ g & -g \end{pmatrix} \begin{pmatrix} d\mu \\ d\sigma^* \end{pmatrix} = \begin{pmatrix} \dfrac{gLZ}{\Theta^2} \\ 1 \end{pmatrix} d\Theta + \begin{pmatrix} -\dfrac{gZ}{\Theta} \\ 0 \end{pmatrix} dL, \tag{27}$$

where g, g', and Ω'' are respectively evaluated at the optimum.

(i) When $d\Theta = 0, d\mu = d\sigma^*$ from the second part of equation (27). Substituting this into the first part gives

$$\frac{d\mu}{dL} = \frac{gZ}{\Theta\Omega''} > 0. \tag{28}$$

(ii) When $dL = 0, d\sigma^* = d\mu - (1/g)d\Theta$, and substituting this into the first part of equation (27) gives

$$\frac{d\mu}{d\Theta} = -\frac{LZ}{\Theta\Omega''}\left(\frac{g}{\Theta} + \frac{g'}{g}\right). \tag{29}$$

The expression within parentheses in the right-hand side of this derivative can be rewritten as

$$\left(\frac{g}{\Theta} + \frac{g'}{g}\right) = \left(\frac{g}{1-G} + \frac{g'}{g}\right) \equiv \chi(\varepsilon).$$

We distinguish two cases. In the first case, $\Theta \geq \frac{1}{2}, g' \geq 0, \chi(\varepsilon)$ is unambiguously positive and $d\mu/d\Theta < 0$. In the second case, $\Theta < \frac{1}{2}$ and $g' < 0$. Because $g(\varepsilon)$ is normal, $g'(\varepsilon)/g(\varepsilon) = -\varepsilon$. On the other hand, the first term within parentheses is known as the inverse Mills's ratio, and we denote it as $\zeta(\varepsilon)$. Hence

$$\chi(\varepsilon) = \zeta(\varepsilon) - \varepsilon.$$

Since we know that

$$\zeta(\varepsilon)(\zeta(\varepsilon) - \varepsilon) \in (0, 1)$$

and that $\zeta(\varepsilon)$ is positive, $\chi(\varepsilon)$ must also be positive[22] and we can unambiguously sign the expression equation (29) to be negative. (Q.E.D.)[23]

This lemma shows that reducing the size of the elite school sector increases individual investment μ. First, more academic skills must be acquired to pass the tougher standard. Second, reducing Θ when $\Theta > H$ increases the probability that a graduate from an elite school matches with a high-tech job, thus increasing the expected returns from entry in an elite school.

We shall hereafter write the optimal level of investment μ in the unconstrained S-regime as

$$\mu = \mu_S(H, \Theta) \tag{30}$$

The above proof shows that, for a given Θ, the difference $\sigma^* - \mu$ stays constant and so does g, at the optimum. Hence we have:

COROLLARY 2. *If the cost of investing in academic skills is quadratic, i.e.,*

$$\Omega(\mu - \mu_0) = \frac{\chi}{2}(\mu - \mu_0)^2, \tag{31}$$

then the optimal choice of education is a linear function of H, given Θ.

Geometrically, the optimal choice of μ for a given H can be expressed by a downward sloping relationship between α_S and μ (recall the relationship equation [17]) in the (μ, α) plane of Figure 1. Using the quadratic investment cost function equation (31), this relationship is drawn as a straight line segment emanating from the point $(\mu_0, \alpha_{\max})$ with slope

$$-\frac{\psi(r+s)\Theta(a_{\max} - a_{\min})}{g(\sigma^* - \mu)\delta(\phi - 1)y}. \tag{32}$$

We shall call this the $E_S E_S$ curve. The geometry given in Figure 1 makes it clear that the interaction between optimal individual investment and the optimal allocation of firms to technologies determines a steady-state equilibrium as an intersection of the $E_S E_S$ curve and the SS curve. It is easy to see that there may be one intersection or no intersection at all, depending on the parameters of the model. Because of condition equation (19), the resulting value of H must not exceed Θ even if an intersection in this regime exists. Moreover, in order for an equilibrium to be locally stable the slope of the $E_S E_S$ curve given by the expression equation (32) must be less than that of the SS curve, which is shown to be given by:

$$\frac{d\alpha_S \mu}{d\mu} = -\frac{s\tau\beta_g}{y(\phi - 1)(1 - \delta)}, \tag{33}$$

i.e., the $E_S E_S$ curve must be steeper than the SS curve.

We can summarize the foregoing discussion as

Proposition 3. *An interior locally stable steady-state equilibrium in the unconstrained S-regime exists under a quadratic investment cost function and a given value of* Θ, *with* $\Theta \geq H$, *if there exists a pair* (μ^*, H^*) *such that*

(i) $\underline{\mu} < \mu^* < 1, 0 < H^* \leq \Theta$

(ii) $H^* = \dfrac{\alpha_{\max} - \alpha_S(\mu^*)}{\alpha_{\max} - \alpha_{\min}}$

and

$$\mu^* = \mu_S(H^*, \Theta).$$

(iii) $\dfrac{\psi(r+s)\Theta(a_{\max} - a_{\min})}{g(\sigma^* - \mu^*)\delta} > \dfrac{s\tau\beta_g}{(1-\delta)}$

There is at most one locally stable steady-state equilibrium in the unconstrained S-regime.

As illustrated in Figure 1, for an interior equilibrium with $\underline{\mu} < \mu^* < 1$ to exist, the configuration of parameters must be such that the $E_S E_S$ curve intersects the $\mu = \underline{\mu}$ line above and the $\mu = 1$ line below the SS curve.

In the unconstrained S-regime, separations are exogenous and firms fill their vacant positions by hiring new school graduates. While high-tech firms strictly prefer to hire graduates from elite schools, low-tech firms hire graduates indifferently from either type of school. High-tech firms have higher productivity and pay their employees more than low-tech firms, which pay the reservation wage. There is no interfirm mobility from the low- to the high-tech sector. If we interpret high managerial ability as the ability to attract and organize not only trainable workers from elite schools but also large capital stock, we can characterize the equilibrium in terms of firm size, measured by the capital–labor ratio. While large firms typically choose the H-technology, small and medium firms choose the L-technology.

THE CONSTRAINED S-REGIME

In the previous subsection we have assumed that the share of new graduates from elite schools, Θ, is at least as high as the share of firms hiring graduates from elite schools, H. When $\Theta < H$, the behavior both of firms and of individuals operating in the S-regime is affected.

To see why, assume that initially $\Theta = H$ and that Θ is reduced. Consider first firms. When $\Theta < H$, there are too few graduates from elite schools relative to the available vacancies in the high-tech sector. Hence, some firms are constrained to fill their vacancies by hiring experienced workers from the market, who are cheaper to train than unexperienced graduates from ordinary schools. Letting $\rho = \Theta/H$ be the probability of filling a vacancy with graduates from elite schools, expected profits in the constrained S-regime are

$$\pi_{si} = \phi y(1-\delta) - \rho\frac{s\tau(1-\beta_g\mu)}{\alpha_i} - (1-\rho)\frac{s\tau\lambda}{\alpha_i} \tag{34}$$

and condition equation (12), which separates the S- from the M-regime, still holds. When ρ is less than 1, there is endogenous turnover from low- to high-tech firms also in the S-regime, because some firms in the high-tech sector hire experienced workers and pay them more than in low-tech firms.

Using equation (34), the number of high-tech firms is given by

$$\alpha_i \geq \frac{s[\rho\tau(1-\beta_g\mu) + (1-\rho)\tau\lambda]}{y(\phi-1)(1-\delta)} = \alpha_{SC}. \tag{35}$$

Since the probability ρ is decreasing in H, equation (35) implies that the optimal number of high-tech firms is strictly increasing in the level of individual investment μ, even when $\Theta < H$. It also implies that, for given μ, $(\partial H/\partial\Theta) > 0$.[24]

When Θ is reduced below H, overall profits fall, both because some of the high-tech firms have to fill their vacancies with experienced workers, who are more costly to train than graduates from elite schools,[25] and because some other firms switch from the H- to the L-technology, which was less profitable before the reduction in Θ. Since low-tech firms are unaffected by the change, both overall profits and H, the number of high-tech firms, decline.

Turning to individuals investing in education, the expected return from access to an elite school in this regime is

$$EU_G = E_H - \Omega(\mu - \mu_0) \tag{36}$$

because all graduates from elite schools can find a job in the high-tech sector. Since high-tech firms hire either graduates from elite schools or experienced workers, the expected return from an ordinary school is

$$EU_B = E_L' - \Omega(\mu - \mu_0) \tag{37}$$

where

$$rE_L' = \delta y + \gamma(E_H - E_L) - sE_L$$

and

$$\gamma = \frac{s(H-\Theta)}{1-H}$$

and respectively the steady-state return from a job in the low-tech sector and the endogenous quit rate, obtained as the ratio of the $s(H-\Theta)$

vacancies filled by hiring experienced workers from the low-tech sector to the number of low-tech firms. Compared to the unconstrained regime, there are two differences. First, graduates from elite schools are certain to end up in the high-tech sector. Second, graduates from ordinary schools can find a job in the high-wage sector by quitting a low-tech firm, after acquiring the necessary labor market experience.

Plugging equations (36) and (37) into equation (24) and maximizing with respect to investment μ yields

$$g(\sigma^* - \mu)\left[\frac{(\phi - 1)\delta y}{(r + s + \gamma)}\right] = \Omega'(\mu - \mu_0). \tag{38}$$

Compared to equation (25), there are two important differences. First, a reduction in Θ, given H, *reduces* individual investment μ.[26] The reason is that a lower value of Θ, by increasing γ, increases the probability of finding a job in a high-tech firm even without graduating from an elite school. This reduces the incentive to invest in academic skills.

Second, for a given value of Θ, individual investment μ *declines* when H increases. An increase in the number of H firms raises the endogenous quit rate γ, thus raising the probability of being hired in a high-tech firm even without graduating from an elite school. Hence, μ falls. In Figure 1, the E_SE_S curve in the constrained S-regime is upward sloping while the SS curve is downward sloping (see equation [35]). If an intersection between the two curves exists in this regime, with $\Theta < H$, it must be unique and a proposition similar to Proposition 3 holds. In particular, the upward-sloping E_SE_S must be steeper than the downward-sloping SS curve for the unique interior equilibrium to be locally stable.

THE M-REGIME

As in the constrained S-regime, nonzero quits are possible in the steady-state equilibrium of this regime. These quits occur because high-tech firms pay wages that are strictly higher than the reservation wage and prefer to fill their vacancies with experienced workers. These workers must come from low-tech firms, where wages are lower.[27] Since workers are homogeneous, the endogenous quit rate is defined, in equilibrium, by equation (10), with $M = H$.

Using equations (9) and (11), the choice between the H- and the L-technology in this regime depends on the following condition

$$\alpha_i \geq \frac{s\lambda\tau}{y(\phi - 1)(1 - \delta)} = \alpha_M \tag{39}$$

so that all firms with managerial ability higher than α_M choose the H-technology. The shares of firms selecting the H- and L-technologies are again determined by equation (16), except that α_M replaces α_S. Notice that α_M does not depend on μ. Hence, in this regime the share of high-tech firms, H, is independent of the level of individual investment in academic skills, μ.

Recalling that $\beta_g \underline{\mu} = 1 - \lambda$ when $\mu = \underline{\mu}$, and assuming that the S-regime is unconstrained, it is immediate to show that

$$\alpha_M = \alpha_S(\underline{\mu}). \tag{40}$$

In Figure 1, α_M is a constant line in the domain of the M-regime. We shall call it the MM curve. On the whole, the curve representing the critical value of α that determines the share of high-tech firms in the M- and in the unconstrained S-regime has a discontinuity at $\mu = \underline{\mu}$.[28]

Turning to the choice of education by individuals, notice that high-tech firms in this regime prefer to hire experienced workers rather than new school graduates. On the other hand, low-tech firms are indifferent to the type of school each new hire has graduated from. Since elite schools do not provide additional returns, there is no individual incentive to get into these schools and to accumulate academic skills by choosing $\mu > \mu_0$.

Thus the privately optimal level of educational effort in the M-regime is equal to μ_0, the minimum level of μ in terms of cost, quite independently of the distribution of firms among available technologies. In Figure 1, this choice is represented by the vertical line $\mu = \mu_0$. We call it the $E_M E_M$ curve. It is immediate to see that a steady-state equilibrium is established by the intersection of $E_M E_M$ and MM curves, (μ_0, α_M). More formally, we have

PROPOSITION 4. *A steady-state interior equilibrium exists in the M-regime if*

$$\alpha_M < \alpha_{\max}.$$

There is at most one such an equilibrium, and, if it exists, it is locally stable.

If an equilibrium exists in the S-regime with $\mu > \underline{\mu}$, then it follows that the number of high-tech firms is strictly higher in this regime than in the M-regime. By default, the share of low-tech firms is higher in the M-regime.[29] If we characterize the equilibrium in terms of firm size, with large firms typically choosing the H-technology and small and medium firms choosing the L-technology, the M-regime features both significant labor market flows from small to large firms and the limited role played by the schooling system in the matching of new entrants with private industry, which prefers experienced workers to new graduates of relatively low average quality.

THE POSSIBILITY OF MULTIPLE REGIME EQUILIBRIA

We have seen that there is at most one locally stable interior equilibrium in the S-regime (with $\mu > \mu_0$) and that there is also at most one locally stable interior equilibrium in the M-regime. This result can be summarized in the following proposition.

PROPOSITION 5. *Depending on the parameters of the model, the economy can be characterized by* (i) *a single S-regime equilibrium,* (ii) *a single M-regime equilibrium,* (iii) *multiple regime equilibria, or* (iv) *no equilibrium.*

An example of multiple regime equilibria, that is, an equilibrium in the unconstrained S-regime (S-equilibrium), and an equilibrium in the M-regime (M-equilibrium), is illustrated in Figure 1. In such a case, historical accident decides which equilibrium the economy actually falls in. In the S-equilibrium, investment μ tends to be high because expected returns to schooling are high and large firms hire graduates from elite schools. In the M-equilibrium, investment μ is low and labor market turnover is relatively high.

3. GOVERNMENT POLICY

A key feature of the decentralized Nash equilibrium described in our model is the assumption that each agent (individual or firm) is too small to take into explicit account the effect of her own action on the optimal decision of other agents. This has implications both on the equilibrium level of educational investment μ and on the optimal number of high-tech firms.

To see why, consider the unconstrained S-regime and recall that H in this regime is an increasing function of μ. While an increase in effort by a single individual has little effect on H, a coordinated and symmetric increase in μ increases the number of firms hiring from elite schools. This in turn makes individual investment more attractive. As shown by Cooper and John (1988), the presence of positive spillovers in equations (8) and (24) implies that equilibria can be ranked in a Pareto sense, with the high μ equilibrium being Pareto superior to the low μ equilibrium.[30]

Since equilibria in the unconstrained S-regime can be Pareto ranked by investment in education and investment μ increases when Θ falls, reducing the size of the elite-school sector in this regime improves both national output and economic welfare. By reducing Θ when $\Theta > H$, the government increases both μ and H, thus cutting the gap between Θ and H. A key implication is that, in the unconstrained S-regime, a government that cares only about efficiency should set Θ at the lowest level consistent with condition equation (19), that is, at $\Theta = H$.

Next, suppose that $\Theta = H$ and assume that the government further reduces Θ below H. The important question here is whether such a move leads to a Pareto improvement. The answer is negative. We have already shown that firms in the S-regime are either worse off or as well off when Θ is reduced below H. It remains to be shown that individuals lose from a reduction of Θ below H. To do so, we compute the marginal change of expected utility EU in the constrained S-regime when μ is optimally chosen and Θ is marginally reduced. Using the envelope theorem and recalling that H changes when Θ varies, the marginal change in expected utility is equal to

$$\frac{\partial EU}{\partial \Theta} = \frac{(\phi - 1)\delta y}{r + s}\left[1 - \frac{\gamma}{r + s + \gamma}\right] * \left\{1 - \frac{s(1 - \Theta)}{(r + s + \gamma)(1 - H)}\left[1 - \frac{1 - \Theta}{1 - H}\left(\frac{\partial H}{\partial \Theta} + \frac{\partial H}{\partial \mu}\frac{\partial \mu}{\partial \Theta}\right)\right]\right\}. \quad (41)$$

This derivative is positive when the expression within braces is positive, that is, when

$$\frac{s(1 - \Theta)}{(r + s + \gamma)(1 - H)}\left[1 - \frac{1 - \Theta}{1 - H}\left(\frac{\partial H}{\partial \Theta} + \frac{\partial H}{\partial \mu}\frac{\partial \mu}{\partial \Theta}\right)\right] < 1.$$

Using the definition of γ and the fact that $(\partial H/\partial \Theta)$, $(\partial \mu/\partial \Theta)$ and $(\partial H/\partial \mu)$ are positive in the constrained S-regime, the above condition can be written as

$$-\frac{s(1 - \Theta)^2}{(1 - H)}\left(\frac{\partial H}{\partial \Theta} + \frac{\partial H}{\partial \mu}\frac{\partial \mu}{\partial \Theta}\right) < r(1 - H).$$

Since the expression within parentheses is positive, this condition is always satisfied. Hence, when $\Theta = H$ and the government reduces Θ below H, expected utility falls. There are two effects at work. First, a lower Θ reduces the probability of passing the tougher entry standard, and both $\text{Prob}\{\sigma \geq \sigma^*\}$ and expected utility EU fall. Second, a reduction in Θ affects both directly and indirectly, by reducing μ and H, the probability that experienced workers from ordinary schools find a job in the high-tech sector. Since the former effect prevails, expected utility falls.

The foregoing discussion shows that, in the constrained S-regime, the government can improve welfare by raising Θ. Since $(\partial H/\partial \Theta)$ in note 24 is positive and less than 1 when Θ is close to H, an increase in Θ increases H by less, closing the gap between the two variables.[31]

To summarize, we have shown that, when Θ is larger than H, the government has an incentive to reduce Θ, thus reducing the difference between Θ and H. We have also shown that, when $\Theta = H$, there is no incentive to cut Θ further, because a reduction in Θ below H reduces economic welfare. Finally, when $\Theta < H$, the government can increase welfare by increasing Θ. It follows that government policy in the S-regime can be characterized by the proposition below:

PROPOSITION 6. *The optimal S-equilibrium is the equilibrium that satisfies Proposition 3 with Θ strictly equal to H.*

Recall that an assumption made at the outset was that workers who attend schools and subsequently enter the low-tech sector only to move to a high-tech firm later are not cheaper to train than similar workers coming from ordinary schools. We have justified this assumption by arguing that the relative advantage of being a new graduate from an elite school rapidly decays with labor market experience. Notice that graduates from elite schools are hired by low-tech firms only when $\Theta > H$, that is, when there are too many graduates from elite schools with respect to the number of available vacancies. An implication of Proposition 6 is that, in the optimal S-equilibrium, all graduates from elite schools find a job in the high-tech sector. It also follows that, in the S-regime, our assumption about training costs is not overly restrictive.

Finally, consider the M-regime. In this regime, individual investment is at its minimum level, μ_0, and the number of M-firms, H, is constant. The absence of positive spillovers between H and μ implies that high μ equilibria in the M-regime cannot be ranked as Pareto superior to low μ equilibria. Quite the contrary, higher μ equilibria in this regime reduce welfare because the allocation of firms to technologies is unchanged but the cost of investment in education Ω increases. Hence, net national output falls as μ increases between μ_0 and $\bar{\mu}$.

If the economy is located in a M-equilibrium and the government wishes to increase both the share of high-tech firms in the economy and investment in education μ, it can only do so by a coordinated increase in investment μ over $\bar{\mu}$, which shifts the economy from the M- to the S-regime and induces firms to switch their hiring policies from reliance upon experienced workers to the selection of new graduates from elite schools. Therefore, changes in educational policy must be coordinated with a policy that induces firms to hire graduates from the best schools.

Should the government pursue such a policy? The answer is positive if economic welfare increases. Let the government set Θ in the S-regime to achieve the optimal S-equilibrium and let this equilibrium be described by the pair (μ^*, H^*). Since a move from the M- to the S-regime increases the number of firms adopting the complex technology, both average productivity and average wages increase. Moreover, firms are at least as well off in the S-regime as in the M-regime. To see why, notice that in the interior S-equilibrium $\alpha_S(\mu^*) < \alpha_M$ if $\mu^* > \underline{\mu}$. Firms with $\alpha_i \geq \alpha_M$, which would have chosen the H-technology in the M-regime, gain from the switch, because training costs are lower in the S-regime. On the other hand, firms with $\alpha_S(\mu^*) \leq \alpha_i < \alpha_M$, which would have selected the L-technology in the M-regime, also gain by shifting to the H-technology in the S-regime, because of equation (15). The remaining lot, with $\alpha_i < \alpha_S(\mu^*)$, is as well off in either regime. Hence, overall profits increase.

While firms as a whole gain from the shift, workers could lose and end up with a lower expected utility. In the M-regime, investment in education μ is at its minimum level, the cost of investing in academic skills Ω is zero, and individuals who work in the low-tech sector can expect to find a job in the high-tech sector with a nonzero probability q. In the S-regime, individuals have a higher probability of finding a job in the larger high-wage sector at the price of higher effort in the schooling system ($\Omega > 0$ because $\mu > \mu_0$). In this regime, however, failure to find a job in the S-sector means to be trapped in the low-tech sector, because high-wage firms do not hire experienced workers.

Individuals are at least as well off in the S-regime as in the M-regime if their expected utility there (equation [24]) is at least as high as their expected utility in the M-regime, given by

$$E_L = \frac{\delta y}{r+s} + \frac{q}{r+s}\left[\frac{(\phi - 1)\delta y}{r+s+q}\right].$$

With $\Theta = H^*$, this is the case if the following condition holds

$$[\text{Prob}\,\sigma \geq \sigma^*]\frac{(\phi - 1)\delta y}{(r+s)} - \Omega(\mu^* - \mu_0) \geq \frac{q}{r+s+q}\frac{(\phi - 1)\delta y}{(r+s)}. \quad (42)$$

The expression on the left-hand side is the expected gain from participation in the tournament for entry in elite schools in the S-regime, evaluated at the optimal S-equilibrium (μ^*, H^*), and must be positive to induce individuals to join the entry tournament. The expression on the right-hand side is the difference between expected returns from employment in a low-tech firm in the M- and in the S-regime and is also positive with positive turnover q. Inequality equation (42) is more likely to be satisfied when the turnover rate q in the M-regime is low (the share of high-tech firms in the M-regime is low).

In the presence of lump sum transfers, the move from the M- to the S-equilibrium improves economic welfare if the gains made by firms are sufficient to compensate the eventual losses made by individuals. Since overall profits from the shift increase as μ increases in the S-regime, while eventual individual losses remain unchanged because of the envelope theorem, the likelihood of a welfare gain is higher when μ is relatively high and the size of the elite-school sector is relatively small.

4. Conclusions

We conclude by going back to the original question as to whether the size of the elite-school sector matters for economic performance and welfare. We have shown that the economic interactions among the decision to invest in academic skills, the allocation of firms to technologies, and the labor market can generate multiple-regime equilibria. In one regime, the size of the elite-school system matters, individuals invest in academic skills, and graduates from elite schools find jobs in the high wage sector of firms adopting complex technologies. In another regime, the size of the elite-school sector does not matter, individuals do not invest in academic skills, and the matching of workers to high wage jobs occurs through labor market turnover.

If the economy is located in the latter regime, the government can shift it to the former regime, where both average output per head and average wages are higher, only if it succeeds in shifting the hiring policies of firms using complex technologies from the reliance upon experienced labor to the recruitment of new school graduates. Hence, educational policy that varies the size of the elite-school sector must be coordinated with a policy that induce firms to hire from the best schools. Since firms are willing to hire from the best schools only when individual investment in academic skills is high, a coordinated increase in individual investment in academic skills is crucial to push the economy toward the regime with higher productivity. This regime switch also increases economic welfare if the profit gains made by firms as a whole are sufficient to compensate the eventual losses made by workers both because of the lower labor market turnover and because of the higher costly investment in education.

Notes

This is a substantial revision of a paper that circulated with the title "Education, Training and Labor Market Structure: Italy and Japan in a Comparative Perspective." We are grateful to two anonymous referees, to James Poterba, Nicholas Baigent, Andrea Boltho, Daniele Checchi, Ronald Dore, Charles Horioka, Hideshi Itoh, Bruno Parigi, Marcus Rebick, Paul Ryan, Toshiaki Tachibanaki, Vittorio Valli, Charles van Marrewijk, Alessandro Vercelli, Hiroshi Yoshikawa, and audiences in Graz, Osaka (Kansai Labor

Workshop), ISER Osaka, Naples, Rotterdam (Erasmus), Siena, and Venice for comments, criticisms and suggestions. Giorgio Brunello also thanks the Institute for Social and Economic Research, Osaka University, which provided an efficient research environment. The usual caveats apply.

1. See OECD (1995, 1997).

2. See Barro and Lee (1992); Bertola and Coen Pirani (1995). Mankiw et al. (1992) use a production function approach and relate real output per head to the rate of human capital accumulation, measured by secondary school enrollment rates.

3. Card and Krueger (1990) present evidence on the relationship between school quality and earnings.

4. Previous work related to the current study includes Redding (1996), who focuses on the interaction between human capital investment and Research and Development in a model of endogenous growth.

5. The assumption of homogeneous ability rules out interesting issues that can only be properly dealt with in a separate paper.

6. This is a useful normalization with no significant consequences. The important assumption is that formal education in ordinary schools is less efficient in enhancing the trainability of individuals with given academic skills.

7. In a broad sense, skills developed in firms using the L-technology are partially transferable to the H-technology. See Stevens (1995) for a discussion of transferable skills. In this paper, we assume that labor market experience reduces training costs equally for all movers, independently of their education. This is equivalent to assuming that the relative advantage of being a new graduate from an elite school rapidly decays with labor market experience. We shall briefly come back to this assumption in Section 3.

8. See Rosen (1976) and the references therein for a similar interpretation of the economic role of education. In this paper, we assume that the cost of on-the-job training is fully borne by firms. More in general, and following Backer, costs and returns are shared by individuals and firms.

9. See Brunello and Ishikawa (1996) for a model with nonzero training costs in the L-technology.

10. Notice that these inequalities hold for any value of $\mu \in [\mu_0, 1]$.

11. See the discussion in Cooper and John (1988).

12. By optimal allocation we mean that each firm in the market selects the technology that yields the highest profit for a given value of μ.

13. In his discussion of hold-up theories, Malcomson (1997: 1918) argues that "hold-up is an issue because turnover costs and specific investments generate rents to continued employment. Training costs create rents only when they are specific to the employer." See also Pissarides (1990); Lindbeck and Snower (1988).

14. This is equivalent to assuming that employees cannot commit on a wage set before training costs are sunk.

15. Hiring another employee while the negotiation continues requires that the firm sinks additional training costs.

16. See Pissarides (1990) for a similar assumption.

17. A less appealing alternative to wage bargaining is that firms adopting the complex technology pay efficiency wages. This approach is discussed in Brunello and Ishikawa (1996).

18. As pointed out by a referee, an alternative characterization of wage determination in low-tech firms is that these firms pay a wage $w_L = y$, thus making zero profits. Nothing of substance changes in the rest of the paper provided that

$$w_H = \phi\delta y > w_L = y$$

as we assume hereafter.

19. The number of vacancies in high-tech firms is sH, and the number of graduates from elite schools is $s\Theta$.

20. See Malcomson (1984) for a detailed discussion of similar tournaments.

21. We are supposing here that the government sets the standard σ^* passively given the decision of individuals. Alternatively we could assume that the government sets σ^* by acting as a Stackelberg leader. The qualitative features of the comparative static properties discussed below, however, are not affected.

22. See Greene (1991): 718.

23. If individuals perceive that a reduction in Θ increases L, the change in individual investment μ is

$$\frac{d\mu}{d\Theta} = -\frac{LZ}{\Theta\Omega''}\left(\frac{g}{\Theta} + \frac{g'}{g}\right) + \frac{gZ}{\Theta\Omega''}\frac{\partial L}{\partial \Theta}.$$

This derivative is larger, in absolute value, than equation (29).

24. More in detail we have

$$\frac{\partial H}{\partial \Theta} = \frac{s\tau(\lambda + \beta_g\mu - 1)}{s\tau(\lambda + \beta_g\mu - 1)\frac{\Theta}{H} + H(\alpha_{\max} - \alpha_{\min})[y(\phi - 1)(1 - \delta)]} > 0.$$

25. Recall that equation (12) holds in this regime.

26. When $\Theta \leq \frac{1}{2}$, a plausible assumption when $\Theta < H, g' < 0$ and $(\partial\mu/\partial\Theta) > 0$. When $\Theta > \frac{1}{2}, g' > 0$ and $(\partial\mu/\partial\Theta)$ is positive if the following condition holds:

$$\frac{g}{r + s + \gamma}\frac{s}{1 - H} - \frac{g'}{g} > 0.$$

In the rest of the paper, we assume that this condition is satisfied.

27. Exogenous separations are permanent flows out of the labor force.

28. When we consider the constrained S-regime,

$$\alpha_M = \alpha_{SC}(\underline{\mu}).$$

29. This result does not depend on whether the S-regime is unconstrained or not.

30. Firms are either better off or as well off when μ increases in this regime. Using the envelope theorem, utility in equation (24) is increasing in μ because $\partial H/\partial\mu > 0$.

31. More precisely, $\partial H/\partial\Theta < 1$ if

$$\rho > 1 - \frac{(\alpha_{\max} - \alpha_S)}{2(\alpha_M - \alpha_S)}.$$

Since $\alpha_M > \alpha_S$ when interior equilibria exist, this condition is certainly satisfied when ρ is close to 1.

References

Barro, R., and J. Lee. 1992. Source of economic growth. Carnegie Rochester Conferences on Public Policy 40: 1–46.

Bertola, G., and D. Coen Pirani. 1995. Market Failures, Education and Macroeconomics. Mimeo. University of Turin.

Brunello, G., and T. Ishikawa. 1996. Education, Training and Labor Market Performance: Italy and Japan in a Comparative Perspective. Institute of Social and Economic Research Discussion Paper 427. Osaka University.

Card, D., and A. Krueger. 1990. Does school quality matter? Returns to education and the characteristics of public schools in the United States. Journal of Political Economy 100: 1–40.

Cooper R., and A. John. 1988. Coordinating coordination failures in Keynesian models. The Quarterly Journal of Economics 3, 103: 441–63.

The Economist. 1997. All must have degrees. 10 May.

Greene, W. 1991. Econometric Analysis. New York: McGraw-Hill.

Lindbeck, A., and D. Snower. 1988. The Insider-Outsider Theory of Employment and Unemployment. Cambridge, Mass.: MIT Press.

Malcolmson, J. 1984. Work incentives, hierarchy and internal labor markets. Journal of Political Economy 92: 486–507.

———. 1997. Contracts, hold-up, and labor markets. Journal of Economic Literature 35: 1916–57.

Mankiw G., D. Romer, and P. Weil. 1992. A contribution to the empirics of economic growth. The Quarterly Journal of Economics 2: 407–38.

OECD. 1995. Education at a Glance. Paris: OECD.

———. 1997. Education Policy Analysis. Paris: OECD.

Pissarides, C. 1990. Equilibrium Unemployment Theory. Oxford: Blackwell.

Redding, S. 1996. The low-skill, low-quality trap: Strategic complementarities between human capital and R&D. The Economic Journal 106: 458–70.

Rosen, S. 1976. A theory of life earnings. Journal of Political Economy 84, 4: S44–S67.

Stevens, M. 1995. Transferrable training and poaching externalities. In Acquiring Skills: Market Failures, Their Symptoms and Policy Responses, A. Booth and D. Snower. Cambridge: Cambridge University Press.

II. Family, Generations, and Savings

5. Imperfection in the Capital Market and the Institutional Arrangement of Inheritance

1. Introduction

In the theoretical literature of the life-cycle savings model originating from Irving Fisher's conception of optimal intertemporal consumption behavior, it has been customarily assumed that the capital market is perfect; that is, one can borrow or lend freely in the capital market. This assumption has also been made in the models of Yaari (1964), Meade (1965), and Atkinson (1965), which include the bequest motive upon which our analysis is based.[1] One of the important implications of these analyses, though unnoted, is that under the assumption of a perfect capital market the optimal program is neutral with respect to the actual form in which inheritance is bequeathed. Namely, the same optimal program can be followed no matter whether the bequest is given as a gift *inter vivos* or as a transfer at death if one adjusts the amount of borrowing and lending suitably in the capital market.

When there is imperfection in the capital market, this neutrality property is no longer expected to be true. The purpose of this paper is to examine the impact of imperfection in the capital market on the welfare of individuals, to examine whether or not we can give any prediction with regard to the types of inheritance arrangements that may appear, and, finally, to examine some of the welfare implications of inheritance taxation, under the assumption of a certain representative type of capital market imperfection.

Our analysis proceeds as follows. The first two sections evaluate the effects of imperfection in the capital market on the optimum path of consumption and the optimum amount of bequests under alternative inheritance schemes. The third section uses the results of the preceding

Originally published in *The Review of Eonomic Studies* (July, 1974): 383–404.

sections to discuss the patterns of choice of inheritance arrangement and also examines some qualitative effects of inheritance taxation. Finally, the fourth section presents some qualificatory remarks of the present analysis.

2. The Nature of the Problem

INSTITUTIONAL NEUTRALITY OF THE YAARI-ATKINSON MODEL

By following Yaari (1964) and Atkinson (1965), we consider an individual born at economic age 0 and dying at economic age L. He bears e^{nH} children at economic age H.[2] The capital market is assumed to be perfect, and the individual is postulated to plan his consumption path and bequest by solving the following problem:

$$\text{maximize} \int_0^L u(c_t^v)e^{-\delta t}\,dt + e^{-\delta L}\phi(b_L^v) \tag{1}$$

$$\text{s.t.}\quad \dot{b}_t^v = rb_t^v + w - c_t^v \quad b_{t=0}^v = b_0^v, = I^v \tag{2}$$

where c_t^v: consumption at time t of generation v
b_t^v: financial wealth at time t of generation v
r: market rate of interest (assumed to be constant)
w: wage earnings (assumed to be constant)
I^v: present value of bequests to be received at time $L-H$ by generation v.

The optimum program of consumption and bequest is characterized by the following conditions:[3]

$$\frac{\dot{c}_t}{c_t} = \frac{r-\delta}{\varepsilon(c_t)}, \quad \text{where } \varepsilon(c) = -\frac{u''(c)c}{u'(c)} > 0 \tag{3}$$

$$u'(c_L) = \phi'(b_L). \tag{4}$$

Throughout this paper we assume that $r - \delta > 0$.[4] This implies from (3) that the optimum consumption level increases throughout the life span. The characteristics of the optimum program can then be depicted by Figure 1. In the figure, an individual starting from initial financial wealth b_0 (the point A) accumulates his wealth during the first period of his life (until he reaches the point C) and, then, decumulates his wealth during the second period of his life until his death, when he leaves the total bequests, b_L (the point B).

With regard to inheritance arrangements, three assumptions are made: (i) the actual transfer of bequests is made at the time of the donor's (parent's) death (to be hereinafter called bequest at death), and

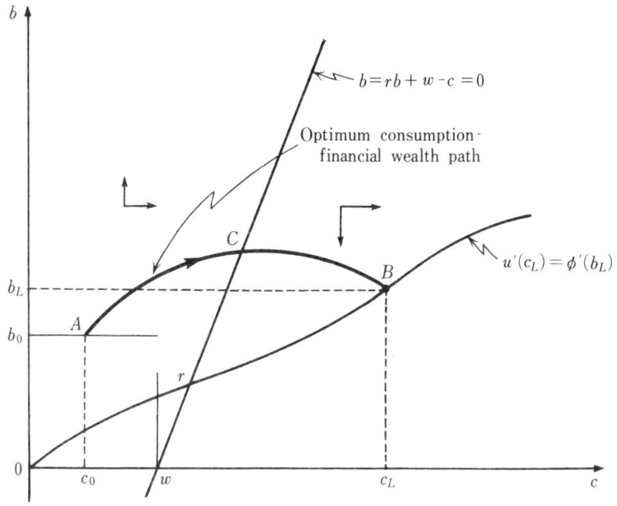

Figure 1

this arrangement is repeated over consecutive generations; in other words, a current generation receives a bequest from a previous generation at age $L-H$ and leaves a bequest to the next generation at age L; (ii) the bequests are equally divided among children (thus the per capita bequest, denoted by $\tilde{b}_L^v$, is expressed as $\tilde{b}_L^v = e^{-nH}b_L^v$); (iii) the amount of bequests received at economic age $L-H$, $\tilde{b}_L^{v-1}$, is perfectly known.[5] These assumptions and the assumption of a perfect capital market imply that an individual can furnish an initial financial wealth which equals the present value of bequests. Namely,

$$b_0^v = I^v = e^{-r(L-H)}\tilde{b}_L^{v-1}$$
$$= e^{-(r(L-H)+nH)}b_L^{v-1} \quad (5)$$

obtainable at his economic birth by borrowing in the capital market.[6]

It is easy to see, however, that so long as the capital market is perfect the optimum consumption and bequest program for an individual are independent of the particular forms through which inheritance is bequeathed. For instance, assumptions (i) and (iii) can be replaced by (i′), the actual transfer of bequests is made at the time of donee's (children's) birth (hereafter to be called gift at birth), and his arrangement is repeated over generations; thus, a current generation receives as a gift at birth the amount of the discounted value of the bequest ($I^v = e^{-r(L-H)}\tilde{b}_L^{v-1}$) from a previous generation at age 0 and leaves a gift at birth of $I^{v+1} = e^{-r(L-H)}\tilde{b}_L^v$ to each member of the next generation at age H. Moreover, any other kind of gift *inter vivos*, schemes, or combinations of gifts *inter vivos* and bequests at death that give the equivalent amount (i.e., a sum whose cumulated value at the time of death equals the planned level of bequest) will sustain the same optimum program.[7] In this sense, the Yaari-Atkinson problem under the perfect capital market assumption is perfectly neutral with respect to the institutional arrangement of inheritance. I shall henceforth refer to the optimum consumption and bequest program derived for Yaari-Atkinson problem as the basic optimum program. An important property associated with this program is that, under a certain weak condition to be satisfied, the level of consumption at each moment of time and the level of bequest are higher, the higher the level of inheritance. Formally,

PROPOSITION 1.[8] *If the value of* $(1 - \varepsilon'(c)c/\varepsilon(c))$ *does not change its sign for all* $c > 0$ *(hereafter to be called the Assumption A), then*

$$\frac{\partial c_t}{\partial I} > 0 \quad \textit{for all } t \textit{ such that } L \geqq t \geqq 0, \tag{6}$$

and

$$\frac{\partial b_L}{\partial I} > 0. \tag{7}$$

Using (7) of this proposition, we can express the level of total bequest, b_L^v, as a monotonic increasing function of I^v, given w and r.

$$b_L^v = F(I^v; w, r), \quad \text{where } F' > 0. \tag{8}$$

The relationships (8) and (5) define the mechanism of financial wealth transmission over generations.[9]

THE OPTIMUM PROGRAM UNDER AN IMPERFECT CAPITAL MARKET

We must now consider what happens to the optimum program if the capital market is not perfect. The imperfection of the capital market that we are primarily concerned with in the following is that one can dissipate one's financial wealth but can never undertake net borrowing.[10] If we introduce the variable net financial wealth, to be denoted by z_t, to represent the level of financial wealth provided that no borrowing is or was[11] done (the precise relation between the variables z_t and b_t will be made clear below), then the above definition of imperfection is mathematically expressed by:

$$z_t \geqq 0 \quad \text{for all } L \geqq t \geqq 0. \tag{9}$$

Then the problem that an individual faces is characterized by (1) subject to (2) and (9). The imposition of this new constraint implies that one can never obtain more satisfaction than with a perfect capital market.

Within the modified framework an individual's optimum program is, in general, no longer independent of the particular type of inheritance arrangement. Under certain types of inheritance arrangements the non-negative financial wealth constraint (9) may not be effective, and, therefore, the basic optimum program, i.e., the optimum program possible under a perfect capital market, can be pursued. However, under certain other types of inheritance arrangements the constraint (9) may become effective, so that the individual must be content with a program that gives less satisfaction (i.e., total utility level) than the basic optimum program. In the following, let us refer to this circumstance as "sub-optimality," where the term "sub" refers to a comparison with the basic optimum program. By assuming that individuals behave rationally, we can expect the development of an inheritance arrangement that is immune from sub-optimality. Thus, institutional forms of inheritance become an explicit variable of concern. Since the various institutional forms noted above are not the kind that can be represented by a simple single dimensional parameter, we shall confine ourselves to analysis of the most basic case where there are two alternative schemes of inheritance, namely either to leave the bequest entirely at death (bequest at death) or to give an equivalent amount at birth (gift at birth).

Within this limited framework we shall deal with the problem of choosing an inheritance arrangement in two steps. In the first step (Section 3), we shall examine under what forms of inheritance and under what other conditions the above-defined sub-optimality will actually occur, by assuming that either institutional form of inheritance is, for reasons that do not concern us at this stage, maintained over consecutive generations. In the second step (Section 4), we shall relax this last assumption and examine various criteria that lead to the actual choice of institutional forms by individual generations.

3. Consumption and Bequests under Alternative Systems of Inheritance

We begin by investigating the conditions for the occurrence of sub-optimality under the alternative schemes of inheritance arrangement—gift at birth and bequest at death. Before proceeding to a formal discussion, let us spell out the results intuitively.

Recalling the nature of imperfection in the capital market, it appears quite naturally that whether the restriction of borrowing in the market induces sub-optimality or not depends critically on the size of financial wealth that an individual inherits from the previous generation. On the one hand, within the system of gift at birth the individual leaves his bequests early in his life. This imposes a special strain on him to accumulate assets fast, and unless he receives a large enough inheritance at the start of his life, the non-negativity wealth constraint becomes binding, resulting in sub-optimality. On the other hand, within the system of bequest at death inheritance arrives late in life. With borrowing restricted, this will hurt the individual if ultimately he is due to receive a large inheritance, for he cannot "get his hands" on the wealth he would like to spend in the early part of his life; hence, the sub-optimality.

Thus, if we classify individuals according to the size of the financial wealth that they inherit (to be precise its present value), I, then those individuals at the lower end of the scale are likely to suffer from sub-optimality under gift at birth, and they would prefer the system of bequest at death; similarly, those individuals in the upper end of the scale are likely to suffer from sub-optimality under bequest at death, and they would prefer the system of gift at birth. In the following, we shall substantiate this intuitive argument and, at the same time, compare the characteristics of the consumption path and the size of bequest under sub-optimality with those of the basic optimum program.

THE CASE OF GIFT AT BIRTH

Under the arrangement of gift at birth, there is an inflow of gift from the previous generation at age 0 and an outflow of gift to the heirs at age H. Let us define the "gift adjusted" optimum wealth path associated with the basic optimum program, to be denoted by ${}^{G}\hat{S}_t (L \geqq t \geqq 0)$, by

$$ {}^{G}\dot{\hat{S}}_t = r\,{}^{G}\hat{S}_t + w - \hat{c}_t \tag{10} $$

$$ {}^{G}\hat{S}_H = \hat{b}_H - \hat{b}_L e^{-r(L-H)}, \tag{11} $$

where $\hat{c}_t$ $(0 \leqq t \leqq L)$ and $\hat{b}_t$ $(0 \leqq t \leqq L)$ are the paths of consumption and wealth along the basic optimum program (the solution to problem [1] subject to [2] only). ${}^{G}\hat{S}_H$ in (11) expresses the net financial wealth left after the optimal size of gift (associated with the basic optimum program) is made. Thus, ${}^{G}\hat{S}_t$ $(t \geqq H)$ as defined by (10) and (11) represents the net financial wealth level for the rest of the current generation's lifetime.[12] On the other hand, since inheritance is obtained at birth, $\hat{b}_t$ $(H \geqq t \geqq 0)$ represents the net financial wealth level until the time of the birth of one's children. In sum, the path of net financial wealth, ${}^{G}\hat{Z}_t$, for the problem (1) subject to (2) only, and when inheritance is made through gift at birth, is expressed as:

$$
{}^{G}\hat{Z}_t = \begin{cases} \hat{b}_t & \text{for } 0 \leqq t < H \\ {}^{G}\hat{S}_t & \text{for } H \leqq t \leqq L. \quad \text{(See Fig. 2.)} \end{cases} \tag{12}
$$

It can now easily be shown that (for a proof see Appendix 1):

PROPOSITION 2. *For any net financial wealth path ${}^{G}\hat{Z}_t$ associated with the optimum solution to problem* (1) *subject to* (2) *and that satisfies the constraint $I \geqq 0$, the necessary and sufficient condition for ${}^{G}\hat{Z}_t \geqq 0$ for all $0 \leqq t \leqq L$ is ${}^{G}\hat{S}_H \geqq 0$.*

Therefore, if the circumstance is such that the solution to (1) subject to (2) satisfies the condition ${}^{G}\hat{S}_H \geqq 0$, then constraint (9) becomes ineffective, and thus, the basic optimum program can be pursued without ever becoming infeasible. The nature of the variable ${}^{G}\hat{S}_H$ can be illuminated by solving (10) with the use of (2) and (11) to get

$$
{}^{G}\hat{S}_H e^{-rH} = \int_H^L \hat{c}_s e^{-rs}\, ds - w \int_H^L e^{-rs}\, ds, \tag{13}
$$

which is clearly a function of I $(= b_0)$. If we differentiate (13) with respect to I and then apply Proposition 1, we obtain:

PROPOSITION 3. *Under Assumption A, ${}^{G}\hat{S}_H$ is a monotonically increasing function of I.*

Therefore, there may exist a critical level, say $\underline{I}$, such that sub-optimality will occur for the individuals with inheritance less than $\underline{I}$.[13] This confirms the first statement of the intuitive argument made above.

The next task is to investigate closely the nature of the modified optimum program under sub-optimality by assuming that positive $\underline{I}$ exists. For the class of individuals whose inheritance level is below $\underline{I}$, let us impose an additional constraint

$$
{}^{G}S_H e^{-rH} + \int_H^L c_s e^{-rs}\, ds - w \int_H^L e^{-rs}\, ds \geqq 0 \tag{14}
$$

to problem (1) subject to (2). It can be seen that (14) becomes an effective substitute for the full constraint (9).[14] It is intuitively clear that it never pays for this class of individuals to hold more ${}^{G}S_H$ than is necessary. Formally, we can show (for a proof see Appendix 2) that

PROPOSITION 4. *If $I < \underline{I}$, then the modified optimum program for the problem defined by* (1) *subject to* (2) *and* (9) *is characterized by:*

(i) $^{G}S_H = 0$ (15)

$$\text{(ii)} \begin{cases} \begin{cases} c_t(I) < \hat{c}_t(I) & \text{for } 0 \leqq t \leqq H-0 \\ c_t(I) > \hat{c}_t(I) & \text{for } H \leqq t \leqq L \end{cases} \\ b_L(I) < \hat{b}_L(I) \end{cases} \tag{16}$$

where $\hat{c}_t(I)$ and $\hat{b}_L(I)$ refer to the levels of c_t and b_L along the basic optimum program corresponding to the same I.

The economic content of this proposition is fairly obvious. As we have intuitively noted earlier, for an individual with inheritance I less than $\underline{I}$, the need to make the transfer of wealth at age H imposes a special strain of accumulating wealth in the first period (i.e., from his birth to the birth of his children) at a much faster rate than is necessary when constraint (9) (or [14]) is not imposed. Thus, during the first period, the optimum level of consumption is uniformly lower than that associated with the basic optimum program. Furthermore, this strain leads to a level of bequest that is lower than that associated with the basic optimum program. On the other hand, since during the remainder of his lifetime the individual is relieved of the role to accumulate wealth in preparation for bequest, he can now enjoy a consumption path uniformly higher than that under the basic optimum program. Finally, it is clear that this special strain of early accumulation is smallest when $^{G}S_H = 0$.

Figure 2 describes the situation where sub-optimality arises. In the figure, the solid curves ($\hat{b}$ and $^{G}\hat{S}$) represent the net financial wealth path along the basic optimum program. The basic optimum program as depicted in the figure is not feasible, however, for it will result in a negative net financial wealth holding after the optimum quantity of bequests have been transferred in the form of gifts at birth (at age H). The modified optimum program, on the other hand, is represented by the dotted curves (b and $^{G}\hat{S}$). It gives both a zero net financial wealth level and a jump in the consumption level at age H, when the transfer takes place.

THE CASE OF BEQUEST AT DEATH

Under the arrangement of bequest at death, an inflow of inheritance from the older generation occurs at age $L - H$, and an outflow of wealth to the younger generation occurs at age L. Thus, an individual starts from a zero net financial wealth level. Let us define the "bequest adjusted" optimum wealth path associated with the basic optimum program, to be denoted by $^{B}\hat{S}_t$ ($L \geqq t \geqq 0$), by

$$^{B}\dot{\hat{S}}_t = rB_{S_t} + w - \hat{c}_t \tag{17}$$

$$^{B}\hat{S}_{L-H} = \hat{b}_{L-H} - \tilde{b}_L^{-1}, \tag{18}$$

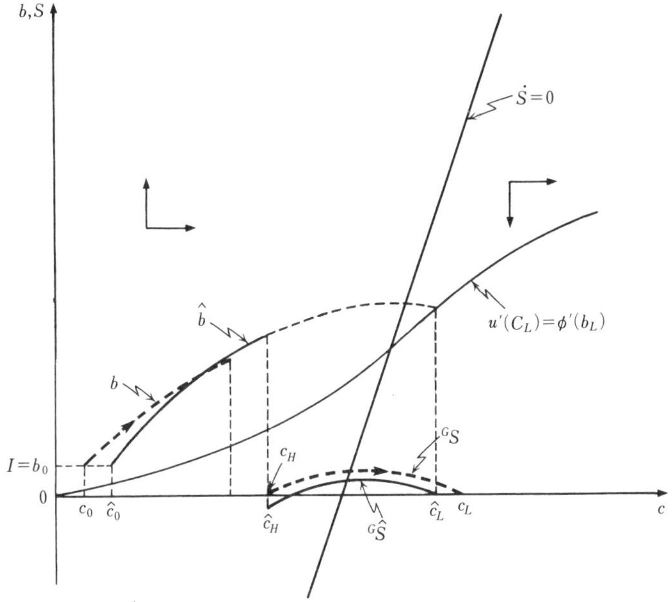

Figure 2

where $\hat{c}_t$ $(0 \leqq t \leqq L)$ and $\hat{b}_t$ $(0 \leqq t \leqq L)$ are the paths of consumption and financial wealth along the basic optimum program, and $\tilde{b}_L^{-1} = \tilde{b}_L^{v-1} = b_L^{v-1}.\, e^{-nH}$ (by [5]) is the size of bequest expected at age $L - H$. Analogous to the previous case, ${}^B\hat{S}_t(0 \leqq t < L - H)$ defined by (17) and (18) (note that ${}^B\hat{S}_0 = 0$) describes the net financial wealth path for this interval when the basic optimum program is pursued. Using the expression above, the path of net financial wealth, ${}^B\hat{Z}_t$, for problem (1) subject to (2) only, and when inheritance is made through bequest at death is summarized by:

$$
{}^B\hat{Z}_t = \begin{cases} {}^B\hat{S}_t & \text{for } 0 \leqq t < L - H \\ \hat{b}_t & \text{for } L - H \leqq t \leqq L. \quad \text{(See Fig. 3.)} \end{cases} \tag{19}
$$

It is then clear that exactly parallel propositions to the previous case hold under the present system of inheritance. (Proofs are omitted.) First we have:

Proposition 5. *For any net financial wealth path ${}^B\hat{Z}_t$ associated wih the optimum solution to problem* (1) *subject to* (2) *and that satisfies constraint $I \geqq 0$, the necessary and sufficient condition for ${}^B\hat{Z}_t \geqq 0$ for all $0 \leqq t \leqq L$ is ${}^B\hat{S}_{L-H} \geqq 0$.*

Second,

PROPOSITION 6. *Under Assumption A,* $^{B}\hat{S}_{L-H}$ *is a monotonically decreasing function of I.*

We conclude (See Appendix 3.) that in this case there exists a critical level of inheritance, to be denoted by $\bar{I}$, above which the non-negativity constraint (9) becomes effective. Thus, individuals with an inheritance (I) greater than $\bar{I}$ will suffer from sub-optimality. This confirms the second part of the intuitive argument made at the beginning of this section.[15]

For the class of individuals with inheritance levels above $\bar{I}$, let us impose an additional constraint:

$$^{B}S_{L-H} \cdot e^{-r(L-H)} = \int_0^{L-H} w \cdot e^{-rs}\,ds - \int_0^{L-H} c_s \cdot e^{-rs}\,ds \geqq 0. \tag{20}$$

This is added to problem (1) subject to (2). For exactly the same reason as in the previous case (See note 14.), this constraint (20) becomes an effective substitute for the full constraint (9). We then have:

PROPOSITION 7. *If* $I > \bar{I}$, *then the modified optimum program for the problem defined by* (1) *subject to* (2) *and* (9) *is characterized by:*

(i) $^{B}S_{L-H} = 0$ (21)

(ii) $$\begin{cases} \begin{cases} c_t(I) < \hat{c}_t(I) & \text{for } 0 \leqq t \leqq L-H-0 \\ c_t(I) > \hat{c}_t(I) & \text{for } L-H \leqq t \leqq L \end{cases} \\ b_L(I) > \hat{b}_L(I) \end{cases} \tag{22}$$

where $\hat{c}_t(I)$ *and* $\hat{b}_L(I)$ *refer to the levels of* c_t *and* b_L *along the basic optimum program corresponding to the same I.*

The reasons for the second part of proposition (22) can be explained as follows. For the class of individuals to which the present proposition applies, the optimum consumption level for the case without constraint (9) is sufficiently high after the initial period of life. Therefore, the presence of constraint (9) places a special strain to reduce consumption initially ($0 \leqq t < L-H$). This *under*-consumption during the first period, in turn, yields both *surplus* wealth and an earlier effective date to start preparation for a bequest, enabling one to achieve a uniformly higher level of consumption during the second period and a higher level of bequest than in the case of the basic optimum program. This part of the proposition has an interesting welfare implication to be discussed at the end of the next section.

On the other hand, the explanation of the first part of proposition (21) is the same as in the previous case. $^{B}S_{L-H} = 0$ gives the least

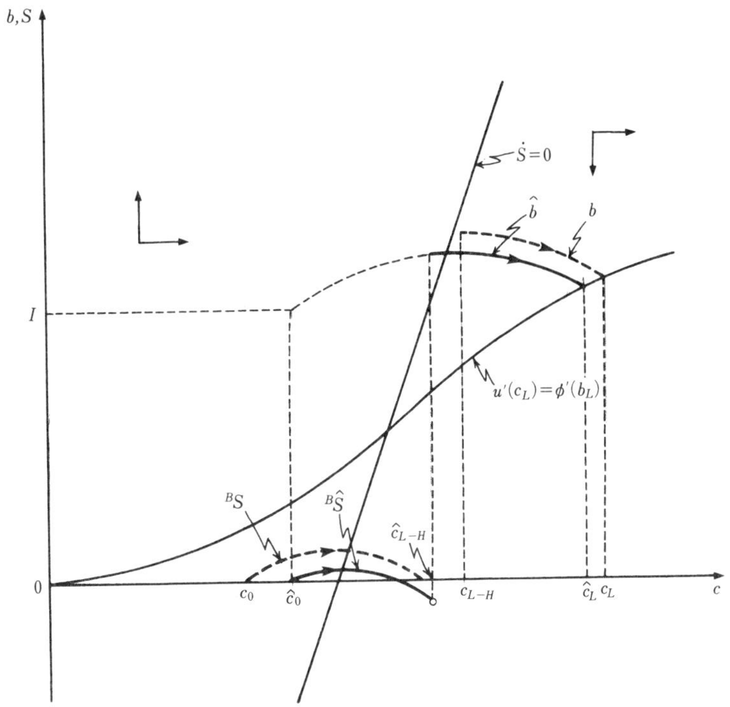

Figure 3

"strain" of under-consumption that is possible during the first period. The situation where sub-optimality occurs, is described in Figure 3. As in the previous case, the solid curves $({}^{B}\hat{S}, \hat{b})$ represent the net financial wealth path along the basic optimum program. The basic optimum program as depicted in the figure is not feasible for it will lead to a negative net financial wealth holding before the receipt of bequests at age $L-H$. The modified optimal program, on the other hand, is represented by the dotted curves $({}^{B}S, b)$. It gives both a zero net financial wealth level and a jump in the consumption level at age $L-H$.

In the above we have examined the character of any modification to the optimum consumption and bequest program that may be induced by the imperfection of the capital market under each alternative institutional form of inheritance. As a result, we have derived a critical level of inheritance (I) for each scheme: $\underline{I}$ for the gift at birth system, and $\bar{I}$ for the bequest at death system. We can easily show (For a proof see Appendix 3.):

PROPOSITION 8. *$\tilde{\underline{I}} < \bar{I}$ where $\tilde{\underline{I}}$ is defined by* $\tilde{\underline{I}} = \max(0, \underline{I})$.

Table 1. The Conditions for the Occurrence of Sub-optimality

Titles of class	Inheritance level	Inheritance arrangement	Occurrence of sub-optimality
The lower inheritance class	$0 < I < \underline{I}$	Gift at birth	Yes
		Bequest at death	No
The middle inheritance class	$\underline{I} \leq I \leq \bar{I}$	Gift at birth	No
		Bequest at death	No
The upper inheritance class	$I' < I$	Gift at birth	No
		Bequest at death	Yes

This completes the confirmation of the intuitive discussion made earlier, and we now arrive at the principal conclusion of the present section.

PROPOSITION 9. *The occurrence of sub-optimality depends upon the level of inheritance and the form of inheritance that is maintained. The conditions for occurrence of sub-optimality can be summarized by Table 1.*

Thus, a rational individual would:

(a) *prefer the system of bequest at death if he is in the lower inheritance class* (*assuming that the lower inheritance class exists*);

(b) *prefer the system of gift at birth if he is in the upper inheritance class*;

(c) *be indifferent between the two systems of inheritance if he is in the middle inheritance class.*

4. Choice of Inheritance Arrangement and the Effects of Inheritance Taxation

In the conclusion of the previous section, we have deliberately used the term "prefer," since the argument of the previous section is based on the assumption that a certain inheritance arrangement is maintained for reasons external to our concern, and thus the arrangement that happens to be maintained may not coincide with the one that avoids sub-optimality. Moreover, since the amount of inheritance varies over generations, the institutional arrangement that is preferable for one generation may not be preferable for subsequent generations. This point leads us to consider inheritance arrangements as an object of choice by each generation.

THE POSSIBILITY OF CHOICE

Let us assume that each generation is free to choose the method by which it leaves its bequest to the next generation and, for simplicity's sake, assume that the alternatives given are either to leave it wholly in terms of a gift at birth or to leave it wholly in terms of a bequest at death. We then observe:

PROPOSITION 10. (i) *When the form through which an individual receives inheritance is bequest at death, the feasibility of the basic optimum program does not depend on the form by which he leaves his inheritance if the birth of his children is not prior to the death of his parents* (*i.e.*, $H \geqq L - H$). *The same property does not hold if the birth of his children is prior to the death of his parents* (*i.e.*, $H \geqq L - H$).

(ii) *When the form through which an individual receives inheritance is gift at birth, the basic optimum program is feasible under the choice of bequest at death for leaving his inheritance, no matter what inheritance class he belongs to and no matter whether or not the birth of his children precedes the death of his parents* (*i.e.*, $H \gtreqqless L - H$).

The first part of the proposition is easily verified when we note in Figure 3 that the feasibility of the basic optimum program is solely determined by the nature of the net financial wealth path during the first period $[0, L - H]$ of the life-span, and thus, so long as H is not smaller than $L - H$, it does not depend on the form in which the bequests are transferred to the next generation (See proof of Proposition 2 in Appendix 1.). We shall in the following concentrate on what seems to be an empirically more plausible case of $H \geqq L - H$.[16] In such a case, the above "independence" property (i) implies that, if the form by which inheritance is received is a gift at birth, then the feasibility of the basic optimum program for the current generation is solely determined by the previous generation; in other words, the infeasibility, if it occurs, cannot be rectified by any choice of inheritance forms. In contrast, the second part of the proposition is obvious, for the choice of bequest at death simulates exactly the situation possible under a perfect capital market. If we integrate these considerations with Proposition 9, we obtain Table 2 showing the relationship between the types of inheritance and the feasibility of the basic optimum program for each inheritance class.[17]

Table 2. Feasibility of the Basic Optimum Program (Case $H \geqq L - H$)

The form in which inheritance is received		Gift at birth		Bequest at death	
The form in which inheritance is left		Gift at birth	Bequest at death	Gift at birth	Bequest at death
Inheritance classes	Lower	No	Yes	Yes	Yes
	Middle	Yes	Yes	Yes	Yes
	Upper	Yes	Yes	No	No

As the table clearly shows, whether the arrangement chosen by the previous generation permits feasibility of the basic optimum program for the current generation depends, in general, upon the size of inheritance transmitted from the previous generation as well as on the choice of inheritance arrangement by the current generation. This point leads us to consider the nature of wealth transmission over generations.

INTERGENERATIONAL WEALTH TRANSMISSIONS

For the sake of simplicity, let us follow Atkinson in, first, adopting a small country assumption so that the rate of interest and wage rate remain constant over generations, and, second, assuming explicitly that individuals over different households and generations have an identical utility function (an implicit assumption we have so far made). Then, the solution of $\hat{b}_L(I^v)$ associated with the basic optimum program, together with (5), defines a relation:

$$I^{v+1} = F(I^v) \quad I^0 = \text{given}, \quad v = 0, 1, 2, \ldots \tag{23}$$

that describes the process of inheritance transmission over generations. Atkinson has characterized, under the assumption of constant elasticity utility functions, three possible types of long-run solutions to this equation system (Atkinson, 1971: 212–13): (i) the case with a single globally stable equilibrium (when $\mu > \varepsilon$ or when $\mu < \varepsilon$ and $r < n$); (ii) the case with no equilibrium and the inheritance level permanently rising (can occur only when $\mu < \varepsilon$ and $r > n$); (iii) the case with two equilibria; the lower being locally stable and the upper being locally unstable (can occur only when $\mu < \varepsilon$ and $r > n$). While sub-optimality under the imperfection of the capital market modifies the functional form of $F(\cdot)$ in (23) for the relevant range of inheritance (I), and may thus alter the location and possibly the number of equilibrium points, we shall assume in the following that the impact of sub-optimality is not so strong as to require a modification of Atkinson's general characterization.[18] However, without further specification of parameters we cannot a priori tell where the equilibrium points (if they exist) lie in relation to the inheritance classes we defined in the previous section.

CHOICE OF INHERITANCE ARRANGEMENTS UNDER ALTERNATIVE VALUE HYPOTHESES

Let us now proceed to our central problem of how the choice of inheritance arrangements is made. This choice in general affects the feasibility of the basic optimum program for the next generation as well as for the bequeathing generation. The notion that the bequest motive arises to some degree out of altruistic concern on the part of one generation for its heirs leads us naturally to expect that individuals may possibly take into account the impact of their choice of inheritance form on the welfare of their heirs when they make their choice.

We shall introduce three criteria of choice: (i) intragenerational rationality: the feasibility of the basic optimum program for the current generation; (ii) intergenerational rationality: the feasibility of the basic optimum program for the next generation; (iii) institutional inertia: the propensity to follow the same arrangement as that chosen by the previous generation. With these we define two systems of lexicographic ordering to represent individuals' values:[19] the first system, which we designate as the institutional inertia hypothesis, first weighs the criterion of intragenerational rationality and, second, that of institutional inertia. Since the form in terms of which individuals receive their inheritance is predetermined for each generation, this hypothesis always gives a definite choice. Thus, this system involves a critical evaluation of the family tradition rather than blind conformity to it; however, being critical is only motivated by the concern for one's own welfare, and the psychological tie to the past dominates the concern for the welfare of the next generation (as far as the form of inheritance is concerned). The second system, which we designate as the intergenerational rationality hypothesis, first weighs the criterion of intragenerational rationality, second, that of intergenerational rationality, and, third, that of institutional inertia. Thus, the altruistic concern for future generations has priority over the psychological tie to the past. The two hypotheses share the property that the intragenerational rationality is the first criterion to be considered.

Let us now turn to the task of examining the patterns of inheritance arrangement chosen under each value system.

Institutional Inertia Hypothesis. By applying the rules of ordering under this hypothesis to Table 2, the patterns of choice by each generation under the institutional inertia hypothesis can be summarized by Table 3. Since the choice becomes determinate prior to intergenerational concern (if it ever exists) the patterns of inheritance arrangements as described by Table 3 are independent of the inheritance class to which the next generation will belong.

On the other hand, by combining the results of Table 3 and the characterization of the wealth transmission processes, the patterns of choice in the long run are derived as follows.

PROPOSITION 11. (a) *The households remaining in the lower inheritance class for over a generation, or which have remained in the lower inheritance class for over a generation and are now moving up to the*

Table 3. Choice of Inheritance Forms under the Institutional Inertia Hypothesis

I^v	If individuals receive gift at birth	If individuals receive bequest at death
Lower inheritance class	Bequest at death	Bequest at death
Middle inheritance class	Gift at birth	Bequest at death
Upper inheritance class	Gift at birth	Bequest at death^{sub}

NOTE: The superscript "sub" in this and the subsequent tables indicates that the institutional form chosen suffers from sub-optimality.

middle or the upper inheritance class, maintain the choice of bequest at death; (b) *among households in the middle or upper inheritance class,* (i) *those whose ancestors originated from the lower inheritance class, or from the middle or the upper inheritance class with bequest at death, maintain bequest at death;* (ii) *those whose ancestors originated from the middle or the upper inheritance class with gift at birth maintain gift at birth.*

Thus, no matter what the actual mobility pattern of the economy (as characterized by Atkinson) is, the persistence of either institutional arrangement over generations will result. In the extreme case where ancestors of all households belong to the lower inheritance class, the economy will exhibit the persistence of bequest at death. One further remark: the possible persistence of bequest at death in the upper inheritance class implies an equalization in the distribution of real lifetime income (as measured by utility) for a given distribution of inheritance (I) as compared with the case of a perfect capital market; however, at the same time it implies an aggravation of inequality in the long-run distribution of real income, again as compared with the case of a perfect capital market. This antinomous character is the straightforward implication of the sub-optimality phenomenon (cf. Proposition 7), which, once suffered, cannot be rectified on account of myopia and institutional inertia on the part of individuals.

Intergenerational Rationality Hypothesis. By applying the rules of ordering under this hypothesis to Table 2, this time noting the fact that choices depend, in general, on the inheritance class to which the next generation belongs, we obtain the patterns of choice by each generation as summarized in Table 4. In comparison with the case of the institutional inertia hypothesis (Table 3) we note that the presence of intergenerational concern as the second-stage criterion particularly affects the choice of individuals whose heirs are to belong to the upper inheritance class.

Table 4. Choice of Inheritance Forms under the Intergenerational Rationality Hypothesis

Inheritance class of the current generation	The form by which inheritance is received	Inheritance class of the next generation		
		Lower	Middle	Upper
Lower	Gift at birth	Bequest at death	Bequest at death	Bequest at death
	Bequest at death	Bequest at death	Bequest at death	Gift at birth
Middle	Gift at birth	Gift at birth	Gift at birth	Gift at birth
	Bequest at death	Bequest at death	Bequest at death	Gift at birth
Upper	Gift at birth	Gift at birth	Gift at birth	Gift at birth
	Bequest at death	Bequest at death^{sub}	Gift at birth^{sub}	Gift at birth^{sub}

NOTE: Although the result of choice is indicated for all entries of the table, some entries are actually irrelevant depending on the particular mobility pattern of the economy as implied by the parameters of the utility function, the population growth rate, and the rate of interest.

Using Table 4, the long-run patterns of choice are described as follows.

PROPOSITION 12. (a) *The households remaining in the lower inheritance class for over a generation maintain the choice of bequest at death;* (b) *among households remaining in the middle inheritance class,* (i) *those whose ancestors originate from the middle inheritance class or from the lower inheritance class with bequest at death maintain the choice of bequest at death over generations;* (ii) *those whose ancestors originate from the middle inheritance class or from the upper inheritance class maintain the choice of gift at birth over generations;* (c) *households remaining in the upper inheritance class for over a generation maintain the choice of gift at birth.*

We notice that the long-run patterns of choice in the lower and middle inheritance classes are similar to those of the previous case. Thus, the major difference between the implications of the institutional inertia and the intergenerational rationality hypotheses lies in that the rational intergenerational concern in the latter hypothesis eliminates sub-optimality in the long run for the upper inheritance class. Thus, the scheme of financial wealth transmission over generations under the intergenerational rationality hypothesis turns out to be identical with that in the perfect capital market case.[20]

THE EFFECTS OF INHERITANCE TAXATION

The preceding discussion shows that, so long as one's own welfare is the first to be counted in the ordering scale, individuals' choice of

Table 5. Long-run Choice of Inheritance Forms under Inheritance Taxation

Inheritance class	Under death duties	Under gift *inter-vivos* tax
Households remaining in the lower inheritance class	Either maintenance of gift at birth[sub] or alternation of gift at birth and bequest at death, depending on the magnitude of the duty	Maintenance of bequest at death
Households remaining in the middle inheritance class	Maintenance of gift at birth	Maintenance of bequest at death
Households remaining in the upper inheritance class	Maintenance of gift at birth	Maintenance of bequest at death

NOTE: The remark made in Table 4 applies also to this table.

behavior will in the long run actually lead to the desirable inheritance arrangement as derived in Section 3 for each inheritance class (though with some exceptions under the institutional inertia hypothesis). It is then clear that imposition of death duties or a gift *inter vivos* tax has differential welfare effects among the inheritance classes.[21] The patterns of choice adjusted after either form of inheritance tax is imposed are summarized in Table 5.[22] Note that, since inheritance taxation affects the welfare of the current generation directly, tax considerations dominate the effect of the difference in the second-stage criterion between the two hypotheses and thus the modified patterns of choice under the two hypotheses are the same.[23]

As seen in the table, when death duties alone are imposed, the lower inheritance class cannot escape the effect of death duties and is hurt both intra- and intergenerationally.[24] Also, in the case where the institutional inertia hypothesis applies, the imposition of death duties functions as a signal to rectify sub-optimality among the upper inheritance class. On the other hand, when a gifts *inter vivos* tax alone is imposed, the upper inheritance class is hurt by sub-optimality. Thus, while the imposition of a gifts *inter vivos* tax may contribute to the intragenerational equality of the distribution of real income, it may, at the same time, aggravate the distribution of real income in the long run (cf. Proposition 7). In view of this analysis, the attempts to equalize the distribution of real income both in the short run and in the long run require stronger forms of taxation than the ones discussed here, e.g., integrated wealth transfer tax, not to mention a capital levy.[25,26]

5. Qualificatory Remarks

This analysis is based on several restrictive assumptions. First, we note that the restrictive character of the utility functional and of the assumption of constancy of the rate of interest and wage earnings. Furthermore, the assumption of the same preference patterns and wage earnings over generations and over the cross-section of households may be admitted *only* as a controlled standard of comparison.[27] On the one hand, when differences in the preference parameters exist among the cross-section of households we observe the following: (a) the sub-optimality consideration implies that, among the households with the same inherited wealth, those households with a higher time preference and, hence, higher consumption during the early part of life tend to be much more anxious to *receive* inheritance in the form of a gift *inter vivos* than those with a lower time preference (this tendency of course holds true for those households whose time preference parameter exceeds the rate of interest ($\delta > r$)—the case that we have not analyzed explicitly in this paper). This desire to receive bequests early will, in fact, be realized in the long run under the intergenerational rationality hypothesis; (b) the possibility of sub-optimality becomes less acute for those households with less care for bequest (smaller μ) in the lower end of the inheritance scale and for those households with more care for bequest (larger μ) in the upper end of the inheritance scale, and vice versa; this is simply because the desired bequest will be small relative to lifetime wealth. On the other hand, when wage earnings differ among households the critical limits of inheritance $\underline{I}$ and $\bar{I}$ for the occurrence of sub-optimality depend on the level of wage earnings. Unfortunately, however, the nature of this dependence is not generally determined.

Second, the assumption that the only alternative forms of inheritance arrangement available are transfer of the entire bequest at death and that at the birth of children is quite restrictive. A more realistic assumption would be to assume that transfer can be made partly at birth and partly at death. Moreover, one may also wish to allow the possibility of a continuous gift *inter vivos* at least for some phase of the life-span (e.g., during the education period). These generalizations obviously decrease the relevant range of the inheritance scale over which sub-optimality occurs.

Third, we note the very restrictive character of the definition of capital market imperfection that we have so far assumed. This assumption, however, can be relaxed without affecting the essence of our analysis. First, it is clear that the non-negativity constraint on net financial wealth can straightforwardly be replaced by a more general condition that the net financial wealth must always be above a certain lowerbound, say $\underset{\sim}{b}$. Second, we can suppose a more realistic case where this lowerbound $\underset{\sim}{b}$ varies with the level of inheritance (I), i.e., $\underset{\sim}{b} = \underset{\sim}{b}(I)$ and that $\underset{\sim}{b}'(I) \leqq 0$.[28] This modification alters the manner in which the

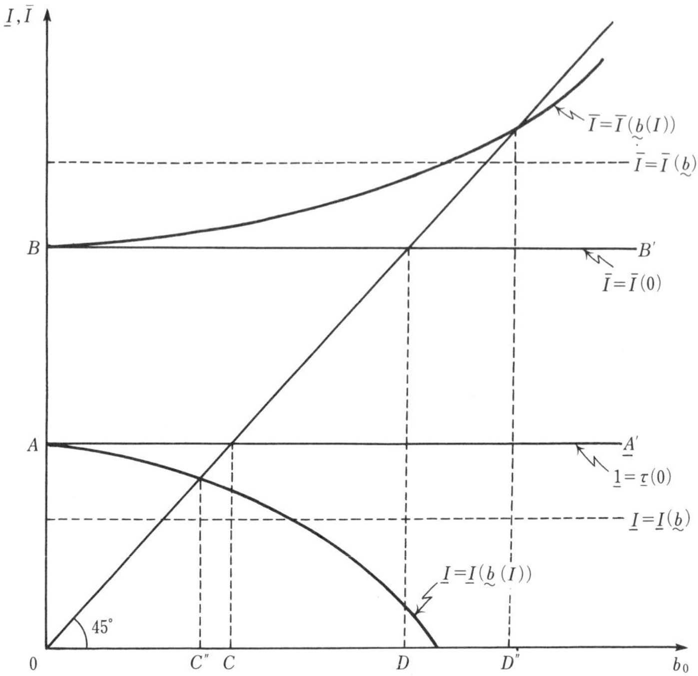

Figure 4

critical levels of inheritance for the occurrence of sub-optimality, namely $\underline{I}$ under gift at birth and $\bar{I}$ under bequest at death, are determined. This is explained in Figure 4, whose horizontal axis measures the amount of inheritance received (I) and whose vertical axis measures the critical levels of inheritance, $\underline{I}$ and $\bar{I}$.

Under the original assumptions, the critical levels $\underline{I}$ and $\bar{I}$ are given at the levels A and B, respectively, and they are uniform over the entire inheritance scale (i.e., the horizontal lines AA' and BB'). Thus, as viewed on the horizontal axis, individuals with inheritance less than C suffer from sub-optimality under the system of gift at birth and those with inheritance greater than D suffer from sub-optimality under the system of bequest at death. The horizontal strip defined by AA' and BB' widens (as the dotted curves in the figure show) when the non-negativity constraint is replaced by the existence of a negative but still a uniform lowerbound $\underset{\sim}{b}$, resulting in a narrower range for the occurrence of sub-optimality. When the assumption of a variable lowerbound $\underset{\sim}{b} = \underset{\sim}{b}(I)$ (with $\underset{\sim}{b}'(I) \leqq 0$, $\underset{\sim}{b}(0) = 0$) is introduced, the wealthier class finds it easier to borrow than does the less wealthy class, and we obtain the schedules of the critical values: $\underline{I} = \underline{I}(\underset{\sim}{b}(I))$ and $\bar{I} = \bar{I}(\underset{\sim}{b}(I))$ as AA' and BB''. It can then be seen that the points C'' and D'' on the horizontal axis corresponding to the intersection of these schedules and the 45° line define the critical levels of inheritance for sub-optimality under the generalized assumption of imperfection. We must note, however, that, depending upon the nature of the relationship $\underset{\sim}{b} = \underset{\sim}{b}(I)$, C'' and D'' may not necessarily exist (in which case the situation is the same as under a perfect capital market) or there may be multiple C'''s and D'''s (in which case the lower and upper inheritance classes are defined as the union of disjoint intervals on the inheritance scale). This, however, is the only modification necessary under the generalized definition of capital market imperfection and the rest of the analysis can proceed just in the same manner as in the previous section.[29]

Finally, we note the possibility that much of actual gifts *inter vivos* is carried out in the form of providing education (an alternative form of wealth) to children; this aspect has been completely left out of consideration in this paper.[30] Transparent analysis of this aspect and, furthermore, incorporation of uncertainty elements and other motives (e.g., the motive to control wealth) as discussed by Shoup (1966: 17–25) provide rich themes for further study.

Mathematical Appendix

Appendix 1. Proof of Proposition 2

(*Sufficiency*). Suppose $\hat{c}_L$ is such that

$$\begin{aligned} {}^G\dot{\hat{S}}_L &= r\,{}^G\hat{S}_L + w - \hat{c}_L \\ &= w - \hat{c}_L < 0 \quad (\text{since } {}^G\hat{S}_L = 0). \end{aligned}$$

Then *either* there exists no t such that ${}^G\hat{S}_t \leqq 0$, in which case no problem arises, *or* there exists t_0 $(0 \leqq t_0 < L)$ such that ${}^G\hat{S}_{t_0} = 0$ and that

$$\begin{cases} {}^G\hat{S}_t > 0 & \text{for all } t > t_0 \\ {}^G\hat{S}_t < 0 & \text{for all } t < t_0. \quad \text{(See Fig. 2.)} \end{cases}$$

However, since by our assumption, ${}^G\hat{S}_H \geqq 0$, we have $t_0 \leqq H$. Therefore,

$${}^G\hat{S}_t \geqq 0 \quad \text{for all } t \geqq H.$$

On the contrary, suppose $\hat{c}_L$ is such that

$${}^G\dot{\hat{S}}_L = w - \hat{c}_L \geqq 0.$$

Then, as is clear from Figure 2, we have

$${}^{G}\dot{\hat{S}}_t > 0 \quad \text{for all } 0 \leqq t \leqq L$$

and therefore,

$${}^{G}\hat{S}_t < 0 \quad \text{for all } 0 \leqq t < L.$$

However, this contradicts the assumption that ${}^{G}\hat{S}_H \geqq 0$.

Combining the previous two paragraphs,

$${}^{G}\hat{S}_H \geqq 0 \text{ implies } {}^{G}\hat{S}_t \geqq 0 \text{ for all } t \geqq H.$$

That $I = b_0 \geqq 0$ and ${}^{G}\hat{S}_H \geqq 0$ assure $\hat{b}_t \geqq 0$ for all $0 \leqq t \leqq H$ is obvious.

(*Necessity*) Obvious. This completes the proof of Proposition 2.

APPENDIX 2. PROOF OF PROPOSITION 4

Consider the following variational problem with respect to a parameter ξ (to be called Problem [ξ]).

Problem (ξ)

$$\text{maximize} \int_0^L u(c_s)e^{-\delta s}\,ds + e^{-\delta L}\phi(b_L) \tag{1}$$

$$\text{s.t.} \int_0^H c_s e^{-rs}\,ds + b_L e^{-rL} = w\int_0^H e^{-rs}\,ds + I - \xi \tag{A-1}$$

$$\int_H^L c_s e^{-rs}\,ds - w\int_H^L e^{-rs}\,ds = \xi. \tag{A-2}$$

It is easily seen that this problem is separable into the following two isoperimetric problems, to be called Problem (ξ^1) and Problem (ξ^2).

Problem (ξ^1)

$$\underset{\left\{\substack{\{c_s\}\\ (0\leqq s<H)\\ b_L}\right\}}{\text{maximize}} \int_0^H u(c_s)e^{-\delta s}\,ds + e^{-\delta L}\phi(b_L)$$

s.t. (A-1)

and

Problem (ξ^2)

$$\underset{\left\{\substack{\{c_s\}\\ (H\leqq s\leqq L)}\right\}}{\text{maximize}} \int_H^L u(c_s)e^{-\delta s}\,ds$$

s.t. (A-2).

Let us first investigate the character of the optimum program for each of the two intervals, i.e., Problem (ξ^1) and Problem (ξ^2).

Problem (ξ^1)

The necessary conditions for the optimum for this interval $[0, H)$ are given by:

$$u'(c_t) = \lambda^1 e^{(\delta - r)t} \quad \text{for } 0 \leqq t \leqq H \tag{A-3}$$

$$\phi'(b_L) = \lambda^1 e^{(\delta - r)L}, \tag{A-4}$$

where λ^1 is a Lagrangean constant that depends upon the value of ξ (for given I). It has the economic interpretation of the marginal utility of wealth as of age L in the context of Problem (ξ^1). We can now apply Proposition 1 to our Problem (ξ^1) to obtain:

$$\frac{\partial b_L}{\partial \xi} < 0, \ \frac{\partial c_t}{\partial \xi} < 0 \quad \text{for all } \xi, \text{ and all } H > t \geqq 0. \tag{A-5}$$

However, from (A-3)

$$u''(c_t)\frac{\partial c_t}{\partial \xi} = \frac{\partial \lambda^1}{\partial \xi} e^{(\delta - r)t}.$$

Thus,

$$\frac{\partial \lambda^1}{\partial \xi} > 0 \quad \text{for all } \xi. \tag{A-6}$$

Let us write λ^1 as $\lambda^1 = \lambda^1(\xi; I)$. Then $\lambda^1(0; I)$ is the minimum for all $\xi \geqq 0$. Moreover,

$$\lambda^1(0; I) > \lambda^1({}^G\hat{S}_H(I)e^{-rH}; I), \tag{A-7}$$

where ${}^G\hat{S}_H(I)e^{-rH}$ is the discounted value of the net financial wealth at age H along the basic optimum program and is negative in the presently assumed circumstance of $I < \underline{I}$. As to the level of consumption $c_t = c_t(\xi; I)$ $(0 \leqq t \leqq H)$, and the level of bequest $b_L = b_L(\xi; I)$, we obtain from (A-5) that, for any $\xi > 0$:

$$c_t(\xi; I) < c_t(0; I) < c_t({}^G\hat{S}_H(I)e^{-rH}; I) \equiv \hat{c}_t(I) \tag{A-8}$$

and

$$b_L(\xi; I) < b_L(0; I) < b_L({}^G\hat{S}_H(I)e^{-rH}; I) \equiv \hat{b}_L(I). \tag{A-9}$$

Problem (ξ^2)

The necessary condition for optimality in the interval $[H, L]$ is given by:

$$u'(c_t) = \lambda^2 e^{(\delta - r)t} \quad H \leqq t \leqq L, \tag{A-10}$$

where λ^2 is a Lagrangean constant that depends upon the value of ξ (for given I). (It has an interpretation analogous to that of λ^1.) Since it is easily verified that equation (6) of Proposition 1 holds for the problem where there is no bequest motive ($\phi_{b_L} \equiv 0$), we can apply this proposition to our problem to conclude that:

$$\frac{\partial c_t}{\partial \xi} > 0 \quad \text{for all } \xi \text{ and all } H \leqq t \leqq L. \tag{A-11}$$

On the other hand, from (A-10) we have

$$u''(c_t)\frac{\partial c_t}{\partial \xi} = \frac{\partial \lambda^2}{\partial \xi} e^{(\delta - r)t}.$$

Therefore,

$$\frac{\partial \lambda^2}{\partial \xi} < 0 \quad \text{for all } \xi. \tag{A-12}$$

Thus, if we write λ^2 as $\lambda^2 = \lambda^2(\xi; I)$, then $\lambda^2(0; I)$ is the maximum for the range $\xi \geqq 0$. Moreover,

$$\lambda^2(0; I) < \lambda^2({}^G\hat{S}_H(I)e^{-rH}; I). \tag{A-13}$$

As to the consumption path $c_t = c_t(\xi; I)$ $(H \leqq t \leqq L)$ we have, from (A-11), that for all $\xi > 0$ and $H \leqq t \leqq L$:

$$c_t(\xi; I) > c_t(0; I) > c_t({}^G\hat{S}_H(I)e^{-rH}; I) \equiv \hat{c}_t(I). \tag{A-14}$$

We are now ready to prove Proposition 4. To prove the first part of the proposition, we first note that for the problem (1) subject to (2) only (without [14] or [9]) optimality requires the two constants λ^1 and λ^2 to be identical, i.e.,

$$\lambda^1({}^G\hat{S}_H(I)e^{-rH}; I) = \lambda^2({}^G\hat{S}_H(I)e^{-rH}; I). \tag{A-15}$$

With the use of (A-15) we combine (A-6), (A-7), (A-12) and (A-13) to obtain:

$$\begin{aligned}\lambda^2(\xi; I) &< \lambda^2(0; I) < \lambda^2({}^G\hat{S}_H(I)e^{-rH}; I)\\ &= \lambda^1({}^G\hat{S}_H(I)e^{-rH}; I) < \lambda^1(0; I) < \lambda^1(\xi; I),\end{aligned} \tag{A-16}$$

where $\xi > 0$ and $I < \underline{I}$.

It is clear from (A-16) above and the strictly concave character of the programming problem that, among all $\xi \geqq 0$, the *optimum optimorum* for the problem (ξ) is obtained at $\xi = 0$, where the divergence of the Lagrangean constants (marginal utility of wealth as of time L) for the two intervals λ^1 and λ^2 is the least possible. This proves the first part of our proposition.

To prove the second part of the proposition, we merely have to note in the inequalities (A-8), (A-14), and (A-9) that the *optimum optimorum* program of consumption and bequest is given by $c_t(0; I)$ $(0 \leqq t \leqq L)$, with discontinuity at age H, and $b_L(0; I)$. This completes the proof of Proposition 4.

APPENDIX 3. PROOF OF THE PROPOSITION 8

From Propositions 3 and 6 we know that

$$^G\hat{S}_H(I)e^{-rH} = \int_H^L \hat{c}_s(I)e^{-rs}\,ds - w\int_H^L e^{-rs}\,ds$$

increases monotonically with respect to I, and that

$$^B\hat{S}_{L-H}(I)e^{-r(L-H)} = \int_0^{L-H} we^{-rs}\,ds - \int_0^{L-H} \hat{c}_s(I)e^{-rs}\,ds \tag{A-17}$$

decreases monotonically with respect to I. In order to prove Proposition 8, we will show $^B\hat{S}_{L-H}(\tilde{I}) > 0$. There are two cases to consider.

(i) Case $\tilde{I} = \underline{I} > 0$

From the definition of $\underline{I}$, we have

$$\int_H^L \hat{c}_s(\underline{I})e^{-rs}\,ds = \frac{w}{r}e^{-rH}(1 - e^{-r(L-H)}). \tag{A-18}$$

By comparing (A-18) with (A-17), we realize that:

$$^B\hat{S}_{L-H}(\underline{I})e^{-r(L-H)} \gtreqless 0$$

according as

$$e^{rH}\int_H^L \hat{c}_s(\underline{I})e^{-rs}\,ds \gtreqless \int_0^{L-H} \hat{c}_s(\underline{I})e^{-rs}\,ds.$$

However, since $\hat{c}_s$ is, under our assumption that $r - \delta > 0$, strictly increasing with respect to time, it is clearly obtained that

$$\int_H^L \hat{c}_s(\underline{I})e^{-r(s-H)}\,ds > \int_0^{L-H} \hat{c}_s(\underline{I})e^{-rs}\,ds. \tag{A-19}$$

This proves the proposition for the case $\tilde{I} = \underline{I}$.

(ii) Case $\tilde{I} = 0$.

In this case, we merely note that (A-18) holds with strict inequality:

$$\int_H^L \hat{c}_s(0)e^{-rs}\,ds > \frac{w}{r}e^{-rH}(1 - e^{-r(L-H)}).$$

Thus, the inequality (A-19) again holds and, therefore,

$$^{B}\hat{S}_{L-H}(0)e^{-r(L-H)} > 0.$$

This completes the proof of Proposition 8.

Notes

This paper derives from chapters 7 and 8 of the author's doctoral dissertation (1972). He is grateful to Professors Kenneth Arrow, Anthony Atkinson, Geoff Heal, Jürg Niehans, an anonymous referee, and the participants of the seminars at the Johns Hopkins University and Queen's University for their valuable comments and suggestions on the previous drafts. He also gratefully acknowledges the financial support from the Woodrow Wilson Foundation and the National Science Foundation under its grant GS–37899.

1. The above statement should be qualified somewhat, for Atkinson considers a form of imperfection where the lending and borrowing rates of interest differ. However, he does not discuss the effect of this imperfection on the forms of inheritance arrangements as we do below. The effects of such a form of imperfection on consumption and savings behavior are analyzed by Tobin and Dolde (1971).

2. Implicit in these statements are the assumptions that (i) there is no distinction between males and females, so that the terms "he" and "parents" can be used interchangeably, and (ii) length of life is certain. For an attempt to extend the life-cycle savings model toward the case where there is uncertainty with respect to lifetime, see Yaari (1965).

3. Atkinson (1971: 210). Unless otherwise explicitly noted, I shall in the remainder of the paper omit the cumbersome superscript v. It is always to be understood that variables refer to the generation v.

4. This follows Atkinson (1971: 210). As has been suggested by a referee, the validity of the following analysis depends on the condition that $r \geqq \delta$.

5. This assumption presupposes a certain degree of altruism on the part of parents, for lack of communication concerning the size of bequests (not to say of gifts *inter vivos*), so that bequests are treated as windfall income by children, will result in less lifetime utility for them than the case where the size of inheritance is known beforehand. For a detailed discussion on this aspect, see Ishikawa (1972), chs. 3–5.

6. For convenience, I shall henceforth adopt the convention of measuring the level of inheritance by its present value (at time 0) I.

7. It is here assumed that the form of inheritance arrangement in itself is not relevant with regard to an individual's satisfaction. Therefore, the individual will take it that the transfer of a given size of bequest at age L and the transfer of the discounted value of that amount at age H (note that lending is still allowed) have equivalent effects on the welfare of his heirs.

8. This is nothing but a corollary to Atkinson's (1971: 214–15) analysis of the effects of a capital levy on the level of the consumption path.

9. In the special case where the utility function belongs to the class of constant elasticity functions:

$$u'(c) = c^{-e}$$

$$\phi'(b_L) = Ab_L^{-\mu} \quad \varepsilon, \mu \geqq 0$$

this proposition is readily proved (cf. Atkinson, 1971: 211) to obtain b_L and c_0 as:

$$b_L = f(I; w, r) \quad f' > 0$$

$$c_0 = g(I; w, r) \quad g' > 0.$$

10. As will be shown in section 5, "non-negativity" itself is not essential for the present analysis. What is essential is that there exists an upper limit to the size of borrowing. This upper limit may depend on the size of the household's wealth.

11. The expression "was" is meant to cover the case of a perfect capital market; in which case the amount borrowed is subtracted to arrive at net financial wealth.

12. By integrating (10) (with the use of [11]) and (2) and comparing the results with each other, we immediately see that ${}^{G}\hat{S}_L = 0$, which is another way of saying that bequests are transferred completely by gift at birth.

13. In the case of constant elasticity utility functions (cf. note 9 above) the necessary and sufficient condition for a positive $\underline{I}$ to exist is given by

$$\frac{w}{r}\theta(r;L)\left\{\frac{\theta(r;H)}{\theta(r;L)} - \frac{\theta(r-\gamma;H)}{\theta(r-\gamma;L)}\right\} < f(0)\left\{1 - \frac{\theta(r-\gamma;H)}{\theta(r-\gamma;L)}\right\},$$

where $\gamma = (r-\delta)/\varepsilon$ and $\theta(\alpha;\tau) = \int_0^\tau e^{-\alpha u}\,du$. Since the bracket in the left-hand side of the above inequality is positive (for, it is not so difficult to prove that, for $G(\beta;\xi)$ defined by

$$G(\beta;\xi) = (1-e^{-\beta\xi})/(1-e^{-\beta M}), \quad \partial G(\beta;\xi)/\partial\xi > 0$$

for any $\beta > 0$ and any ξ such that $0 < \xi < M$), this condition is not necessarily always satisfied.

14. Constraint (14) is only a necessary condition for (9) to hold. However, the modified optimum program under the additional constraint (14), to be discussed in the following, can be shown easily to satisfy constraint (9). (The proof is similar to the one employed in the case of Proposition 2.) Therefore, the modified program under constraint (14) coincides with that under the full constraint (9).

15. In the constant elasticity utility function case:

$$\begin{aligned} {}^{B}\hat{S}_{L-H}e^{-r(L-H)} &= \frac{w}{r}\theta(r;L)\left\{\frac{\theta(r;L-H)}{\theta(r;L)} - \frac{\theta(r-\gamma;L-H)}{\theta(r-\gamma;L)}\right\} \\ &\quad - \frac{\theta(r-\gamma;L-H)}{\theta(r-\gamma;L)}y(I;w,r), \end{aligned} \tag{N-1}$$

where $y(I;w,r)$ is defined by

$$y(I;w,r) = \{Bf(I;w,r)\}^{\mu/g}e^{-\gamma L} - \frac{w}{r}\theta(r;L) \ (B\text{: constant}).$$

Since $y(\cdot)$ is an increasing function of I, it is clear that ${}^{B}\hat{S}_{L-H}$ is monotonically decreasing with respect to I. Furthermore, since the first term in the right-hand side of (N-1) is positive (cf. note 13 above) and that

$$y(0;w,r) < 0 \quad \text{and} \quad y(\infty;w,r) = \infty,$$

we know that there exists a unique critical value $I > 0$.

16. Within the framework of the Yaari-Atkinson model where there is no room for individuals' educational investment, we may interpret economic birth (i.e., economic age 0) to correspond to physical age, say, 15. Similarly economic age H, when parents give economic birth to children, may be regarded as to correspond to physical ages, say, between 40 and 50 (assuming that they give physical birth to children between their physical ages 25 to 35). Finally, economic age L, when parents die may be regarded as to correspond to physical age, say 65. Thus, within this model, we may plausibly assume $H \geqq L - H$).

17. The modified optimum program of consumption and bequest for the upper inheritance class under the cirumstance that an individual receives inheritance in the form of bequest at death is independent of the choice of inheritance arrangement that he makes.

18. It is to be noted that this assumption merely permits us to avoid formidable taxonomies. It in no way affects the results of our analysis below.

19. A similar kind of lexicographic ordering is also used in John Rawls's (1971) ethical principles.

20. In order to evaluate the effect of intergenerational concern in isolation, it may be worthwhile to examine the patterns of choice under a variant of the intergenerational rationality hypothesis whose third stage of the ordering system is randomness (so that either form is adopted with the equal probability of one-half) rather than institutional

inertia. Under this new hypothesis the patterns of choice in the long run are summarized as follows. (For details of proofs see Ishikawa [1972: ch. 8].) (a) Among the households remaining in the lower inheritance class, two-thirds of them choose bequest at death and the remaining one-third choose gift at birth; (b) among the households remaining in the middle inheritance class half of them choose bequest at death and the remaining half choose gift at birth; (c) the households remaining in the upper inheritance class maintain the choice of gift at birth.

This confirms that allowing intergenerational concern as a second stage of the ordering eliminates sub-optimality in the long run, independent of the third-stage criterion.

21. In the case of a perfect capital market, the institutional neutrality property implies that death duties or a gift *inter vivos* tax, when imposed alone, will be completely avoided by all inheritance classes, and therefore they have no welfare effects on individuals whatever.

22. Since we are only interested in the qualitative effects of inheritance taxation, we need not explicitly specify the exact way in which either tax is imposed. On the expenditure side, however, we assume that the tax revenue is used only in a neutral manner with regard to the distribution of income. It is to be noted that the pattern of choice under taxation that appears in the long run does not depend upon when the tax is imposed.

23. This statement also holds under the variant of the intergenerational rationality hypothesis.

24. This statement is true no mater which of the alternatives indicated in Table 5 is taken after death duties are imposed. As far as the level of bequest is concerned, both sub-optimality in the lower class range and endurance of death duties imply a diminution in the level of bequest (though the concept of bequest relevant in the latter case is net-of-tax bequest). Cf. Atkinson (1971: 215–18).

25. For proposals advocating the integration of death duties and gift *inter vivos* taxes, see Shoup (1966: 14f) and Meade (1965: 54–58, esp. 54–55).

26. For an evaluation of the effects of a capital levy and integrated wealth transfer tax, see Atkinson (1971: 214–16).

27. The effects of differences in individuals' value systems on the distribution of earnings and property income both in the short run and in the long run are discussed in Ishikawa (1972), chs. 5 and 9, under the perfect capital market assumption.

28. I am indebted to a referee for suggesting to me the possibility of generalizing the notion of imperfection in this direction.

29. As an alternative way of defining an imperfection in the capital market, we may consider the possibility that the borrowing rate of interest (which in our formulation becomes infinite above a certain upper limit of borrowing), though finite, depends on the financial wealth level itself. However, as has been noted by Blinder (1971: ch. 2, appendix 2), this formulation permits few practical results.

30. For a detailed analysis of choice behavior between education and financial assets under a perfect capital market, see Ishikawa (1972: chs. 3–5).

References

Atkinson, A.B. 1971. Capital taxes, the redistribution of wealth and individual savings. Review of Economic Studies 38 (April): 209–27.

Blinder, A.S. 1971. Towards an economic theory of income distribution. Ph.D. dissertation. M.I.T.

Ishikawa, T. 1972. The dynamics of wealth accumulation and education under different family institutions as determinants of the size distribution of income. Ph.D. dissertation. Johns Hopkins University.

Meade, J.E. 1965. Efficiency, Equality and Ownership of Property. Cambridge, Mass.: Harvard University Press.

———. 1966. Life-cycle savings, inheritance and economic growth. Review of Economic Studies 33 (Jan.): 61–78.

Rawls, J. 1971. A Theory of Justice. Cambridge, Mass.: Harvard University Press.
Shoup, C.S. 1966. Federal Estate and Gift Taxes. Washington, D.C.: Brookings Institution.
Tobin, J., and W.C. Dolde. 1971. Wealth, liquidity and consumption. In Consumer Spending and Monetary Policy, Monetary Conference Series 5. Boston: Federal Reserve Bank of Boston.
Yaari, M.E. 1964. On the consumer's lifetime allocation process. International Economic Review 5 (Sept.): 304–17.
———. 1965. Uncertain lifetime, life insurance, and the theory of the consumer. Review of Economic Studies 33 (April): 137–50.

6. Family Structures and Family Values in the Theory of Income Distribution

Real and socially important inequality is associated with the differences among children of differentially situated parents in the degree of access to opportunities to acquire such lifetime income streams.

Such differences in opportunity raise two different kinds of problems. The first is that to define a standard for a tolerable degree of inequality of opportunity facing individuals of the same age cohort, it is necessary to refer to the life history of a family over more than one generation. The difficulties we have with the welfare economics of this problem are associated with the neglect in our basic welfare economics theory, of the fundamental realities of parental choice and parental ambitions—or lack of them—for children. We also ignore the realities of children's appreciation both of the limitations of their parents and their own opportunities to exploit their parents' useful qualities while escaping from parental limitations.

—*Harry G. Johnson (1972: S285)*

1. Introduction

The purpose of this paper is to provide a microeconomic analysis of some of the basic family institutional factors in the determination of the size distribution of income in both the short run and the long run. More specifically, I would like to analyze explicitly the effects of parent-child relationships in two dimensions—the structure of economic de-

Originally published in *Journal of Political Economy* 83, 5 (1975): 987–1008.

cisions within the household constituted by parents and children, and the existence of altruistic concern for children's welfare on the part of parents—on the levels of education and financial wealth that are transmitted over generations. I shall base my discussion on a generalized model of the household that integrates the models of investment in human capital (Mincer, 1958; Becker, 1962, 1967; Ben Porath, 1967) and of life-cycle savings (Yaari, 1964; Meade, 1966; Atkinson 1971).

In Section 2, I present the model of the household, in particular typifying family value orientations concerning children's welfare. Section 3 compares, among households with alternative value types, the levels of education and financial wealth that the family leaves to its next generation. My main section, 4, examines the long-run effects of the household behavior discussed previously on the distribution of wealth and also discusses factors influencing the patterns of economic mobility among households. Extensions and qualifications of my analysis are discussed in Section 5.

2. A General Model of Household Family Structures

Let us assume that each individual has an economic life of L years. An individual is defined as *economically born* (i.e., economic age 0) when he is graduated from infancy and thus joins the potential labor force (say, corresponding to physical age 5). A certain number, e^{nH}, of children are economically born at economic age H.[1] At each moment of time, an individual has a choice of spending the *fixed* number of hours available working, which gives him earnings, or spending the time taking education and formal training, which does not give immediate earnings but increases his later earning capacity.[2] He also has the opportunity to lend or borrow in a perfect capital market. Thus, the individual at each moment receives his income as a sum of wage earnings, if any, and the interest payment (positive or negative) on his net financial wealth and spends it between consumption and savings, that is, the increment in financial wealth.

To define the character of the family household, we assume that individuals remain in the paternal household for a certain initial period, say I years, of their life, to be called the period of dependence (See Fig. 1.). The paternal household is an authoritative organization in that (a) the length of the period of dependence is determined by parents; (b) during this period of dependence, children are subject to their parents' decisions, particularly concerning children's levels of consumption and education; and (c) any earnings that children obtain during the period of dependence are pooled with the family resources.[3] At the

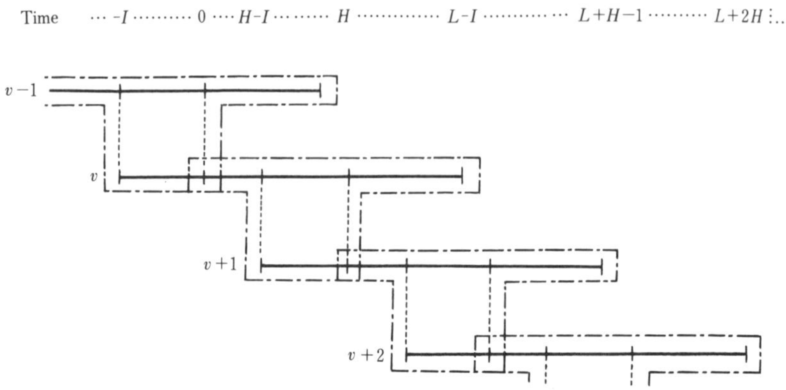

Figure 1

end of this period, each child becomes independent of his parents and starts a new household of his own.[4] One of the important consequences of independence is that children may then be able to revise the program of their education as planned and pursued by their parents. I shall not at first go into the question of how the length of the period of dependence, I, is determined but, rather, treat it as an exogenously given constant.[5] Since parents die when children's economic age becomes $L - H$, I is clearly bounded from above by $L - H$. It also seems plausible to assume that I is bounded by H, the economic age at which children economically bear their children. Thus, in effect we assume $0 \leq I \leq \min(H, L - H)$.[6]

Finally, as a condition regulating the overall independence of a household, we impose the solvency constraint to the effect that each household must not end itself with negative holdings of financial wealth.

EDUCATIONAL INVESTMENT OPPORTUNITY

We shall characterize the educational investment opportunity by a simple functional relationship between the annual wage earnings, w, and the total number of years of education, E, $w = w(E)$, defined for each household. This function will be referred to as the earnings capacity schedule of the household.[7] To keep matters simple, we assume that the function $w(\cdot)$ is well behaved, and we ignore uncertainty, learning, and obsolescence effects.

We then consider two possibilities with regard to the flexibility of the educational process. The first is the case where individuals can take their education only consecutively and are not allowed to return to school once they leave. The second is the case where individuals can take education in any intermittent manner, so that individuals can harvest the results of education already attained in the form of increasing earnings during each period they choose to work. We define the former case as the case of inflexible education and the latter as the case of flexible education. I have elsewhere shown (Ishikawa, 1972: ch. 2; 1975), however, that as long as education is merely an investment opportunity, the two frameworks give exactly the same optimal program of education; that is, individuals will take education consecutively from the initial period even though they are allowed to take it intermittently ex ante. The distinction of these two cases nevertheless becomes important when we consider revision of education by children.

Let us denote the discounted sum of earnings when an individual's time horizon is T years and when he takes E consecutive years of education by $V(E, T)$, namely,

$$V(E,T) = \int_E^T w(E)e^{-rt}\,dt = \frac{w(E)}{r}(1 - e^{-r(E-L)}), \tag{1}$$

where r is the rate of interest (assumed to be constant). We also denote the level of E which maximizes this expression by $E^*(T)$. (We will neglect the possibility of a corner solution, so that $E^*(T)$ is defined by $|\partial V/\partial E|_{E=E^*(T)} = 0$.) Thus, in both flexible and inflexible cases, the optimal length of education is obtained as $E^*(T)$. It can be shown that

$$0 < dE^*(T)/dT < 1. \tag{2}$$

FAMILY VALUE ORIENTATIONS

We shall contrast two types of family values in the household. The first is called parental altruism, which designates the parents' gratuitous concern for their children's welfare *after* the latter become independent.[8] It will be expressed, first, by the parents' bequest motive (cf. Yaari 1964), with equal weight given to each child, and, second, by their willingness to provide perfect information about the level of their bequests (or to make gifts *inter vivos* directly) to their children at the time of independence. These two conditions either directly or through borrowing in the capital market facilitate the initial wealth to children when they start a new household.

The second is called parental self-satisfaction, which designates parents' wish to enjoy family wealth by themselves and to have no concern for their children's welfare after they become independent. Thus, there exists no bequest motive, and the two generations become completely independent financially after the children start their own households.

THE MODEL OF HOUSEHOLD BEHAVIOR

We now express the present assumptions in formal terms. Let us take the time origin as the moment of independence of generation v, which we take to be parents (cf. Fig. 1), and denote the consumption and holding of financial wealth of generation v at time t by c_t^v and b_t^v. Let us further denote the level of education of generation v as planned by generation $v-1$ by ${}^{v-1}E^v$ and the level of education of generation v that is realized (after a possible revision) by ${}^vE^v$. Then the lifetime budget constraint for generation v is expressed by

$$\int_0^{L-I} c_t^v e^{-rt}\,dt + \int_{H-I}^{H} e^{nH} c_t^{v+1} e^{-rt}\,dt + b_{L-I}^v e^{-r(L-I)}$$
$$= b_0^v + h_0^v + e^{nH} h_0^{\prime v+1}, \tag{3}$$

where

$$h_v^0 = \begin{cases} \displaystyle\int_{{}^vE^v - {}^{v-1}E^v}^{L-I} w^v({}^vE^v) e^{-rt}\,dt & \text{if } I \geq {}^{v-1}E^v \\ \displaystyle\int_{{}^vE^v - I}^{L-I} w^v({}^vE^v) e^{-rt}\,dt & \text{if } I < {}^{v-1}E^v \end{cases} \tag{4}$$

and

$$h_0^{\prime v+1} = \begin{cases} \displaystyle\int_{H-I+{}^vE^{v+1}}^{H} w^{v+1}({}^vE^{v+1}) e^{-rt}\,dt & \text{if } I \geq {}^vE^{v+1} \\ 0 & \text{if } I < {}^vE^{v+1} \end{cases} \tag{5}$$

and where $w^v(\cdot)$ and $w^{v+1}(\cdot)$ refer to the earnings capacity schedules of generation v and generation $v+1$. The term h_0^v defined by (4) represents the human wealth or the present value of the future earnings stream for generation v at time 0. As mentioned earlier, it is possible to revise the education program in the case of flexible education and in the case of $I \leq {}^{v-1}E^v$ under inflexible education. In such cases, the value of h_0^v is determined by generation v. Then, denoting the additional number of years of schooling taken by generation v by ${}^v\tilde{E}^v$, we express the realized level of education ${}^vE^v$ as ${}^vE^v = {}^v\tilde{E}^v + {}^{v-1}E^v$. On the other hand, the term $h_0^{\prime v+1}$ defined by (5) represents the human wealth of each member of generation $v+1$ at time 0 that accrues in the family resource pool.

In addition to the budget constraint (3), we have the solvency constraint, expressed by

$$b_{L-I}^v \geq 0. \tag{6}$$

The household with parental altruism plans to leave bequests of wealth, defined as the sum of financial wealth and human wealth at the time of independence bequeathed equally to each child. By assuming that parents expect the planned level of children's education, ${}^{v}E^{v+1}$, even if it exceeds I, to be realized, the planned bequest per child, say, j^{v} (and W^{v}_{L-I} for all of the children), is expressed by[9]

$$j^{v} = W^{v}_{L-I}e^{-nH}$$
$$= \begin{cases} i^{v} + \displaystyle\int_{H}^{L+H-I} w^{v+1}({}^{v}E^{v+1})e^{-r[t-(L-I)]}\,dt & \text{if } I \geq {}^{v}E^{v+1} \\ i^{v} + \displaystyle\int_{H-I+{}^{v}E^{v+1}}^{L+H-I} w^{v+1}({}^{v}E^{v+1})e^{-r[t-(L-I)]}\,dt & \text{if } I < {}^{v}E^{v+1}, \end{cases} \quad (7)$$

where

$$i^{v} = b^{v}_{L-I}e^{-nH} \quad (8)$$

represents the per child share of the bequest of financial wealth.[10] On the other hand, the initial wealth of generation v, denoted as W^{v}_{0}, is expressed by

$$W^{v}_{0} = b^{v}_{0} + h^{v}_{0} = \begin{cases} b^{v}_{0} + \displaystyle\int_{{}^{v}E^{v}-{}^{v-1}E^{v}}^{L-I} w^{v}({}^{v}E^{v})e^{-rt}\,dt & \text{if } I \geq {}^{v-1}E^{v} \\ b^{v}_{0} + \displaystyle\int_{{}^{v}E^{v}-I}^{L-I} w^{v}({}^{v}E^{v})e^{-rt}\,dt & \text{if } I < {}^{v-1}E^{v}, \end{cases} \quad (9)$$

where b^{v}_{0} is the present value of the bequest of financial wealth to be given at time $L - H - I$ to each child by generation $v - 1$ that cannot be borrowed in the perfect capital market or is given in the form of a gift *inter vivos*, that is,

$$b^{v}_{0} = i^{v-1}e^{-r(L-H-I)} = b^{v-1}_{L-I}e^{-[nH+r(L-H-I)]}.\text{[11]} \quad (10)$$

By employing the additively separable utility function customarily used in the literature,[12] we describe the behavior of the household with parental altruism by the following:

$$\max U_{A} = \int_{0}^{L-I} u^{v}(c^{v}_{t})e^{-\delta t}\,dt + \int_{H-I}^{H} e^{nH}u^{v+1}(c^{v+1}_{t})e^{-\delta t}\,dt$$
$$+ e^{-\delta L}e^{nH}\phi(j^{v}), \quad (11)$$

subject to (3), (6), and (10).

We shall, on the other hand, express the value of parental self-satisfaction by the parental attitude to consume as much as possible under the solvency constraint (6), namely,

$$b^{v}_{L-I} = 0. \tag{12}$$

This implies from (10) that

$$b^{v}_{0} = 0.^{13} \tag{13}$$

Now the behavior of the household with parental self-satisfaction is described by

$$\max U_S = \int_0^{L-I} u^v(c^v_t)e^{-\delta t}\,dt + \int_{H-I}^{H} e^{nH}u^{v+1}(c^{v+1}_t)e^{-\delta t}\,dt, \tag{14}$$

subject to (3), (12), and (13).

3. Determination of the Levels of Education and Bequest in the Household

Let us examine the household behavior on education and bequest within the framework described above.

EDUCATION AND EARNINGS

When, as in our model, education is viewed only as an opportunity for investment, maximization of lifetime earnings can be pursued independently of consumption and bequest programs (à la Fisher [1930]). Moreover, children's education level is determined independently of their parents' wealth per se. This is a general conclusion that applies to any type of household described above.

On the one hand, in the case of the household with parental altruism, rewriting the budget constraint (3), using (4), (5), (7), and (9), into the form

$$\int_0^{L-I} c^v_t e^{-rt}\,dt + \int_{H-I}^{H} e^{nH}c^{v+1}_t e^{-rt}\,dt + e^{nH}j^v e^{-r(L-I)}$$
$$= W^v_0 + e^{nH}e^{-r(L-I)}V({}^vE^{v+1}, L)^{14} \tag{15}$$

and associating it with the utility function (11) make it clear that parents plan for their children the level of education that maximizes the present value of their children's earnings for their entire life-spans (which in this specific sense is optimal). This planned level will in fact be realized by children when they become independent, that is, ${}^vE^{v+1} = {}^{v+1}E^{v+1} = E^*(L)$. Similarly, by assuming the same value type for grandparents (generation $v-1$), the parents realize the level of education ${}^{v-1}E^v = E^*(L)$ planned by grandparents.[15] This result holds regardless of the time at which children become independent and of whether or not educational institutions are flexible.[16]

On the other hand, in the case of a household with parental self-satisfaction, the level of education planned by parents, ${}^{v}E^{v+1}$, is $E^*(I)$ and is not optimal for children. As can be seen from (3), (5), (12), and (14), this is because parents' sole concern with regard to the education of children is to extract the maximum contribution from children to the household resource pool during the I years that the children remain in the parental household. Since the education of children planned by parents ceases before children become independent [i.e., ${}^{v}E^{v+1} = E^*(I) < I$], $E^*(I)$ becomes the terminate level unless the educational institution is flexible. When it is flexible, children will reattend school to make the best of the opportunity then available and will realize the educational level $E^*\{L - [I - E^*(I)]\}$, which is less than the level $E^*(L)$ that is optimal in view of the entire span (See Fig. 2.).[17]

There is one important qualification of the result of the parental self-satisfaction case just stated. Would it not be better (i.e., a Pareto move) for both parents and children if parents planned the level of education that was optimal for children in terms of the entire life-span, $E^*(L)$, in return for payment later by children of at least the amount that they would otherwise have contributed to the household?[18] In fact, as long

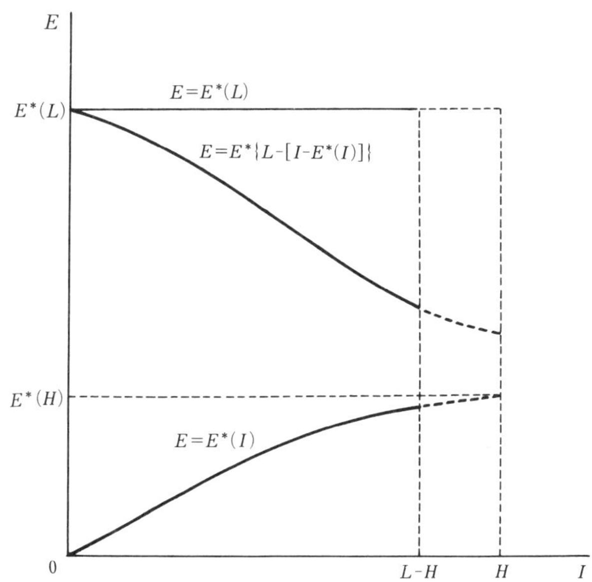

Figure 2

as the educational opportunity is productive enough,[19] this arrangement would make both generations better off. However, parents will not have the incentive to do so if they recognize at the same time that there is nothing to guarantee repayment by children.[20] Hence, unless it is accompanied by a legal sanction to enforce repayment, such an arrangement would not materialize.

BEQUEST OF FINANCIAL WEALTH

The household with parental altruism leaves a certain level of bequest consisting of financial wealth and human wealth to children. The problem of determining the level of the bequest is structurally identical to that of Atkinson (1971), except for the minor modification introduced by the solvency constraint (6). We can then show that the bequest per child is an increasing function of the initial wealth of parents and that there exists a certain level of j, say $\hat{j}$ (≥ 0), under which the solvency constraint (6) becomes effective and the bequest consists only of human wealth, that is,

$$j^{\nu} = \begin{cases} A(j^{\nu-1}; w, r), \quad A' > 0, & \text{for } j^{\nu-1} > \hat{j} \\ \int_{H}^{L+H-I} w[E^{*}(L)]e^{-r[t-(L-I)]}\,dt, & \text{for } j^{\nu-1} \leq \hat{j}. \end{cases} \tag{16}$$

Under the assumption that every generation of a household is identically situated except for initial wealth, equation (16) describes the process of wealth transmission over generations of the household. Since the level of human wealth will be maintained at the same level, any change in the amount of wealth transmitted is mediated by financial wealth. The dynamics of this transmission process follows the basic patterns characterized by Atkinson (1971: 212–13) under the assumption of constant utility functions:

$$\begin{aligned} u'(c) &= c^{-\varepsilon}, & \varepsilon &= \text{constant} > 0, \\ \phi'(j) &= Kj^{-\mu}, & K, \mu &= \text{constants} > 0. \end{aligned} \tag{17}$$

Depending on the relative magnitudes of the parameters of the utility function (ε, μ),[21] the rate of interest (r), and the rate of fertility (n), there are three possibilities: (1) The case with a single, globally stable equilibrium. (2) The case with two equilibria, the lower locally stable and the upper locally unstable. The upper equilibrium level thus serves as a threshold point. That is, if initially the wealth level of a household is above the upper equilibrium level, the wealth level rises permanently over generations; on the other hand, if initially the wealth level of the household is below the upper equilibrium level, the wealth level will decrease over generations and converge on the lower equilibrium level. (3) The case where there is no equilibrium and where the ever higher level of the (gross) bequest is transmitted from generation to generation. Case 1 occurs if the consumption of the future generation is a "necessity" relative to the consumption of the current household ($\mu > \varepsilon$) or if the consumption of the future generation is relatively a "luxury good" ($\varepsilon > \mu$), but at the same time the size of the family grows rapidly enough ($r \leq n$) so that the increased level of the total (gross) bequest is fragmented into smaller portions in per capita terms. Either case 2 or 3 occurs if the consumption of the future generation is relatively a "luxury good" ($\varepsilon > \mu$) and if the size of the family grows relatively moderately ($n < r$).[22] In the case of the household with parental self-satisfaction, the bequest of financial wealth is definitionally zero.[23]

4. Family Values, Educational Environments, and the Size Distribution of Income

The preceding sections have discussed the effects of different family structures and family values on the levels of education and bequest for each generation. The dependence of the level of a generation's bequest on that of the bequest of the previous generation in the case of a household with parental altruism defines a wealth transmission mechanism through which the long-run change of household wealth can be analyzed. In the following, we shall discuss the qualitative implications of the foregoing model on the distribution of income both for a generation and for the long run.

Among the numerous variables affecting the level of income in our model, our attention will be focused on the effects of different family values and educational environments (so far fixed), first, regarding them as exogenously given and, second, taking account of the possibility that they are influenced by the level of wealth of the previous generation (See Fig. 3.).

Let us start by assuming that households are identical except possibly for the level of bequest given by the ancestral generation (relevant under parental altruism) and then relax this restrictive assumption step by step. Within the framework where this basic assumption holds and where household value is parental altruism, the economy is characterized by perfect equality of earnings and by inequality of financial wealth depending on the distribution of bequests. The inequality in the financial wealth holdings and the associated property income increase or decrease according to the magnitude of the parameters that regulate the stability patterns of the wealth transmission paths discussed above.

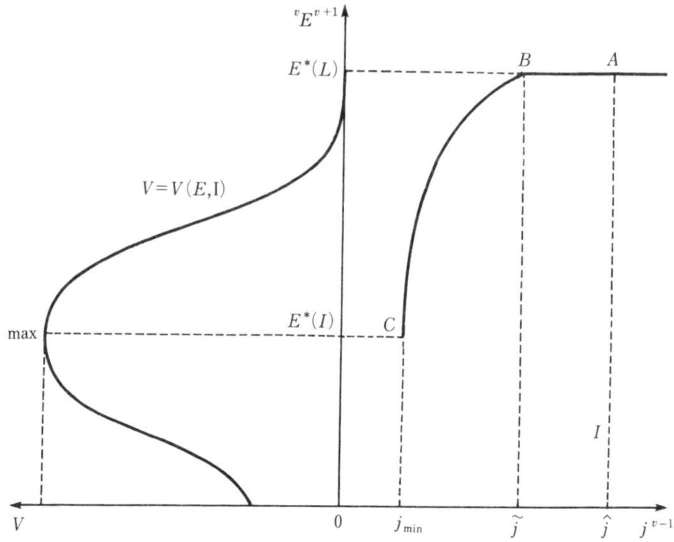

Figure 4

be fundamental; rather, it might be a problem of realizing one of the two value types. More specifically, poor families may not be able to realize the value of parental altruism even if they potentially possess it, so they are forced to behave as if they possessed parental self-satisfaction, or a value close to it.

The tendency just described, together with the other possible extended reasons mentioned above, makes the distribution of parental altruism likely to be positively correlated with the wealth position of households. This makes both earnings and property income positively correlated with parental wealth and, therefore, makes the distribution of income in the short run more unequal than in the case where values are distributed independent of wealth position. The same effect applies to the distribution of income and wealth in the long run.

EDUCATIONAL ENVIRONMENT FACTORS

The Case Where Educational Environment Is Given Exogenously. Apart from the degree of flexibility of educational institutions, we have thus far assumed that the educational environment is fixed and common for all households. Specifically, the earnings capacity schedule $w = w(E)$ has been assumed to be common for all households and generations. The functional form of this schedule can be interpreted to reflect intelligence and the qualities of schools and other social environments, such as home, peers, and community, to which household members are subject. Therefore, there is no empirical reason to expect that earnings capacity schedules are common among different households.

Let us express the difference in the educational environment summarily by the difference in the output elasticity function of earnings capacity with respect to the total number of years of schooling,

$$\gamma(E) = \frac{E}{w}\frac{dw}{dE}.$$

For the sake of simplicity, let us henceforth assume that the elasticity $\gamma = \gamma(E)$ is constant with respect to E; therefore, differences in the household educational environment can be represented by differences in the value of the elasticity γ among households. Then, in the case where all households' value is characterized by parental altruism, the level of education attained is approximated by

$$E \simeq \gamma/r. \tag{19}$$

Equation (19) implies that, when γ is symmetrically distributed, the level of education is approximately symmetrically distributed. Furthermore, under the same assumption, it can be shown (proof omitted) that, as long as the distribution of γ is such that the distribution of earnings exhibits single modality, the distribution of earnings is characterized by a positive skewness in the weak sense that the inequality "mode earnings < median earnings < mean earnings" holds.

The Case Where Educational Environment Is Influenced by the Wealth Position of the Parental Household. Recent empirical studies on educational opportunity indicate quite strongly that the economic position of the household positively affects the quality of educational environment for children through various channels (e.g., Bowles, 1972). If we interpret the term "quality" in narrow economic terms and incorporate the above observation into our framework by expressing the efficiency parameter γ as an increasing function of the initial wealth level of the parental household,

$$\gamma^{\nu+1} = \gamma(W_0^{\nu}) \quad \text{and} \quad \gamma'(\cdot) > 0, \tag{20}$$

then it is obvious that the levels of children's education and earnings under either parental altruism or parental self-satisfaction are increasing with respect to the initial wealth of the parental household.[28] Incorporation of relationship (20) modifies the stability patterns of the wealth transmission process under parental altruism in such a way that the cases that previously produced equalizing tendencies in the long run (i.e., $\mu > \varepsilon$, or $\varepsilon > \mu$ and $n > r$) now admit the possibility of multiple equilibria where the lowest equilibrium point is stable.[29] Therefore, inequality in educational opportunity may conceivably more than offset the equalizing force coming from the low wealth elasticity of bequest or the high rate of fertility and thus may make permanent strata of income and wealth classes.

THE TWO ASPECTS COMBINED

When we combine the present discussions of the dependence of apparent family values and educational environment on the wealth position of the household, we are likely to see the possibility of a strongly or weakly stratified society in the long run with very rich households continuing to accumulate wealth through inheritance and higher education, on one end of the scale, and poor households, on the other end, remaining stationary with little or no inheritance of financial wealth and with little education. The possible equalizing forces of a relatively low wealth elasticity of (gross) bequest and a relatively high fertility rate may not be sufficient to circumvent this tendency.[30]

5. Concluding Remarks: Extensions and Qualifications of the Analysis

The foregoing analysis is based on various restrictive assumptions. I conclude this paper by indicating some of the important limitations of my model and speculating on topics for further research.

Some of the limitations concern the nature of the family household considered in this model. We have assumed that the household is an authoritative institution where children are completely subordinate to parents' decisions during the first I years of life and that the length of dependence is determined exogenously. Alternatively, and perhaps more realistically in modern Western society, we can assume a more democratic household where children, as they become mature, are given an increasing amount of autonomy and/or room for discussion with parents concerning their economic affairs.[31] It is then natural to assume that children reserve the right to alter their parents' preconceived age of independence. Let us see how the preceding analysis is modified when this occurs. It is clear that when parents have parental altruism and are rich enough to realize that value, there will be no incentive on the part of children to alter the age of independence their parents have determined, as long as children and parents have no conflict over children's consumption patterns during the period parents expect children to be dependent. In this case, no change will be necessary in the analysis. However, when parents have parental self-satisfaction or when they have parental altruism but are not rich enough to realize it (see the previous section), the analysis calls for modification. Children who recognize their low future economic perspective as the result of low planned education then have economic incentives (aside from the possible conflict over consumption patterns mentioned above) to become independent of the household as quickly as possible so as to avoid the limitation of the parental household.[32] Of course, the time children actually leave will depend on various other factors, including the rapidity of children's maturity and their psychological ties to parents. Nevertheless, to the extent that children do leave the household earlier, inequality in the distribution of earnings will be reduced, and inequality in the distribution of wealth in the long run will be reduced accordingly.

With regard to the nature of education, we have thus far assumed that education is merely an opportunity for investment. However, it seems more realistic to assume that educational achievement as measured by length of schooling or by the economic ability that schooling facilitates gives direct satisfaction to individuals by way of accessibility to more information and control of environment and/or fulfillment of status consciousness. Elsewhere (Ishikawa, 1972), I have shown that schooling is then planned at the level where the marginal utility loss arising from decreased lifetime earnings (when one more year of schooling is taken) is exactly offset by the marginal increment in the direct utility of educational achievement obtained. Therefore, its planned level now depends on initial household wealth and is pushed beyond the point where the investment value is maximized.[33] However, there are no major changes in the results of the preceding analysis.

Another aspect of education concerns the implicit treatment of educational institutions in the model. Our assumptions amount to saying that schools are provided as manna.[34] There are two stages of extensions to render the framework more realistic. The first and more comprehensive approach is to incorporate the educational supply sector, either private or public (or both), explicitly into the model and consider the equilibrium of the demand for and supply of schools through either competitive market forces in the case of private schools or a Lindahl-type voluntary exchange mechanism in the case of public schools. The second, less comprehensive but more manageable approach is to treat educational supply as exogenous to the system but to assume that direct costs of education are collected either privately in the form of tuition and other fees or publicly in the form of taxes according to the quality of schooling. On the one hand, privately collected direct costs of education are not difficult to incorporate into our model. In fact, under our assumption of a perfect capital market, incorporation of this does not cause any substantial modification of our analysis. On the other hand, in the case of public financing of schools, different redistributional effects arise according to how taxes are imposed and how schools are utilized among households.[35] Presumably, the closest we come to distributionally neutral taxation in our framework is in the case of a crude "benefit principle" where educational costs are allocated among households in such a way that the discounted sum of taxes collected during each household's education period equals some constant (over households) proportion of the present value of the lifetime earnings stream that will be received by members of the household taking education.[36] However, this scheme is not as practical as one would imagine, for schooling comprises only a part of the entire educational environment, and interactions with other components of educational environment make it extremely difficult to disentangle and identify the pure contribution of schools in raising lifetime earnings. In any case, to the extent that the actual financing of public schools is not performed in this manner, taxation schemes should be explicitly incorporated into our model and their redistributional effects evaluated accordingly.

With regard to the assumption of a perfect capital market under which our analysis has been conducted, it has been widely acknowledged that the capital market is actually imperfect, especially with regard to financing education, since the result of education is embodied in human beings, and in contemporary society they cannot be made the object of exchange in the market and thus can never be made collateral.[37] Although the recent tendency on the part of private institutions of higher education to introduce student tuition loan programs can rightly be interpreted as an effort to remove imperfections in the field of educational finance, its effect is still partial, for the indirect cost of education is not taken care of.[38] In order to cope with actual circumstances and to evaluate various educational subsidy programs, my theoretical framework ought to be extended to explicitly incorporate imperfections of the capital market.[39]

My final remark concerns the most important limitation of this analysis, namely, the fact that the analysis has been confined to the personal sector of the economy. No explicit account of the formation of the market wage rate and the market rate of interest, and of the character of their change over time, has been made; rather, the analysis has been based on the "small country" assumption of constant market wage rate and market rate of interest. If, instead, we assume that the economy is not really "small" and that physical capital equipment and "educated labor" are substitutable inputs in the overall spectrum of techniques in the economy, we should expect the market wage rate to rise and the market quasi rent of capital equipment to fall when physical capital investment proceeds faster than the rise in the supply of "educated labor," and vice versa. Constant rate of interest (which then equals the quasi rent of capital equipment) and constant market wage rate are realized when the economy stays on a steady growth path, and the latter, in turn, is possible only when the personal sector has a steady state so that the wealth level of each household becomes stationary.[40] According to the discussion of Section 3, such a circumstance is obtained only when every household's wealth transmission process converges over generations to a stable equilibrium level. These conditions may be regarded as very stringent. Development of a full dynamic model that includes the corporate and educational sectors and the determination mechanism for the wage rate and the rate of interest is left for future research.[41]

NOTES

This paper originates from the major part of my doctoral dissertation. I am very grateful to Professors Kenneth Arrow, Peter Newman, and Jürg Niehans for their valuable criticisms and suggestions during the course of my research. I am also indebted to Professors Alan Blinder, Zvi Griliches, Shoichi Rohyama, Lester Thurow, the participants of the Harvard–M.I.T. seminar on mathematical economics, and in particular Professor Gary Becker for their helpful comments and helpful discussions. Becker's comments were particularly stimulating in the course of revision. Financial support from the Woodrow Wilson Foundation and the National Science Foundation under grant GS–37899 is also gratefully acknowledged.

1. In this model, I do not distinguish between males and females. Thus, the terms "he" and "parents" are used interchangeably.

2. I shall, for the sake of simplicity, neglect in this paper the familiar work-leisure choice problem. The extension of this problem into the life-cycle savings model is done in Blinder (1971: ch. 3) and Weiss (1972).

3. The characterization of the family with authoritative or sovereign parents is different from that of the family characterized by Becker (1974). Becker draws the surprising conclusion that "when one member cares sufficiently about other members to be the head, all members have the same motivation as the head to maximize family opportunities and to internalize fully all within-family 'externalities' regardless of how selfish (or, indeed, how envious) these members are" (1974: 1080) and argues that identification of the family "head's" utility function as that of the entire family does not require the family "head" to be sovereign (Becker 1974: n. 29). However, his conclusion does not seem to be generally valid once we note the ambiguous nature of the definition of family "head." More specifically, his conclusion depends crucially on the implicit assumption that the family head "who cares sufficiently about other members" is financially richer than other members, so that his altruistic optimum requires him to transfer income to others in net.

4. To be precise, it is the time point conceptualized by parents such that, from this moment, (a) economic decision making, more specifically decisions pertaining to children's consumption, saving, and education, is transferred to children; (b) any earnings that children obtain accrue to themselves; and (c) any further economic support that parents give to children is done as a part of inheritance. It does not necessarily coincide with geographical separation, acquisition of first job, or marriage, which are frequently discussed in the social mobility literature.

5. Further discussion of this point follows in the concluding section.

6. The case of $I = 0$, where each individual becomes an independent decision maker at the moment of economic birth, is customarily assumed in the literature on investment in human capital and on life-cycle savings.

7. The factors regulating this schedule are discussed in Section 4 below.

8. This may reflect the more fundamental paternal love of children or parental concern for the economic prosperity of the family as a historically continuous entity. The latter interpretation corresponds to the use of the term "altruism" in biology; see Trivers (1971) and Boorman (1973).

9. Strictly speaking, "bequest" here expresses the object of parental concern and should be construed as a gross concept, for the human wealth component contains a portion that is not directly contributed by parents. The *net* bequest can be defined as the sum of financial wealth and net increment in human wealth resulting from parents' action, as compared with the case where they do not have the bequest motive. This distinction between gross and net concepts becomes important when we measure the actual degree of parents' bequest motive from empirical data (see n. 22 below).

10. The effects of methods of inheritance division other than the equal-division rule adopted here on the long-run distribution of wealth are analyzed by Stiglitz (1969) and Blinder (1973). For a discussion of inheritance tax schemes to induce equal-inheritance division, see Meade (1965: 54–59).

11. Note that in (9), human wealth is defined in terms of the realized level of education, ${}^{v}E^{v}$. The possibility of revision in the education program implies that $W_0^v(W_0^{v+1})$ does not automatically equal $j^{v-1}e^{-r(L-H-I)}(j^v e^{-r(L-H-I)})$, although the corresponding relation for financial wealth (eq. [10]) always holds true.

12. It will become clear that this restrictive form of the utility function is immaterial for the discussion of the level of education.

13. We may alternatively interpret parental self-satisfaction as containing valuation of accumulation of financial wealth for its own sake (even until the moment of death) as motivated by miserliness, power consciousness, or fulfillment of duty psychologically imposed by religion. Mathematically, we can add a wealth valuation term, say $\psi(b_{L-I}^v)$ to the utility functional (eq., [14]). In this case, the accumulated financial wealth at death may be donated as charitable contributions, or it may alternatively be left unspecified and subsequently divided up by the heirs, which becomes windfall income. Although I shall not go into detailed analysis of such a case in this paper (See Ishikawa, 1972.), note that the household behavior toward children's education is unchanged under such a modification of interpretation.

14. Formally, the right-hand side of this equation corresponds to Becker's (1974) social income concept.

15. This accords with the following statement by Becker: "Children have their decisions guided, however, as well as partly financed, by their parents, and as long as parents receive some monetary or psychological benefit from an increase in their children's economic well being, parents have an incentive to help children make wise decisions" (Becker, 1967: n. 22). A similar statement is found in Becker (1974: 1077).

16. Even if we extend the definition of altruism to imply that children's earnings do not enter the family income pool, the outcome on the choice of education can easily be shown to be immaterial.

17. From (4), we have

$$h_0^v = \int_{{}^{v}E^{v}-E^*(I)}^{L-I} w^v({}^{v}E^v)e^{-rt}\,dt$$

$$= \frac{e^{rE^*(I)}}{r}\left[w^v({}^{v}E^v)e^{-r\{L-[I-E^*(I)]\}}\right].$$

Hence, the maximum of h_0^v is obtained at ${}^{v}E^{v} = E^*\{L-[I-E^*(I)]\}$. In the customarily discussed case of $I = 0$ (purely individualistic household), it does not matter which value the household has, for even under parental self-satisfaction, children have L years left to consider their education program (See Fig. 2.).

18. I am indebted to a participant of the Harvard–M.I.T. seminar and Professor Becker for pointing out this qualification to me.

19. The condition for Pareto improvements is that the increases of children's earnings for the period after they become independent is larger than the amount that compensates the decrease of earnings that are contributed to the resource pool of the parental household. Mathematically, this is expressed by

$$w[E^*(L)][e^{-rE^*(L)} - e^{-rL}] > w[E^*(I)][e^{-rE^*(I)} - e^{-rL}]$$

for the case of inflexible education and

$$w[E^*(L)]e^{rI}[e^{-rE^*(L)} - e^{-rL}] > w[E^*(I)]\{e^{-r[E^*(I)-I]} - 1\}$$
$$+ w(E^*\{L - [I - E^*(I)]\})(e^{-rE^*\{L-[I-E^*(I)]\}} - e^{-r(L-I)})$$

for the case of flexible education. Note that these conditions are not automatically satisfied.

20. The reasons for this are as follows: (a) Since parents have no altruistic concern for their children, they have no moral basis to expect anything reciprocal from children. (b) Even under the assumptions of a perfect capital market and an authoritative household, we preserve the notion of independence strictly to disapprove of parents' having the right to mortgage their children's future earnings. The situation here is analogous to the difficulty in Samuelson's (1958) perishable-good economy of the occurrence of a transfer of goods from the old to the young in the absence of money or other social compacts.

21. The case $\varepsilon > \mu$ implies that the household allocates an increasing portion of its wealth (defined by the right-hand side of eq. [15]) to (gross) bequest as its wealth level rises. In such a case, we may say that the consumption of the future generation is a "luxury good" relative to the consumption of the current household or, equivalently, that the latter is a "necessity" relative to the former.

22. In the special case of $\varepsilon = \mu$, function (16) becomes piecewise linear and case 1 holds if the rate of fertility, n, is sufficiently smaller than the rate of interest, r; otherwise (and certainly for the case $r \geq n$), either case 2 or 3 holds.

As has been lucidly pointed out by Becker (1974), an apparent high elasticity of *net* bequest (i.e., actual contribution by parents [cf. n. 9 above]) with respect to wealth may not necessarily be incompatible with a low wealth elasticity of *gross* bequest. Therefore, empirical investigations that would establish the wealth elasticity of the bequest expenditure could not in itself rule out the possibility that the consumption by future generations is a "necessity" relative to the consumption of the current household, i.e., $\varepsilon \leq \mu$.

23. Under the alternative interpretation of self-satisfaction noted in n. 13 above, there results transmission of financial wealth of the form

$$i^v = \begin{cases} B(I^{v-1}; r, w) \quad B' > 0, & \text{for } i^{v-1} > \hat{\imath} \\ 0 & \text{for } i^{v-1} \leq \hat{\imath} \end{cases} \qquad (\hat{\imath} \geq 0)$$

whose stability patterns follow that of (16).

24. As a result of a survey study on conjugal cohesion, Scanzoni (1970) finds that the presence of empathetic affection between conjugal members increases as the economic position of the household improves. We can safely expect that the empathetic concern among parents will naturally extend to their children.

25. It seems plausible to assume that the minimum consumption constraint (18) becomes effective only after the solvency constraint (6) became effective. However, this assumption is not crucial for the conclusion to follow.

26. The locus BC in Figure 4 is mathematically defined by

$$\int_0^{L-I} \hat{c}^v e^{-rt}\, dt + \int_{H-I}^{H} \hat{c}^{v+1} e^{nH} e^{-rt}\, dt$$
$$= e^{-r(L-H-I)} j^{v-1} + e^{nH} e^{-r(H-I)} V({}^{vEv+1}, I),$$

where $0 \leq j_{\min} \leq j^{v-1} \leq \bar{j}$ and where $j_{\min}$ expresses the value of j^{v-1} corresponding to

${}^{v}E^{v+1}E^{*}(I)$, that is, when maximum contribution is extracted from children. This is the minimum level of initial wealth that the household must have for its survival.

27. Needless to say, as long as the educational system is flexible, children can revise their education programs after they become independent (just as in the case of parental self-satisfaction).

28. There may be significant diminishing "marginal returns" in relationship (20) so that the variance of the distribution of earnings may be kept within a finite range in the long run.

29. This cases occurs if relationship (20) is significant; otherwise, the case of a single globally stable equilibrium holds. The case $\varepsilon > \mu$ and $r > n$ admits, as before, either no equilibrium or two equilibria.

30. See Blau and Duncan (1967). For detailed discussion of the effects of differences in fertility rates on the distribution of income, see Ishikawa (1972: ch. 9).

31. The conflict between parents and children over children's economic affairs that arises out of differences in their preference patterns are discussed in Griliches (1973) and Leibenstein (1974). For an analogous discussion in the field of biology, see Trivers (1974).

Also note that school education trains children for self-direction, although Kohn (1969) finds, from the results of various survey studies, that emphasis on such training is more prevalent among schools that have students from white-collar backgrounds.

32. Of course, when conflict exists, children have incentives to become independent early, as Griliches (1973) discusses. In the case of households with parental self-satisfaction, there remains the possibility that a rational contract (to replace the more paternalistic arrangement considered in Section 3) will develop between parents and children so that the optimal level of education for children is planned in return for payment later of its opportunity cost. However, again, as long as there is no legal sanction to guarantee the enforcement of the contract, parents are unlikely to engage in such an arrangement. On the other hand, in the case of households with parental altruism but with too little wealth to realize it, no such possibility exists unless children or parents can borrow funds by mortgaging the children's future earnings (which is totally unrealistic). Therefore, parents would feel powerless over the welfare of children, as in the case of the mother in a popular elegy:

> My children will go
> As soon as they grow,
> Well, there ain't nothin' here now to hold them. [Bob Dylan]

33. One complication that arises here is that, if the consumption element of education is sufficiently large in the household's preference structure so that the total length of education exceeds $E^{*}(\infty)$ years, then, as I show elsewhere (Ishikawa, 1972, 1975), the optimal education strategy under flexible education actually contains an intermission in the education process, taking $E^{*}(\infty)$ consecutive years of schooling first and then postponing the remaining years of schooling until as late as possible.

34. I am indebted to Professor Rohyama for stressing this point and providing suggestive interpretations.

35. An interesting case study of such redistributional effects is provided by Hansen and Weisbrod (1969).

36. Note that households' decisions on education are not affected by this scheme of taxation, unless educational achievement is valued by them for its own sake.

37. See Friedman (1962: 102) and Becker (1967: 9–10, 33). The difficulty is increased when we note the highly risky nature of educational investment, an element that is completely ignored in this analysis.

38. See Hartman (1972) and Nerlove (1972) for evaluations of the existing programs and various proposals.

39. For the effects of imperfections in the capital market on life-cycle savings behavior, see Tobin and Dolde (1971) and Ishikawa (1972, 1974).

40. The same conditions appear in the model of Stiglitz where households accumulate wealth according to a nonlinear savings function (Stiglitz, 1969: 389–90).

41. For an interesting attempt in this direction, see Atkinson (1974).

References

Atkinson, A.B. 1971. Capital taxes, the redistribution of wealth and individual savings. Review of Economic Studies 38 (April): 209–27.
———. 1974. A model of the distribution of wealth. Unpublished. University of Essex and M.I.T.
Becker, G.S. 1962. Investment in human capital: A theoretical analysis. Journal of Political Economy 70, 5, suppl. (Oct.): 9–49.
———. 1967. Human Capital and the Personal Income Distribution: An Analytical Approach. Woytinski Lecture 1. Ann Arbor: University of Michigan Press.
———. 1974. A theory of social interactions. Journal of Political Economy 82 (Nov./Dec.): 1063–93.
Ben Porath, Y. 1967. The production of human capital and the life cycle of earnings. Journal of Political Economy 75 (Aug.): 352–65.
Blau, P.M., and O.D. Duncan. 1967. American Occupational Structures. New York: Wiley.
Blinder, A.S. 1971. Towards an economic theory of income distribution. Ph.D. dissertation. M.I.T.
———. 1973. A model of inherited wealth. Quarterly Journal of Economics 87 (Nov.): 608–26.
Boorman, S.A. 1973. A frequency-dependent natural selection model for the evolution of social cooperation. Ph.D. dissertation. Harvard University.
Bowles, S. 1972. Schooling and inequality from generation to generation. Journal of Political Economy 80, 3, suppl. (May/June): S219–51.
Fisher, I. 1930. The Theory of Interest. New York: Macmillan.
Friedman, M. 1962. Capitalism and Freedom. Chicago: University of Chicago Press.
Griliches, Z. 1973. Economic problems of youth. In Youth: Transition to Adulthood. Report of the Panel on Youth of the President's Science Advisory Committee, Office of Science and Technology, Executive Office of the President. Washington, D.C.: Government Printing Office.
Hansen, W.L., and B.A. Weisbrod. 1969. Benefits, Costs, and Finance of Public Higher Education. Chicago: Markham.
Hartman, R.W. 1972. Equity implications of state tuition policy and student loans. Journal of Political Economy 80, 3, suppl. (May/June): S142–71.
Ishikawa, T. 1972. The dynamics of wealth accumulation and education under different family institutions as determinants of the size distribution of income. Ph.D. dissertation. Johns Hopkins University.
———. 1974. Imperfection in the capital market and the institutional arrangement of inheritance. Review of Economic Studies 41 (July): 383–404. Reprinted in this volume.
———. 1975. A note on the optimal spacing properties in a simple Jevonian model of educational investment. Quarterly Journal of Economics 89 (Nov.): 633–42. Reprinted in this volume.
Johnson, H.G. 1972. The alternatives before us. Journal of Political Economy 80, 3, suppl. (May/June): S280–89.
Kohn, M. 1969. Class and Conformity. Homewood, Ill.: Dorsey.
Leibenstein H. 1974. Towards a Significantly (but Not Radically) New Theory of Consumption. Discussion Paper 343. Cambridge, Mass.: Harvard Institute of Economic Research.
Meade, J.E. 1965. Efficiency, Equality and Ownership of Property. Cambridge, Mass.: Harvard University Press.
———. 1966. Life-cycle savings, inheritance and economic growth. Review of Economic Studies 33 (Jan.): 61–78.
Mincer, J. 1958. Investment in human capital and personal income distribution. Journal of Political Economy 66 (Aug.): 281–302.
Nerlove, M. 1972. On tuition and the costs of higher education: Prolegomena to a conceptual framework. Journal of Poltical Economy 80, 3, suppl. (May/June): S178–218.

Samuelson, P.A. 1958. An exact consumption-loan model of interest with or without the social contrivance of money. Journal of Political Economy 66 (Dec.): 467–82.
Scanzoni, J.H. 1970. Opportunity and the Family. New York: Free Press.
Stiglitz, J. 1969. Distribution of income and wealth among individuals. Econometrica 37 (July): 382–97.
Tobin, J., and W.C. Dolde. 1971. Wealth, liquidity and consumption. In Consumer Spending and Monetary Policy. Monetary Conference Series 5. Boston: Federal Reserve Bank of Boston.
Trivers, R.L. 1971. The evolution of reciprocal altruism. Quarterly Journal of Biology 46: 35–57.
———. 1974. Parent-offspring conflict. American Zoologist 14: 249–64.
Weiss, Y. 1972. On the optimal lifetime pattern of labour supply. Economic Journal 82. (Dec.): 1293–1315.
Yaari, M.E. 1964. On the consumer's lifetime allocation process. International Economic Review 5 (Sept.): 304–17.

7. The Bonus Payment System and Japanese Personal Savings

1. Introduction

In this paper we examine an oft-posed conjecture that the institutional form of worker compensation called bonus in Japan is contributing significantly to a high personal savings rate by international standards (with the average of 20.0 percent during 1958–78). The only close statistical study, so far, addressing this specific question is that of Mizoguchi (1964: ch. 3).[1] By comparing the Family Income and Expenditure Survey (hereinafter abbreviated as FIES) data on worker family households for various years, Mizoguchi has found that the annual consumption expenditure of households has a remarkably stable relationship with family head's regular income, the ratio being 1.2–1.3. Furthermore, even when households are decomposed into quintile groups by the size of income, this stability holds for each group except for the lowest quintile. He then argued that households' regular consumption habits are formed on the basis of family head's regular income, and consequently, an increase in the ratio of temporary income (including the incomes of other members of the household and bonus payments as the major parts) to the family head's income is bound to raise the rate of savings (See also Mizoguchi [1973: ch. 3].).

In the present paper we will investigate this question from three different angles. First, we will make a detailed probe into the recent (time series of) FIES cross-section data on worker households that have become much richer since the time of Mizoguchi's study. Our main ob-

Coauthored with Kazuo Ueda, Bank of Japan. Originally published in *The Economic Analysis of the Japanese Firm*, ed. by Masahiko Aoki, pp. 134–92. (Amsterdam: North Holland, 1984).

jective here is to obtain separate estimates for the marginal propensities to consume bonus income, on the one hand, and nonbonus income, on the other. Second, we shall make a time-series analysis of a unique survey data (Survey on the Movement of Consumption, prepared by the Economic Planning Agency) that contains data on households' expectations on bonus income. Using this data and estimating the length of the planning horizon of households in dispensing with the bonus income, we directly estimate the transitoriness of the bonus income. This task thus provides us with a direct test of the permanent-income–life-cycle savings hypothesis. Third, we evaluate the effect of the bonus payment system on savings at the macro level. For this purpose, we have newly constructed aggregate time-series data on bonus earnings for the period 1958–78, using the same data source as the data on employee compensation in the national income accounts (NIA).

The major conclusions that emerge from our study are as follows. First, the permanent-income–life-cycle hypothesis does not seem to apply to Japanese worker households. They are not rational maximizing economic agents. This conclusion follows from our analyses of both the survey data and the cross-section data. Our data suggests that households distinguish bonus earnings from the rest of their income and regard them as a sort of buffer income, capable of being dispensed with discretionarily. Moreover, in the normal years of stable growth, households seem to follow a conventional rule of thumb that dictates saving about half of their bonus income. This interpretation, which we term the habit–buffer-income hypothesis, is a further elaboration of the viewpoint implicitly held by Mizoguchi and recently explicitly stated by Shinohara (1959).

Second, in a quantitative dimension, the marginal propensity to consume bonus income is significantly lower than that of nonbonus income. Studies at three different levels all point to the same conclusion, that the marginal propensity to consume bonus income is (except for the "turning point" years of 1975–76 as suggested by the cross-section study) roughly one-half (0.5), whereas consumption of regular wage income is 0.7. This roughly 20 percent difference in the marginal propensity to consume is the source of quantitative effects of the bonus payment system on Japanese personal savings. We should, however, not exaggerate the quantitative importance of this effect, for simple arithmetic would suggest that its contribution to the aggregate personal savings rate would not be more than a few percentage points. Therefore, the cause of internationally high personal savings rates yet remains an open question. Our conclusion thus qualifies the intuitive suggestion of the importance of the bonus effect so often made by Japanese economists.[2]

The organization of the paper is as follows. The following section presents an overview of the movement of the rate of personal savings and its relationship with the relative magnitude of bonus earnings in the aggregate wage income. The cross-section analysis is presented in Section 3, while the time-series analysis of the survey data is presented in Section 4. Section 5 gives the analysis of aggregate time-series data, together with the result of simulation concerning the quantitative effect of bonus income. Section 6 summarizes the implications of our analysis and also states various qualifications on our results. Finally, the Data Appendix provides an account of our estimation procedure for aggregate bonus income series.

2. Movement of Personal Savings and Bonus Earnings: An Overview

Let us now turn to a brief overview of the movement of the personal savings rate and its relationship with the share of bonus earnings in the aggregate employment income. The basic personal savings concept employed here is identical with that of the national income accounts (hereinafter abbreviated as NIA), namely the difference between personal disposable income and personal consumption, including expenditures on consumer durables.[3] The period of study is 1958 through 1978, for which we have estimated the aggregate bonus income series.

Figure 1 summarily depicts the now familiar movement of the personal savings (S) over personal disposable income (DY) and the movement of various factors that have previously been suggested to explain the former. We immediately notice that the personal savings rate series had a definite upward trend until the mid-1970s, starting from 14.8 percent in 1958, with distinctive rises in 1961 and during the four years 1973–76, reaching the peak of 25.2 percent in 1974. Since 1975, it has been declining, and some more recent statistics suggest that by 1980 it had declined to a pre-1973 level.[4]

Out of numerous studies conducted in the past to explain (i) the very high personal savings ratio by international standards, and/or (ii) the trend increase in the rate of personal savings up till the mid-1970s, we have taken up the following four factors for examination. They are: (a) the so-called rate of growth effect (Ohkawa and Rosovsky, 1973: 171–72), (b) the importance of the self-employed sector (Shinohara, 1959; Komiya, 1963; Mizoguchi, 1964), (c) the desired financial asset and stock adjustment effect (Mizoguchi, 1970: ch. 3, 1973: ch. 4), and (d) the effect of bonus earnings (Komiya, 1963; Mizoguchi, 1964; Shinohara, 1981).

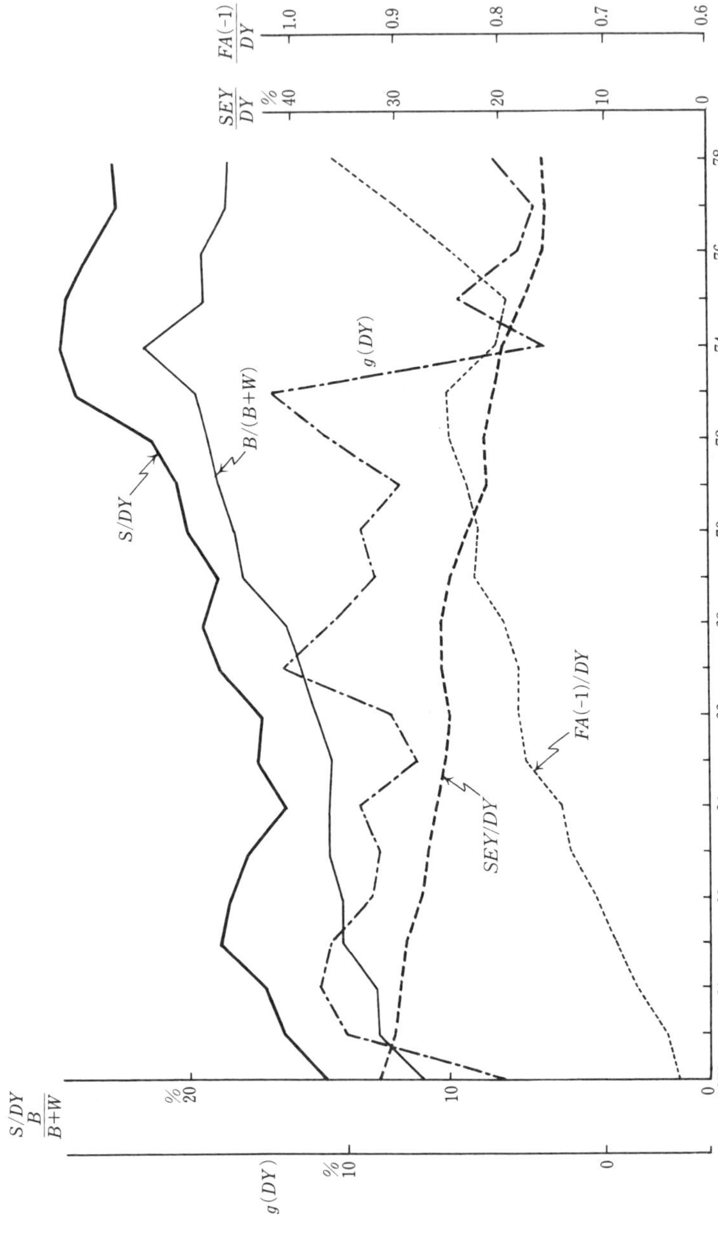
S/DY
B/(B+W)
g(DY)
SEY/DY
FA(-1)/DY
1958
60
62
64
66
68
70
72
74
76
78
%
20
10
0
40
30
0.6
0.7
0.8
0.9
1.0

Figure 1

Implicit in the rather vague terminology of the "rate of growth" effect is the notion of habit persistence or of permanent income, which produces lagged consumption responses to a growth in income. This factor is represented in Figure 1 by the curve $g(DY)$, which expresses the annual rate of growth of real personal disposable income (i.e., $g(DY) = (DY - DY(-1))/DY(-1))$. Comparison of this curve with the curve representing the rate of savings reveals two particularly noteworthy features.

First, for years before 1974, it appears generally true that acceleration in the growth of income resulted in a quick rise in the savings rate, which is an observation consistent with many theoretical hypotheses on savings, including the permanent-income hypothesis and the habit-persistence hypothesis. Yet when the movements of the two series are contrasted more closely, we notice that there exists a lagged response on the part of the savings rate to the rate of growth of disposable income. More specifically, within the period of 1958–74, there are ten turning points in the $g(DY)$ curve. However, in six cases out of ten, these points are followed with a lag of one year by the turning points (in the same direction) of the savings rate curve. Thus, the relation between the rate of growth of personal disposable income and the rate of personal savings is not that simple. Moreover, after 1974, there no longer seems to be any correlation between the two.

Second, and more fundamentally, we must face the fact that any good theory of Japanese personal savings ought to be able to explain not only why they are high (query [i] above), but also why they show a marked long-run increasing trend (query [ii] above) up until 1974. The view stressing merely the rate of growth effect seems to fail on this ground, for even if we again disregard the years after 1974 and concentrate on the period of rapid growth, no clear trend in the rate of growth of personal disposable income is discernible. High average growth rates during this period may very well explain high savings rates, yet they fail to explain their trend increase. We thus have two points of reservation on the simple view stressing the rate of growth.

The last point applies even more to the second factor. As Mizoguchi (1964, 1970) has shown on the basis of FIES data, self-employed households (both agricultural and nonagricultural) do save more than worker households, as expected. Nevertheless, while it may partly answer the above query (i), it certainly does not answer our query (ii). The proportion of self-employed income (SEY) in personal disposable income exhibits a continual decline from 32.1 percent in 1958 to 15.9 percent in 1978 (the scaling for this graph is given in the right-hand margin of Fig. 1).

Concerning the third factor, we notice a clear positive trend in the

$FA(-1)/DY$ curve, which expresses the ratio of beginning-of-the-year net financial assets of the individual sector over the current-year personal disposable income, or for short, the net financial wealth/income ratio. This ratio fell down significantly from the trend during 1974–76. It has been suggested that: (a) in the face of high growth rates in income, a high rate of savings is required just to maintain the net financial wealth/income ratio intact (Mizoguchi, 1973: ch. 3), which is a straightforward implication of the familiar Harrod-Domar formula, and (b) individuals have a notion of the desired net financial wealth/income ratio and that the Japanese economy is still undergoing a period of transition, trying to reach a high target ratio (Economic Planning Agency, *Annual Economic Report*, 1970, as referred to by Mizoguchi, 1973). Clearly, if (b) were actually the case, it would help in one way to answer our query (ii). Moreover, this hypothesis has another apparent appeal, the off-trend rise in the rate of savings during 1973–76 corresponds well with the off-trend decline in the net financial wealth/income ratio during 1974–76, making the interpretation that the former was caused by the latter conceivable. (Flow of Funds Accounts, Bank of Japan). While this explanation is certainly suggestive, we must yet see if it derives from a more basic hypothesis about individuals' consumption behavior, or if it is a mere statistical correspondence. Important as it is, a careful analysis of this point is left beyond the scope of the present paper.[5]

Now we come to the fourth factor, the effect of bonus earnings on personal savings. The graph $B/(B+W)$ in Figure 1 depicts the estimated ratio of bonus earnings B over total employee compensation $(B+W)$ in the NIA. (W will hereinafter be referred to as the regular wage income.)[6] As we can see from the figure, the ratio of bonus income over total earnings, or for short, the "bonus earnings ratio" shows a steady upward trend until 1974, starting from 10.9 percent in 1958, reaching 21.9 percent in 1974, and then declining to 18.5 percent in 1978. The average bonus earnings ratio during the entire sample period turns out to be 16.6 percent.[7,8] We immediately observe a high correlation between the movement of the savings rate (S/DY) and the bonus earnings ratio ($B/(B+W)$). Moreover, this high correlation extends over the period after 1974. The simple correlation coefficient between these two variables is 0.92. This provides *prima facie* evidence that the relative magnitude of bonus income in total earnings might have a significant contribution in answering our basic queries (i) and (ii). In fact, an aggregate consumption function we estimate in Section 5 shows a positive and significant effect of bonus income on savings.

Discerning readers, however, may still question that this close correspondence might indeed be a spurious one, caused by a high positive correlation between the bonus earnings ratio and the rate of corporate profit (or the share of corporate profits in national income), on the one hand, and a high positive correlation between the latter and the rate of personal savings on the other. However, this argument, while theoretically plausible, does not turn out to be relevant in our case. In the first place, the correlation coefficient between the share of (after-tax) corporate profits in national income and the rate of personal savings turns out to be –.57. In the second place, while the correlation coefficient between the share of the (after-tax) corporate profits before bonuses are paid out and the bonus earnings ratio is 0.47, indeed suggesting the presence of a profit-sharing element,[9] the correlation coefficient between the (after-tax) corporate profits (after bonuses are paid out) and the bonus earnings ratio is –.45. (For the source of these calculations, see Table 1.)

Table 1. Bonus, Corporate Profits, and Personal Savings

Year	(1) $B/(B+W)$	(2) $(P+B)/NY$	(3) P/NY	(4) S/DY
1958	.109	.114	.0602	.148
1959	.127	.123	.0600	.165
1960	.129	.153	.0916	.173
1961	.142	.155	.0876	.189
1962	.141	.146	.0758	.185
1963	.146	.140	.0658	.178
1964	.146	.145	.0707	.163
1965	.145	.130	.0544	.175
1966	.151	.145	.0655	.173
1967	.156	.159	.0794	.189
1968	.162	.174	.0922	.196
1969	.180	.182	.0918	.190
1970	.182	.190	.0969	.202
1971	.189	.183	.0817	.206
1972	.193	.175	.0722	.215
1973	.198	.154	.0453	.247
1974	.219	.124	–.0046	.252
1975	.194	.148	.0332	.249
1976	.196	.157	.0407	.241
1977	.186	.160	.0465	.229
1978	.185	.173	.0628	.230

SOURCE: Calculated from national income account series and our estimates for bonus income series. See also Table A2 in Data Appendix.

NOTES:
B = after-tax bonus income, W = after-tax regular wage income,
P = after-tax corporate profits, NY = national income,
S = personal savings, DY = disposable income.
Column (1): Bonus earnings ratio
Column (2): Share of after-tax corporate profits before bonus payment in national income
Column (3): Share of after-tax corporate profits after bonus payment in national income
Column (4): Average personal savings ratio

What then is the source of the close association between the rate of personal savings and the bonus earnings ratio? Could we say that the movement of the latter explains the former? Two familiar theoretical explanations immediately come to mind. One is based on the permanent-income hypothesis. This hypothesis holds that the propensity to consume permanent income is higher than that of transitory income. Then, a rise in the proportion of transitory income to total income will raise the rate of savings. An interpretation of bonus effects on savings can therefore be proposed; it is just this increase of transitory income that bonus earnings are creating. The second is the habit-persistence hypothesis. It holds that, in the short run, individuals' consumption patterns are geared to historically formed habits, and it takes time to adjust these habits to an increase in income. Furthermore, the more temporary the nature of income increases are, the more slowly (if ever) do they induce revision of consumption habits. Then, just as in the case of the permanent-income hypothesis, a rise in the proportion of temporary income will raise the rate of savings.[10]

In order for these two hypotheses to be applicable to our context, bonus incomes must fluctuate relatively more than regular components of income, so that there are good reasons for them to be regarded as either transitory or temporary in character. That this is in fact the case can be shown at two levels: one at the aggregate level and the other at an industry level. Table 2 gives the figures of growth rates for both the bonus and regular wage income (real, per capita) series, together with their means and standard deviations. The standard testing procedure suggests that the bonus income series exhibits significantly larger fluctuations than regular wage components. The result is much more pronounced when we look at the corresponding figures at an industry level. Table 3 provides the means and standard deviations of the growth rates of both income series by major industry and by size of establishments. Also presented are the F-test statistics with respect to the null hypothesis that both series have identical variances against the alternative that one has a larger variance than the other series. As we see from the table, except for the utility industry for which we observe an opposite tendency (though barely significant), there is a strong indication that bonus income series fluctuate much more wildly than the regularly paid counterparts even at a micro level.

What emerges from our following study, however, is neither the permanent-income hypothesis nor the habit-persistence hypothesis in its pure form. Our explanation is a modification of the latter, and we name it the habit–buffer-income hypothesis. It holds that, at least in the short run, habitual spending rules govern individuals' consumption

Table 2. Growth Rates of Aggregate Regular Wage and Bonus Incomes (Real and Per Capita)

Year	Regular wage	Bonus
1959	5.9 (%)	25.9 (%)
1960	11.5	14.5
1961	10.1	20.5
1962	10.6	12.1
1963	7.8	9.1
1964	8.8	12.2
1965	7.1	5.2
1966	8.6	12.4
1967	9.1	15.3
1968	8.4	12.6
1969	7.7	21.3
1970	10.5	15.1
1971	7.8	9.8
1972	7.9	10.7
1973	8.3	13.9
1974	2.3	15.8
1975	7.2	−7.9
1976	1.7	2.5
1977	4.8	−1.3
Mean	7.7 (%)	11.7 (%)
Std. Dev.	2.6	7.7

SOURCE: NIA and our own estimates of bonus income series.
NOTE: Growth rates for each year are calculated by comparing the figures of the current year with those of the previous year.
The figures of each year are for the fiscal year. For institutional reasons they reflect the sum of summer bonuses and winter bonuses of each year more accurately than figures of the calendar year.
Real and per-capita figures are obtained after an adjustment with respect to consumer price index (base = 1970) and number of the population.

behavior. More specifically, we shall pose the following to this working hypothesis.

(i) Households hold a convention stipulating that they save a certain proportion of their income, which may possibly differ for different income categories.
(ii) Households' consumption habits are a historical result of such conventional behavior.
(iii) Bonus incomes are regarded by households as a very different kind of income from other parts of their income. Namely, they are a sort of buffer income that allows them to dispense with it much more freely and discretionarily.
(iv) Under normal circumstances, where the conventional mode of behavior defined in (i) satisfies the level dictated by the consumption

Table 3. Fluctuations in the Growth Rates of Regular Wage and Bonus Earnings: By Industry and by Size of Establishment, 1959–79; Real and After-Tax, per Regularly Employed Worker

Period	Mining	Construction	Manufacturing	Wholesale & retail	Finance & insurance	Transp. & communic.	Utility	Service
(Establishment Size: 30 or more employees)								
Regular wage								
1959–79	4.70 (%)	5.18 (%)	4.86 (%)	4.70 (%)	4.13 (%)	4.43 (%)	4.26 (%)	
	(3.78)	(2.43)	(3.98)	(5.96)	(2.87)	(2.99)	(5.47)	
1959–74	5.15	5.83	5.36	5.51	4.06	5.14	4.13	
	(3.31)	(2.38)	(4.11)	(6.56)	(2.84)	(2.87)	(4.80)	
1975–79	3.27	3.18	3.28	2.10	4.37	2.18	4.69	4.45# (%)
	(5.19)	(1.34)	(3.41)	(2.24)	(3.29)	(2.36)	(4.69)	(4.17)
Bonus earnings								
1959–79	7.40	7.49	8.01	7.35	6.41	6.97	5.80	
	(11.13)	(7.56)	(9.08)	(8.32)	(4.20)	(6.95)	(4.86)	
1959–74	9.90	8.30	11.22	9.73	7.22	9.25	7.93	
	(11.09)	(8.40)	(6.65)	(7.86)	(4.37)	(5.51)	(3.13)	
1975–79	−0.61	4.91	−2.27	−0.27	3.80	−0.33	−0.99	3.97#
	(7.30)	(3.14)	(8.56)	(4.38)	(2.32)	(6.35)	(2.37)	(9.42)
Test statistic								
1959–79	+8.67**	+9.68**	+5.20**	+1.95	+2.14*	+5.40**	−1.27	
1959–74	+11.23**	+12.46**	+2.62*	+1.44	+2.37	+3.69**	−2.35	
1975–79	+1.98	+5.49	+6.30	+3.82	−2.01	+7.24*	−11.20**	+5.10*

Table 3 – continued

(Establishment Size: 5–29 employees)

Regular wage								
1959–79	6.52 (%)	5.78 (%)	6.05 (%)	5.56 (%)	5.29 (%)	4.91 (%)	4.52 (%)	
	(5.26)	(3.54)	(3.05)	(4.56)	(3.47)	(3.82)	(5.78)	
1959–74	7.40	6.87	7.10	6.67	5.78	5.08	4.29	
	(3.76)	(2.32)	(2.65)	(4.37)	(3.57)	(3.13)	(6.12)	
								5.41# (%)
1975–79	3.73	2.30	2.68	2.01	3.71	4.38	5.25	5.23
	(8.54)	(4.77)	(1.23)	(3.37)	(2.92)	(5.97)	(5.03)	
Bonus earnings								
1959–79	16.40	9.13	12.12	9.39	7.79	6.76	5.48	
	(25.82)	(9.26)	(11.22)	(11.62)	(7.47)	(8.18)	(5.27)	
1959–74	20.90	12.36	15.72	12.43	9.44	9.06	7.07	
	(25.80)	(7.57)	(10.15)	(10.92)	(7.74)	(7.44)	(6.24)	
								4.69#
1975–79	20.01	−1.18	0.59	−0.31	2.53	−0.58	3.91	(9.79)
	(22.26)	(6.26)	(4.99)	(8.55)	(2.97)	(6.18)	(2.87)	
Test statistic								
1959–79	+24.10**	+6.84**	+13.53**	+6.49**	+4.63**	+4.59**	+1.18	
1959–74	+47.08**	+10.65**	+14.67**	+6.24**	+4.70**	+5.65**	+1.04	
								+3.50
1975–79	+6.79*	+1.72	+16.46**	+6.44*	+1.03	+1.07	−3.07	

SOURCE: *Maigetsu Kinrō Tōkei* (Monthly Labor Statistics) and other sources.
NOTE: "Year" refers to the fiscal year for the same reason as stated in Table 1. For the service industry, the figures refer to the period 1972–79. *Test* statistic refers to the ratio of variance between the two series. Test of $\mathrm{var}(g(B)) = \mathrm{var}(g(W))$ against $\mathrm{var}(g(B)) > \mathrm{var}(g(W))$ is indicated by the symbol (+) in front of the number, whereas that against $\mathrm{var}(g(W)) < \mathrm{var}(g(B))$ is indicated by the symbol (−) in front. Rejection of the null hypothesis at a significance level of 5% is indicated by (*) and that at a significance level of 1% is indicated by (**). Standard deviations are in parentheses. (#: 1972–79).

habit, which in turn, is defined by (ii), bonus earnings are regarded as a convenient source of savings, and thus savings flow out at a higher rate than other parts of income.

That households conceive bonus income to be a convenient source of savings and households follow a convention of assigning a fixed rate of savings on bonus income have been argued by Shinohara (1981), which he termed the lump-sum–income hypothesis, albeit on quite an intuitive basis. Our hypothesis can, in fact, be regarded as a further elaboration of his hypothesis, with ours having the qualifications (ii), (iii), and (iv). While in normal years of stable income growth the two hypotheses differ little, they become quite different (and, we argue, Shinohara's becoming unsuccessful) when the economy faces a major downward shock. This point becomes quite relevant when we try to interpret the experience of the major downturn period of 1974–76 (See the next section.).

The similarity and dissimilarity between our hypothesis and the original Duesenberry-Modigliani-Brown habit-persistence hypothesis can now be stated as follows. The similarity, of course, lies in that we accept already formed consumption habits to persist over time, or put differently, we accept past consumption to have a lasting influence on present consumption. While accumulated savings would facilitate a source of buffer in the habit-persistence world, we are, in effect, adding the current bonus income as an additional source of buffer to the list. On the other hand, we differ from the pure habit-persistence world in not regarding savings as a totally passive residual, but rather allowing households to have some degree of "telescopic faculty" (albeit not in such sophisticated form as in the permanent-income hypothesis) and allow this to participate in the formation of habit itself.

On the other hand, the crucial distinction between the permanent-income hypothesis and our hypothesis (and the habit-persistence hypothesis) lies in the former's emphasis on the households' forecasting capacity and optimal intertemporal choice behavior. One of our purposes in this paper is to test the validity of such a presumption directly.

3. Cross-Section Estimates of the Effects of Bonus

One obvious way of evaluating the effect of bonus payments on household savings is through the use of cross-section data. Detailed statistical data on composition of income and consumption expenditure of worker households are available in Japan every year since 1963 (for a population sample covering the whole nation) in the form of the

Family Income and Expenditure Survey (FIES). Of particular interest for our purposes are the data on households that are simultaneously classified by levels of different income categories. Two such classification tables are compiled in the FIES Annual Reports, one by level of annual household income, and another, by level of household head's regular wage income. Availability of the former table dates back to 1963, while that of the latter only dates back to 1969. In this section, we will try to extract as much information as possible from time series (over the period of 1969–80) of these two bodies of data.[11]

The major limitations of our data are that they are only one-way classification tables, and no cross-classification or joint frequency tables (not to mention individual household data) are available. It is well known that simple cross-section regressions relying solely on data from one-way tables are bound to give misleading estimates (Haitovsky, 1973; Maddala, 1977: 268–74). In order to overcome this limitation we must devise some method to extract information on the joint distribution of two types of income. The basis of the method we propose to employ is the well-known empirical fact that income distribution, when roughly the top and the bottom 10 percent are taken out, follows closely the lognormal distribution (Aitchison and Brown, 1957; Lydall, 1968). This empirical law also holds for our two series of data.

For illustrative purposes we have depicted in Figure 2 the plots of cumulative income distribution on a lognormal probability paper for three representative years (1970, 1975, and 1980). The plots are done for both household head's regular wage income (expressed by ▲) and for total household income (expressed by ○). The total household income of each year follows the lognormal law quite closely, even toward the very bottom of the distribution. On the other hand, the household head's regular wage income follows the lognormal law in the range above the bottom 6–8 percentile of the distribution. We notice that there is a mass of households with none or very little household head regular wage income. In any case, this finding suggests that we may regard the distribution of these two types of income as approximately bivariate lognormal.

MODEL

In view of the nature of the income data discussed above, we shall now suppose that the household's regular income (W) and the household's total income (Y) of each year can be approximated by a bivariate lognormal distribution such that:

$$(\log W, \log Y) \sim N(\mu, \Sigma) \tag{1}$$

where

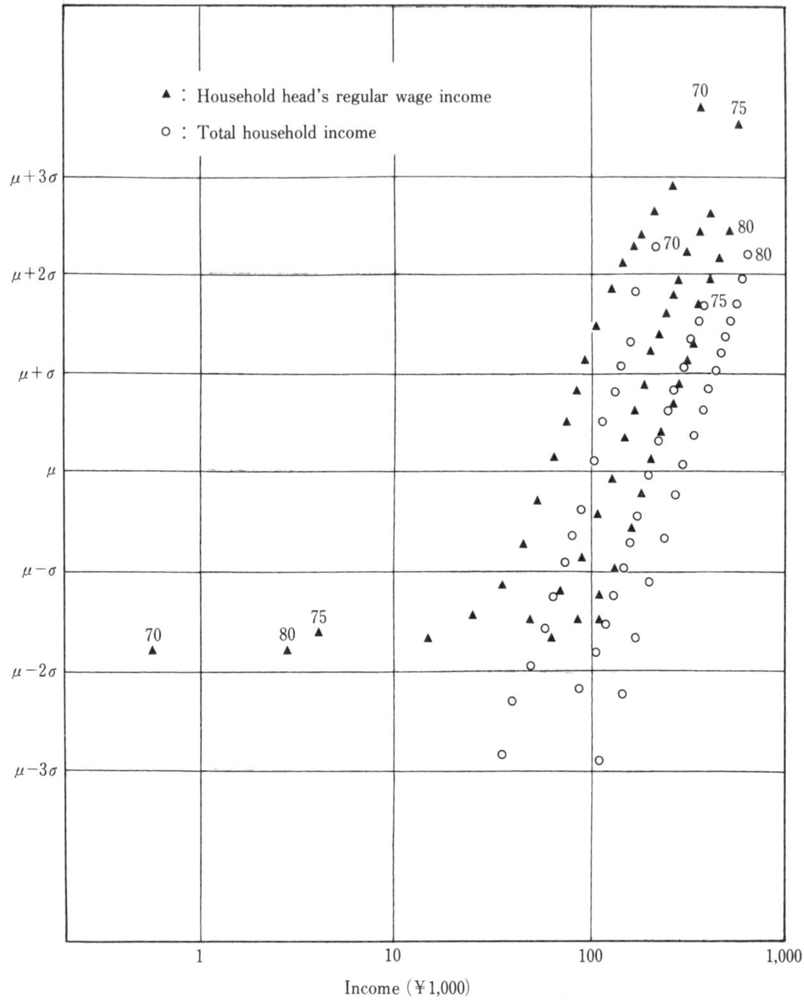

Figure 2

$$\mu = (\mu_w, \mu_y), \quad \Sigma = \begin{pmatrix} \sigma_{ww} & \sigma_{wy} \\ \sigma_{wy} & \sigma_{yy} \end{pmatrix}.^{12}$$

Then by a well-known theorem on the normal distribution, the conditional distribution of log Y (hereinafter expressed by a lower-case letter y) given log W (hereinafter expressed by w) is normal with

$$y|w \sim N\left(\mu_y + \frac{\sigma_{wy}}{\sigma_{ww}}(w - \mu_w), \sigma_{ww} - \frac{\sigma_{wy}^2}{\sigma_{yy}}\right), \tag{2}$$

while that of w given y is

$$w\,|\,y \sim N\left(\mu_w + \frac{\sigma_{wy}}{\sigma_{yy}}(y - \mu_y), \sigma_{yy} - \frac{\sigma_{wy}^2}{\sigma_{ww}}\right). \tag{3}$$

We observe that the expressions for the conditional means $E(y\,|\,w)$ and $E(w|y)$ in (2) and (3), correspond exactly to the manner in which our one-way classification data are presented. Thus, the parameters of the lognormal distribution (1) are readily estimable (up to a multiplicative constant); we discuss the method shortly.

We next assume that the consumption of a household unit is a function, common to all households, of household regular income (W) and the bonus income, to be denoted by $B = Y - W$. More specifically, we assume the following log-linear function

$$c = \alpha w + \beta x + \gamma, \tag{4}$$

where $c = \log C$, $x = \log\{1 + (B/W)\}$, and $\gamma = \log \bar{C}$.[13] Equivalently, it can be expressed by

$$c = \bar{C}W^{\alpha}\{1 + (B/W)\}^{\beta} = \bar{C}W^{\alpha-\beta}Y^{\beta}. \tag{4'}$$

The meaning of this functional form can be summarized as follows: (i) the elasticity of consumption with respect to income with the proportion of bonus income remaining constant is α; (ii) the (partial) elasticity of consumption with respect to income, $\eta_B\left(\equiv \dfrac{B}{C}\dfrac{\partial C}{\partial B}\right)$ is (after simple algebra) $\beta \cdot (B/Y)$ whereas that with respect regular income, $\eta_W\left(\equiv \dfrac{W}{C}\dfrac{\partial C}{\partial W}\right)$ is $\alpha - \beta(B/Y)$; (iii) The average propensity to consume expressed by $C/Y = \bar{C}W^{\alpha-1}\{1 + (B/Y)\}^{\beta-1}$ declines with the rise in the bonus income ratio (B/W) (Y being held constant) if $\alpha > \beta$. Thus the magnitude of β is of central importance in the evaluation of the putative bonus effect on savings.

By noting the identity $x = y - w$, we can transform equation (4) into

$$c = (\alpha - \beta)w + \beta y + \gamma. \tag{5}$$

However, since (w, y) is bivariately normally distributed, c $(= \log C)$ also becomes normally distributed, and the conditional distributions of c given w and c given y can also be deduced from the conditional distribution of y given w and w given y, respectively. In consequence, we have the following expressions for the conditional mean of consumption:

$$E(c|w) = \left(\alpha - \beta + \beta \cdot \frac{\sigma_{wy}}{\sigma_{ww}}\right) w + \beta\left(\mu_y - \frac{\sigma_{wy}}{\sigma_{ww}}\mu_w\right) + \gamma \tag{6}$$

$$E(c|y) = \left(\beta + (\alpha - \beta) \cdot \frac{\sigma_{wy}}{\sigma_{yy}}\right) y + (\alpha - \beta)\left(\mu_w - \frac{\sigma_{wy}}{\sigma_{yy}}\right) + \gamma. \tag{7}$$

With this form we are now able to confront the data available and estimate the parameters of the consumption function. An important feature of our model is that yearly fluctuations of the distribution of (W, Y) are corrected in the estimation process by substituting the estimated values of the distribution parameters (done for each year) into equations (4) and (5) as yearly shifting factors.

DATA AND METHOD OF ESTIMATION

The above discussion reduces to the following four estimating equations.

$$y_1^{it} = \frac{\sigma_{wy}^t}{\sigma_{ww}^t} w_1^{it} + \left(\mu_y^t - \frac{\sigma_{wy}^t}{\sigma_{ww}^t}\mu_w^t\right) + u_1^{it} \tag{8}$$

$$w_2^{jt} = \frac{\sigma_{wy}^r}{\sigma_{yy}^t} y_2^{jt} + \left(\mu_w^t - \frac{\sigma_{wy}^t}{\sigma_{yy}^t}\mu_y^t\right) + u_2^{jt} \tag{9}$$

$$c_1^{jt} = \alpha^t z_{11}^{it} + \beta^t z_{12}^{it} + \gamma^t + v_1^{it} \tag{10}$$

$$c_2^{jt} = \alpha^t z_{21}^{jt} + \beta^t z_{22}^{jt} + \gamma^t + v_2^{jt} \tag{11}$$

where

$$z_{11}^{it} = w_1^{it},$$

$$z_{12}^{it} = \left(\mu_y^t - \frac{\sigma_{wy}^t}{\sigma_{ww}^t}\mu_w^t\right) + \left(\frac{\sigma_{wy}^t}{\sigma_{ww}^t} - 1\right) w_1^{it}$$

and

$$z_{21}^{it} = \frac{\sigma_{wy}^t}{\sigma_{yy}^t} y_2^{it} + \left(\mu_w^t - \frac{\sigma_{wy}^t}{\sigma_{ww}^t}\mu_y^t\right)$$

$$z_{22}^{jt} = y_2^{jt} - z_{21}^{jt}$$

$$(i = 1, 2, \ldots, i_t),\ (j = 1, 2, \ldots, j_t),\ t = 1969, \ldots, 1980.$$

All variables that appear in the above equations are in natural logarithms. The variables with subscript 1 and superscript i refer to observations provided by the table classified by W, while those with subscript 2 and superscript j refer to observations provided by the table classified by Y. The coefficients α, β, and γ of the consumption function carry a superscript t in order to allow for a possibility that household behavior might change from year to year. In view of the above discussion we have discarded certain observations that correspond to the bottom 6–8 percentile group in regular income and the very top 1 percentile group in both income categories. The chosen numbers of observations i_t and j_t for each year range from 12 to 15, and the total sum of i_t's and j_t's over the 1969–80 period is 339.[14] The final term in each equation is a random disturbance term that is assumed to be independently and identically distributed over different classification ranges (i, j) and time periods (t). In addition, we assume that the distribution of v_1^{it} and v_2^{jt} are identical.[15]

The procedure of estimation is as follows. First, we estimate the coefficients of equations (8) and (9), i.e., $(\sigma_{wv}^t/\sigma_{ww}^t)$, $(\sigma_{wy}^t/\sigma_{yy}^t)$, $(\mu_y - (\sigma_{wy}^t/\sigma_{ww}^t)\mu_w^t)$, and $(\mu_w^t - (\sigma_{wy}^t/\sigma_{yy}^t)\mu_y^t)$ for each year ($t = 1969, \ldots, 1980$) by applying the ordinary least squares method to each equation. Second, we substitute the yearly point estimates of these coefficients into equations (10) and (11) (thus correcting for yearly changes in income distribution), and then obtain estimates for the coefficients α, β, and γ of these equations. Since equations (10) and (11) have exactly the same form (i.e., linear in parameters α, β, and γ), and since, by assumption, disturbance terms v_1^{it} and v_2^{it} have identical forms of distribution, we can pool the two equations together, and estimate α, β, γ's by using ordinary least squares with the number of observations being $i_t + j_t$. All income variables used in the estimation process are real (deflated by consumer price index $1975 = 1.00$) and adjusted for taxes and social security contributions.[16,17]

ESTIMATION RESULTS

The results of estimating the parameters of the consumption function are given by Table 4 and 5.[18] Each table gives the estimates based on regressions carried out separately for each year. The difference between the two tables lies in that Table 4 refers to the case where the dependent variable, consumption, includes all durables, while Table 5 refers to the case where the dependent variable is nondurables consumption.

The features of the yearly estimates of the coefficients can be summarized as follows. First, the estimates of coefficient α are relatively stable over the years, all of them lying in between .77 and .89 in the case of consumption including durables and between .74 and .85 in the case of nondurables.

Second, quite in contrast, the estimates of coefficient β are rather volatile over the years. While the normal range of β (for both consumption categories) seems to be .5–.6, there are distinctive subsets of years for which the actual estimates deviated substantially from the

Table 4. Estimated Parameters of the Consumption Function, by Year, Consumption Expenditure Including Durables

Year	$\hat{\gamma} = \log \bar{C}$	$\hat{\alpha}$	$\hat{\beta}$	$(\alpha \hat{-} \beta)$	s.e./mean	SSR	# of observ.
1969	1.632	.853	.536	.317	.0635	.105	29
	(.293)	(.025)	(.211)	(.217)	11.93		
1970	1.958	.824	.554	.270*	.0411	.044	29
	(.190)	(.016)	(.097)	(.102)	11.90		
1971	2.060	.812	.778	.034	.0290	.020	27
	(.150)	(.013)	(.105)	(.108)	11.91		
1972	2.523	.775	.638	.138	.0407	.038	26
	(.236)	(.021)	(.136)	(.145)	11.91		
1973	1.946	.829	.471	.358*	.0357	.029	26
	(.223)	(.019)	(.129)	(.137)	12.04		
1974	1.361	.853	1.420	−.567	.0776	.138	26
	(.571)	(.051)	(.291)	(.325)	11.91		
1975	.770	.891	1.931	−1.040**	.0821	.182	30
	(.462)	(.041)	(.264)	(.286)	11.98		
1976	2.315	.778	1.375	−.597**	.0429	.050	30
	(.257)	(.023)	(.148)	(.174)	12.03		
1977	2.553	.775	.597	.178	.0418	.046	29
	(.286)	(.025)	(.147)	(.162)	12.02		
1978	2.556	.773	.610	.163	.0275	.019	28
	(.219)	(.020)	(.118)	(.132)	12.01		
1979	1.496	.871	.193	.678**	.0366	.036	30
	(.305)	(.027)	(.165)	(.186)	12.03		
1980	1.942	.829	.481	.348*	.0328	.028	29
	(.239)	(.021)	(.136)	(.146)	12.16		

NOTE: Standard errors in parentheses. * indicates significance at 5% level, whereas ** indicates significance at 1% level (in column 5).

seeming norm. The years 1974–76 are one such subset of years, while 1979 is another. Curiously enough, these two sets of years correspond to the years corresponding to the period of (and the period immediately ensuing) the so-called first and second oil crises. The direction of deviation in these two periods is, however, just the opposite. While the estimate of β for 1979 is quite low, the corresponding estimates go sky high during the 1974–76 period.

Third, except for years 1974–76, the estimate of α is greater than that of β, indicating the existence of an independent effect of bonus payments on savings, as expected. However, as the last column of Tables 4 and 5 show, the standard error of the estimate of the differential $(\alpha - \beta)$ is also high, and only in four cases out of nine (for which we find positive difference) do we find $(\alpha - \beta)$ to be significantly different from 0.

Similarity of estimated coefficients over the period excluding 1974–76 suggests a possibility of pooling observations across years. In fact, using the F-test on linear restrictions among parameters (taking the

Table 5. Estimated Parameters of the Consumption Function, by Year, Consumption Expenditure Excluding Durables

Year	$\hat{\gamma} = \log C$	$\hat{\alpha}$	$\hat{\beta}$	$(\alpha \hat{-} \beta)$	s.e./mean	SSR	# of observ.
1969	1.759	.834	.540	.294	.0507	.067	29
	(.234)	(.020)	(.169)	(.174)	11.84		
1970	2.073	.808	.492	.316**	.0449	.053	29
	(.208)	(.018)	(.106)	(.111)	11.81		
1971	2.150	.798	.712	.086	.0355	.030	27
	(.183)	(.016)	(.129)	(.133)	11.81		
1972	2.514	.768	.675	.093	.0422	.041	26
	(.245)	(.022)	(.141)	(.151)	11.82		
1973	1.753	.838	.447	.391*	.0428	.042	26
	(.267)	(.023)	(.155)	(.164)	11.95		
1974	1.790	.813	1.292	−.479	.0690	.110	26
	(.508)	(.046)	(.259)	(.289)	11.83		
1975	1.258	.846	1.867	−1.021**	.0760	.156	30
	(.428)	(.038)	(.245)	(.265)	11.90		
1976	2.544	.754	1.284	−.530**	.0480	.062	30
	(.288)	(.025)	(.166)	(.180)	11.95		
1977	2.883	.740	.620	.120	.0442	.051	29
	(.302)	(.027)	(.155)	(.171)	11.94		
1978	2.774	.750	.584	.166	.0415	.043	28
	(.331)	(.030)	(.117)	(.200)	11.93		
1979	1.680	.848	.237	.611**	.0399	.043	30
	(.333)	(.030)	(.180)	(.203)	11.95		
1980	1.926	.825	.466	.359	.0468	.057	29
	(.342)	(.029)	(.194)	(.208)	12.08		

NOTE: Standard errors in parentheses. * indicates significance at 5% level, whereas ** indicates significance at 1% level (in Column 5).

critical significance level to be 5 percent), we have come to the following conclusion:

(i) In the case of expenditures including durables, all non-1974–76 years can be pooled together; 1974–76 are distinctly different years from the rest and cannot be pooled among themselves.

(ii) In the case of nondurables expenditures, pooling of all non-1974–76 years is rejected; however, pooling of observations for 1969–73 and 1977–78, on the one hand, and pooling of those for 1979–80, on the other, are justified. Again, 1974–76 proved to be distinctly different from the rest and cannot be pooled even among themselves.[19]

Statement (ii) confirms our casual grouping of estimation results into three subsets (except that 1980 is also to be considered in the same subset as the year 1979). We designate the first as normal years; the second, post–first oil shock recession years (1974–76); and the third, post–second oil shock years (1979–80). However, according to statement (i), the distinctiveness of the post–second oil shock years does not present itself clearly in the case of consumption including durables. In any case, the results of estimation under an alternative way of pooling are presented in Table 6, together with the F-statistics. And, in view of the maxim not to pool observations too easily, we shall in the following discuss our results on the basis of pooling in a manner suggested in statement (ii) (namely, to pool the seven years 1969–73, 1977–78, and the two years 1979–80 separately), which passes the test for both categories of consumption used in the regression. We shall continue to designate the same seven years as normal years.

The major findings from Table 6 are as follows. First, for the period of normal years and for the post–second oil shock years (1979–80), β is estimated to be significantly less than α. This is the singlemost important evidence that households treat bonus income differently from other parts of income and that the bonus payment system exerts a positive effect on the savings of the worker households.

Second, the quantitative magnitude of this effect can perhaps more easily be ascertained by transforming these estimates into estimates of elasticities and marginal propensities to consume out of bonus and nonbonus incomes. This task is done in Table 7. For normal years, the figures in the table are calculated in the following manner. Since we know that the average bonus income ratio (i.e., after-tax bonus/disposable income ratio averaged over the sample) is 23.5 percent while the average propensity to consume disposable income (again over the sample) is 79.0 percent, the point estimate of the partial elasticity of consumption with respect to bonus income is $\hat{\eta}_B = (.519)(.235) = (.130)$, while the marginal propensity to consume bonus income (evaluated at the sample mean) is $\text{MPC}_B = (C/B)\hat{\eta}_B \equiv \{(C/Y)/(B/Y)\}\hat{\eta}_B = .437$. The corresponding figures for nonbonus income, i.e., $W + T + R$, are $\hat{\eta}_W = .821 - .130 = .685$, and MPC_W (evaluated at the sample mean) $= \{C/(W + T + R)\}\hat{\eta}_W = (.790/.765)(.685) = .707$. Furthermore, the elasticity of consumption with respect to household disposable income when the bonus income ratio remains constant, denoted by $\eta_Y|_{\overline{(B/W)}}$, is .821. This implies the marginal propensity to consume (at the sample mean), MPC_Y, of $(.790)(.823) = .644$. Similar calculations are performed for other parts of the table. They show that during the normal years there is about 27 percent difference in terms of marginal propensity to consume (or 28 percent difference in the case of nondurables, both evaluated at the sample mean) between bonus and nonbonus incomes.

Third, for normal years the difference in consumption categories affects the estimate of β more than that of α. It suggests that expenditure on durables responds to bonus income much more than other parts of income, which confirms our intuition.

Table 6. Estimated Parameters of the Consumption Function, Pooled Regressions

Period	Depend. Var.	$\hat{\gamma} = \log \bar{C}$	$\hat{\alpha}$	$\hat{\beta}$	$(\alpha \hat{-} \beta)$	s.e./mean	SSR	# of observ.	F-Statistic
1969–73	C	2.017	.821	.519	.302**	.0412	.423	253	$F^{24}_{226} = 1.50$
		(.077)	(.007)	(.045)	(.048)	11.99			
&									
1977–80	NDC	2.048	.812	.479	.333**	.0461	.530	253	$F^{24}_{226} = 2.27^{**}$
		(.086)	(.008)	(.050)	(.054)	11.90			
1969–73	C	2.082	.815	.552	.263**	.0422	.340	194	$F^{18}_{173} = 1.25$
		(.086)	(.008)	(.050)	(.053)	11.96			
&									
1977–78	NDC	2.146	.803	.511	.292**	.0449	.386	194	$F^{18}_{173} = 1.73$
		(.092)	(.008)	(.054)	(.057)	11.87			
	C	1.773	.845	.365	.408**	.0345	.067	59	$F^{3}_{53} = 0.77$
		(.185)	(.016)	(.102)	(.113)	12.09			
1979–80									
	NDC	1.819	.835	.376	.459**	.0431	.104	59	$F^{3}_{53} = 0.68$
		(.230)	(.020)	(.128)	(.141)	12.02			
	C	1.412	.847	1.558	−.771**	.0759	.479	86	$F^{6}_{77} = 3.78^{**}$
		(.265)	(.023)	(.147)	(.160)	11.98			
1974–76									
	NDC	1.767	.813	1.447	−.634**	.0724	.435	86	$F^{6}_{77} = 4.19^{**}$
		(.253)	(.022)	(.140)	(.152)	11.90			

NOTE: Standard errors in parentheses. In column 2, C designates expenditure including durables while NDC designates nondurables expenditure. In columns 6 and 10, * indicates statistical significance at 5% level, while ** indicates statistical significance at 1% level. In column 10, statistical significance implies rejection of pooling observations.

Table 7. Estimated Elasticities and Marginal Propensities to Consume out of Different Components of Income

Period	Bonus/ income	Depend. var.	Cons./ income	η_W	η_B	MPC_W	MPC_B	$MPC_Y\|_{\overline{B\|W}}$
1969–73 & 1977–78	.235	C	.790	.685	.130	.707	.437	.644
		NDC	.734	.683	.120	.655	.375	.589
1974	.237	C	.745	.514	.339	.502	1.066	.636
		NDC	.697	.507	.306	.463	.960	.567
1975	.220	C	.749	.466	.425	.448	1.447	.667
		NDC	.706	.435	.411	.394	1.319	.597
1976	.228	C	.776	.464	.314	.466	1.069	.604
		NDC	.730	.461	.293	.436	.938	.550
1979–80	.221	C	.781	.764	.081	.766	.286	.660
		NDC	.739	.752	.083	.713	.278	.617

NOTE: This table is constructed by using the point estimates of parameters in Tables 4–6, and using the mean characteristics of our samples for respective periods. "Income" referred to in columns 2 and 4 of the table is the household disposable income. As in previous tables, C designates expenditures including durables and NDC designates nondurables expenditures.

The question yet remaining is what happend in the "deviant" years, especially 1974–76. These are the first years of serious and long-lasting depression that this country experienced since the start of the rapid growth era. Simultaneously, these years mark an important turning point in the long-run behavior of Japanese personal savings. While the households' average savings rate reached its peak in 1974 and maintained its high level during 1975–76, the trend clearly began to decline. (See Figure 1. This feature is also true of FIES data on worker households.) What we observe from Tables 4–7 is, however, a wide deviation of micro from macro behavior, or else, a wide deviation of the marginal from the average behavior. The marginal propensity to consume bonus income (evaluated at the sample mean) is roughly two to three times that of the normal years.[20] It implies, ceteris paribus, that households with relatively high bonus income spent a lot, while those with relatively low bonus income saved a lot. And, as Figure 3 shows, since households with high bonus income are relatively more concentrated in the high disposable income class and vice versa, this tended to lower the savings rate of the upper disposable income class, while raising that of the lower income class.

At any rate, this extremely high β coefficient or extremely high marginal propensity to consume bonus income seems to be the culprit

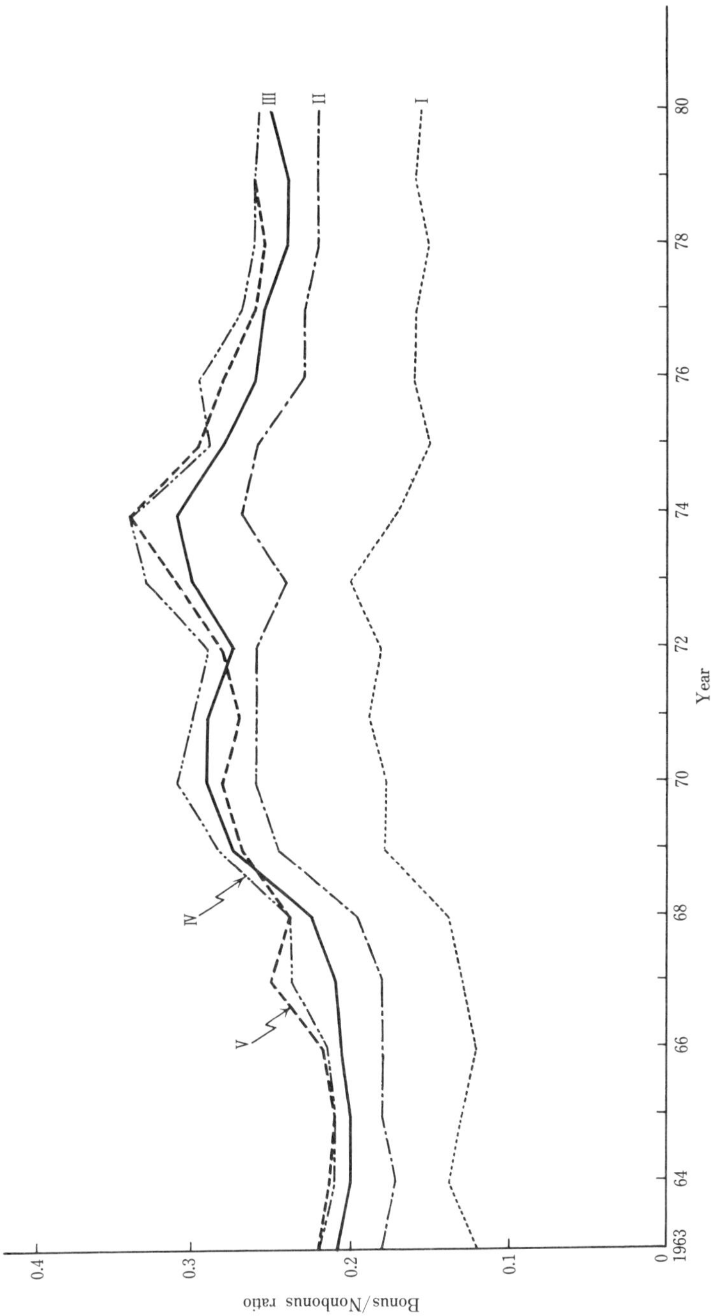

Figure 3. Bonus/nonbonus ratio of annual total income quintile groups

in the now familiar paradox among Japanese economists that, during 1974 and 1975 (though more pronounced in 1975), the average rate of savings declined as the annual income (Y) quintile rose, while the savings rate (in proportion to disposable income) rose with the quintiles of the household heads' regular wage income (W).[21] In fact, using the estimates for the coefficients of equations (8) through (11), we can reconstruct the emergence of the paradox. First, we note that the relationship between consumption and disposable income as seen from the table classified by Y is nothing but our equation (11), or its more formal equivalent (7). On the other hand, the same relationship as seen from the table classified by W can easily be derived by combining (8) and (10) (or, equivalently, [6] and the expression for $E(y|w)$ in [3]).

Together, we have:

$$E(c|y) = \{\beta + (\alpha - \beta)S_2\} \cdot y + \{(\alpha - \beta)C_2 + \gamma\} \tag{12}$$

$$E(c|w) = \{\beta + (\alpha - \beta)/S_2\} \cdot E(y|w) + \{\gamma - (\alpha - \beta)C_1/S_1\} \tag{13}$$

where

$$S_1 = (\sigma_{wy}/\sigma_{ww}), \quad S_2 = (\sigma_{wy}/\sigma_{yy}),$$

$$C_1 = \mu_y - \frac{\sigma_{wy}}{\sigma_{ww}}\mu_w, \quad C_2 = \mu_w - \frac{\sigma_{wy}}{\sigma_{yy}}\mu_y.$$

The fitted equations for each year of the 1974–76 period (using our yearly estimates of parameters $(S_1\ S_2, C_1, C_2, \alpha, \beta, \gamma))$ are given in Table 8. In this table, the estimated slope coefficient being greater than 1 implies that the average savings rate declines as income rises. It is then clear that our model exactly reproduces the features of the savings

Table 8. Reconstruction of the Savings Paradox

Year	Table referred	Expenditures including durables	Expenditure excluding durables
1974	Classified by Y	$c = 1.019\ y - .414$	$c = .953\ y - .207$
	Classified by W	$c = .683\ y + 3.715$	$c = .669\ y + 3.281$
1975	Classified by Y	$c = 1.150\ y - 1.969$	$c = 1.100\ y - 1.431$
	Classified by W	$c = .631\ y + 4.419$	$c = .591\ y + 4.840$
1976	Classified by Y	$c = .919\ y + .827$	$c = .879\ y + 1.223$
	Classified by W	$c = .632\ y + 4.366$	$c = .624\ y + 4.365$

SOURCE: Estimated parameters for equations (8)–(11).

NOTE: The variables in the equations are in natural logarithms. (c, y) in upper equations of each entry refers to $E(c|y)$ and y, while (c, y) in lower equations of each entry refers to $E(c|w)$ and $E(y|w)$. (Cf. equations (12) and (13) in the text.)

paradox discussed above: This feature is more prononunced in 1975 and disappears in 1976. We also note that equations using nondurables expenditures show no paradox for 1974, but do so in 1975.[22,23]

We propose to interpret these abnormal phenomena as the working of the "ratchet" effect, or the historically formed consumption habit asserting itself as in the habit-persistence hypothesis, plus the households' perception of bonus income as buffer income which admits of discretionary allocation. More specifically, in terms of our habit–buffer-income hypothesis, they are construed as a temporary deviation from the households' conventional spending behavior in the face of a severe downward shock (i.e., a rapid decline in the growth of real income and that use of bonus income as buffer income maintains the level of expenditure dictated by consumption habit. (The reader is referred back to the conceptual discussion at the end of Section 2.) But because of the very fact that spending of bonus income was largely a protective measure and that the low savings rate of the upper income class (with ample source of buffer income) was offset (and presumably more than offset) by the high savings rate of the lower income class, the aggregate savings rate did not have to drop sharply; in fact, it achieved one of the highest levels in history. One immediate consequence of this is that we cannot interpret the close aggregate relationship between the bonus/income ratio and the personal savings rate observed in Figure 1 as a simple and direct causal relationship. Although the hump in the bonus income ratio around 1974–76 corresponded very well with the hump in the personal savings rate of the same period, what went on inside the micro world of the household was precisely the opposite.

Now we are left with an interpretation of the low estimates for the years 1979–80. We propose to interpret this as a rather normal response to the exogenous shock of the second oil crisis. Where this shock differed from the first oil shock is that, by this time, the economy had already adjusted, and households had already adapted their consumption habits, to a slow rate of growth, if not a prolonged stagnation. Thus the second oil shock did not have to trigger the buffer mechanism similar to that of the 1974–76 period to protect the already-formed consumption habits. Rather, it acted to depress household expectations about the future, and thus to restrain their consumption. The households following our habit–buffer-income hypothesis would naturally choose to save a large proportion of their bonus income.

It now seems to be pertinent to comment on the works of earlier writers. Mizoguchi argued (based on a study of 1951–60) that household consumption is very much geared to the household head's regular wage income (with a remarkably stable ratio of 1.2 to 1.30), and that an increase in bonus payments does not systematically increase consumption, but rather increases savings. Although this proportionality relationship largely continued to hold throughout the 1960s, the years since 1969 have witnessed a steady decline in this ratio. Hence, it is fair to say that the thrust of Mizoguchi's argument has now lost its power. We do, however, share the basic spirit with Mizoguchi's argument (though implicit) in that bonus income is regarded by households as a different source of income that allows them to decide allocation between consumption and savings discretionarily.

Shinohara's lump-sum–income hypothesis, on the other hand, is in accord with our hypothesis for most of our period of study. But Shinohara's view clearly fails to explain the experience of 1974–76. This is the kind of pitfall one sometimes falls into if one looks only at the correlation of aggregate data series.

Incidentally, this pitfall can further be exploited to argue against the rationality of worker households. By concentrating on the observations of the 1970s, some Japanese economists have found a negative association between corporate retained earnings and the personal savings at an aggregate level. Then they rather complacently accepted this to be evidence in favor of the "substitution" or the "ultra-rationality" hypothesis; that is, households substitute corporate savings for their own savings.[24] The negative correlation observed for the decade of the 1970s, however, is very much a consequence of the striking contrast between relatively high personal savings (discussed just above), on the one hand, and the very low corporate profits, on the other, during the period 1974–76. Our present study clearly invalidates these economists' interpretations. In fact, since we know from the Family Savings Survey that the corporate share holding is concentrated in the upper income groups (e.g., in 1980, the top quintile group among worker households held 39.9 percent of all corporate stock held by the household sector, including self-employed households), and that these groups contain, with higher density, those households that received large bonus incomes and spent much on consumption during the 1974–76 period, what we actually have at the micro level is a positive, and not a negative, correlation between the corporate savings and personal savings. This is exactly opposite to what we see at the macro level.

4. Evidence from Survey Data: A Test of the Permanent-Income Hypothesis Interpretation of the Bonus Effect on Savings

So far, we have pointed out that the system of bonus payments seems to exert strong positive effects on personal savings. However, we have not made clear the mechanism by which an increase in bonus income increases savings. In this section, we attempt to shed some light on this point. More specifically, we would like to examine the plausibility of the interpretation of a permanent-income–life-cycle theory of the bonus effect on savings. This theory holds that a transitory increase in income is disbursed over a long period of time and thus it increases consumption by a smaller amount than a permanent increase in income. Hence, if bonus payments are regarded as a more transitory source of income than others, an increase in the share of bonuses in total income leads to an increase in the personal savings rate.

In order to test such a hypothesis, we need to know the manner in which consumers decompose income changes into permanent and transitory components. Usually, we make assumptions about the process whereby consumers generate expectations of future income, and then test the permanent-income hypothesis (hereinafter abbreviated as PIH) jointly with these assumptions. Recently, we have witnessed an increase in attempts to test the PIH jointly with the hypothesis of rational expectations.[25] Some have largely accepted the joint hypothesis, while others have rejected it. One difficulty with such an approach is that a rejection of the joint hypothesis does not by itself make clear which one of the two hypotheses is responsible.

In this section, we attempt to overcome this difficulty, at least partially, by using survey data on expectations of future income. We still have to assume something about the expectation formation process of consumers. In that sense, results of our analysis depends on the plausibility of such assumptions. However, the assumptions we shall be making are much less stringent than the ones used in previous works.[26] Thus, loosely speaking, we can test the PIH almost independently of assumptions about expectations. In addition, comparison of income expectations with actual incomes enables us to test the hypothesis about income expectations.

Our major findings are:

(i) Expectations on bonuses do not satisfy restrictions imposed by the rational expectation assumption.

(ii) The PIH is rejected; the propensities to consume out of permanent and transitory bonus incomes are approximately the same.

(iii) Nonetheless, the propensity to consume out of bonus income is very low—about 46 percent (irrespective of whether a bonus income is permanent or transitory).

The first two findings cast serious doubt about the view of the permanent-income–life-cycle theory that individuals are rational agents, maximizing intertemporal utility functions with expectations of future income reflecting all available information in an optimal manner. According to the first finding, individuals do not use all available information in forming expectations of future bonus payments. The second finding indicates that the distinction between permanent and transitory incomes is not a useful guide in determining current consumption, thus leading to a rejection of the framework in which individuals are forward-looking rational agents.

The third finding shows clearly that the system of bonus payments exerts significant effects on household savings. However, the explanation of the effects must be sought outside the realm of the permanent-income–life-cycle hypothesis. One possible interpretation of these results is the existence of a conventional spending rule whereby consumers assign a smaller propensity to consume to bonuses than other incomes.

SPECIFICATION

As stated above, our analysis focuses on the major theoretical implication of the PIH that the propensity to consume permanent income is higher than that of transitory income. In other words, if households are behaving under PIH, then they must be somehow decomposing the current bonus income (denoted by B_t) into a permanent component (denoted by B_t^P) and a transitory component (denoted by B_T^{TR}). An increase in the transitory component increases the household's wealth (upon which consumption is based) less than an increase in the permanent component. Consequently, the propensity to consume out of B^{TR} will be smaller than that out of B^{P-}. And to the extent that B^{TR} is larger relative to B_t^P, we obtain a strong contribution of bonus payments on personal savings.

The problem then is how households decompose income into two parts. We shall approach this problem by making an assumption that households suppose the permanent bonus income B_t^P to follow a martingale process except for a constant linear time trend,[27] and the transitory component B_t^{TR} to be a serially uncorrelated random noise with mean 0. Then B_t is construed as the sum of these two stochastic processes. After all, this seems to be a very natural formalization of the concepts of permanent and transitory incomes. Nevertheless, to the extent that the above involves a certain behavioral assumption, our study depends on the validity of this conception.

Households under PIH (and life-cycle hypothesis, LCH) determine their consumption on the basis of their perceived wealth, which, in this case, is the present value of present and expected future bonus income over the households' time horizon of T periods. This present value, which we denote by V_t, is formally expressed as:

$$V_t = B_t + \frac{E_t(B_{t+1})}{1+r} + \cdots + \frac{E_t(B_{t+T-1})}{(1+r)^{T-1}} \tag{14}$$

where $E_t(\cdot)$ expresses households' expectation as of time t, and r is the real rate of interest.

We next rewrite (14) using our assumptions about B_t. From the definition of B^P and B^{TR}, we have

$$B_{t+s} = B^P_{t+s} + B^{TR}_{t+s} \quad 1 \leqq s \leqq T-1.$$

Then, the assumptions about the stochastic properties of B^P and B^{TR} imply

$$\left.\begin{aligned} &E_t(B^{TR}_{t+s}) = 0 \\ &\text{and} \\ &E_t(B^P_{t+s}) = B^P_t + \beta \cdot s \quad 1 \leqq s \leqq T-1 \end{aligned}\right\} \tag{15}$$

where β ($\beta > 0$) expresses the linear growth trend. Using these to rewrite (14), we obtain

$$V_t = \left\{ \frac{1 - \left(\frac{1}{1+r}\right)^T}{1 - \frac{1}{1+r}} \right\} B^P_t + B^{TR}_t$$

$$+ \beta \left\{ \frac{1}{r} \sum_{s=1}^{T-1} \left(\frac{1}{1+r}\right)^{s-1} \left(1 - \left(\frac{1}{1+r}\right)^{T-s}\right) \right\}. \tag{16}$$

Let us now suppose more specifically that consumption of bonus income, denoted by C_t, is determined as k ($0 < k \leqq 1$) times the annuitized value of this "perceived bonus wealth" plus a random component (corresponding to transitory comsumption). That is,

$$C_t = k\{B^P_t + g(r, T)B^{TR}_t + \beta f(r, T)\} + u_t \tag{17}$$

where

$$g(r, T) = \frac{1 - \frac{1}{1+r}}{1 - \left(\frac{1}{1+r}\right)^T} \tag{18}$$

denotes the appropriate annuitization factor,

$$f(r, T) = g(r, T) \left\{ \frac{1}{r} \sum_{s=1}^{T-1} \left(\frac{1}{1+r}\right)^{s-1} \left(1 - \frac{1}{1+r}\right)^{T-s} \right\},$$

and u_t is a random term with mean zero.

Perhaps a word of explanation is necessary for the notion of "consumption of bonus income." For a rational household, total consumption is a function of total perceived wealth, and, in general, no parts of consumption are earmarked to particular categories of income. However, under the Friedman-type proportional consumption function adopted here (which assumes homotheticity of utility function in the background), households can unambiguously trace consumption of "bonus wealth," and moreover, it is independent of other parts of their perceived wealth. This is what we have as our C_t here.[28]

In terms of equation (17), the essence of the PIH is that the coefficient $g(r, T)$ is significantly less than unity. In fact, so long as $T > 2$ (i.e., so long as households are forward looking) we can see from (18) that $g(r, T) < 1$ and, as $T \to \infty$, $g(r, T) \to r/(1+r)$.

We now come back to the important question of how individuals divide B_t into B_t^P and B_t^{TR}. Note that our foregoing assumptions about the stochastic properties are not, by themselves, sufficient to yield information about how, in fact, households estimate the realized values of B_t^P and B_t^{TR} after the realized value of B_t is observed. Usually, we specify the information set possessed by households at each moment in time and determine the breakdown of B_t into B_t^P and B_t^{TR}. Fortunately, however, our survey questionnaire gives direct data on households' expected bonus income for the next period, or $E_t(B_{t+1})$ to use the above notation. As we now show, we can use this data to infer B_t^P and B_t^{TR}. From the martingale property,

$$E_t(B_{t+1}) = \beta + B_t^P \tag{19}$$

and from the identity

$$B_t = B_t^P + B_t^{TR}$$

we have

$$B_t^{TR} = B_t - (E_t(B_{T+1}) - \beta). \tag{20}$$

By substituting (19) and (20) into (17), we obtain the final estimating equation:

$$C_t = kE_t(B_{t+1}) + kg(r, T)(B_t - E_t(B_{t+1})) + \bar{C}' + u_t \tag{21}$$

where $\bar{C}'$ is a constant term relating to the trend factor.

We can now confront the model with the data, and test the validity of the PIH. We do so by estimating (21) and seeing whether or not $g(r, T)$ is significantly less than 1. If indeed it turns out to be smaller than 1, households' behavior is consistent with the PIH. On the other hand, if $g(r, T)$ is equal to 1, then households are in effect determining today's consumption on the basis of today's income only; hence, the PIH is rejected.

DATA

The Survey of Movements in Consumption (Shōhi Dōkō Chōsa) has published answers to questionnaires on expected bonus income for each half year (i.e., before the summer bonus or winter bonus time). They ask worker households (the sample size averages roughly 5,000 households) ahead of time as to what level of bonus income they expect to receive and what fraction of the income they plan to spend. After bonuses have been paid, they ask what the actual level of bonus income and consumption out of them[29] had been. Such data are available from 1966 to the first half of 1973 and then from 1976 to 1981.[30]

Thus, the time unit of analysis is one-half year. We interpret the data as individuals reporting $E_{t-1}(B_t)$ and $E_{t-1}(C_t)$ right before bonus periods and B_t and C_t after bonuses have been paid.[31]

Before we estimate equation (20), let us digress for a moment to examine the properties of the expectations series $E_{t-1}(B_t)$. In particular, let us briefly discuss whether or not the bonus expectations satisfy the rational expectations assumption in view of its widespread use in recent literature. As many users of survey data have done,[32] we estimate the following equation:

$$B_t = \alpha + \beta E_{t-1}(B_t) + \varepsilon_t. \tag{22}$$

If expectations are rational, α should be equal to zero, β to one, and ε_t should be serially uncorrelated. The result is the following:

$$\begin{aligned} B_t = \underset{(.0972)}{.321} + \underset{(.0381)}{.911}\ E_{t-1}(B_t) \end{aligned}$$

$$R^2 = .961, \quad \text{D.W.} = 1.51.$$[33]

Thus, all three of the restrictions the rational expectations assumption imposes are rejected. People tend to underestimate bonus payments; errors in expectations are (although mildly) serially correlated. This result indicates at least the danger of using the rational expectations assumption in the analysis of the consumption function.

Of course, in our case we do not have to assume anything strong about expectations, thanks to the availability of the survey data.

ESTIMATION RESULTS

Preliminaly estimations indicated that there is a serial correlation in the error term of equation (20). Consequently, the error term was assumed to follow a first order autoregressive process and the equation was estimated using nonlinear least squares.[34] The estimation result is shown in Table 9.

Table 9. Estimated Parameters of Consumption Function

$\hat{k}$	$\hat{g}$	$\hat{\bar{C}}'$	$\hat{\rho}$	s.e.	mean of C_t
.460 (.0528)	.941 (.0661)	.0534 (.0607)	.626 (.206)	.0655	1.32

NOTES: s.e. is the standard error of the regression. Standard errors are in parenthesis. $\hat{\rho}$ is the estimated first order serial correlation coefficient.

First, the table shows that g is not significantly different from one. Hence, the PIH is rejected. In other words, the average time horizon of worker households is about one-half year. This means that the distinction between permanent and transitory income does not play a major role in the behavior of these worker households.

Second, the propensity to consume bonuses, irrespective of whether a bonus income is permanent or transitory, is about .46 and is quite low. Thus, households do save a lot of their bonus income, but this effect does not come from the transitoriness of bonus income, nor the type of household behavior hypothesized by the life-cycle theory.

One conceivable explanation of our results is, as stated in earlier sections, that consumers have formed a "habit," accordingly they save a larger amount from bonus income than other income; moreover, at least in the short run (and in normal times), they do not adjust this habit to changes in the stochastic nature of bonus payments. The consumption function estimated here has become quite similar to the usual Keynesian consumption function in which the major determinant of current consumption is current income. But ours differs from the Keynesian formulation in that current consumption not only depends on current income, but also on the breakdown of income into bonus and nonbonus income.[35] Our next task would be to explore in depth the historical circumstances that led to the formation of such a habit and the possibility of changes in the habit as economic environments surrounding individuals evolve over time. But this is left beyond the scope of the present work.

5. The Effect of Bonus Income on Savings at the Macro Level

In the previous two sections, we analyzed household savings behavior using microdata and survey data that cover only a fraction of the total households. In this section, we turn to macrodata and study the major determinants of aggregate savings of the household sector. This is important because there are many interesting macroeconomic problems directly or indirectly related to the behavior of aggregate savings. Of course, movements of aggregate savings are a reflection of savings behavior at the microlevel. Thus, analysis of worker households might give a reasonable first order approximation of aggregate savings behavior. However, the ratio of nonworker households to total households is still more than 30 percent; hence, if these households behaved differently from worker households, we would still need an analysis of aggregate savings.[36]

For these reasons, we shall estimate a simple aggregate consumption function in this section in order to obtain a rough idea about the determinants of aggregate consumption and the quantitative significance of each. The specification of the consumption function will include most of the variables that were discussed in Section 2. We are especially interested in studying the extent to which the bonus system has increased savings. Thus, in the last part of the section, we shall carry out a simulation that will show clearly the effects of bonuses on savings.

SPECIFICATION

Following the discussion in Section 2, we specify an aggregate consumption function as follows:

$$C_t = \alpha_0 + \alpha_1 A_t + \alpha_2 W_t + \alpha_3 B_t + \alpha_4 S_t + u_t. \tag{23}$$

The notations mean C_t, aggregate consumption; A_t, financial wealth; W_t, regularly paid wages; S_t, income of the self-employed; u_t, error term uncorrelated with included right-hand side variables. All variables are deflated by the consumers' price index.

Several aspects of the specification call for an explanation. First, we have not followed the usual practice of using distributed lag formulation of income variables. Such a practice is often justified by lagged adjustments of expectations or consumption habits. However, our analysis in Section 4 indicated that, at least in the case of bonuses, current income is the major determinant of current consumption. Also, specifications that included lagged consumption terms in equation (24) (in order to introduce, roughly, the effects of adjustment lags) either did not lead to major changes in estimates or produced unreasonable results. Consequently, we decided to use only current income variables in the equation.

Second, income variables appear separately in the equation. This is to allow for differences among propensities to consume from various income sources. It would be hard to believe that the estimate of .460 we obtained for the propensity to consume bonus income in Section 4 applies to all income sources.

The wealth variable represents income from assets. As discussed in

Section 2, this variable played an important role in some previous work in explaining large increases in the savings rate in the mid-1970s. Our specification attempts to estimate the significance of such an effect along with other effects.

DATA AND ESTIMATION RESULT

The period of study is 1958 to 1978 on a semi-annual basis. This choice of time reflects our conclusion in Section 4 that the average time horizon of households is one-half year. Aggregate bonus earnings were estimated by multiplying the level of bonuses per person by the number of regularly employed workers (For details, see the Appendix.). The beginning period of net household wealth was constructed by taking the cumulated sum of surpluses in financial transactions of the individuals' sector (using Flow of Funds Accounts of the Bank of Japan). This corresponds to the FA(−1) variable introduced in the previous section. Therefore, wealth here includes only financial wealth and the latter was used as a proxy for total wealth. Other variables come from NIA.

Equation (23) was estimated by OLS with a dummy variable taking one in the second half of each year added. The dummy variable was introduced in order to capture the seasonality in consumption not explained by included variables. The result of the estimation is the following:

$$\begin{aligned} C_t = \underset{(2.541)}{15.593} + \underset{(.0225)}{.1098A_t} + \underset{(.0961)}{.6645W_t} + \underset{(.1539)}{.3759B_t} \\ + \underset{(.0890)}{.6997S_t} - \underset{(2.073)}{7.862D_t}. \end{aligned} \tag{24}$$

$R^2 = .9985$, s.e. $= 2.861$, D.W. $= 1.474$, where standard errors are in parentheses.[37] All variables are of the right sign and are significant. In particular, the propensity to consume bonus income is .376 and lower than the spending propensities from other incomes.[38] The corresponding number we obtained in Section 4, .460, is slightly higher than this, but within one standard error of the current estimate. In any case, this result supports the view that the bonus system has had positive effects on the savings rate.

The propensity to consume income of the self-employed is about the same as that of those paid regular wages. This result then rejects the view that fluctuations in the income of the self-employed exert significant effects on the savings rate. Equation (24) also shows that the propensity to consume regular wages is about .66, which is very close to what we obtained in our cross-section study. This is fairly low by international standards—a finding that partially explains the high savings rate in Japan relative to other countries. The propensity to consume net household wealth seems very large. This, however, is probably due to the fact that A_t includes only financial assets. The statistical significance of this variable shows the importance of the effects of inflation or wealth accumulation on savings. In sum, the estimation result clearly supports the view that an increase in bonus earnings relative to regular wages increases savings.

SIMULATION

Using the estimation result, we may determine quantitatively the effect of bonuses on savings. For this purpose we ran the following simulations. We calculated the rate of savings for the sample period assuming that all bonus income had been paid in the form of regular wages.

Such a calculation can be done at least in two ways. We may assume that household wealth is exogenous, or else the effect of changes in savings (on the path of wealth) may be taken into account. Since the wealth variable here includes only financial wealth, it is not clear how we should calculate its time path when the time path of consumption changes. Because of this difficulty, we report only the result of the first simulation, although in theory, the second simulation would be more accurate.[39]

Figure 4 shows the simulated path along with the actual savings rate.[40] It is immediately clear that bonus payments have exerted positive effects on the rate of savings. The difference between the actual and simulated savings rates were, on average, equal to 3.0 percentage points. Consequently, we conclude that the Japanese personal savings rate would have been (at least) about 17 percent (on average) if bonus income had been paid as regular wages.[41]

This numerical figure of *at most* 3 percentage points (on average) seems quite modest. It certainly does not meet the expectation so often expressed about the effect of the bonus payment system. Moreover, as Figure 4 makes clear, its effect is not strong enough to wipe out the strong increasing trend in the rate of savings (up until the mid-1970s) even if the bonus payment system had not existed. In short, it does not explain our query (ii) raised in Section 2. In particular, our simulated path shows that there were large increases in the savings rates of 1973 and 1974, even after the effects of bonus income had been eliminated. These remarks reinforce our criticism of Shinohara's view made in Section 3.

6. Conclusion

We are now ready to state our conclusion briefly and also some qualifications of the present work. We have confirmed in the present paper

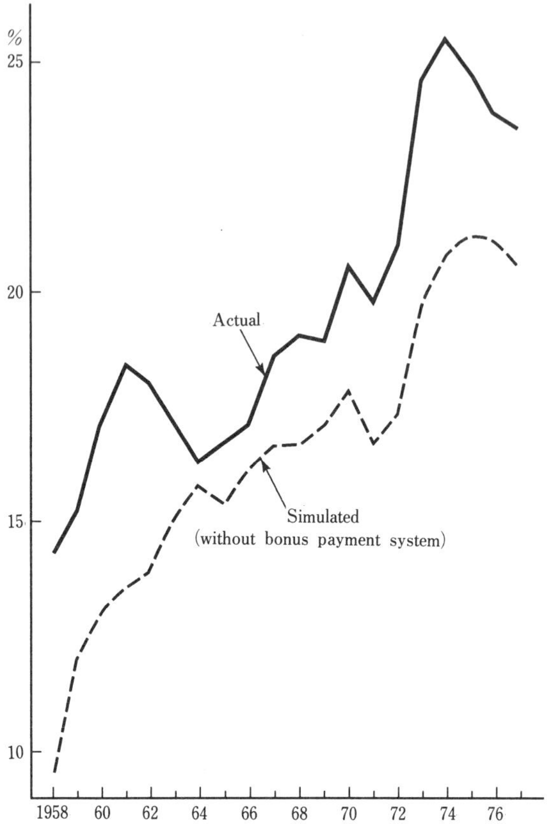

Figure 4. Actual and simulated rates of savings

that the bonus payment system has exerted a statistically significant effect on Japanese personal savings (namely, an approximately 20-percent difference in terms of the marginal propensity to consume as compared with other parts of income). However, the quantitative magnitude of its contribution to the aggregate rate of personal savings is rather small, at most 3 percentage points (on average) for the period of 1958–78, when the aggregate rate of personal savings averaged 20 percent.

On the theoretical side, we have seen from our study of the survey data that this effect on bonuses does not come from the permanent-income–life-cycle hypothesis behavior of individuals. This conclusion has been reinforced by our cross-section study which showed further evidence that household behavior is incongruent with the implications of the permanent-income–life-cycle hypothesis. As an alternative, we have suggested what we termed the habit-buffer–income hypothesis—that, at least in the short run and under normal economic conditions, households follow a convention of spending some fixed proportion of different components of income. We do not claim we have proved this hypothesis, yet we believe it is a workable and plausible inductive hypothesis waiting to be tested further.

It is important to note that by arguing against the permanent-income–life-cycle hypothesis and also suggesting that people follow conventional spending rules in the short run we do *not* imply that they have no concern for the future. We see clearly from individual answers to various survey questionnaires[42] that Japanese households do seem to be aware of their savings objectives (and in this sense their savings are purposive), giving thought to their expected future needs. But the point is that their foresight capacity of telescopic faculty (à la Irving Fisher) is fairly limited, and it is also very costly to calculate and respond to every flow of new information.[43] Thus, households may set some mild notion of "savings goals" and, on the other hand, resort to such conventional rules of spending as we discussed in the present paper. Under normal economic conditions, this ensures satisfying both already formed consumption habits (or the life space of consumption) and psychological obligations to abide by their "savings goals." Here we have left open how people decide the specific proportion of income they set aside to spend. Determination of this ratio surely must relate to their long-run objectives.

We have also indicated the role of wealth in governing Japanese household savings behavior, albeit in a manner different from the postulates of the permanent-income–life-cycle theories. It seems that, in the context just stated, the role of wealth should be studied. These long-run aspects, and the manner in which household wealth plays a role, shall be the next topic of our study.

Data Appendix

We have estimated the (quarterly) aggregate time-series data on bonus earnings by following as closely as possible the manner in which the employment income of NIA is estimated. In making this estimation we have relied heavily on the *Source Materials for Estimating NIA*, published by the Economic Planning Agency in 1970 (hereinafter *SM*). In this appendix, we shall provide a brief account of the estimation procedure.

The NIA estimate the employment income by (employee compensation) dividing the economy into the following 13 major industry categories: A = Agriculture, B = Forestry, C = Fishery, D = Mining,

E = Construction, F = Manufacturing, G = Wholesale and Retailing, H = Banking and Insurance, I = Real Estate, J = Transportation and Communication, K = Electricity, Gas, and other utilities, L = Service, and M = Government. These industries are then regrouped as the agricultural sector (consisting of A, B, and C), the nonagricultural and nongovernmental sectors (consisting of D through L) and the government sector (consisting of M).

Our first major assumption is that bonus earnings within the agricultural sector are negligible. While this may not be true literally, this assumption was necessary because there are no readily available data on bonuses for the agricultural sector. We regard this as an acceptable assumption because the proportion of employed workers in this sector is negligible. (According to the 1975 Census, workers [including managers] in the agricultural sector are 0.47 million, while those in the nonagricultural sector are 36.5 million.)

As for the nonagricultural sector, NIA employ *Monthly Labor Statistics* (hereinafter *MLS*) as the primary source of material for estimating employment income. MLS give monthly data on both the total wages of regularly employed workers and the size of regular employment for each industry (D through L). These numbers are given according to the size of establishments (*not* firms), namely those with 5–29 employees and those with 30 or more employees. It also gives decomposition of total wage payment figures divided into two components: the regularly paid and specially paid portions. The latter portion is primarily constituted by bonus payments. Being unable to decompose further, we have assumed that the specially paid portion of wage payments and bonus earnings are identical. The bonus figure per employee obtained for each establishment-size class is then multiplied by the corresponding number of regular employees to give total bonus payments for each industry (D through L [for the establishment-size classes 5–29 employees and 30 and more employees]).

The remaining task for this sector is to estimate the total bonus payments for establishments with 1–4 employees. Although *MLS* do not cover this class on a monthly basis, they conduct a special survey for this class once each year (at the end of July). From this survey, we obtained (for each industry) the figure of the total special payments (which, by our assumption, equals bonus payments) made during the preceding year (i.e., from August of the previous year to July of the current year) to regular employees (per worker) and the figure of the number of employees. In estimating the quarterly (and annual) series of regular employees, we have assumed that these yearly payments followed the same monthly pattern as that observed for establishments with 5–29 employees. This assumption is the same as that of the NIA in estimating the quarterly series of total wage payments made to this establishment size class (cf. *SM*: 18–23).

The above constitutes the basic procedure of estimating bonus earnings in the nonagricultural and nongovernmental sectors. For certain parts, however, we have had to resort to somewhat more ad-hoc procedures. First, NIA treat specially the public school (both national and local) employees (both teachers and administrators) that are already covered by *MLS* under the title of the service (L) industry. Namely, by using the Census of Establishments (conducted every three years) data, it estimates the proportion of public school employees within the entire service sector and deducts this portion from the number of employees that *MLS* give. It derives the figures from the fiscal year books of the Ministry of Education (*SM*: 52–53). Although this seemed to be too contrived and perhaps an unnecessary procedure, we have followed the same. Since the bonus payments pattern for this group of workers is identical with other government employees, we will describe the procedure of estimating bonus earnings for this group in the next subsection.

Second, there exists a difficulty in that *MLS* did not have figures for the service industry prior to 1970. NIA thus resorted to an ad-hoc method of multiplying wage figures in the Wholesale and Retailing industry (G) by the ratio of wages in the service industry to the C industry. This ratio is available in the Survey of Wages and Salaries of Private Employees (Minkan Kyūyo Jittai Chōsa, Office of Personnels). Our conclusion was that this method results in a significant underestimation of wages in the service industry. Hence, we obtained the ratio of wages in the two industries from a different source. That is, *MLS* report annual bonus earnings for the two industries for establishments with 1–4 employees. From this we obtained the wage ratio in the two industries and then proceeded the same way as NIA, assuming that the ratio applies to all establishment-size classes.

We also faced some difficulty in estimating the number of regular workers in the L industry since *MLS* do not report this prior to 1970. Thus, we first obtained total employment (including part-time workers) from the Survey of Labor Force and then applied to this the proportion of regular workers in total employment available in the Census of Establishments.

GOVERNMENT SECTOR

The NIA restrict the coverage of industry M (government) to those establishments providing general government services. Annual figures of the total employment earnings of this sector are available in NIA yearbooks. (They were obtained directly from government sources.) The bonus payments of central government employees are determined by law (Office of Personnel). For example, it was stipulated that in fiscal year 1975 public employees were to receive as bonus payment 2.0 months' worth of their regular salary (the basic part of salary plus certain parts of allowance) in June, 2.7 months' worth in December, and 0.5 months' worth in March. In addition, while each year public employees' salaries are adjusted by approval of the recommendation made by the Office of Personnel (usually in December), the adjustment usually goes back to earlier months and the cumulated amount is paid then. These payments may very well be regarded as a form of bonus. By collecting information on these payments for each fiscal year, we have divided annual total earnings of government employees into the regularly paid part and the bonus part. The assumptions we made are that the bonus ratio and the proportion of salaries on which the bonus ratio is applied are the same between the national and local governments. We have also applied exactly the same method to public school employees.

AFTER-TAX BONUS PAYMENTS

The figures obtained above were inclusive of all taxes on bonus earnings. We then used the average income tax ratio for the salaries of each year we obtained from the annual financial reports of national and local governments to derive the after-tax bonus earnings. For example, in 1975 this ratio amounted to 3.77 percent for national government taxes and to 2.45 percent for local government taxes.

CONSISTENCY WITH CROSS-SECTION DATA

The ratio of bonus earnings derived over the entire employment income in the NIA is contrasted in Table A-1, with the corresponding ratio obtained by the FIES figures, which apply to family households (excluding single person households) that are drawn from a sample of cities with populations over 50,000. As the corresponding Figure A-1 shows, our estimated series are consistently lower than the FIES series. This difference in the two estimates may be explicable by the fact that FIES households are a more restricted sample, in the sense that they are older in age and wealthier than all households. However, it is at once noticable that the two series are almost parallel. This shows that our estimates are at least consistent with the FIES estimates.

Table A-1. Correspondence of the Bonus Earnings Ratio between FIES and NIA (%)

Year	FIES	NIA (our estimate)
1958	14.3	10.9
1959	15.4	12.7
1960	17.1	12.9
1961	17.5	14.2
1962	18.0	14.1
1963	18.8	14.6
1964	18.6	14.6
1965	18.7	14.5
1966	19.3	15.1
1967	19.7	15.6
1968	20.2	16.2
1969	22.3	18.0
1970	23.4	18.2
1971	22.8	18.9
1972	22.4	19.3
1973	23.7	19.8
1974	24.5	21.9
1975	21.8	19.4
1976	21.7	19.6
1977	21.1	18.6
1978	20.4	18.5

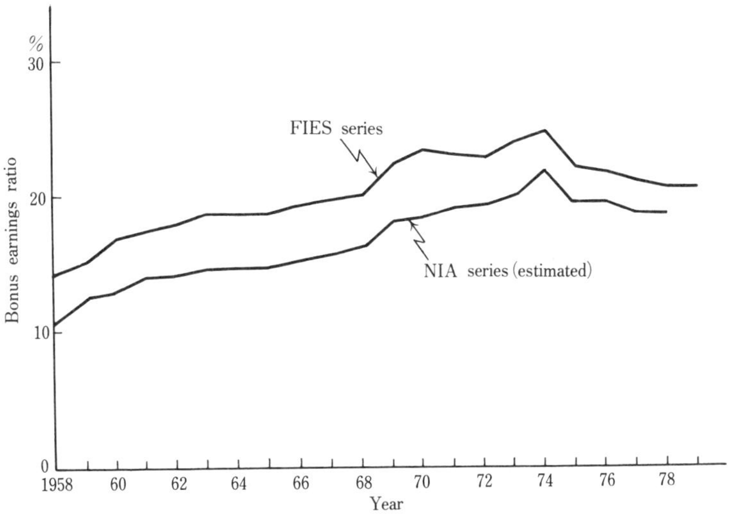

Figure A-1

Table A-2. Annual Data

Year	Consumption (C)	Nondurables consumption	Household net financial wealth (A)	Regularly paid wages (W)	Bonus earnings (B)
1958	128.9	122.2	95.7	77.0	9.4
1959	138.9	130.4	107.9	82.2	12.0
1960	152.8	143.5	123.6	91.8	13.6
1961	165.7	155.0	140.5	101.4	16.8
1962	181.5	169.0	158.2	114.1	18.7
1963	198.9	185.2	177.5	123.9	21.2
1964	222.0	207.2	197.0	136.9	23.4
1965	234.5	218.9	219.4	148.7	25.3
1966	254.1	237.0	240.4	161.4	28.6
1967	279.9	259.9	269.8	178.9	33.0
1968	306.7	282.9	303.8	196.4	38.0
1969	336.2	312.9	343.5	211.9	46.5
1970	362.5	337.3	373.8	237.2	52.9
1971	389.0	360.4	407.5	263.2	61.4
1972	424.9	395.5	459.6	286.2	68.3
1973	460.1	428.6	520.9	322.1	79.6
1974	467.0	434.7	503.0	325.6	91.3
1975	496.0	465.7	524.1	359.1	86.3
1976	517.9	485.0	576.0	369.7	89.9
1977	540.0	510.4	628.9	389.8	89.1
1978	561.8	528.4	699.5	402.2	91.4

NOTE: All data are in terms of billion yen divided by consumer price index: 1970 = 100.0

Table A-3. Expected and Actual Values of Bonus Payments per Average Worker Household

Year	Expected	Actual
1966s	54.8	59.0
1966w	73.1	77.8
1967s	60.5	64.5
1967w	76.3	86.8
1968s	67.6	74.2
1968w	91.1	98.5
1969s	77.5	87.6
1969w	114.6	115.8
1970s	92.3	102.8
1970w	123.3	141.0
1971s	116.2	133.2
1971w	151.3	175.6
1972s	129.7	147.5
1972w	179.3	201.7
1973s	154.5	178.4
1976s	268.0	291.6
1976w	395.7	352.8
1977s	360.1	351
1977w	428	438
1978s	376	367
1978w	444	453
1979s	387	383
1979w	448	466
1980s	417	408
1980w	481	496
1981s	420	407
1981w	485	501

SOURCE: Shōhi Dōkō Chōsa
NOTE: Figures are in units of thousand yen; s = summer; w = winter

NOTES

This is an extended and revised version of the paper presented at the Rokko Econometric Conference held in Kobe, July 1981. We are indebted to Joaquim de Andrade, Henry Farber, Robert Feldman, Alberto Giovannini, Nils Gottfries, Mervyin King, Susumu Koizumi, Masao Kuroda, Stephen Marglin, Franco Modigliani, Jurg Niehans, Terukazu Suruga, and Martin Weitzman for their helpful suggestions and criticisms at various stages of our research. We are also indebted to the National Income Department of the Economic Planning Agency and the Statistics and Information Department of the Ministry of Labour for their generous support and aid in our data collection process. Finally, we would like to thank Atsuko Ohashi for her skillful and perseverant research assistance, and Margaret Leclair for kindly editing the English of our manuscript.

1. Most of Mizoguchi's works published earlier in Japanese were assembled and published in English (1970). For example, we find the same material as noted here in chapter 5 of (1970).

2. In particular, we differ from Shinohara (1981) in terms of overall evaluation of the bonus effect.

3. We did, however, face the problem of discontinuity of data in the NIA after 1977, as EPA switched to the new System of National Accounts (SNA) series. In order to ob-

components, for which no decomposition is available.) Since these categories of income are much closer to the household head's regular wage income in nature than the true bonus income (except for the proviso just noted), this limitation of data may introduce a serious bias in estimating the elasticity of consumption with respect to bonus income. In order to rectify this bias we have adopted the following procedure. Let our "bonus incomes," B, be further divided into the true bonus income B', "wife and other household members' wage incomes," T', and "return from assets and business income," R' (all tax adjusted), so that $B = B' + T' + R'$ holds. Recalling equation (4′), the true model for consumption behavior is now expressed by:

$$C = \bar{C}' \cdot (W + T' + R')^{\alpha'} \left(1 + \frac{B'}{W + T' + R'}\right)^{\beta'}$$

where the variable W, i.e., the household head's regular wage income, remains unchanged. This functional form, however, can easily be rewritten as

$$C = \bar{C}' \cdot W^{\alpha'} \left(\frac{Y}{W}\right)^{\beta'} \left(1 + \frac{T' + R'}{W}\right)^{\alpha' - \beta'}$$

or taking the natural logarithm of both sides,

$$C = (\alpha' - \beta')w + \beta' y + (\alpha' - \beta')q + \gamma'$$

where $\gamma' = \log \bar{C}'$ and $q = \log\left(1 + \frac{T' + R'}{W}\right)$. The new term $(\alpha' - \beta')q$ represents the adjustment factor necessary to correct the bias from inaccurate measurement. The foregoing formulas (6) and (7) should then be modified accordingly, with $(\alpha' - \beta')E(q \mid w)$ and $(\alpha' - \beta')E(q \mid y)$ added to the right-hand side respectively. The final estimation equations are, again, a little modification of the equations (10) and (11):

$$C_1^{it} = \alpha^t(z_{11}^{it} + q_1^{it}) + \beta^t(z_{12}^{it} - q_1^{it}) + \gamma^t + v_1^{it}$$

$$C_2^{jt} = \alpha^t(z_{21}^{jt} + q_2^{jt}) + \beta^t(z_{22}^{jt} - q_2^{jt}) + \gamma^t + v_2^{jt}.$$

18. The estimates of the coefficients of equations (8) and (9) that were used in the estimation of the parameters of the consumption function presented here are given in Table N1.

19. We have also tried pooling the years 1969–73, 1977–78, and 1980 together. However, the result did not pass the F-test for the case of nondurables.

20. There is another evidence in support of this finding. Although, for some mysterious reason, the survey data (Shōhi Dōkō Chōsa), which we will examine in the next section, do not have bonus-related questions for most of the periods in question, the data for the winter-bonus period of 1976 is available, and it suggests a higher propensity to consume out of bonus than other years. More specifically, the actual average propensity to consume out of the winter bonus of that year was about 55 percent over all income classes, which was about 10 percent higher than the corresponding figures for normal years.

21. See Kosai and Ogino (1980: 192–98) and Akabane (1981: 77–85). While the former accepts the paradox as a fact and attempts an explanation, the latter dismisses it as a statistical artifact, allegedly caused by the unreliableness of the data coming from the table classified by annual household income. However, the basis of that allegation rested mostly on the fact that the behavior of individual consumption items as given by the table in question fluctuated much. But, in our view, this is not a fair allegation. We all know that narrow items of expenditure data can fluctuate much. What we have shown in our paper is that, even though we corrected for possible fluctuation in the componentwise distribution of income, we still obtain this paradox. Hence, we believe that Akabane's allegation is unfounded and the paradox is real.

22. Kosai and Ogino's explanation (1980) seems to have relied too much on the role played by the durables consumption. While we agree that it was an important factor, we would still argue that the main explanatory factor lay elsewhere. As described here, the

Table N-1. Estimated Lognormal Parameters (Standard errors in parentheses)

Year	S_1	S_2	C_1	C_2
1969	.746	.786	3.412	2.138
	(.024)	(.019)	(.284)	(.228)
1970	.723	.770	3.722	2.323
	(.027)	(.022)	(.323)	(.259)
1971	.743	.766	3.457	2.395
	(.013)	(.017)	(.152)	(.209)
1972	.769	.824	3.163	1.728
	(.020)	(.037)	(.242)	(.445)
1973	.756	.729	3.344	2.869
	(.022)	(.022)	(.263)	(.276)
1974	.769	.708	3.193	3.130
	(.017)	(.018)	(.200)	(.217)
1975	.800	.751	2.807	2.634
	(.158)	(.025)	(.192)	(.303)
1976	.803	.764	2.759	2.492
	(.021)	(.015)	(.254)	(.178)
1977	.760	.719	3.280	3.041
	(.019)	(.023)	(.225)	(.277)
1978	.812	.797	2.650	2.110
	(.013)	(.019)	(.157)	(.223)
1979	.760	.774	3.274	2.400
	(.019)	(.012)	(.226)	(.151)
1980	.771	.708	3.142	3.197
	(.025)	(.026)	(.297)	(.317)

NOTE: Estimated equations:

$$y_1^{it} = S_1^t \cdot w_1^{it} + C_1^t + u_1^{it}$$
$$w_2^{jt} = S_2^t \cdot y_2^{jt} + C_2^t + u_2^{jt}$$

where

$$S_1^t = (\sigma_{wy}^t / \sigma_{ww}^t), \quad S_2^t = (\sigma_{wy}^t / \sigma_{yy}^t),$$
$$C_1^t = \mu_y^t - (\sigma_{wy}^t / \sigma_{ww}^t) \cdot \mu_w^t$$
$$C_2^t = \mu_w^t - (\sigma_{wy}^t / \sigma_{yy}^t) \cdot \mu_y^t$$

paradox does not disappear in the case of year 1975, even if we subtract durables consumption.

23. Obviously, the type of behavior just described is not explicable within the strict confines of the permanent-income hypothesis. There is an additional reason that works against this hypothesis. The preceding years of sharp inflation have considerably reduced the real value of household financial wealth. However, since the holding of financial wealth is concentrated among households with high annual income (e.g., in 1980, according to the Family Savings Survey, the top-income quintile group among worker households held 31.3 percent of total financial net worth of the household sector [including the self-employed households] as opposed to 8.5 percent held by the bottom-income quintile group [again among worker households]), high annual income households were the ones which have been affected most by the inflation. Nevertheless, they tended to consume much, which is against the implication of the permanent-income hypothesis. Furthermore, it is clear that one cannot defend the hypothesis by resorting to the shelter of liquidity constraints.

24. A representative of these studies is Kosai (1981).

25. This literature includes contributions by Hall (1978), Flavin (1981), Hall and Mishkin (1982), and Hayashi (1982).

26. If survey data were not available, we would be obliged to assume that the stochastic model proposed below corresponds to the true representation of payments—an assumption much stronger than the one used here. See, for example, Hall and Mishkin (1982) for use of such a procedure.

27. This is much more general than the Muthian framework (Muth, 1961) where B_t is supposed to be generated as

$$B_t = (B_{t-1} - v_{t-1}) + u_t + v_t$$

with u_t representing a permanent shock and v_t representing a transitory shock.

28. Under a more general utility function, C_t must be interpreted to mean the amount of consumption that would have to be (marginally) cut back if the "bonus wealth" were not present. In general, C_t would depend on the magnitudes of other parts of wealth, and the consumption function (17) would have to be modified accordingly. We are indebted to Nils Gottfries for a helpful discussion on this point.

29. We interpret the households' answers to this question (as to "consumption out of bonus") to mean the amount of consumption out of annuitized "bonus wealth," a theoretical notion discussed previously. (See also n. 28.) In effect, we are assuming that households are much more rational than the persons who actually prepared this question.

30. Strangely enough, the survey does not give data for the very period in which our cross-section studies in the previous section detected irregularities.

31. Strictly speaking, the time the actual amount of bonus is reported and the time the expectation of the next bonus payment is reported are not the same. During most of the sample period, the former was February and August and the latter was May and November. Clearly, this tends to produce overestimation of the permanent component and underestimation of the temporary component of bonus changes, possibly resulting in biased estimates of the coefficients. Since it was not obvious how this problem could be avoided, we ignored the problem in the estimation result reported below.

32. See, for example, B. Friedman (1980).

33. The D-W statistic reported takes into account the gap in the sample.

34. The equation was estimated in the following form:

$$C_t = \rho C_{t-1} + k'({}_tB_{t+1} - \rho \cdot {}_{t-1}B_t) + k' \cdot g \cdot (B_t - \rho B_{t-1} - {}_tB_{t+1} + \rho \cdot {}_{t-1}B_t) + c'' + \varepsilon_{t-1}$$

and

$$u_t = \rho u_{t-1} + \varepsilon_{t-1}.$$

35. In this section, we have not estimated an equation that explains consumption out of total income. However, it would be reasonable to assume that the propensity to consume out of regular wages is different from that out of bonus income. We will leave this part to Sections 3 and 5.

36. On the other hand, we are assuming in this section that aggregation biases are fairly small so that the analysis of macrodata give meaningful results.

37. Equation (24) indicates the existence of a mild serial correlation. When the equation was corrected for serial correlation, the coefficient on bonuses turned out to be unreasonably high—.764. However, when a distributed lag is introduced to the W variable, the estimation result came fairly close to (24) even after correction for serial correlation. This suggests that consumption responds sluggishly to regularly paid wages but not to bonuses. This seems to be broadly consistent with the analysis of the consumption habit carried out so far in this paper. A careful analysis of such a hypothesis is left for future work.

38. The analysis in Section 3 indicated that during the mid-1970s the propensity to consume out of bonus was much higher than in other periods. This possibility was tested here by splitting the sample at the end of the 1960s into two. The estimation result showed that, in fact, there was an increase in the propensity to consume out of bonuses in the latter period. However, the increase was not statistically significant because of large standard errors.

39. Note that such a simulation tends to overestimate the effects of bonus income on savings.

40. The figure shows the average of two half-year numbers for each year.

41. The average of the actual savings rate for the sample period of this simulation was about 20 percent.

42. Representative examples of survey questionnaires are found in the Economic Planning Agency's Survey on the Movement of Consumption used in Section 4 and Bank of Japan's Public Opinion Polls with regard to Savings (Chochiku ni kansuru Seron Chōsa), which is conducted annually.

43. The spirit here is similar to the so-called satisfying approach or Leibenstein's convention approach (Leibenstein, 1982).

References

Aitchison, J., and J. Brown. 1957. Log-Normal Distribution. Cambridge: Cambridge University Press.

Akabane, T. 1981. Hijōshiki no Nihon Keizai-Ron (On Japanese Economy from a Non-Commonsensical Viewpoint). Tokyo: Nihon Keizai Shimbun.

Brown, J.M. 1952. Habit persistence and lags in consumer behavior. Econometrica 20 (July).

Duesenberry, J. 1949. Income, Saving and the Theory of Consumer Behavior. Cambridge, Mass.: Harvard University Press.

Flavin, M. 1981. The adjustment of consumption to changing expectations about future income. Journal of Political Economy 89 (October).

Friedman, B. 1980. Survey evidence on the "rationality" of interest rate expectations. Journal of Monetary Economics 6 (October).

Friedman, M. 1957. A Theory of the Consumption Function. Princeton: Princeton University Press.

Haitovsky, Y. 1973. Regression Estimation from Grouped Observations. London: Griffin.

Hall, R. 1978. Stochastic implications of the life cycle-permanent income hypothesis: Theory and evidence. Journal of Political Economy 86 (December).

Hall, R., and F. Mishkin. 1982. The sensitivity of consumption to transitory income: Estimates from panel data on households. Econometrica 50 (March): 461–82.

Hayashi, F. 1982. The permanent income hypothesis: Estimation and testing by instrumental variables. Journal of Political Economy 90 (October).

Houthakker, H.S., and L. Taylor. 1970. Consumer Demand in the United States, second and enlarged ed. Cambridge, Mass.: Harvard University Press.

Komiya, R. 1963. The supply of personal savings. In Sengo Nihon no Keizai Seichō (Economic Growth of Postwar Japan), ed. by R. Komiya. Tokyo: Iwanami.

Kosai, Y. 1980. Kojin chochiku to sonota chochiku no kankei. (The Relationship between Personal Savings and Other Savings). Chochiku Jihō 127 (March).

Kosai, Y., and Y. Ogino. 1980. Nihon Keizai Tenbō (Japanese Economy in Perspective). Tokyo: Nihon Hyoron Sha.

Leibenstein, H. 1982. The prisoners' dilemma in the invisible hand: An analysis of intrafirm productivity. American Economic Review 72 (May).

Lydall, H. 1968. The Structure of Earnings. Oxford: Oxford University Press.

Maddala, G.S. 1977. Econometrics. New York: McGraw-Hill.

Marglin, S.A. 1983. Growth, Distribution and Prices. Cambridge, Mass.: Harvard University Press.

Mizoguchi, T. 1964. Shōhi Kansū no Tōkei-teki Bunseki (A Statistical Analysis of the Consumption Function). Tokyo: Iwanami.

———. 1970. Personal Savings and Consumption in Postwar Japan. Tokyo: Kinokuniya.

———. 1973. Chochiku no Keizai-Gaku (The Economics of Saving). Tokyo: Keisō Shobō.

Modigliani, F. 1949. Fluctuations in the saving-income ratio: A problem in economic forecasting. In Studies in Income and Wealth 11. New York: National Bureau of Economic Research.
Muth, J. 1961. Rational expectations and the theory of price movements. Econometrica 29 (July): 315–35.
Ohkawa, K., and H. Rosovsky. 1973. Japanese Economic Growth. Stanford: Stanford University Press.
Shinohara, M. 1959. The structure of savings and the consumption function in postwar Japan. Journal of Political Economy 67 (December).
———. 1981. Chochiku ritsu no nazo (The puzzles of savings rate). Chochiku Jihō 127.
Weitzman, M. 1982. Some macroeconomic implications of alternative compensation systems. Discussion Paper, M.I.T. (December).

8. Savings and Labor Supply Behavior of Aged Households in Japan

1. Introduction

It has long been suggested that one of the major causes of the internationally high savings rate of Japanese households lies in the high saving propensity of aged households (Kanamori, 1961; Komiya, 1963; Shinohara, 1963; Mizoguchi, 1973; and more recently, Horioka, 1984). As compared with the situation where aged households dissave or save little, they are contributing substantively to the country's household savings.

Early opinions differed, however, as to why aged households exhibited a high savings rate. Kanamori suggested an interpretation of this as expressing the strength of traditional culture and morality. Komiya instead suggested that it reflected the labor market practice of seniority wages giving high earnings to aged workers, while at the same time, consumption needs declined as households aged, and furthermore, those aged people who were retired were subsumed by their adult children's households. Shinohara (1963) suggested an additional interpretation that, since the dispersion in employee earnings between large-size and small-size firms increases as workers age, the high savings rate of the elderly reflects the behavior of high income earners with a higher propensity to save.[1] Komiya's last point implicitly meant that the observed high savings ratio of the elderly was partly an artifact due to a sample selection problem. This possible bias has been emphasized again by Ando et al. (1986) and Hayashi (1986), who then jointly took up a detailed anatomy of merged households.

Mizoguchi (1973), on the eve of the rapid expansion and increase of

Originally published in *Journal of the Japanese and International Economies* 2 (1988): 417–49.

public pension coverage and benefits in Japan, suggested that the delay in the full implementation of the public pension system and the concomitant high labor participation rate of the elderly lay was the major reason for the high savings rate of the elderly. The aspect of labor supply has been taken up by Ishikawa (1987), who, through cross-classification of the microdata, showed that savings rates, even when income class is controlled for, indeed varied much between working and nonworking households, the latter showing a small degree of financial dissaving.

This paper examines closely the two routes by which aged individuals affect overall household savings. First, it extends my previous analysis by presenting a more detailed analysis of the interrelationship between labor supply and savings behavior of independent aged households. Second, it evaluates the degree by which the subsumed elderly people within the younger generation's households affect the latter's savings rate. We would then hope to answer the following questions. Does the declining employment ratio of the aged in Japan reduce the savings rate of this group, and if so, by how much? Does the traditional extended family really act as a preserver of household savings?

A brief outline of the paper is as follows. Section 2 gives a broad overview of the demographic and economic characteristics, and their time-series changes, of the aged population in Japan and confirms three distinctive characteristics noted above: first, the (internationally) high ratio of aged persons living in their children's or kin's dwelling units; second, their high labor force participation rate; and third, their high propensity to save.

Section 3 examines the net impact the first characteristic described above has on the savings behavior of the younger generations. While there is some evidence that the presence of aged parents reduces the savings rate of the younger household as a whole, its negative effect is washed away when we take account of other evidence that the aged parents greatly assist the young in homeownership.

Section 4 analyzes the labor supply and savings behavior of the aged population that maintain independent households. By estimating a simultaneous employment probability *cum* savings equations system, we show that the two decisions are indeed endogenous, that, *ceteris paribus*, the working households save 13 percent more than the nonworking households as a proportion of noninterest income (evaluated at the mean of income distribution), which together with the high propensity to work, raises the observed average savings rate of this age class. The detected endogeneity implies, however, that any exogenous shock toward reduction of employment invites an offsetting increase in the savings rate, leaving the savings rate of this class virtually unchanged.

Table 1. Changes in the Demographic Characteristics of Household Types for Population Aged 65 and Above, 1970–85

	1970	1975	1980	1985
Number of households containing elderly persons				
Single-person family	41.0	60.0	84.6	116.0
	(7.0)	(8.7)	(10.5)	(12.5)
Independent nuclear family	161.8	208.3	257.1	317.2
	(27.6)	(30.6)	(31.8)	(34.3)
Two-generation family	34.5	47.7	56.6	64.4
	(5.9)	(6.9)	(7.0)	(7.0)
Three-generation family	349.9	370.0	409.5	427.5
	(59.6)	(53.8)	(50.7)	(46.2)
Total	587.2	688.1	807.8	925.2
	(100.0)	(100.0)	(100.0)	(100.0)
Proportion of all households	(21.7)	(22.0)	(23.7)	(25.4)
Number of elderly persons				
Institutionalized	23.2	33.2	45.1	57.6
	(3.1)	(3.7)	(4.2)	(4.6)
Single-person family	41.0	60.0	84.6	116.0
	(5.5)	(6.8)	(7.9)	(9.3)
Independent nuclear family	211.6	281.5	356.6	454.4
	(28.6)	(31.8)	(33.5)	(36.4)
Two-generation family	42.2	59.3	70.9	82.0
	(5.7)	(6.7)	(6.7)	(6.6)
Three-generation family	421.3	452.5	507.5	536.8
	(57.0)	(51.0)	(47.7)	(43.1)
Total	739.3	886.5	1,064.7	1,246.8
	(100.0)	(100.0)	(100.0)	(100.0)
Proportion of entire population age 15 and over	(9.3)	(10.4)	(11.9)	(13.2)

SOURCE: Population Census, 1970, 1975, 1980, 1985.
NOTE: Unit = 10,000 households or persons; figures in parentheses indicate percentage of total. Each category of household may contain kin other than parents as additional members. Households that consist only of siblings are classified as "independent nuclear family."

Section 5 gives a summary of the analysis and discusses problems for future inquiry.

2. Characteristics of the Aged Population

According to the 1985 Population Census, there are 12.5 million people aged 65 and over in Japan, and this group constitutes 13.2 percent of the nation's population aged 15 and over. As the total figures in Table 1 show, this group has been increasing steadily in both absolute and relative terms.[2] A quite similar picture holds for the number of households. In 1985, there were 9.3 million households that had at least one member aged 65 and over, and this constitutes just about a quarter of all households.

Table 1 also shows the changes in the classification of household types over time. (The upper part of the table refers to the number of households falling into each category, while the lower part of the table refers to the number of aged individuals belonging to each category of household.) In 1985, in terms of numbers of individuals, roughly half of the aged individuals belonged to independent generation families (institutionalized, single-person, or independent [core] families), while the rest of the aged population lived with younger-generation families (as two-generation or three-generation families).[3] Although the proportion of aged people living with their children's families is still (internationally) very high, we observe a clear time trend such that: (i) both single-person households and independent (core) families of the aged generation are increasing, and (ii) three-generation families are rather rapidly decreasing. In fact, the rates of change in the relative composition of household types that have been observed for the last 15 years are so steady that, other things being equal, the proportion of independent generation families will outnumber that of two- and three-generation households combined within the coming decade.

Turning to the labor force participation rate of aged individuals, we observe from the Labor Force Survey that the participation rate for men aged 65 and over was just about 50 percent in 1970, and declined since then until reaching 37 percent in 1985.[4] (See also Seike [1986] for detailed analysis of the figures.) Still, this figure is internationally very high. In fact, the comparable figures for men aged 65–69 are 65 percent for Japan (1980), 28 percent for the United States (1980), and 17 percent for France (1977), while for women aged 65–69 the corresponding figures are 27 percent for Japan, 15 percent for the United States, and 9 percent for France (Economic Planning Agency, 1981: table II-4-5).

The decline in the labor force participation rate seems to have been influenced by the spread of the public pension system. Table 2, compiled from Ministry of Labour (1981) (a report on the special large-scale sample survey conducted in 1980 on the employment condition of the aged), shows how individuals aged 65–69 evaluate their own livelihood resources. While detailed responses are available only for healthy individuals (constituting 83.3 and 78.9 percent for men and women, respectively), 20.8 percent of men and 16.5 percent of women evaluate that they are healthy, living economically independent of their children, and supported primarily by pension benefits. These numbers are certainly adjusted upward when we add individuals who are ill but otherwise fall into the same category. This data source has been put to close statistical scrutiny by Motokawa and Mori (1981), Seike (1986), and Tachibanaki and Shimono (1985), all showing cross-sectionally statistically significant effects of public pension benefits on labor supply.

Table 2. Livelihood Resources as Evaluated by Individuals Aged 65–69, 1980

	Men			Women		
Livelihood resources	Total	Working	Not working	Total	Working	Not working
Healthy						
Support by self or spouse	62.2	48.1	14.1	30.6	15.9	14.7
Earnings more than half of total individual income	39.3	39.3	—	12.6	12.6	—
Earnings zero or less than half of total individual income	22.9	8.8	14.1	18.0	3.3	14.7
Major nonearnings income source						
Pension benefits	20.8	7.7	13.1	16.5	3.0	13.5
Others	2.1	1.1	1.0	1.5	0.3	1.2
Support by children	14.7	6.8	7.9	32.3	8.6	23.7
Earnings more than half of total individual income	4.9	4.9	—	5.0	5.0	—
Earnings zero or less than half of total individual income	9.8	1.9	7.9	27.3	3.6	23.7
Major nonearnings income source						
Pension benefits	9.5	1.8	7.7	26.5	3.5	23.0
Others	0.3	0.1	0.2	0.8	0.1	0.7
Support by other means	4.0	1.2	2.8	5.8	1.3	4.5
Ill or in poor health	16.7	3.5	13.2	21.1	2.0	19.1
Not classifiable	2.4	1.7	0.7	10.2	2.2	8.0
Total	100.0	61.8	38.7	100.0	30.0	70.0

SOURCE: Compiled from Ministry of Labour (1981), Table 16.
NOTE: Unit = percentage.

Furthermore, as reported by Seike (1986: 11–12), recipients of a major category of public pension benefits (*rōrei-nenkin* within the *Kōsei Nenkin* system) increased from roughly half a million people in 1970, to two million in 1980, and three million in 1984, while, at the same time, the average amount of benefit per recipient (*including* those receiving reduced benefits because of the earnings test) increased from ¥14,000 per month in 1970, to ¥100,000 per month in 1980, and to ¥116,000 per month in 1984 (in real terms this means a threefold increase between 1970 and 1984). Since the average monthly consumption level for aged couples in 1984 is ¥174,000 (National Survey of Family Income and Expenditure [NSFIE], vol. 7, table 44), such a benefit level indeed seems to provide an incentive for the recipients to retire from the labor force. Note, however, that the number (3 million) of recipients of that benefit is relatively small as compared with the total aged population of 12.5 million, and this no doubt corresponds to the fact that a large part of the aged population works to earn its living.[5]

The decline in the rate of labor force participation and the concomitant decline in the employment ratio also seem to have been caused by the demand side of the labor market. Although Seike carefully remarks that the tightness of the job market for the aged, as measured by the job vacancy/job desire ratio, has not changed much for the recent 20 years (with the exception of just before the first oil shock), with the ratio hovering around 0.1, such an observation cannot be viewed as conclusive evidence that the demand side does not play a role in the decline of the labor force participation ratio. This is because the job vacancy/job desire ratio measure (which is calculated on the basis of individuals and jobs registered at public employment offices) does not reflect the existence of *discouraged* workers.[6]

Table 3, again compiled from the same Ministry of Labour survey, provides a check as to how large the number of discouraged workers might possibly be. Among individuals aged 65–69, 16 percent of men and 15 percent of women are not working and yet simultaneously

Table 3. Labor Force Participation Status and Reasons for Not Working Currently among Individuals Aged 65–69, 1980

Labor force participation status	Men		Women	
Working full time	61.3		30.0	
	(50.2)		(15.1)	
Not working	38.7		70.0	
Willingly retired	(22.7)		(55.1)	
Desiring work	(16.0)		(14.9)	
(5)/(3)	0.413		0.213	
Reason those desiring work are not working currently				
All reasons	16.0	100.0	14.9	100.0
Illness	5.3	33.1	5.2	34.8
Family circumstances	0.8	5.3	3.6	24.1
No desirable job available	8.5	53.0	4.8	32.5
Skills and experience inapplicable	(4.1)	(25.7)	(0.9)	(6.0)
Working hours unsuitable	(1.3)	(8.0)	(1.0)	(6.8)
Pay insufficient	(0.4)	(2.5)	(0.1)	(1.0)
Other reasons	(2.7)	(16.8)	(2.8)	(18.7)
Other or reasons not classifiable	1.4	8.5	1.3	8.5

SOURCE: Ministry of Labour (1981), Tables 2 and 10.
NOTE: Unit = percentage.

"desire work." The lower half of the table gives the reasons reported by this group of individuals for not currently working. About a third is because of illness, and clearly this subgroup is correctly counted out of the labor force. Among the rest, just about half of the men and a third of the women (8.5 percent of the total men and 4.8 percent of the total women, both aged 65–69) state that they are somehow discouraged. It is worth noting that 4.1 percent of the total male population complains that they cannot utilize their accumulated skills and experience. Unfortunately, we do not know if those individuals, "discouraged" for non-health reasons, are actually *seeking* work, which is the major criterion for being included or excluded from the labor force statistics. Yet the hypothesis that aged individuals are increasingly falling into the category of discouraged workers (thus excluded from the labor force) certainly seems to be worth further testing. This is, however, beyond the scope of this paper.

Finally, we note the generally high savings rates of aged households. According to the 1980 Family Income and Expenditure Survey (FIES), employee households whose head is aged 65 or above have an average propensity to save (out of disposable income) of 13.6 percent. While this is 10 percentage points lower than the peak average propensity to save shown by households with heads aged 40–44, it is still a far cry from the textbook characterization of aged people who dissave.[7]

Twofold criticisms have been mounted of such an observation. First, because of the Statistics Bureau's criterion of identifying the household head as the principal earner of the household, many aged persons who are living with their children become hidden in the children's households. Therefore, the possible dissaving of the aged does not show up (Komiya, 1963). Second, there is a tendency for high income or large wealth holding individuals to form independent core families. In fact, Ando et al. (1986) give evidence that the probit equation of aged individuals living with their children carries a negative significant coefficient on the wealth level of the aged. These two factors are adduced as giving a serious upward bias to the savings rate of aged households.

These are valid criticisms. The aged households in the official statistical classification contain independent nuclear families as well as two- or three-generation families (by the definition of the Population Census) whose oldest generation is rich enough to surpass the income of the younger parents (or of the nonmarried children in the case of old nuclear families). In contrast, households whose head belongs to a younger age group may be nuclear families, or two- or three-generation families which contain an older generation parent (or parents) who earn(s) less than the younger generation. If we also take account of Ando et al.'s (1986) and Hayashi et al.'s (1988) evidence that the elderly people who form independent nuclear families are on average more wealthy than similarly aged individuals, then there is an inherent selection bias that renders the aged households in the official classification prone to be high income and high savings households.[8]

Unfortunately, because of the data deficiencies of the Family Savings Survey (FSS) that (a) the ages of individual household members are not known and therefore independent nuclear families vis-à-vis extended families are not identifiable, (b) the compositions of income earned and assets owned by individual household members are not known, and (c) single-person households are excluded entirely from the sample, we cannot directly evaluate the magnitude of these selection biases and devise ways to avoid them. Whether a randomly chosen elderly individual is saving or dissaving is thus not answerable by our data.[9]

The effect of the elderly population on overall household savings can, however, still be analyzed using the official statistical classification of household age groups by separating the problem into two steps: first, evaluate the extent to which elderly people subsumed in the younger generation's households affect the latter's savings behavior as a whole, and second, evaluate the determinants of the savings behavior of the aged households as they appear on the surface of the sample data. There are three basic presumptions for justifying such a research strategy. First, the subsumed elders in the younger generation households are an *economically inactive* population (who have ceased to be independent economic decision makers), whereas the aged household heads appearing in the data, regardless of whether they are living with children, are an economically active population. Second, whether a particular elderly person or couple is economically inactive (subsumed) is determined by noneconomic factors such as condition of health, death of a spouse, and closeness of personal affection between the members of different generations. Third, the variables we consider as determinants of saving, in particular, employment status and the factors which determine that status (which is the focus of our study below) involve household choices that occur strictly within the realm of the economically active status. Thus whether a household head chooses to be employed or retired is unrelated to his or her becoming subsumed in the children's household.

To the extent that the second assumption does not strictly hold in reality so that economic factors actually influence the probability of elders becoming economically inactive, our research leaves some room for bias in the analysis of each step.[10] Yet in view of our chosen focus, not to answer whether the elderly are saving or dissaving per se but to explain the sources of variations in the savings behavior among the economically active elderly population, the validity of the analysis depends more on the less questionable third assumption. Therefore, as a first approximation we shall conduct the following analysis by ignoring the above possible bias, and leave the analysis of its impact for a future occasion with a richer set of data.

The following section deals with the effect of the subsumed aged parent(s) on the savings rate of households headed by the younger generation. The analysis of the economically active elderly is relegated to Section 4.

3. The Effect of the Presence of Elders on the Savings Behavior of Households Headed by the Younger Generation

Available data limitations restrict us to two kinds of cross-tabulated tables in the 1984 NSFIE. The samples are for employees (excluding corporate managers) only. The first table cross-classifies households by the household head's age, by who is working in the household (WKSPOUSE = 1 if spouse is working, = 0 if not; WKOTHERS = 1 if member other than spouse is working, = 0 if not), and by the presence of children and aged family members (CHILDREN = 1 if children are present, = 0 if not; PARENT = 1 if aged parent(s) are present, = 0 if not). The second table, on the other hand, cross-classifies households by income level (DY),[11] by homeownership status (HOME = 1 if owner, = 0 if renter, and in addition, DETACHED = 1 if owner of an independently detached house, = 0 if not), and by the presence of children and aged family members (CHILDREN and PARENT defined above).

The results of the weighted OLS regressions of the average saving propensity on these dummy variables are shown in Tables 4 and 5. Table 4 shows that the supposed negative effect of the presence of aged parents on household savings increases as the age of the household head rises (for the age group 50–59, the effect is to lower the savings ratio by 1.9 percent), but that the effect is hardly statistically significant.

Table 5 is more informative. When we control the homeownership status (HOME and DETACHED), in addition to income (DY), a statistically significant negative effect appears. Thus the presence of aged parents amounts to lowering the savings rate by 1.5 to 1.7 percent *in net* after the specified controls (see regressions (3) and (4)).

It may not be appropriate, however, to evaluate this effect under control of homeownership status. It is often suggested that parents living together with a child's family offer their own house in which to

Table 4. The Effect of the Presence of Aged Parents on the Savings Rate of Merged Households: Working Members and Head's Age Controlled; Employee Households with Head's Age 30–59, 1984

	(1) Age 30–39	(2) Age 40–49	(3) Age 50–59	(4) Age 30–59
Constant	0.127	0.105	0.082	0.124
	(6.63)**	(6.92)**	(7.19)**	(10.2)**
AGE40S	—	—	—	−0.019
				(−2.43)*
AGE50S	—	—	—	−0.041
				(−3.91)**
WKSPOUSE	0.083	0.066	0.068	0.072
	(7.65)**	(9.28)**	(6.09)**	(10.3)**
WKOTHERS	0.015	0.037	0.121	0.069
	(0.59)	(3.26)**	(9.15)**	(6.40)**
CHILDREN	−0.022	−0.007	−0.039	−0.014
	(−1.12)	(−0.48)	(−2.76)*	(−1.24)
PARENT	0.002	−0.010	−0.019	−0.013
	(0.14)	(−1.12)	(−1.43)	(−1.52)
df	9	9	9	35
Mean dep.	0.137	0.134	0.132	0.135
SSR	0.00320	0.00154	0.00385	0.01690
R^2 adj.	0.825	0.883	0.906	0.787

SOURCE: National Survey of Family Income and Expenditure, 1984 (Vol. I, Part 1, Table 23).
NOTE: Dependent variable = total savings rate. Figures in parentheses give *t* ratios; * and ** indicate statistical significance at 5 and 1 percent, respectively. Employees do not include corporate managers.

live. Actually 92.9 percent of the households with elderly parents living with their children (i.e., PARENT = 1) in the sample own an independently detached house, while only 53.4 percent of the nuclear households (i.e., PARENT = 0) own an independently detached house.[12] More direct evidence is given by regressions (5) through (7) that take the net financial asset/(monthly) disposable income ratio (NFAY) as the dependent variable. As can be seen from regression (5) (and also from regressions [6] and [7]), NFAY decreases significantly for owner–dweller households (note also that ownership of an independently detached house recovers about two-thirds of this negative effect), and we can easily allude to (i) the substitution of real assets for financial assets, and/or (ii) the incurrence of financial debt as the likely causes. However, regressions (6) and (7) reveal that the presence of aged parents significantly offsets this decrease. Moreover, the fact that the estimated coefficient on PARENT × DETACHED in (7) is larger than that on PARENT in (6) with virtually no changes in the coefficients of the other variables indicates that the effect of the presence of aged parents occurs in combination with homeownership, or more specifically, independently detached house ownership. A natural interpretation of this is that the effect in question arises *because* parents

Table 5. The Effect of the Presence of Aged Parents on the Savings Behavior of Merged Households: Income Level and Homeownership Controlled; Employee Households, 1984

Dependent variable	*S* (Total savings rate)				NFAY (Net finan. asset/disp.income)		
	(1)	(2)	(3)	(4)	(5)	(6)	(7)
Constant	0.238	0.172	0.176	0.176	33.3	32.1	32.4
	(9.88)**	(11.7)**	(12.0)**	(12.1)**	(13.1)**	(14.1)**	(14.2)**
HOME	—	0.0754	0.0614	0.0753	−18.7	−18.7	−18.5
		(6.49)**	(9.90)**	(6.61)**	(−9.32)**	(−10.4)**	(−10.3)**
DETACHED	—	−0.0191	—	−0.0157	12.7	11.4	11.0
		(−1.75)		(−1.45)	(6.71)**	(6.71)**	(6.39)**
CHILDREN	0.161×10^{-4}	−0.0191	−0.0185	−0.0186	−10.4	−10.5	−10.5
	(−0.490)	(−2.55)**	(−2.51)**	(−2.53)**	(−8.01)**	(−9.11)**	(−9.07)**
PARENT	0.815×10^{-6}	—	−0.0165	−0.0150	—	5.49	—
	(−0.030)		(−2.33)*	(−2.11)*		(4.92)**	
PARENT × DETACHED	—	—	—	—	—	—	5.67
							(4.83)**
1/DY	−30.6	−19.3	−20.3	−20.2	−3396.2	−3092.3	−3131.1
	(−6.07)**	(−6.46)**	(−6.80)**	(−6.80)**	(−6.57)**	(−6.64)**	(−6.71)**
SE	0.0375	0.0261	0.0258	0.0257	4.51	4.03	4.05
R^2adj.	0.351	0.685	0.693	0.696	0.628	0.703	0.701

SOURCE: National Survey of Family Income and Expenditure, 1984 (Vol. I, Part 1, Table 32).
NOTE: See Table 4. $N = 97$. Mean of the dependent variable (S) = 0.130; (NFAY) = 8.09.

provide the house (or the detached house), thereby alleviating the financial burden of homeownership for the child's household. Indeed the sum of the coefficients on DETACHED and PARENT × DETACHED in (7) almost completely offsets the coefficient on HOME.

Thus it would be a significant overestimate of the negative effect of the presence of parents on savings to believe the figures of −1.5 to −1.7 percent obtained in regressions (3) and (4). The polar alternative of excluding the controls on household ownership altogether (regression [1]) suggests that this effect is completely zero. While the truth must lie somewhere in between, it is most likely that the effect is nil and statistically insignificant.

All the foregoing discussions based on Tables 4 and 5, however, are subject to the qualification that all the relevant explanatory factors on savings are effectively controlled; the validity of this is surely to be questioned. Notice that the age and the size of the working members in the household, which have been controlled in obtaining Table 4, were not controlled in obtaining Table 5, and conversely, that income and homeownership status, which have been controlled in obtaining Table 5, were not controlled in obtaining Table 4. While the final resolution must await the future availability of the original microdata, we may note that (i) the bias arising from not controlling for homeownership is very small, as argued in the previous paragraph, and (ii) the age and size of the working members are significantly correlated with the income for worker households, thus making the bias arising from not controlling for these variables probably very small. In short, we expect our discussion to survive through the expansion of the set of explanatory variables.

Our tentative conclusion is thus as follows. The presence of aged parents does not affect the savings rate of the younger generation households that accommodate them. The primary reason appears to be that the parents tend to provide the young with a house (and more likely an independently detached house) in which to live, which offsets the otherwise negative effect (estimated at around −1.5 to −1.7 percent) on the merged household's savings.

4. A Simultaneous Equations Model of the Employment and Savings Behavior of Aged Households

In my previous work (Ishikawa, 1987), I made a cross-tabulation analysis of the savings propensity of (economically active) aged households using the FSS microdata (for the period 1976–84). Its main finding was that, even controlling for income (i.e., two-year average of disposable income), the savings rate is greatly affected by the presence of a working elderly person in the family. Households with no working elderly members on average save very little and financially dissave (albeit at a small rate), while those with working members continually save at a relatively high rate (See note 7 for numbers.).

Theoretically, the most well-known hypothesis that links the high employment rate to the high savings rate of the households is the prototype life-cycle savings hypothesis. Within that framework, the employment period and the savings period are equated a priori, and retirement from work immediately means the start of asset decumulation. Obviously, therefore, the more delayed the retirement is, the higher the average savings rate of households above any specified age becomes. But then the question simply reduces to an explanation of delayed retirement for Japanese households. (Recall Mizoguchi's [1973] argument noted earlier that the high employment ratio among the elderly associated with low public pension benefit levels was the major reason for their high savings rate.) Furthermore, it would easily lead to the prediction that the ongoing decline in the labor force participation rate would bring about a decrease in the savings rate of the elderly (although it may simultaneously invite a greater effort for saving by younger households).

Once we allow for the existence of a precautionary motive and/or a bequest motive besides the basic consumption smoothing motive, however, there is no necessity that the employment period be identical to the savings period.[13] Employment and saving would both serve the same end. In such a circumstance, the decline in the employment ratio, or equivalently, the tendency for earlier retirement, may not necessarily lower the savings rate of aged households. To anticipate our conclusion, this is indeed the picture that we obtain from our data.

In order to examine the possible interaction between employment and savings behavior of the household, we shall estimate a simultaneous equations model, consisting of a probit equation explaining the 1–0 choice of employment by the household head, and a savings ratio equation that includes this qualitative dummy variable as a jointly endogenous variable. Using this model, we wish to see:

(a) to what extent the actual degree of labor supply by the elderly contributes to the savings rate of aged households as a whole;

(b) if employment is endogenous in explaining the savings propensity, or if it is truly exogenous;

(c) to what extent the future savings behavior of the aged is affected in the advent of various institutional changes regarding support for the elderly, e.g., changes in social security institutions.

THE MODEL

The model we consider is expressed by

$$\mathrm{DLP}_i^* = Z_i\gamma - u_i \tag{1}$$

$$S_i = X_i\beta + \mathrm{DLP}_i \cdot \alpha + v_i \tag{2}$$

$$\begin{aligned} \mathrm{DLP}_i &= 1 \quad \text{if } \mathrm{DLP}_i^* \geq 0 \\ &= 0 \quad \text{if } \mathrm{DLP}_i^* < 0. \end{aligned} \tag{3}$$

The subscript i refers to each household ($i = 1, \ldots, N$). DLP_i^* measures the potential labor supply pressure of the household. Although DLP_i^* is not directly observable, we interpret the ex post observation that the household is actually employed (namely $\mathrm{DLP}_i = 1$) to have arisen because the potential pressure has surpassed a certain threshold value, which is chosen here to be 0. As seen from (1), $\mathrm{DLP}_i^* \geq 0$ is equivalent to $Z_i\gamma \geq u_i$. Z_i is a vector of observable explanatory variables, while u_i is an unobservable disturbance (error) term. S_i is the total savings rate as defined by the sum of financial savings and real savings (mainly housing investment) divided by disposable income, (X_i, DLP_i) is the vector of explanatory variables, and v_i is an unobservable error term. The contents of the vectors Z_i and X_i are specified later.

As for the error terms (u_i, v_i), we suppose that they are independent for each i, and that they follow an identical joint normal distribution,

$$(u_i, v_i) \sim N[(0, 0), \Sigma],$$

where

$$\Sigma = \begin{bmatrix} 1 & \rho\sigma \\ \rho\sigma & \sigma^2 \end{bmatrix}. \tag{4}$$

We also suppose that the explanatory variables (X_i, Z_i) are statistically independent of (u_i, v_i). As usual with the standard probit analysis, the variance of u_i is normalized to 1. ρ is the correlation coefficient between u_i and v_i. As is easily seen from (1)–(3), any joint endogeneity between S_i and DLP_i is reflected in the correlation between these error terms. On the other hand, $\rho = 0$ implies that (so long as X_i is independent of v_i) DLP_i is independent of v_i, and hence, it is exogenous in the explanation of S_i.

Our strategic concern in the estimation is the coefficients α and ρ. Because we allow the error terms to be mutually correlated, the entire model (1)–(3) is estimated simultaneously.[14] In the following, we shall exploit assumption (4) in obtaining the maximum likelihood estimate for the coefficient vector $(\alpha, \beta, \gamma, \rho, \sigma^2)$. We shall not go into detail on the methodology, but rather satisfy ourselves by writing down the concentrated log-likelihood function that can be derived as

$$\log L(\alpha, \beta, \gamma, \rho, \sigma) = -\frac{N}{2}\{\log(2\pi + 1)\} - N \log \sigma$$
$$+ \sum_{i=1}^{N} \left\{ \mathrm{DLP}_i \cdot \log \Phi\left(\frac{Z_i \gamma}{\sqrt{1-\rho^2}} - \frac{\eta}{\sigma^2} v_i \right) \right.$$
$$\left. + (1 - \mathrm{DLP}_i) \cdot \log \left[1 - \Phi\left(\frac{Z_i \gamma}{\sqrt{1-\rho^2}} - \frac{\eta}{\sigma^2} v_i \right) \right] \right\}$$

where

$$\eta = \frac{\rho\sigma}{\sqrt{1-\rho^2}}, \qquad v_i = S_i - X_i\beta - \mathrm{DLP}_i \cdot \alpha,$$

and $\Phi(\cdot)$ expresses the cumulative distribution function of a standardized normal variable. We employed an iterative optimization procedure to obtain the actual estimates.[15] A similar model has been developed by Lee and Trost (1978) in a slightly more general context of switching regression models and has been applied to the estimation of the household's choice of owner–renter housing tenure choice. Our model is formally a special case of that model.

DATA

The data base for our study is the six reinterview sets of the FSS microdata for 1976–77, and 1979–80 through 1983–84, obtained by formal permission from the Statistics Bureau. Each household in the sample was interviewed at the end of each year for two consecutive years. In our study, the flow variables, such as disposable income (YAVR), disposable noninterest income (WAVR), and savings (SAVR) refer to the two-year average of *real* quantities. All the household attributes (See Table 6.) in addition to employment status (DLP) refer to those of the second year. All the stock variables, the financial asset (FA), the financial debt (FD), and the net financial asset (NFA = FA − FD), refer to the *real* value at the end of the first year. All the real values refer to the respective nominal values deflated by the consumption price index (that is normalized as 1 in 1980). The variable S_i appearing in (2) is calculated as $\mathrm{SAVR}_i/\mathrm{YAVR}_i$. By employing the two-year average magnitudes we expect that some part of each household's year-to-year variations in flow variables is eliminated. (Nevertheless, the remaining variations in the savings rate among households still appear to be large.)

Table 6. Mean Sample Characteristics of the FSS Data for Households with Household Heads Aged 65 and Over, 1976–84

Attribute	Variable	Sample mean
Sample size	N	1,386
Household attributes		
Head's age	AGE	70.9
Size of household	SIZE	3.07
Dweller status and location of residence		
House owner	HOME	0.844
Residence in major metropolitan area	METRO	0.530
House owner in major metropolitan area	METHOME	0.428
Employment status		
Employed	DLP	0.673
As employee (corporate manager included)		0.199
As self-employed		0.474
Income, financial assets, and debt		
Disposable income	YAVR	355.0
After-tax noninterest income	WAVR	317.9
Noninterest income ratio	WAVR/YAVR	0.906
Financial asset/disposable income ratio	FA/YAVR	2.38
Net financial asset/disposable income ratio	NFAY	2.27
Rate of saving		
Total savings ratio	S	0.097
Financial savings ratio	FS	0.072

NOTE: For YAVR and WAVR, income is measured in terms of ¥10,000 (1980). Major metropolitan area refers to Keihin, Chūkyō, Keihanshin, and Kita-Kyūshū metropolitan districts.

Our samples are restricted to those with the household head (= major earner) aged 65 and over. That the head is working, $\text{DLP}_i = 1$ (not working, $\text{DLP}_i = 0$), is judged by the size of the working member being greater than zero (equal to zero, respectively). We do not distinguish between employees and the self-employed.[16]

The major defect of the data for our present purpose is that it does not provide any direct information on the pension benefit receipts of each household. Of course, because our sample periods extend over many years, some portion of the variations, in particular, variations over time in the number of recipients as well as the individual benefit levels, are reflected in the data. Time variations may be picked up by dummy variables, D80 (= 1 for 1979–80 samples) through D84 (= 1 for 1983–84 samples), but the remaining individual variation must be pushed to the error term u_i, and thus some interpretative ambiguity remains unresolved.

Much imputation work was necessary in order to make this data set usable for our purpose. This is briefly explained in the Appendix. All sample data are pooled in the estimation task except for allowing yearly shifts in the constant term of the employment probability equation. The average characteristics of the sample households are summarized in Table 6.

SPECIFICATION OF EXPLANATORY VARIABLES

In view of the available data, we have chosen the vector Z in the probit equation to consist of

$$Z = [1, \mathrm{METRO}, \mathrm{SIZE}, \mathrm{HOME}, \mathrm{AGE}, \mathrm{SQAGE}, \mathrm{FA}, \mathrm{FD}, \text{Yearly Dummies } (\mathrm{D80}, \mathrm{D81}, \mathrm{D82}, \mathrm{D83}, \mathrm{D84})],$$

where all variables other than those previously defined and SQAGE (= AGE squared) are explained in Table 6. In contrast to the previous studies addressed to the employment behavior of aged individuals (references given below), the important variables missing from the above list are the amount of pension benefits received and the condition of health, which are repeatedly found to be significant explanatory variables. The potential market wage offered to the household head is desirable, yet ignored here because no information on the head's past employment history or schooling is available. All these variables are thus pushed into the individual error term u_i.

Among these nonobservable variables, perhaps the most troublesome is the amount of pension benefits. Although, as previously noted, a part of the total variation is expected to be caught by the yearly dummies, the remaining variations among individual households may not be statistically independent of the variables in Z. In particular, these individual variations are likely to be positively correlated with the amount of financial asset (FA), for the variable portion of the benefit depends on the earnings level and the length of job tenure at the time of retirement, and we observe among households a positive correlation between annual earnings and accumulated financial assets. The qualification of this argument is that it is based on the presumption that households do not substitute expected pension wealth for nonpension financial wealth. In fact, the time-series and cross-section evidence of this substitution effect is at best very weak (See Sasaki and Tachibanaki [1985] and references therein.),[17] and we can safely ignore it. In any case, we must exercise care in interpreting the coefficient of FA.

The aged households in our sample on average saved 9.7 percent of their disposable income, its composition being 7.2 percent for financial savings and 2.5 percent for real (mostly housing) savings. While explanation of the composition of savings is also an interesting subject for study, the results for estimating the same model with the financial savings rate as the dependent variable generally are parallel with those for the total savings rate, and hence are omitted from this paper.

Table 7. Maximum Likelihood Estimates of the Employment and Savings Equations

	I		II	
Model	Coeff.	SE	Coeff.	SE
Constant	18.8	6.28	19.1	6.31
METRO	0.269	0.0835	0.269	0.0835
SIZE	0.662	0.0503	0.663	0.0503
HOME	−0.0422	0.108	−0.0450	0.108
AGE	−0.486	0.170	−0.494	0.171
SQAGE	0.00285	0.00115	0.00291	0.00116
FA	0.000148	0.0000502	0.000154	0.0000507
FD	0.000889	0.000280	0.000880	0.000279
D80	−0.193	0.158	−0.188	0.159
D81	−0.135	0.162	−0.132	0.162
D82	−0.303	0.161	−0.298	0.162
D83	−0.415	0.158	−0.411	0.159
D84	−0.675	0.156	−0.668	0.156
Constant	−0.230	0.201	−0.158	0.209
SIZE	−0.0275	0.00808	−0.0284	0.00917
HOME	0.0293	0.0383	0.0355	0.0379
METHOME	−0.0171	0.0226	−0.00850	0.0229
AGE	0.00561	0.00273	0.00550	0.00280
1/YAVR	−21.7	4.91	−24.1	5.00
DLP	0.137	0.0494	0.0909	0.0607
Rho	0.149	0.0586	0.0916	0.0850
NFAY			−0.0142	0.00394
Sigma	0.364		0.362	
log *lkhd.*	−1240.0		−1233.7	

SOURCE: FSS microdata; $N = 1386$.
NOTE: Dependent variable = savings rate. Based on eqs. (1), (2), and (3).

As for the explanatory vector X in the savings rate equation, we take

$$X = [1, \text{SIZE}, \text{HOME}, \text{METHOME}, \text{AGE}, \text{NFAY}, 1/\text{YAVR}].$$

In this list, 1/YAVR corresponds to the constant term in the customary linear savings function. NFAY is defined as NFA (= FA − FD) divided by YAVR.

The result of estimating equations (1)–(3) simultaneously is given in Table 7. (Note that rho and sigma in the table mean the coefficients ρ and σ, respectively.)[18] The table gives estimates for two versions; one in which equation (2) excludes NFAY (Model I), and another in which the same equation includes NFAY (Model II). As far as the estimated coefficients of the employment equation are concerned (i.e., the top portion in Table 7, and similarly for Table 8), there is virtually no change between the two versions. With the exception of those for

HOME and for earlier yearly dummies (D80, D81, and D82), the estimated coefficients are all statistically significant (at least) at the 5 percent level.

Our result conforms well with those of the previous studies (Motokawa and Mori, 1981; Seike, 1982; Tachibanaki and Shimono, 1985; all based on the same microdata set of the Ministry of Labour survey, 1981). The fact that AGE has a negative coefficient and that SIZE and FD both have positive coefficients requires little explanation. The positive coefficient on METRO is perhaps most naturally construed as reflecting the existence of larger opportunities for work in major metropolitan areas. Increasingly large negative coefficients on yearly dummies are consistent with the existence of the declining time trend in the labor force participation rate among aged people, as discussed earlier (the major reason for which might very well be the increased public pension benefits in recent years).

Most notably, our result confirms the property found in previous studies in that level of financial assets (FA) is associated positively with employment probability. Previously, such an association was found even after explicitly taking account of the negative impact of public pension benefits. (See Motokawa and Mori (1981: 12, fig. 6; 13, table 4), Tachibanaki and Shimono (1985: 245, table 5), and Seike (1982: 20, Table 2).) Given our supposition stated earlier that the financial asset holding and the public pension benefit are positively correlated, our own estimate must be understating this positive impact.[19]

In any case, this positive association requires an interpretation. The only interpretation of this finding attempted thus far is that of Seike (1982: 22). He referred to the Greenberg and Kosters study of the negative income tax experiment in suggesting that the positive coefficient may be a reflection of the differences in the preference fields among households concerning financial accumulation (or simply put, differences in the accumulation motive). Namely, in comparing households with similar income, highly "accumulation motivated" households are more likely to have already accumulated a larger financial asset, on the one hand, and are naturally prone to supply more labor, on the other (cf. Greenberg and Kosters, 1973: 20, 30–35). For our convenience, let us call the hypothesis the "motivational difference" hypothesis. It should be noted that Seike merely suggested this as a plausible hypothesis; he has yet to verify it against data. Although a rigorous empirical testing of the above hypothesis requires data of each household's employment and earnings history, which are beyond our reach, we shall attempt a tentative evaluation of it and, at the same time, suggest an alternative to the motivational difference hypothesis.

ESTIMATION RESULT (2): THE SAVINGS BEHAVIOR OF AGED HOUSEHOLDS

The estimated coefficients for the savings rate equation can be read from the lower part of Table 7. There are two reasons why we estimated two versions, one without NFAY (Model I) and another with NFAY (Model II). First, it would facilitate a provisional test of the motivational difference hypothesis. Second, it shows whether the savings rate depends, in addition to income level, on the composition of income or the wealth level itself.

We start by discussing the first. Suppose motivational differences for accumulation lie at the heart of the differences in employment probability that remain even after various household attributes are controlled for. Since NFAY coupled with controls on income level, ownership of real wealth (HOME and METHOME), and other household attributes becomes a proxy variable for the strength of the accumulation motive, we should expect the following for the coefficients of Model I and Model II. (i) The estimate of α for Model I is positive, while that of α for Model II diminishes, if not to zero; (ii) the estimated coefficient for NFAY for Model II must be positive.

When we look at Table 7, we find that (i) is satisfied. In fact, α for Model I is 0.137 and is statistically significantly different (at the 1-percent level) from zero, but once we add NFAY to the equation, α is reduced to 0.0909 and loses statistical significance. On the other hand, (ii) does not hold. The estimated coefficient on NFAY (for Model II) becomes −0.0142 and is statistically significant at the 1-percent level. Hence, we conclude provisionally that the motivational difference hypothesis is not supported by our data. In the following, we shall assume that, once the income level is controlled for, not much difference in the accumulation motive remains among aged households.[20]

We now turn to the second question. The result that the savings rate depends on NFAY suggests that savings behavior might depend not only on total disposable income but also on the composition of income between earned income and interest income. If this is indeed the case, then our equation (2) cannot be judged the appropriate model to evaluate the effect of employment behavior on savings. Hence we try a slightly different form of equation (2),

$$S_i = X_i\beta + DLP_i \cdot (\mathrm{WAVR}_i/\mathrm{YAVR}_i) \cdot \alpha' + v_i, \qquad (5)$$

where $\mathrm{WAVR}_i/\mathrm{YAVR}_i$ expresses the proportion of noninterest (disposable) income to total (disposable) income. We thus suppose that employment affects savings to the extent that it raises the noninterest component of income. The meaning of this modification is perhaps more easily understood by rewriting (5) as follows. By summarizing the term $X_i\beta$ by δ_i, and using the identity $1 = (\text{WAVR}_i/\text{YAVR}_i) + (\text{PAVR}_i/\text{YAVR}_i)$, where PAVR_i denotes (after tax) interest income, we obtain

$$S_i = (\delta_i + \alpha' \cdot \text{DLP}_i)(\text{WAVR}_i/\text{YAVR}_i) + \delta_i(\text{PAVR}_i/\text{YAVR}_i). \quad (5')$$

Effectively we are assuming that the saving propensity from non-interest income depends on whether WAVR_i is, in fact, obtained by employment or obtained from nonemployment sources (mainly pension benefits). (Note that in our data, PAVR_i is directly observable, while WAVR_i is obtained as a residual from YAVR_i.) In the former case, the saving propensity becomes $\delta_i + \alpha'$, while in the latter case it is δ_i. Of course, were we to have direct observation of pension benefits, a more refined formulation (that separates WAVR_i into the true earnings component and the pension benefit component) would become meaningful. However, given the data limitation, we regard (5′) as a first-order approximation. This approximation, however, is buttressed somewhat by the institutional datum of the presence of the earnings test in obtaining qualification for actually receiving benefits (its empirical importance has been attested by Seike [1982]).

The result of simultaneously estimating the new system (1), (5), and (3) is reported in Table 8. Again two versions, one without NFAY (Model III) and another with NFAY (Model IV), are given. The coefficients for the employment equation are virtually unchanged as compared with the previous table. The most important result concerning the savings equation is that, even for the case where NFAY is included (i.e., Model IV), the coefficient α' (of DLP_i) maintains a statistically significant (at the 1-percent level) positive value. ρ also assumes a statistically significant (again at the 1-percent level) positive value, the point estimates being 0.20 for Model III and 0.13 for Model IV. This is clear evidence that the employment status variable acts as an endogenous variable in the determination of savings behavior, which facilitates our answer to query (b) raised in the beginning of this section. For other coefficients, the estimates do not vary much between Model III and Model IV. The coefficient on NFAY itself takes, even under the new formulation, a statistically significant negative value of −0.011.

All variables but HOME and METHOME are statistically significant (while the ownership of a house tends to raise the savings rate, its effect is not statistically significant). The feature that the household size (SIZE) diminishes the savings rate is common for all age groups, and, obviously, it represents the increase in livelihood needs. The positive coefficient on AGE is somewhat surprising (especially vis-à-vis the pure

Table 8. Maximum Likelihood Estimates of the Employment and Savings Equations

Model	III Coeff.	III SE	IV Coeff.	IV SE
Constant	17.6	6.29	18.4	6.32
METRO	0.271	0.0836	0.274	0.0835
SIZE	0.659	0.0501	0.665	0.0496
HOME	−0.0473	0.109	−0.0492	0.108
AGE	−0.455	0.171	−0.476	0.171
SQAGE	0.00265	0.00115	0.00279	0.00116
FA	0.000151	0.0000500	0.000158	0.0000507
FD	0.000975	0.000274	0.00115	0.000256
D80	−0.207	0.158	−0.202	0.158
D81	−0.134	0.162	−0.135	0.162
D82	−0.310	0.161	−0.305	0.162
D83	−0.415	0.158	−0.412	0.159
D84	−0.679	0.155	−0.673	0.156
Constant	−0.334	0.174	−0.245	0.177
SIZE	−0.0355	0.00796	−0.0335	0.00810
HOME	0.0288	0.0381	0.0334	0.0379
METHOME	−0.0147	0.0225	−0.00790	0.0229
AGE	0.00695	0.00251	0.00644	0.00248
1/YAVR	−22.1	4.63	−23.9	4.74
DLP × (WAVR/YAVR)	0.199	0.0376	0.143	0.0442
Rho	0.201	0.0377	0.136	0.0481
NFAY			−0.0113	0.00432
Sigma	0.365		0.362	
log *lkhd.*	−1233.4		−1231.4	

SOURCE: Family Savings Survey microdata; $N = 1386$.
NOTE: Dependent variable = savings rate. Based on eqs. (1), (5), and (3).

life-cycle hypothesis), yet it is also most naturally explained by the fact that living needs decline with advancing age. (Note here that in Japan, direct medical bills for individuals aged 70 and above are heavily aided by the social security system.) The small but negative coefficient on NFAY seems to suggest that households have some accumulation target in mind, rather than pursuing indefinite accumulation.

Based on the estimates of Model IV, let us evaluate how much difference it makes in the savings rate between the households that work and those that do not. If we employ the sample average figures (for the dummy variables, the proportion of households that take the value 1) given in Table 6, the average δ_i becomes 4.1 percent, while the average value of α' ($WAVR_i/YAVR_i$) becomes 13.0 percent. Hence, evaluated on the basis of average household characteristics and the mean level of the income distribution, the average saving propensity for nonworking households is 4.1 percent, and that for working households is 17.1

percent, with a 13.0 percent difference between them. This is the contribution of employment per se, which facilitates our answer to query (a). (Actually, however, the average income is lower for nonworking households, which is why they save very little [around 1.5 percent] and financially dissave on average as noted earlier.)

In sum, employment raises household savings because the preference of households, shown (though tentatively) to be relatively homogeneous in nature, is structured in such a way that households treat employment earnings as a source of continued accumulation up to a certain level. The reason Japanese households exhibit such a preference must be explained on much deeper cultural grounds, but we can speculate that it might further be traced to the precautionary and/or bequest motive discussed in the opening part of the present section.

THE EMPLOYMENT BEHAVIOR AGAIN AND SOME GENERAL IMPLICATIONS

How are we, then, to interpret the positive coefficient on the financial asset (FA) variable in the employment probability equation? We have previously noted that, within the confines of the present data, the motivational difference hypothesis is not positively confirmed. A natural alternative, it seems to me, is to suppose that the level of financial assets (besides the METRO variable noted earlier) acts as a proxy for the household's accessibility to the employment opportunity. For, as we discussed in Section 2, the employment status of aged individuals seems to depend equally as much on the demand side of the labor market as on their own voluntary choice. And, given the highly stratified labor market according to firm sizes and occupations, with large-sized firms and professional occupations having the advantage not merely in terms of earnings levels throughout employment tenure but also in locating employment opportunities after mandatory retirement (which may not arise, of course, in the case of professional occupations), it is easily expected that accumulated financial assets and employment probability are positively correlated, even under homogeneous preference structure. (We may find Shinohara's [1963] point echoed here.)

Our result shows that aged households that are able to secure employment continue to save on average nearly four times as much as those households that are not employed. Although the resulting gap in the wealth level does not widen indefinitely, due to the decelerating factor we found (i.e., the negative coefficient on NFAY), and also due to the ultimate death of the household head, still a significant gap arises in terms of bequeathable wealth to children among households. Inequality of wealth arising from inequality in employment opportunities for the aged is then transmitted over generations.

Second, let us return to the fact of the declining labor force participation rate. In terms of this trend, Japan is no exception among the developed countries. Although our own data cannot verify this directly, there is sufficient evidence from previous studies (referred to earlier) that the recent increase in public pension benefits, and institutional earnings limitations in obtaining qualification for such benefits, lie as a major factor explaining this trend. We have also discussed the imminent and growing difficulty on the part of the elderly to secure agreeable employment opportunities.

If these environmental changes are purely exogenous shocks, then we can employ our estimated model in predicting their effect on the savings rate of aged households. Let us conduct a simple simulation experiment. Starting from the present employment rate (67 percent for our sample), what happens to the savings rate when the exogenous shocks lower the employment rate by 10 or 20 percent? (We assume there are no other changes in the observable exogenous variables such as household attributes.) The extent of the shocks can be evaluated as an upward shift in the mean value of the (marginal) distribution of u_i. Denote this by Δu. By using numbers from the cumulative normal distribution table, the magnitude of Δu that changes the employment ratio from 67 to 57 percent or from 67 to 47 percent is obtained as 0.264 or 0.515, respectively. The effect on the savings rate is evaluated as the sum of (i) the *direct* effect of the change in the employment ratio as expressed by the term $(\alpha' \cdot (\text{WAVR}/\text{YAVR}) \cdot \Delta\text{DLP})$ in (5), and (ii) the *indirect* effect that arises from the existence of a positive correlation between u_i and v_i. Table 9 shows the magnitudes of direct and indirect effects as calculated on the basis of our Model IV estimates. We observe that the two components almost exactly cancel each other out, leaving the net effect on savings virtually zero. Hence, as long as the shocks on employment behavior are purely exogenous, they do not affect the savings rate at all.

Table 9. The Effect of an Exogenous Shock to the Employment Behavior on the Savings Behavior of Aged Households

Changes in the employment ratio	Corresponding Δu	Direct effect $= \alpha'(\text{WAVR}/\text{YAVR}) \times \Delta\text{DLP}$	Indirect effect $= \rho\sigma \times \Delta u$	Change in the average savings ratio
10% decrease	0.264	−0.013	0.013	0.000
20% decrease	0.515	−0.026	0.025	−0.001

NOTE: Initial value of the employment ratio = 0.67.
SOURCE: Based on Model IV coefficient estimates (Table 8).

While the above experiment is quite informative in that the current savings behavior of aged households is very robust, we must exercise care in regarding the kind of institutional changes that we noted above as truly exogenous shocks. Major changes in the social security institutions are likely to affect an elderly person's status of being economically active or inactive (to live independently or become subsumed in their children's households), in which case (as discussed at the end of Section 2) the coefficients of the saving propensity equation themselves would probably change. Such a consideration requires us to go beyond the maintained assumption of the present paper that the choice of the activeness status of the elderly is largely exogenous.

Perhaps a more apt interpretation of the above simulation exercise and, at the same time, of the meaning of the positive correlation between the error terms u_i and v_i lies in the following hypothesis that links the demand side of the labor market and savings behavior: the strong precautionary and/or bequest motives that govern aged households at the root make employment opportunity and the additional effort at saving serve as substitutes in meeting these motives. Thus when employment is inadvertently cut back, one raises the saving propensity to compensate for the loss from the former. In fact, even though public pension coverage and benefits have improved, those who can obtain sufficient benefits are fairly limited, and the risk of uncertain lifetime remains a major factor of concern. In addition, for those who desire to leave a moderate bequest, increased pension wealth may not constitute a reason for reducing personal savings activity. Rigorous testing of such an interpretation, which certainly requires a richer data set that at least includes pension benefits received by the aged households, is left for future study.

5. Concluding Remarks

What is the impact of the elderly on the overall savings rate of Japanese households? We have approached the problem by dividing the elderly population into those who maintain an economically active status (including those who form independent nuclear households and those who live with children and yet earn a high income) and those who are subsumed in their children's household and have become economically inactive.

For the former category of individuals, we have observed that under the control of the household income (and evaluated at the mean of income distribution) there is a difference of about 13 percent in the propensity to save that is attributable to employment, and this difference supplies the leverage by which the internationally high labor force participation (and employment) ratio of aged Japanese can be translated into the high household savings rate. We must be cautious in making a simple calculation, however. This is because we have also observed that the employment behavior is endogenous in the determination of the savings behavior; more specifically, any exogenous shock that generates a 10–20 percent decline in the employment ratio from the current level tends, at the same time, to generate an offsetting increase in the household savings behavior, leading to almost no change in the savings rate (cf. Table 9). Thus ultimately the cause of the high savings rate among the elderly (a fact that has been noted for more than 25 years) does not lie in the high employment ratio itself, but must be sought elsewhere. While we have hinted that a strong precautionary motive and a strong bequest motive probably play a major role, such an idea is yet no more than speculation. We could obtain more mileage in locating this cause if we were able to analyze the source of the above endogeneity, but such a task must await the availability of richer data.

For the second category of aged individuals, we have tried to evaluate the effect of their presence on the younger generation household's savings behavior. Although our analysis that is based on limited cross-classified tables cannot be regarded as conclusive, we have arrived at a provisional conclusion that the presence of parents does not increase nor decrease the younger generation household's savings rate. To be sure, we have found that when homeownership (in addition to income and the presence of children) is controlled for, their presence decreases the younger generation's savings rate by 1.5–1.7 percent, but at the same time we have also found that homeownership by the younger generation is greatly aided (if not outrightly provided) by their aged parents. Therefore, when we take account of this latter effect, the total effect becomes nil. The "family social security" system is thus quite an economical system in terms of preserving aggregate household savings.

As far as the overall household savings rate is concerned perhaps the most important problem that remains to be studied is the impact of changes in the social security system on the choice of living form by the aged (i.e., whether to live independently or to live together), in other words, how much it substitutes for the family social security system. Another important subject is the problem of intertemporal substitutability, which, of course, lies at the heart of the neo-classical decision theory. As long as we admit some length for a planning horizon (if not life-long as the prototype life-cycle hypothesis supposes), it becomes difficult to maintain that the savings behavior of economically active elderly households can be studied independently of the savings behavior of the younger age households. These topics (together with the investigation of single-person households) are left for future study.

Appendix

We summarize the procedure by which the original Family Savings Survey microdata have been put to use in our estimation.

1. Because the original data contain total annual before-tax income (called "annual income") as the sole information on the household income, we have used other information in decomposing earnings and asset (interest) income, and in estimating tax and social security contribution payments. (a) The asset income is estimated by utilizing the information of each household's componentwise financial assets (e.g., various bank and postal savings deposits, bonds, shares) held at the beginning of each year, multiplying by corresponding rates of interest and return obtained from various sources of financial statistics, and then summing them altogether. (b) Before tax earnings (= noninterest income) are then calculated as a residual.[21] (c) Taxes on earnings are estimated by using the information on household size in calculating the tax base, applying the tax tables of each year, separately for national and local taxes, and then summing them up. A proviso is that for self-employed households, actual taxable income (actually grasped by the tax authorities) is assumed to be 70 percent of true taxable income on the basis of the studies by Ishi (1981) and Homma et al. (1984). (d) Taxes on interest income are estimated on the assumptions that (i) postal and *zaikei* (tax-exempt contract savings plans for salaried workers) savings escape taxes completely; (ii) the *maruyū* system (tax exempted small-amount deposits and government debt holdings) is used to its upper limit; (iii) taxes on securities generate on the part of the household a choice of the comprehensive income tax (*sōgō kazei*) or the separate tax at the source (*gensen bunri kazei*); and we have estimated them by supposing that the households are rational tax averters (whose concrete calculations followed the descriptions of *Zeikin Dokuhon* (Tax Reader) published by Daiwa Securities Ltd). (e) Finally, social security contributions and property tax have been estimated by the relationship between the amount of contribution and annual income, and the data of property tax paid by residential locations as reported by FIES (each year).

2. The estimated tax figures are then subtracted from before-tax income figures in obtaining disposable income, after-tax earnings (noninterest income), and after-tax interest income.

3. The amount of savings is defined as financial savings and real investment. Financial savings are calculated by obtaining, for each asset (and debt) item, the difference between holdings at the end of the year and at the beginning of the year (or for items for which flow transactions during the year are reported, the net increment), and then

summing up the differences. Note that FSS includes life insurance that has the character of savings as a category of financial asset, while it excludes cash. The changes in cash holdings have thus been ignored. For the second year as well as the first, the financial asset holdings at the beginning of the year mean those as recalled by households at the end of the year, which admittedly contain memory errors.

4. From the original samples, we have deleted incomplete samples, and also excluded those households whose estimated consumption level (= disposable income − total savings) is less than ¥10,000, or whose reported total financial asset (and debt) figures between the two years (namely those at the end of the first year and those at the beginning of the second year as recalled at the end of the second year) differ substantially. The resulting sample size has become 1,386.

5. We have diverged from the Statistics Bureau's practice by including corporate managers in the group of workers.

6. All nominal figures are deflated by the consumption price index which sets 1980 as unity.

Notes

I am grateful to Professors Susan Collins, Fumio Hayashi, Takatoshi Ito, Masahiro Kuroda, Naoyuki Yoshino, two anonymous referees, and other participants of the Economics of the Japanese Firms Conference, 1980, for helpful comments and suggestions. Financial support from the Ministry of Education and the Japan Economic Research Foundation is gratefully acknowledged.

1. Both of these suggestions are echoed in our interpretation of the estimated simultaneous equations model given in Section 4.

2. According to the Institute of Population Studies (Ministry of Welfare) projection, the relative size of this age group continues to grow at least for another 30 years. See Office of the Prime Minister (1979: 25, Table 1–2–1).

3. In the Population Census, household types are classified by first identifying the *youngest* couples in the household and then observing the kin relationships around them. This is to be contrasted with the practice throughout the consumption and savings surveys of the Statistics Bureau (FIES, FSS, and NSFIE) that households are classified by age groups by identifying the principal earner of the household as the head (no matter whether he/she is young or old) and then classifying households by the head's age.

4. Aged individuals are relatively more heavily present in the agricultural, mixed (agricultural and nonagricultural), and not-working sectors. In fact, in 1985, every other household in these sectors includes at least one aged member, while the same probability for nonagricultural households is only 19 percent. Because of the small and still declining size of the agricultural and mixed sectors, however, these two sectors make up only 20 percent of all (noninstitutionalized) aged individuals. At the same time, 23 percent of aged individuals belong to not-working households, which is a large increase since 1970. (All the figures above are from the Population Census.)

5. Another major category of the public pension system, *Kokumin Nenkin*, currently pays out a benefit of only about ¥50,000 per month per recipient.

6. The official unemployment rate figures for men aged 65 and above (according to the Labor Force Survey, various years) exhibit a picture similar to the job vacancy/job desire ratio figures. In fact, they are relatively constant at around 2 percent since the compilation of unemployment rate figures for that specific age group began in 1975. For the age

class 55–64, the unemployment rate has increased from 3.2 percent in 1975 to 5.2 percent in 1986. (For the age class over 55, for which we have figures from 1970, the unemployment rate has increased from 1.4 percent in 1970 to 4.2 percent in 1986, whereas the same rate for the age class 40–54 increased only slightly during the period in question, namely from 0.9 percent to 1.7 percent.) Why there exists a sudden drop in the unemployment rate between the age class 55–64 and the age class 65 and over remains a puzzle. However, it is natural to interpret the significant rise of the unemployment rate for the age class 55–64 as a symptom indicating that job opportunities for the elderly (i.e., those aged 65 and over) have become increasingly scarce, in spite of the apparently stable and low unemployment figures for the same group noted above. Therefore, it is plausible (though not proof) to argue that there exists a sizable group of discouraged workers among the elderly.

7. My own estimate using the FSS microdata (for the period 1976–84) gives the average figures of 15.8 percent for aged employee households (including corporate managers) and 11.5 percent for self-employed households. (For the ages 35–44 group, the average total savings rate is 19.1 percent for employees and 7.8 percent for the self-employed.) The average financial savings rates for the two groups are 8.5 and 4.7 percent, respectively. For nonworking aged households, the average total savings rate is 1.5 percent and the average financial savings rate is −6.9 percent, and we see evidence of financial dissaving taking place (Ishikawa: 1987, Table 7-3).

8. See Table 3c of Hayashi et al. (1988), which shows that the sum of pension income and business income for old nuclear families is on average about twice that for the dependent old living with children (e.g., for nuclear families with the head aged 65–69, that sum is ¥175,000 while that for dependent old individuals aged 65–69 is ¥93,000). The same table indicates that a part of this difference arises from the fact that the number of elderly members contained in the merged household is smaller than that of old nuclear families, and also by the fact that the former is more dominated by female members.

At the same time we must note the existence of wide disparity in income distribution among elders living independently. Our FSS data indicate that aged households in the official classification do contain in substantive frequency low income and nonworking families. To be more specific, the sample frequency distribution of aged households by type of employment (i.e., employees or nonemployees), income class (i.e., quartiles I [lowest], II, III, and IV [highest], defined for each employment group and over all age groups), and number of working members in the household is given by the following:

	I	II	III	IV
For employee households: 19.3 (%) in the total sample				
One person working	4.6	2.6	1.5	2.7
Two + persons working	1.1	0.9	1.1	4.8
Total	5.7	3.5	2.6	7.5 (%)
For nonemployee households: 80.2 (%) in the total sample				
No person working	24.7	7.4	3.4	.8
One person working	5.0	5.2	3.9	2.9
Two + persons working	4.0	4.6	7.2	11.1
Total	33.7	17.2	14.5	14.8 (%)

Hence, it is not really true that independent elders are uniformly rich individuals. Hayashi et al. (1988) also attest to this fact in panel D of their Table 3c.

9. I am indebted to Fumio Hayashi for incisive comments on this problem that greatly clarified my thinking.

10. Notice that even if the elderly do need economic support from children, this can be realized by external remittances; poverty in itself does not constitute a reason for living together. On the other hand, rich elderly individuals can hire nurses and/or housekeepers even if their health normally does not allow independent living. Also they are perhaps

more conscious of preserving their sense of power and and self-control. Thus they may aid their children's families to obtain housing in the immediate vicinity of their residence (often within the same land space) and obtain the same effect as living together, whereas the normal solution is to live together physically. These are presumably the sources of the positive correlation noted by Ando et al. (1986) and Hayashi et al. (1988) between independent living and wealth holding (or income) of elders.

11. We assume that disposable income (DY) is significantly correlated to "annual income," which is the original classification variable.

12. These numbers are corroborated by the Population Census (1985) data, where the houseowner ratios of single-person, independent, two-generation, and three-generation households (i.e., the same classification as Table 1) are given as 63.8, 81.6, 94.8, and 95.4 percent, respectively.

13. It is well known that existence of the bequest motive, either out of parental altruism (Yaari, 1964, 1965) or out of strategic and control motive (Bernheim et al., 1985), or existence of the precautionary motive within an environment characterized by the uncertainty of lifetime and the lack of actuarially fair annuity insurance (Davies, 1981) can lead to continuation of saving even after retirement.

14. If we were solely interested in obtaining consistent estimates for the coefficients of the model, then Heckman's (1974) two-step estimator should suffice. However, since that procedure is known to underestimate the standard error of coefficients, and since our major interest lies in testing whether there exists a non-zero correlation between the error terms, we proceed to estimate the model simultaneously.

15. Maximization is done by taking as the basis of the correction matrix the sample covariance matrix of the gradient vector, noting the property that asymptotically it converges to the true Hessian matrix. This is known as the B.H.H.H. algorithm. The actual computation was done by writing down a program routine (following Berndt et al., 1974) within the SAS (Version 5) Matrix Procedure. Convergence was always assured for the results presented in Tables 7 and 8.

16. Although there is a tendency for an individual working as self-employed from a young age to continue to work automatically (unless becoming ill), there is also a group of self-employed individuals who have turned themselves from the group of employees after mandatory retirement (according to the Ministry of Labour [1981]; among men, this group constitutes around 6 percent of individuals who were employees at age 55).

17. Using the time series of FIES and FSS data, Sasaki and Tachibanaki estimated the public pension wealth (the expected present value of the *Kōsei Nenkin* and *Haigūsha Kokumin Nenkin* benefits), and then regressed the (private) net financial wealth on the (estimated) lifetime disposable income and the pension wealth. While the authors conclude that there is on the whole some substitutability, this conclusion is far from persuasive; first, while their result shows there exists around 20 percent substitutability between the net financial wealth and the *Kokumin Nenkin* wealth (and this is their major ground for the above conclusion), there is none between the net financial wealth and the *Kōsei Nenkin* wealth, which is itself 5–7 times as large as the *Kokumin Nenkin* wealth; and second, their cohort time-series regressions are quite unstable. It is more appropriate to interpret their result as showing little evidence of substitutability.

18. We have also estimated the probit equation and the savings rate equation separately, the latter using the standard OLS method. The estimated coefficients of both equations are similar except for that of DLP in the savings propensity equation, which carries the value 0.0678 (0.0284) for Model I and the value 0.0472 (0.0288) for Model II (where the numbers in parentheses are the estimated standard errors). For either model, the coefficient estimate of DLP is just about half of the maximum likelihood estimate given in Table 7. This is expected because of the existing positive correlation between u_i and v_i.

19. On the other hand, there may also be a bias working in the opposite direction. Diamond and Hausman (1984) argued that there may exist taste differences among individuals concerning retirement, and naturally those who wish to retire early are likely to have accumulated much financial wealth. This would result in a negative correlation be-

tween FA and the error term, rendering an upward bias in the estimated coefficient of FA. Diamond and Hausman's own test (i.e., the Instrumental Variable estimate in Table VII, p. 97) did not show, however, that there actually existed a large bias in the direction they argued. While their results indicated the existence of some simultaneity, once the simultaneity is controlled for, the amount of financial wealth lowered, rather than raised, the probability of retirement. This finding is qualitatively the same as our finding. It thus appears that the evidence for the magnitude of the bias that Diamond and Hausman argued is yet to be shown.

20. The validity of this test depends on our supposition that any difference in total wealth among households is also reflected in the difference in net financial wealth. If there exists a substantial degree of substitution between real wealth and financial wealth (e.g., owning a *second* house by drawing down financial assets), then this supposition does not hold. (I am indebted to Takatoshi Itō for raising this point.) Because our data contain only a very imperfect measure of real wealth holding, we cannot directly verify this supposition. However, since borrowing capacity is normally limited for most of the elderly population (an exception is the very rich who might also have high net financial wealth in any case), and since redemption of past debts is completed for many of them, we expect this supposition to be a good first approximation of the reality for elderly households. Needless to say, this does not mean that the same supposition holds good for much younger age households.

21. As Ando et al. (1986: 43) suggest, there is a possibility that the reported "annual income" figures do not include interest and dividend income that are not obtained in cash. Therefore, we have prepared another data series that is based on the assumption that "annual income" equals "annual before-tax earnings." However, since the results based on the two series do not differ much, we only report one.

References

Ando, A., M. Yamashita, and A. Murayama. 1986. "Life-cycle" kasetsu ni motozuku shōhi/chochiku no kōdō bunseki: Zenkoku Shōhi Jittai Chōsa ni motozuku Nihon no kakei no kō-chochiku-ritsu no bunseki (An analysis of consumption and savings behavior along the life-cycle hypothesis: An analysis of the high savings rate of Japanese households based on the Family Income and Expenditure Survey). Keizai Bunseki 101: 25–114.

Berndt, E., B. Hall, R. Hall, and J. Hausman. 1974. Estimation and inference in nonlinear structural models. Annals of Economic and Social Measurement (Oct.): 653–65.

Bernheim, B., A. Shleifer, and L. Summers. 1985. The strategic bequest motive. Journal of Political Economy 93, 6 (Dec.): 1045–76.

Davies, J. 1981. Uncertain lifetime, consumption, and dissaving in retirement. Journal of Political Economy 89, 3: 561–77.

Diamond, P., and J. Hausman. 1984. Individual retirement and savings behavior. Journal of Public Economics 23, 1&2 (Feb./March): 81–114.

Economic Planning Agency. 1981. Kokumin Seikatsu Hakusho (White Paper on the living condition of the people of Japan).

Greenberg, D., and M. Kosters. 1973. Income guarantees and the working poor: The effect of work of male family heads. In Income Maintenance and Labor Supply, ed. by G. Cain and H. Watts. Chicago: Rand McNally.

Hayashi, F. 1986. Why is Japan's saving rate so apparently high? In Macroeconomics Annual, pp. 147–200. Cambridge, Mass.: National Bureau of Economic Research.

Hayashi, F., A. Ando, and R. Ferris. 1988. Life cycle and bequest saving: A study of Japanese and U.S. households based on the 1984 JSFIE data and data from the survey of consumer finances 1983. Journal of Japanese and International Economies 2, 4 (Dec.): 450–91.

Heckman, J. 1974. Shadow prices, market wages and labor supply. Econometrica 42, 4 (July): 679–94.

Homma, M., T. Ihori, N. Atoda, and A. Murayama. 1984. Shotoku zei futan no gyōshu-kan kakusa no jittai: Micro-teki approach (The state of occupational differences in tax liabilities: A microeconomic approach). Kikan Gendai Keizai 59: 14–25.

Horioka, C. 1984. The applicability of the life-cycle hypothesis of saving to Japan. Kyoto University Economic Review 54: 31–56.

Ishi, H. 1981. Kazei shotoku hosoku-ritsu no gyōshu-kan kakusa (Occupational differences in the apprehension of taxable income). Kikan Gendai Keizai 42: 72–83.

Ishikawa, T. 1987. Kaikei chochiku no kōzō yōin to kin'yū zeisei (The structural elements of household savings and financial asset taxation). In Nihon Keizai no Makuro Bunseki (A macroeconomic analysis of the Japanese economy), ed. by K. Hamada, A. Horiuchi, and M. Kurada, pp. 177–210. Tokyo: University of Tokyo Press.

Kanamori, H. 1961. Nihon no chochiku-ritsu wa naze takai-ka (Why is the Japanese savings rate high?). Keizai Geppō (Nov.).

Komiya, R. 1963. Kojin chochiku no kyōkyū (The supply of personal savings). In Sengo Nihon no Keizai Seichō (Postwar Japanese economic growth), ed. by R. Komiya, pp. 157–82. Tokyo: Iwanami. English translation available from University of California Press, Berkeley.

Lee, L., and R. Trost. 1978. Estimation of some limited dependent variable models with applications to housing demand. J. Econometrics 8: 357–82.

Ministry of Labour. 1981. Survey of the Employment Condition of the Aged.

Mizoguchi, T. 1973. Chochiku no keizaigaku: Katei kara no hatsugen. (The economics of saving: Voices from the household). Tokyo: Keisō Shobō.

Motokawa, A., and T. Mori. 1981. Kō-nenreisha no shūgyō-ritsu henka ni kansuru yōin bunseki (A factor analysis of the changes in the employment ratio among aged individuals). Rōdō Tōkei Chōsa Geppō 388: 4–22.

Office of the Prime Minister. 1979. Kōreisha mondai no genjō. (The current state of the problems of the aged).

Sasaki, M., and T. Tachibanaki. 1985. Kōteki nenkin seido ga sedai-betsu chochiku-ritsu to shisan keisei ni ataeta eikyō (The effect of the public pension system on the savings rate and wealth formation of different generations). Shakai Hoshō Kenkyū 21, 1 (June): 59–71.

Seike, A. 1982. Nenkin no shūnyū seigen to rōdō kyōkyū (Earnings limitations of pensions and labor supply). Rōdō Kyōkai Zasshi 282 (Sept.): 14–24.

———. 1986. Kōreisha shūgyō no sūsei to kōteki nenkin (Trends in the employment of the aged and public pensions). Rōdō Kyōkai Zasshi 331 (Oct.): 9–16.

Shinohara, M. 1963. Comment (on Komiya's article). In Sengo Nihon no Keizai Seichō (Postwar Economic Growth), ed. by R. Komiya, pp. 183–88. Tokyo: Iwanami. English translation available from the University of California Press, Berkeley.

Tachibanaki, T., and K. Shimono. 1985. Labor supply of the elderly: Their desires and realities about full-time jobs, part-time jobs, self-employed jobs or retirement. Keizai Kenkyū 36, 3 (July): 239–50.

Yaari, M.E. 1964. On the consumer's lifetime allocation process. International Economic Review 5 (Sept.): 304–17.

———. 1965. Uncertain lifetime, life insurance, and theory of the consumer. Review of Economic Studies 32 (April): 137–50.

III. Class Conflict, Work Incentives, and Job Satisfaction

9. Class Conflict, Capital Accumulation, and Distribution of Income

1. Introduction

In this paper, we shall construct an aggregate model of a capitalist economy following the works of Keynes (1936), Kalecki (1939: 54), and Joan Robinson (1962), and analyze the factors governing the motion of the capitalist economy. More specifically, we would like to evaluate the roles that class conflict over the level of real wage[1] play in determining the short-run and the long-run course of the capitalist economy, in particular the rate of capital accumulation and the distribution of income.

This paper consists of six sections. Section 2 discusses the general framework and assumptions of the model. Section 3 characterizes the short-run equilibrium of the economy. Section 4 then turns to the study of dynamics and discusses the basic factors governing the long-run stability of the economy under the assumption of constant real wage rate. Section 5 discusses in particular the case where the growing economy confronts resource bottlenecks, and compares two alternative views as to how the economy might develop after production becomes constrained by the available resources. Section 6 extends the preceding discussion by allowing real wage rate to fluctuate in response to variation in the unemployment ratio, and to evaluate its implications on the dynamic course of the economy. Finally, Section 7 concludes this paper by summarizing the important results and by discussing the limitations of our model, which are to be considered further in our future research.

Originally prepared as Discussion Paper #468 (April 1976), Harvard Institute of Economic Research, Harvard University, Cambridge, Massachusetts.

2. Assumptions of the Model

GENERAL FRAMEWORK

We shall assume a world with one commodity. This commodity is either consumed or turned irreversibly and without any cost into machines, which constitute the sole capital good (to be called *capital*) in this economy. The commodity is produced with the aid of labor and capital. The economy is composed of two economic classes, namely the capitalists who own capital, and workers who provide labor but do not own any capital. The capitalist class entrusts its capital to entrepreneurs who then with a certain degree of autonomy manage corporate activities of production and make investment decisions with a view to realizing the highest long-term returns to the owners of capital.

TECHNOLOGY

We shall assume fixed coefficient technology, with labor coefficient α and capital coefficient β. There occurs an exogenous labor augmenting technical progress at the constant rate of a so that $\alpha_t = \alpha_0 e^{-at}$. Also, we shall assume for the sake of simplicity that capital once accumulated will never depreciate.

DEMAND FOR INVESTMENT

In deriving entrepreneurs' investment demand we shall generally follow Keynes's discussion in his *General Theory* (1936: chs. 11, 12).[2] In Keynes's view, entrepreneurs' state of long-term expectations, namely their subjective evaluation of uncertain future states of the economy, govern the volume of investment by affecting the position of the marginal efficiency of investment schedule. More specifically, we will introduce into our model a variable called the expected rate of excess capacity and to be denoted by μ_t^e, namely the degree of excess capacity expected to prevail in the current period (t), and let it summarize the general psychological atmosphere of the economy as well as govern the long-term expectations of entrepreneurs. Its actual (or ex post) value for the current period, to be called the rate of excess capacity and denoted by μ_t, is defined by the ratio of existing capital stock (K_t) over what is technically required for current production. Therefore,

$$\mu_t = K_t/\beta Q_t, \tag{1}$$

where Q is the volume of production and β is the capital coefficient of production already defined.

We shall make the following assumptions with regard to the expected rate of excess capacity variable, μ^e. First, we assume that entrepreneurs, due to their precautionary motive in the imperfectly competitive product market, desire positively to maintain a reasonable degree of supplementary capacity.[3] Therefore, entrepreneurs will not curb new investment altogether even when their existing capacity is expected to be underutilized for the current period. A rise in the value of this variable, μ^e, does, however, diminish the prospective yield of current investment. Second, we assume that entrepreneurs form expectation of this variable in an adaptive manner, so that

$$\dot{\mu}_t^e = \kappa(\mu_t - \mu_t^e) \qquad \mu_0^e = \text{given}, \quad \kappa > 0. \tag{2}$$

We also assume that the prospective yield (marginal efficiency) of the current investment is decreasing with respect to the relative magnitude of current investment over the existing capital stock, denoted by I_t/K_t. Therefore, in sum, the marginal efficiency of investment schedule is expressed by

$$r_t^e = r^e(I_t/K_t, \mu_t^e) \tag{3}$$

with the assumptions $r_1^e < 0$ and $r_2^e < 0$. Then the entrepreneurial objective implies that they push their investment demand up to the point where the marginal efficiency of investment equals the long-term real rate of interest, i_t. Namely,

$$r^e(I_t/K_t, \mu_t^e) = i_t. \tag{4}$$

By solving this equation (4), we obtain the investment demand function of entrepreneurs,

$$g_t^d = I_t/K_t = g(\mu_t^e, i_t) \qquad g_1 < 0, \quad g_2 < 0. \tag{5}$$

Later in Section 6 we shall extend our discussion to include an additional variable called expected (effective) real wage rate in the marginal efficiency schedule, in which case investment demand also becomes a function of that variable.

Finally, we note two immediate and important implications of the assumptions made thus far. In the first place, the assumption of no depreciation implies that gross investment is identical with net investment. In the second place, the assumption of irreversibility implies that net investment should always be non-negative.

SUPPLY OF SAVINGS

We shall assume that only capitalists save and that they save a constant fraction $s_c (0 < s_c \leqq 1)$ of gross profit income. Thus, by denoting the rate of profit by ρ, we have

$$S_t = s_c \rho_t K_t. \tag{6}$$

We shall interpret independence of management from ownership in a strict manner and assume that entrepreneurs do not have the power to control the propensity to save, s_c.[4]

PRODUCT MARKET

We shall assume as in Kalecki and Joan Robinson that product market is imperfectly competitive (thus diverting from Keynes). The price of the commodity (p_t) is set by imposing a certain mark-up, at the rate of γ_t, on the prime cost of production. Since there is no depreciation of capital goods, prime cost consists only of labor cost. Moreover, as another characteristic of imperfect competition we shall assume that entrepreneurs, being cautious not to lose the current share of the market, shift the change in money wage rate (which is increasing by our assumption made below) onto their price only with a time lag of h ($h \geqq 0$) period. Thus,

$$p_t = (1 + \gamma_t)\alpha_t W_{t-h} \tag{7}$$

where W denotes the level of money wage rate. Kalecki (1954: 17–18, 1971a) suggests a hint that the mark-up ratio (his "degree of monopoly" parameter) reflects the tensions that exist among capitalists themselves as well as between capitalists and workers. For the sake of simplicity, we shall in this paper assume that this ratio is maintained at a constant level, γ.[5]

LABOR MARKET

We shall adopt an assumption taken since Keynes in assuming that labor market is imperfectly competitive, and that money wage rate follows its own historical course reflecting the relative balance of class powers between capital and labor. More specifically, we shall assume a situation where in each period money wage rate is determined from the past but workers bargain and struggle for a higher money wage for the coming period. Thus,

$$\dot{W}_t = \delta_t W_t \quad W_0 = \text{given} \tag{8}$$

where the parameter δ_t reflects the relative balance of class forces.[6] Until Section 6, where this parameter is assumed to respond to the extent of unemployment in the labor market, we will assume that it is maintained constant over time. Hence, $\delta_t = \delta \geqq 0$.

MONETARY SECTOR

In order to isolate the real factors at work, we shall assume that the monetary authority (the Central Bank) adjusts the nominal supply of money in such a way that the real rate of interest i_t remains constant over time at the level i.[7] As an immediate consequence of this assumption, we shall suppress the variable i in the investment function (5), and henceforth write $g^d = g(\mu^e)$.

3. Short-run Equilibrium

At each moment of time, capital stock, K_t, labor population, N_t, labor coeficient α_t, expected rate of excess capacity μ_t^e, and money wage rate, W_t are historically given. In this section, we shall consider the short-run equilibrium of the economy for the case where both capital and labor are not fully utilized. Later in Section 5, we shall extend our analysis to the case where either factor becomes fully utilized.

Rate of Profit

We observe that entrepreneurs' investment demand is determined for the short run by a historically given expected rate of excess capacity, μ_t^e. Therefore, aggregate demand-supply equilibrium is obtained if and only if sufficient savings are created to match the investment demand. However, savings come only out of profits. Thus, combining equations (5) and (6), the aggregate demand-supply equilibrium condition $I_t = S_t$ determines the rate of profit,

$$\rho_t = \frac{1}{s_c} g(\mu_t^e). \tag{9}$$

Real Wage Rate

By combining equations (7) and (8), we obtain the expression for real wage rate, w_t, as

$$w_t = \frac{W_t}{p_t} = \frac{e^{\delta h}}{(1+\gamma)\alpha_t}. \tag{10}$$

Therefore, real wage rate is increasing with respect to the rate of increase in money wage rate, δ (as long as $h \neq 0$), and is decreasing with respect to the mark-up ratio, γ. However, in the special case of zero price adjustment lag ($h = 0$) customarily assumed (as in Kalecki and Joan Robinson), any change in money wage rate is immaterial to the level of real wage rate, and workers can affect real wage rate only indirectly through mark-up ratio γ (whose mechanism we must yet specify).

Another implication of formula (10) is that over time real wage rate increases steadily at the rate of productivity increase, a. For convenience of later discussion, we shall define a variable $\tilde{w}_t$ by $\tilde{w}_t = \alpha_t w_t$. This will be called effective real wage rate, and it expresses real wage rate as paid on efficiency units of labor. The same formula then implies that $\tilde{w}_t$ remains constant over time. Let us write it $\tilde{w}$.

DISTRIBUTIONAL SHARES

By noting the distributional identity of national income in real terms,

$$Q_t \equiv w_t \alpha_t Q_t + \rho_t K_t \tag{11}$$

the distributive share of profits, to be denoted by π_t, is immediately solved as

$$\pi_t \equiv \frac{\rho_t K_t}{Q_t} = 1 - \alpha_t w_t = 1 - \tilde{w}, \tag{12}$$

which in the light of equation (10) can be expressed as

$$\pi_t = 1 - \frac{e^{\delta h}}{1 + \gamma}. \tag{12'}$$

With the assumption of zero price adjustment lag ($h = 0$), this essentially reduces to Kalecki's formula (1954: 28–29) whereby distributive share of the product is *prima facie* explained in terms of the price policy of firms.[8] It is rather unfortunate that Kalecki's formula has been termed the "degree of monopoly" hypothesis of distribution, for certain class struggle elements involved in the parameter γ, which Kalecki himself recognized, are thereby neglected. In our formula (12′), the class struggle element involved in determining distributive shares is also caught by the parameter δ. The constancy of the parameters δ, γ, and h implies that distributive shares remain constant over time. We will hereinafter denote this value by π. Hence, $\pi = 1 - \tilde{w}$.

OUTPUT AND EMPLOYMENT

We have already seen in equation (9) that the aggregate demand-supply equilibrium condition directly determines the rate of profit. This aggregate demand-supply equilibrium, in fact, is attained by adjustment of the volume of output by entrepreneurs. By using our equation (12), let us rewrite S_t in equation (6) as $S_t = s_c \pi Q_t$, where $s_c \pi = s_c(1 - \tilde{w})$ is the average propensity to save. Translated into this form, the equilibrium condition $I_t = S_t$ determines the level of output as

$$Q_t = \frac{1}{s_c \pi} g(\mu_t^e) K_t \tag{13}$$

which is nothing but the familiar Kahn-Keynes multiplier formula. Then the level of employment, L_t, is obtained as

$$L_t = \frac{\alpha_t}{s_c \pi} g(\mu_t^e) K_t. \tag{14}$$

This mechanism is illustrated by Figure 1.

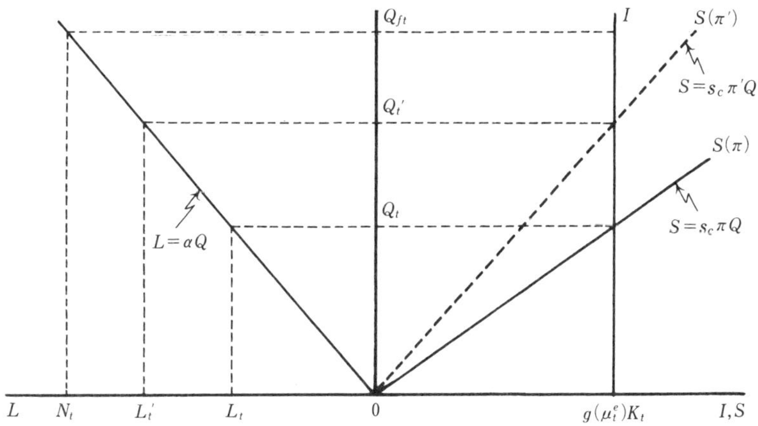

Figure 1

We thus see that by expanding or curtailing the volume of output, entrepreneurs can always (that is, for any given real wage rate) realize the rate of profit given in equation (9), and thereby satisfy their investment desire. Therefore, we have,

$$\dot{K}_t = g(\mu_t^e)K_t. \tag{15}$$

As an important comparative static property, we observe from equations (13) and (14) that higher effective real wage rate ($\tilde{w}$) implies larger output as well as larger employment. (See Figure 1.) Thus when the worker class becomes stronger and succeeds in raising the level of real wage (once for all), they will force the entrepreneurs to expand production and at the same time the volume of employment.[9] To remind us, this paradoxical result holds true only as long as our assumption of underutilized capital and labor resources remains valid.

RATE OF EXCESS CAPACITY

By combining equations (1), (9) and (13), the rate of excess capacity (whose reciprocal gives the rate of capacity utilization) is determined as

$$\mu_t = \frac{s_c\pi}{\beta g(\mu_t^e)}. \tag{16}$$

This value enters into equation (2) and generates a new expected rate of excess capacity for the coming period.

4. Dynamic Process of the Economy

Let us now examine how this economy evolves over time. Under the assumptions of the previous sections, we have already seen that it is the entrepreneur's investment demand that directly determines the rate of growth, and that, together with the relative balance of class forces, determines all the short-run characteristics of the economy. However, since the class force parameter δ and the make-up ratio γ are exogenously given by our assumption, the dynamic path of the economy can be analyzed in terms of variables that affect the investment demand of entrepreneurs alone.[10]

In fact, by substituting equation (16) for μ_t in equation (2), we obtain the following basic dynamic equation of the economy.

$$\dot{\mu}_t^e = \kappa \left\{ \frac{s_c \pi}{\beta \cdot g(\mu_t^e)} - \mu_t^e \right\}. \tag{17}$$

In order to examine how this system develops, we rewrite equation (17) as

$$\dot{\mu}_t^e = \frac{\kappa \mu_t^e}{g(\mu_t^e)} \left\{ \frac{s_c \pi}{\beta \mu_t^e} - g(\mu_t^e) \right\} \tag{18}$$

(note that $g(\mu^e) > 0$ for $\mu^e < \infty$) and consider the graphs of each term within the bracket in the (μ^e, g) space. The first term can be interpreted as expressing the supply of savings in the long run, and, therefore, we will call the graph of $g = \frac{s_c \pi}{\beta \mu^e}$ (which is a rectangular hyperbola) the *LS* curve. On the other hand, the second term expresses the demand for investment both for the short run and for the long run. We will call the graph of $g = g(\mu^e)$ (which is downward sloping) the *LI* curve. Then we observe the following possibilities.

(a) If *LI* curve and *LS* curve intersect, then the intersection point forms a long-run stationary equilibrium. Moreover, if at this point *LI* curve crosses the *LS* curve from below (or, equivalently, if the elasticity of investment with respect to the expected rate of elasticity (η_{μ^e}) at this point is less than 1, then the equilibrium is locally stable; on the other hand, if at this point *LI* curve crosses *LS* curve from above (or equivalently if η_{μ^e} at this point is greater than 1), then the equilibrium is locally unstable. (See Figure 2 for an example of this case.) Depending on how η_{μ^e} varies as μ^e changes, there may be any number of stable and unstable equilibria. However, in the special case of constant η_{μ^e}, there exists at most one equilibrium, and it is globally stable if $\eta_{\mu^e} < 1$, and globally unstable if $\eta_{\mu^e} > 1$. In the

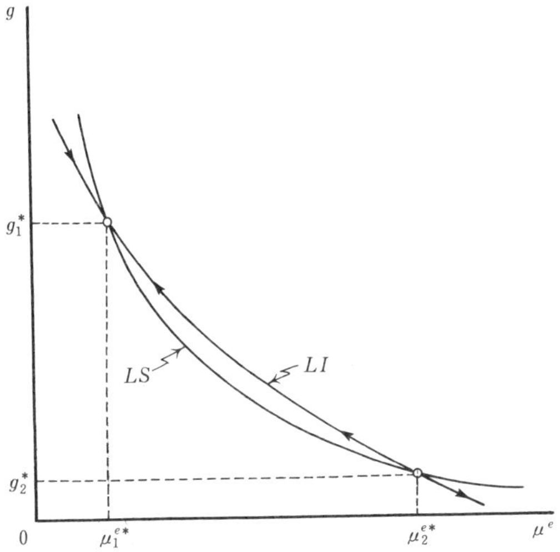

Figure 2

example case depicted in Figure 2, the economy will converge to the stable long-run equilibrium (μ_1^{e*}, g_1^*), if it starts with initial μ^e less than μ_2^{e*}, while it will diverge with an ever-declining rate of growth from the unstable equilibrium (μ_2^{e*}, g_2^*) should it start with initial μ^e greater than μ_2^{e*}. The equilibrium growth rate g_1^* corresponds to what Harrod termed the warranted rate of growth, G_w (or what Joan Robinson [1962] termed the desired rate of growth).

(b) If *LI* curve always stays above *LS* curve (i.e., $\frac{s_c\pi}{\beta\mu^e} > g(\mu^e)$), then the expected rate of excess capacity is always decreasing $\dot{\mu}_t^e < 0$ for all t. In this case, capital accumulation continues to be accelerated and the rate of growth of the economy is ever increasing (until it is checked by the force to be discussed in later sections.) (See Fig. 3.)

(c) If *LI* curve always stays below *LS* curve (i.e., $g(\mu^e) > \frac{s_c\pi}{\beta\mu^e}$), then the expected rate of excess capacity is always increasing. (See Fig. 4.) In this case, capital accumulation continues to be decelerated, and the economy will experience secular stagnation.

The actual occurrence among the three possible cases, of course, depends on the parameters of the *LI* and *LS* curves. However, as one interesting comparative dynamic property, we note that a large enough increase in the share of profit, π, will ceteris paribus shift the *LS* curve

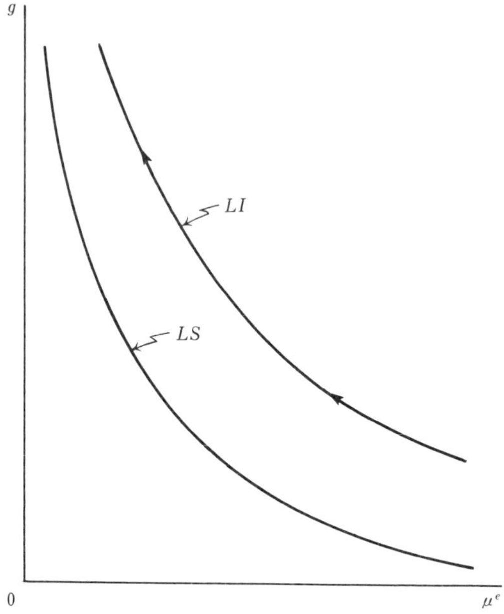

Figure 3

upward and will bring the new situation to be like Figure 4. Then chronical insufficiency of effective demand arises and leads the economy into a state of secular stagnation. Thus a change in the balance of class powers affects the character of the long-run tendency of the economy in a rather paradoxical manner; namely, the more capitalists succeed in obtaining a high profit share, the more likely they are to bring the economy to stagnation. This fact may be interpreted as putting an *objective* constraint on capitalists' power to control the economy. Also, this point seems to clarify as well as qualify the explanation of contradiction in the capitalist economy provided by the underconsumption hypothesis.[11]

We thus conclude that, with a given propensity to save by capitalists, a stable warranted growth equilibrium is possible for this economy only if (a) entrepreneurs' investment demand is not very volatile with respect to their long-term expectations (i.e., $\eta_{\mu^e} < 1$), and (b) the share of profit reflecting the balance of class powers falls within a certain limited range. Otherwise, the economy is unstable in the long run. We finally note that the foregoing analysis holds only as long as our basic

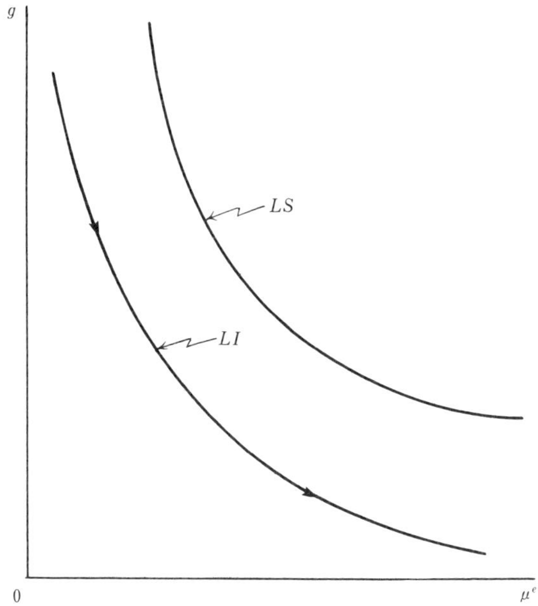

Figure 4

assumption of underutilitized capital and labor resources remains valid. In the next section let us consider what happens when this assumption no longer holds.

5. Restrained Growth Paths

When either capital or labor becomes fully employed, entrepreneurs can no longer realize their desired level of investment by merely controlling the level of output.

First, by noting the definition of the rate of excess capacity variable and equation (16), we see that capital becomes the bottleneck for increasing production whenever the desired rate of growth, $g(\mu^e)$, exceeds $s_c\pi/\beta$, which we call G_c. (See Fig. 5.) Second, labor becomes the bottleneck when the desired amount of output as determined by equation (13) exceeds the full employment output, $Q_{ft} = N_t/\alpha_t$, which only grows at the exogenously given natural rate of growth, $G_n = n + a$. This immediately implies that the desired rate of growth, if it is to be realized without any change in other parts of the system, cannot persistently be above G_n.

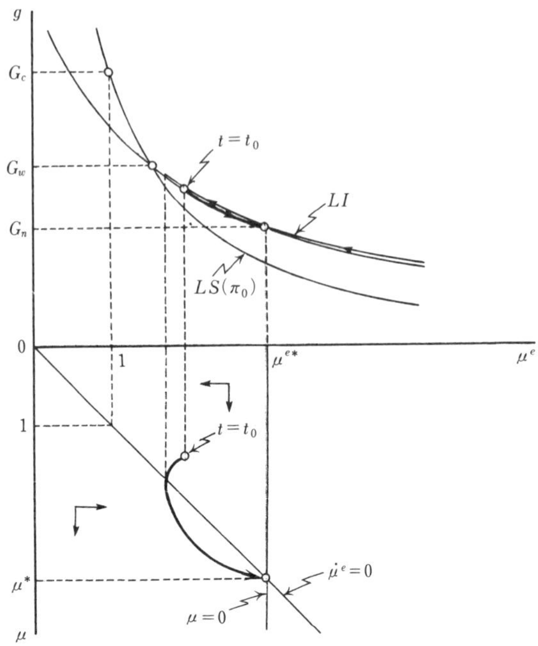

Figure 5. The Kaldor-Kaleckian solution

DYNAMIC ANALYSIS OF THE RESTRAINED GROWTH PATH

Let us assume a case where there exists a stable warranted growth equilibrium with the growth rate G_w. Also, let us assume that initially labor is not fully employed. Then we note that the analysis of the previous section holds without any qualification by the resource constraints if $G_w < G_c$ and $G_w < G_n$. In such a case, the economy tends to the warranted growth equilibrium with a constant degree of excess capacity and growing unemployment of labor. On the other hand, if G_w is greater than either G_c or G_n, or both, then the economy will sooner or later confront the bottleneck either in labor or in capital. Then entrepreneurs' desired rate of growth will no longer be compatible with the given distributive share, π. What will happen then? I shall take up two alternative ways to understand the dynamics that follows.

THE KALDOR-KALECKIAN APPROACH

The first alternative to be taken up is the solution advanced by the works of Kaldor and Kalecki (Kaldor [1956–57, 1959, 1963]; Kalecki

[1971a]). In this approach, entrepreneurs are assumed to have the mighty force to control the distributive shares in such a way that sufficient savings are generated to realize their desired rate of growth. The supposed mechanism by which this mighty force is displayed is as follows: Out of the given constrained output, the entrepreneurs will first secure the desired amount of output, which will be transformed into investment goods and consumption goods for the capitalist class, and then let the workers bid the price competitively for the amount of output that remains.[12]

Let us illustrate this approach by supposing the case where the economy confronts the full-employment constraint at time $t = t_o$ (assuming $G_c > G_w > G_n$). Then, since entrepreneurs satisfy their investment desires, the economy after time $t = t_o$ moves according to the differential equations system;

$$\begin{cases} \dot{\mu}_t^e = \kappa(\mu_t - \mu_t^e) & (19) \\ \dot{\mu}_t/\mu_t = \dot{K}_t/K_t - (\dot{N}_t/N_t + \dot{\alpha}_t/\alpha_t) = g(\mu_t^e) - G_n. & (20) \end{cases}$$

This system has a steady state equilibrium (μ^{e*}, μ^*) such that $\mu^{e*} = \mu^*$ and $g(\mu^{e*}) = G_n$. We then see that, if the speed of adjustment κ is sufficiently large, the system will monotonically converge to this steady state equilibrium; namely the state of balanced growth (Golden Age) equilibrium with capital, employment, and output all growing at the natural rate of growth, G_n.[13] The process of adjustment for this case (i.e., κ sufficiently large) is depicted in Figure 5.

Because entrepreneurs' desired rate of investment exceeds the rate of growth of output, excess capacity will be accumulated ($\dot{\mu}_t > 0$). However, this discourages the entrepreneurs' long-term expectations, i.e., $\dot{\mu}_t^e > 0$ at least after a certain period and leads them to diminish their investment desires. Thus the economy moves down along the *LI* curve until the entrepreneurs' desired rate of capital accumulation is pushed down to G_n.

The distribution of income during this dynamic process of adjustment is given by (using equation [16]),

$$\pi_t = \frac{\beta \mu_t}{s_c} \cdot g(\mu_t^e). \tag{21}$$

This formula, alternatively written as $\pi_t = \frac{1}{s_c} \cdot \frac{g(\mu_t^e) \cdot K_t}{Q_{ft}}$, expresses the relationship that has been called the Kaldorian theory of income distribution (Kaldor, 1956, 1957) for the short run. The movement of the share of profits is described by

$$\frac{\dot{\pi}_t}{\pi_t} = (g(\mu_t^e) - G_n) - \kappa\eta_{\mu e}(\mu_t^e)\left(\frac{\mu_t}{\mu_t^e} - 1\right) \tag{22}$$

from which we observe that, at least for a certain period of time after $t = t_o$, the share of profit increases,[14] and that the share of profit in the long-run equilibrium, $\pi^* = \dfrac{\beta\mu^* G_n}{s_c}$, is greater than that before full employment was reached, π_o.[15]

A similar mechanism operates when the economy confronts the bottleneck of capital instead of the bottleneck of labor (i.e., $G_n > G_n > G_c$ or $G_w > G_n > G_c$). In this case, G_n in equation (20) is replaced by G_c, and if the speed of adjustment, κ, is sufficiently large, then the economy will monotonically converge to the state of capacity-restrained growth equilibrium where output, capital, and employment all grow at the rate G_c.

Thus, in sum, the Kaldor-Kaleckian solution assumes totally different mechanisms of distribution between the case when both capital and labor are underutilized and the case when either resource becomes the bottleneck for expansion. More fundamentally, the mechanism of price and real wage determination based on the assumption of imperfect competition in the product market becomes "defunct" (in Kalecki's own term, Kalecki [1971a: 8, 1971b: 164]) as soon as the resource bottleneck appears, and it is replaced by the mechanism that assumes perfect competition in the wage goods market. This conceptual discontinuity, however, is left unexplained and, moreover, as I shall argue in the following, it is not a justifiable assumption to make in describing the functioning of the capitalist economy. The difficulty does not lie in the logic of the second mechanism itself. For, since, in the capitalist economy, it is the capitalist class that organizes the production process and which, according to the property relationship, appropriates the product, they are in principle[16] able to control the composition of output between consumption and investment purposes (even if the control of the total amount of output is no longer possible due to the lack of resources), and therefore to control indirectly the price and real wage as long as the market is competitive. The difficulty lies in that the switch of the mechanism from one to another requires that capitalists come to agree that they act in concert to change the character of the market, which is not conceivable in the capitalist economy based on the spontaneity of capitalist actions. Indeed, the capitalist economy is characterized not only by the struggle between capitalists and workers, but also by the struggle among capitalists themselves. Thus, the Kaldor-Kaleckian solution outlined here does not provide a logically coherent and meaningful answer to the question we have raised.

MARX–J. ROBINSONIAN APPROACH

An alternative to the Kaldor-Kaleckian solution would be provided by assuming that the workers succeed in resisting the entrepreneurs' pressure to reduce the real wage rate relative to productivity growth so that the distribution of income remains the same as before. In such a case, entrepreneurs can no longer generate sufficient profits to fulfill their investment desires, and capital accumulation becomes constrained by the amount of savings. I shall call this the Marx–J. Robinsonian solution.[17] It constitutes the opposite polar case to the Kaldor-Kaleckian solution.

Let us suppose again that $G_c > G_w > G_n$ and that the economy reaches full employment ceiling at time t_o. Then, after time t_o, the rate of excess capacity is determined as $\mu_t = \dfrac{K_t}{\beta Q_{ft}}$. Moreover, since the share of profits does not change (i.e., $\pi_t = \pi_o$), the rate of profit is given by $\rho_t = \dfrac{\pi_o}{\beta\mu_t}$. Then the rate of capital accumulation, or equivalently, the rate of realized investment, becomes constrained by the savings arising out of profits.

$$\frac{\dot{K}_t}{K_t} = s_c\rho_t = \frac{s_c\pi_o}{\beta\mu_t}. \tag{23}$$

Thus the dynamics of the economy after time t_o are described by the system,

$$\begin{cases} \dot{\mu}_t^e = \kappa(\mu_t - \mu_t^e) & (24) \\ \dfrac{\dot{\mu}_t}{\mu_t} = \dfrac{\dot{K}_t}{K_t} - \dfrac{\dot{Q}_{ft}}{Q_{ft}} = \dfrac{s_c\pi_o}{\beta\mu_t} - G_n. & (25) \end{cases}$$

We easily observe that the system converges monotonically to a long-run steady state equilibrium (μ^{e**}, μ^{**}) such that $\mu^{e**} = \mu^{**} = \dfrac{s_c\pi_o}{\beta G_n}$.[18] (See Fig. 6.) Therefore, after time t_o, the rate of profit, and thus, the rate of capital accumulation continues to decline until the economy converges to a restrained (or what J. Robinson terms the high-level bastard) Golden Age equilibrium where capital, employment, and output all grow at the natural rate of growth, G_n. The rate of profit and the rate of excess capacity (= 1/capacity utilization rate) are then given by G_n/s_c and $s_c\pi_o/\beta G_n$, respectively. During this phase, entrepreneurs' expectation behavior does not play any active role, for their investment desire, although declining as the expected rate of ex-

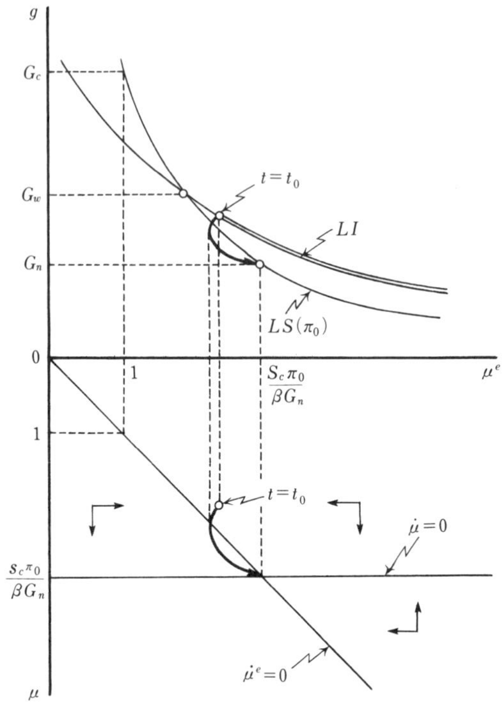

Figure 6. The Marx–J. Robinsonian solution

cess capacity increases, continues to be unfulfilled (even in the Golden Age equilibrium).

A similar mechanism operates when $\min[G_w, G_n] > G_c = \frac{s_c\pi_o}{\beta}$ and the economy confronts the bottleneck of capital, say at time $t = t_o$. In this case, the economy will maintain the capacity restrained growth equilibrium with capital and output growing at the rate G_c and the amount of unemployment growing at $(G_n - G_c)$. The rate of profit is given by $\rho = \pi_o/\beta$. Again the expectation behavior of entrepreneurs no longer plays any active role in this time phase, since their investment desire becomes restrained by the available savings.[19]

Therefore, contrary to the case of the Kaldor-Kaleckian solution, in the Marx–J. Robinsonian solution the character of the income distribution mechanism, and, moreover, the actual distributive share between profits and wages do not change while entrepreneurs' investment desire is no longer fulfilled. It seems that this picture is much closer to what might actually happen in reality than the former one. However, the supposition of unchanged distributive share even when the economy confronts a resource bottleneck seems to be a very strong assumption. We will consider the relaxation of this assumption in the next section.

QUALIFICATIONS OF THE ANALYSIS

The foregoing analysis pertains directly to the case when a stable warranted growth equilibrium exists. However, it is easy to see that the analysis can be applied without any modification to the case when the economy is unstable and is expanding at an ever faster rate (namely, the case of Figure 3). On the other hand, when the economy is unstable and tends steadily toward stagnation (i.e., the case of Figure 4), it is quite likely that the problem in question does not occur at all. The question we must ask then will be quite a different one!

6. Endogenous Fluctuations of Real Wage and the Possibility of a Growth Cycle

Let us extend the Marx–J. Robinsonian approach a little further. Up until now the parameters regulating the effective real wage rate (i.e., real wage rate on the efficiency unit of labor) $\tilde{w}$ remained constant. However, it is perhaps more realistic to assume that workers' strength in bidding up the wage rate depends on the tightness of the labor market. Therefore, we now assume that the rate of increase of money wage rate, δ, depends on the proportion of the labor force employed, L/N, which we call the rate of employment and denote by v, i.e., $\delta = \delta(v)$ $(\delta' \geqq 0)$. The immediate consequence of this is that the effective real wage rate $\tilde{w}$ depends on v. On the other hand, once it is allowed, the variability of the effective real wage rate will certainly affect the position of the marginal efficiency schedule. Therefore, we now assume that the entrepreneurs' investment demand depends on the expected rate of effective real wage, $\tilde{w}^e$, as well as on the expected rate of excess capacity, μ^e, i.e., $g = g(\mu^e, \tilde{w}^e)$, $g_{\mu^e} < 0$, $g_{\tilde{w}^e} < 0$.

As a preliminary to a more general and rigorous analysis to follow, we shall in this paper confine ourselves to the analysis of a special and simplified case. First, we assume that there exists a critical rate of employment, $\bar{v}$ $(\bar{v} \leqq 1)$ such that δ takes on a higher value as $v \geqq \bar{v}$. Formally, $\delta(\cdot)$ is a step function such that

$$\delta = \delta(v) = \begin{cases} \delta_1 & \text{for } \bar{v} > v > 0 \\ \delta_2 & \text{for } 1 \geqq v \geqq \bar{v} \end{cases} \quad \delta_2 > \delta_1. \tag{26}$$

Then, in view of the price equation (7), where we still assume γ and h to be constant, the effective real wage rate at time t, $\tilde{w}_t$, depends in general on the time path of the rate of employment. However, simplification is obtained by our special assumption (26) so that effective real wage rate becomes constant after the rate of employment stays in either of two intervals $(0, \bar{v})$ or $[\bar{v}, 1]$ for more than h period of time. Thus, except for a short period, after v makes the transition from one interval to another the effective real wage rate is solved as

$$\tilde{w} = \tilde{w}(v) = \begin{cases} \tilde{w}_1 = \dfrac{e^{\delta_1 h}}{1+\gamma} & \text{for } \bar{v} > v > 0 \\ \tilde{w}_2 = \dfrac{e^{\delta_2 h}}{1+\gamma} & \text{for } 1 \geqq v \geqq \bar{v} \end{cases} \tag{27}$$

where $\tilde{w}_2 > \tilde{w}_1$ provided that $h > 0$. Second, we assume that the expected rate of effective real wage is formed adaptively (as in equation [2]) but that the adjustment speed is very large. Therefore, in the case where actual effective real wage $\tilde{w}$ changes its value and stays constant thereafter, adjustment of the expected value $\tilde{w}^e$ toward the new value of $\tilde{w}$ requires only a very short period of time (in the order of h or less) to be effectively completed.

Under these special assumptions let us examine the dynamics of the economy by supposing that the set of *LI* and *LS* curves corresponding to the effective real wage rate $\tilde{w}_1$ generates as in Figure 2 a stable warranted growth equilibrium with a growth rate G_w^1, such that $G_c \geqq G_w^1 > G_n$. If we suppose that initially the rate of employment v is less than $\bar{v}$, then the economy moves according to (17) with the investment function corresponding to $\tilde{w}_1$ and $\pi = 1 - \tilde{w}_1$. (See Figs. 10 and 12.) The movement of v is described by (using the relation [16])

$$\dot{v}_t = \left\{ g(\mu_t^e, \tilde{w}^e) - \eta_{\mu^e} \frac{\dot{\mu}_t^e}{\mu_t^e} \right\} - G_n \tag{28}$$

with $\tilde{w}^e = \tilde{w}$. Since $\dot{\mu}_t^e < 0$ in this phase, the employment is increasing faster than the capital stock. Therefore, the economy will sooner or later confront the ceiling of $\bar{v}N_t$ which only grows at the rate G_n. Suppose this occurs at time $t = t_o$ and at $\mu^e = \hat{\mu}^e$. Then, by our assumptions, after a short period of transition the effective real wage rate is increased to $\tilde{w}_2$, and also the expected rate $\tilde{w}^e$ adjusts to this new value. There result downward shifts in both *LI* and *LS* curves.

The dynamic path of the economy that follows depends crucially on the magnitudes of these shifts as well as on where along the *LI* $(\tilde{w}_1)$ curve the economy attains the critical rate of employment $\bar{v}$, namely

$\hat{\mu}^e$. Let us assume initially that the latter is given. The magnitudes of the shifts in LI and LS curves, on the other hand, depend on the size of the increment in effective real wage rate, $\Delta\tilde{w} = \tilde{w}_2 - \tilde{w}_1$, and on the elasticity of the investment demand with respect to the expected rate of effective real wage, $\eta_{\tilde{w}^e}$.[20] The former reflects the strength of the workers in the wage bargaining process while the latter reflects the subjective attitude of entrepreneurs. We first observe for the simple case of η_{μ^e} (<1) and $\eta_{\tilde{w}^e}$ constant that the manner in which the position of the new warranted equilibrium (μ_2^{e*}, G_w^2) depends on these two parameters can be depicted as in Figure 7.[21] Therefore (a) for a given $\Delta\tilde{w}$, the larger is $\eta_{\tilde{w}^e}$, the lower will be G_w^2 and, except when $\eta_{\tilde{w}_e}$ is sufficiently small, the larger will be μ_2^{e*}; (b) for a given $\eta_{\tilde{w}^e}$, the manner in which μ_2^{e*} and G_w^2 depends on $\Delta\tilde{w}$ varies according to the magnitude of $\eta_{\tilde{w}^e}$; namely, if $\eta_{\tilde{w}^e}$ is sufficiently small, then the larger is $\Delta\tilde{w}$, the smaller will be μ_2^{e*} and the higher will be G_w^2; on the contrary, if $\eta_{\tilde{w}^e}$ is sufficiently large, then the larger is $\Delta\tilde{w}$, the larger will be μ_2^{e*} and the lower will be G_w^2.

There are two broad types to the dynamic adjustment path of the economy. The first type (I) is convergence to the Marx–J. Robinson restrained growth equilibrium. The second is a growth cycle which can be classified into two subtypes (IIA, IIB) according to the duration of the cycle. How the occurrence of these cases depends on the parameters just considered is exibited in Figures 8 and 9.[22]

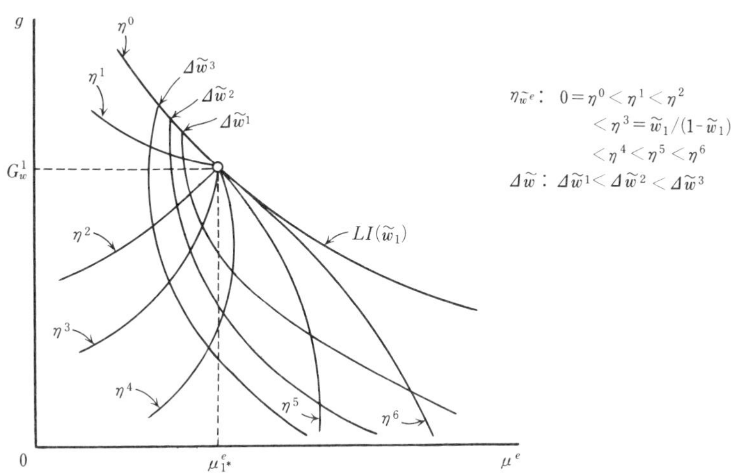

Figure 7

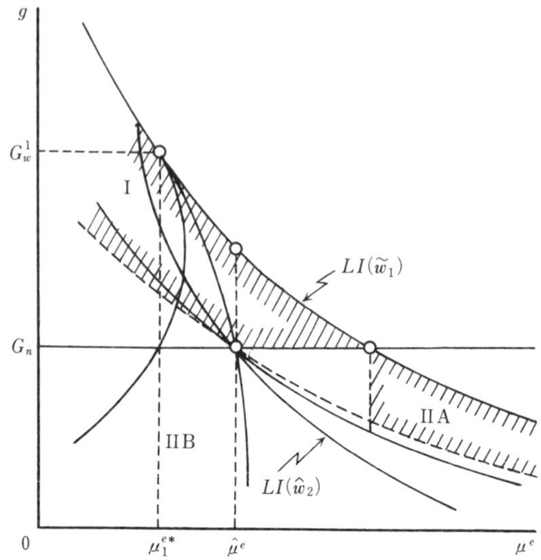

Figure 8

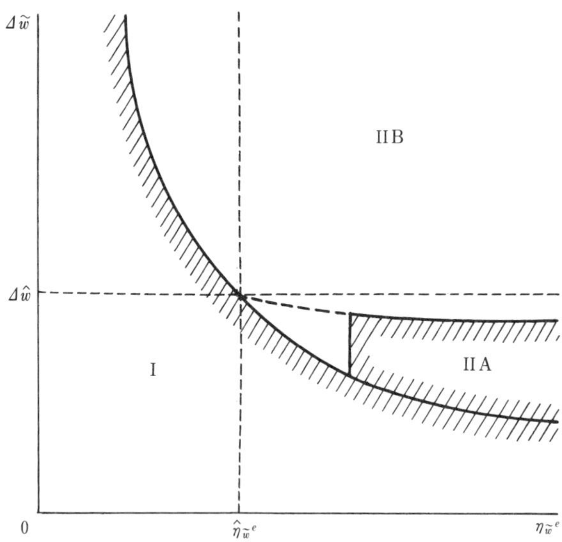

Figure 9

Table 1

		t_0				t_1				t_2
Rate of capital accumulation	↗	MAX	↘		↘	MIN	↗		↗	MAX
Rate of profit	↗	MAX	↘		↘	MIN	↗		↗	MAX
Rate of employment	↗		↗	MAX	↘		↘	MIN	↗	

(Case I) When, for any given $\eta_{\tilde{w}^e}$, $\Delta\tilde{w}$ is sufficiently small, the new warranted growth rate G_w^2 is greater than the natural rate G_n, and the rate of employment continues to increase until the economy reaches the absolute full employment ceiling (i.e., $v = 1$). From then on the dynamic path of the economy is described by the Marx–J. Robinson solution. Namely, capital accumulation is constrained by the available amount of savings, which declines relatively due to the fall in the rate of profit. This process continues until the restrained Golden Age equilibrium is reached where capital, employment and output all grow at the rate G_n. (See Figs. 10 and 11.)

(Case IIA) When $\eta_{\tilde{w}^e}$ is sufficiently large but $\Delta\tilde{w}$ is moderately small (See Figures 8 and 9.), the economy will generate a mild growth cycle around the critical employment path of $\bar{v}N_t$. This case is illustrated by Figures 12 and 13.

Namely, soon after time t_o the economy will start moving down along the $LI(\tilde{w}_2)$ curve. The rate of employment will at first continue to rise, albeit at a reduced rate (see equation [28]). However, due to the decline in the rate of accumulation, it will eventually fall, until, say at time $t = t_1$, its level returns to $\bar{v}$. From then on the dynamic path of the economy is switched back again to $LI(\tilde{w}_1)$. The rate of capital accumulation starts to recover and to increase again, while the rate of employment will for a period of time decrease further but eventually turning upward again. (See Table 1.) Thus there occurs a growth cycle around the balanced growth path with the rate of employment $\bar{v}$ and the rate of growth G_n.

Incidentally, the features of the growth cycle derived here are similar to those of a growth cycle model advanced by Marx (1867: ch. 25).[23] However, to the extent that occurrence of a cycle depends crucially on the intermediation of the state of entrepreneurs' psychology and expectations our model contains a strongly Keynesian element.[24]

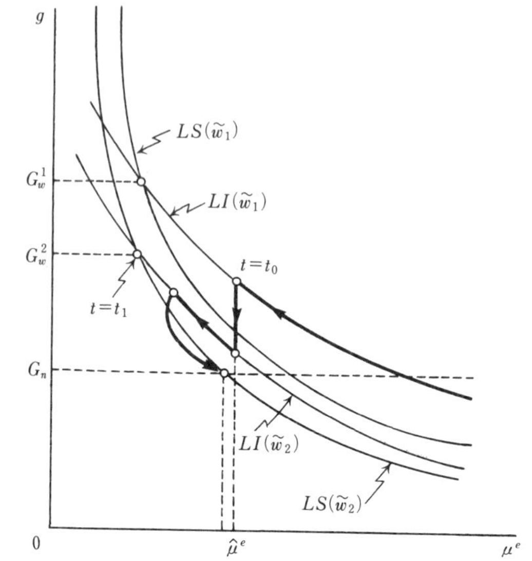

Figure 10

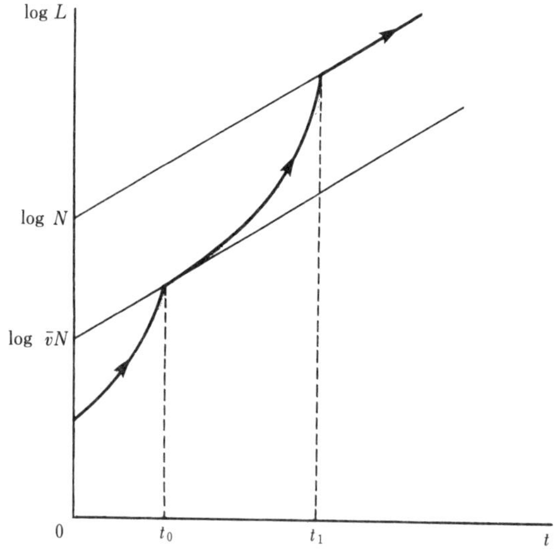

Figure 11

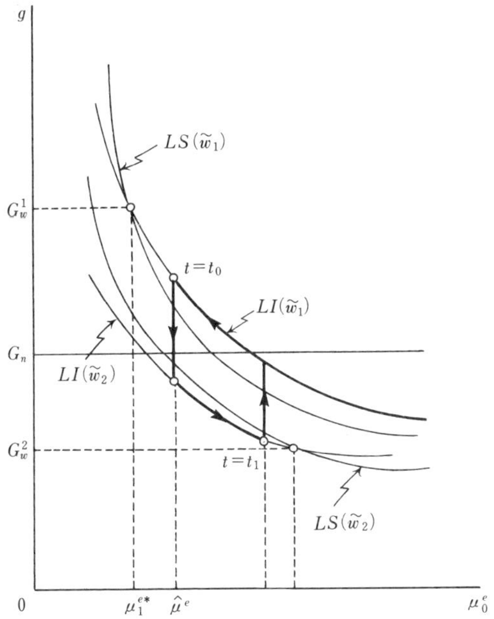

Figure 12

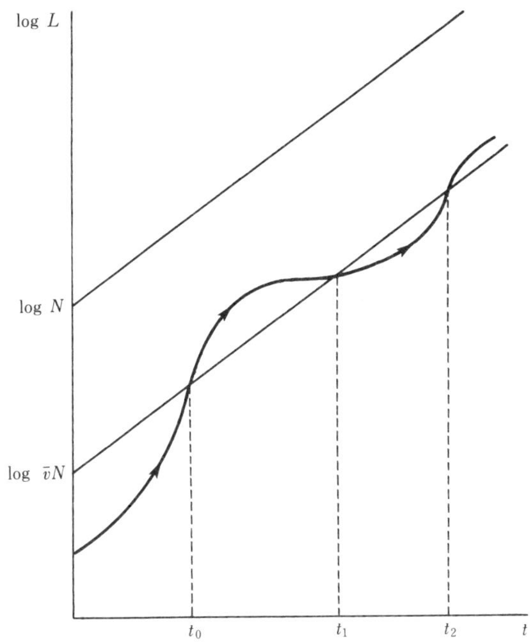

Figure 13

(Case IIB) When the values of $\eta_{\tilde{w}^e}$ and $\Delta\tilde{w}$ are sufficiently large (See Figure 9.) there occurs a growth cycle around a Golden Age path with the employment ratio $\bar{v}$. However, due to volatile fluctuations in the level of investment, the employment ratio fluctuates around the critical ratio $\bar{v}$ quite frequently (at the order of four times the lag, h); hence the cycle has a very short duration. Thus a strong brake to capital accumulation is provided by the workers' wage pressure with the result that the economy maintains a more-or-less constant rate of growth (G_n) and the path of employment does not deviate significantly (in terms of distance) from the critical path $\bar{v}N_t$.

QUALIFICATIONS

Having discussed three conceivable types of dynamic adjustment path to follow after the critical employment level is reached, let us make a few qualificatory remarks on our analysis in the increasing order of generality.

In the first place, recall that our Figure 9 depicting the conditions of the occurrence of alternative cases (I, IIA, and IIB) depends on the specifically given value of $\hat{\mu}^e$, that is, where on the original path $(LI(\tilde{w}_1))$ the critical ratio $\bar{v}$ is reached.[25] In fact, by carefully examining Figure 8, we find that the smaller $\hat{\mu}^e$ is, the smaller will be $\hat{\eta}_{\tilde{w}^e}$ and the larger will be $\Delta\hat{w}$. Thus the closer the economy initially approaches to the warranted growth equilibrium (G_w^1, μ_1^{e*}), the larger will be the set of values $(\eta_{\tilde{w}^e}, \Delta\tilde{w})$ that produces types I and IIA.

In the second place, the rather unrealistic features of the growth cycle of type IIB, namely its extremely short duration, derives primarily from the two simplifying assumptions that we imposed at the start of our analysis in this section. It should be evident that, even if we retain the first assumption of step function for the effective real wage rate (equation [27]), the cycle would become milder and its duration longer (such as in IIA) once we modify our second assumption so that the expected rate of effective real wage is adjusted to a change in the actual rate only at a moderate speed.

In the third place, we have so far discussed the conditions for occurrence of a growth cycle, but have not said a word on the question of magnitude and persistence of the cycle. It is clear that with our present specification there is no possibility of an explosive oscillation; on the other hand, there is no a priori reason to believe that oscillation will be persistent or eventually dampening. However, since examination of this question requires a detailed analysis of other parameters (e.g., the parameter $\hat{\mu}^e$ discussed in a preceding remark) we shall not go into this task in the present paper.

In the fourth place, and finally, we have conducted our analysis on the assumption that the elasticity of investment with respect to the expected rate of excess capacity is less than one (i.e., $\eta_{\mu^e} < 1$) and that a stable warranted equilibrium (G_w^1, μ_1^{e*}) exists. We have also neglected the possible relevance of the full capacity constraint. Just as we have qualified in Section 5, however, we can straightforwardly extend our analysis to the case where the full capacity constraint becomes effective as well as to the case where $\eta_{\mu^e} > 1$ and the basic dynamic force of the economy is unstable.

Implications of our discussion in this section are further considered in the next section.

7. Conclusion

In the present paper, we have constructed an aggregate model of a capitalist economy based on an imperfectly competitive market and examined the role that class confrontation around the level of real wage plays in determining the short-run and the long-run course of the economy, in particular the rate of capital accumulation and the distribution of income.

For the short run we observed the following points.

(1) As long as factors of production (capital and labor) are kept underutilized, entrepreneurs are able to generate sufficient profits to realize their investment desire (which is given in the short run) by controlling the amount of employment and output. Therefore, a higher rate of (effective) real wage is compatible with entrepreneurs' desired rate of profit, and we confirm the point noted earlier by J. Robinson (1942, 1962) and Kalecki (1971a, 1971b) that the higher the workers succeed in raising the real wage rate, the less will they make the number of the unemployed.

(2) However, when either factor of production becomes fully utilized, no further expansion of output is possible. Therefore, higher real wage rate is no longer compatible with desired rate of profit, and the class conflict over real wages and their share in the total output becomes a real one. The Kaldor-Kaleckian hypothesis to resolve this conflict, namely to suppose that the capitalist class has the mighty force always to realize its desired rate of profit at the sacrifice of workers, cannot be regarded as a satisfactory characterization of the capitalist economy.

On the other hand, we observed the following points for the long run.

(3) As a first step of our discussion, assume a constant real wage rate, $\tilde{w}$, reflecting the relative balance of class forces. Then the long-run stability of the economy depends crucially on the volatility of entrepreneurs' investment demand with respect to their long-term expectations (as measured by η_{μ^e}) as well as on the share of wages in the total output (which equals $\tilde{w}$). More specifically, in order for this economy to have a stable warranted growth equilibrium it is necessary that (a) entrepreneurs' investment demand not be very volatile ($\eta_{\mu^e} < 1$) and (b) the share of wages fall within a certain limited range.
(4) One important implication of (3) is that even when condition (a) is satisfied, if the relative balance of class forces is such that the share of wages is sufficiently low, then the economy falls into the state of secular stagnation due to chronical insufficiency of effective demand. In other words, the more the capitalist class succeeds in obtaining a high profit share, the more likely they are to bring the economy to stagnation. This provides an objective constraint on the capitalists' power to extract high profits quite independent from the constraint that workers must be paid their minimum subsistence wages.
(5) On the other hand, if the conditions (a) and (b) are met and, moreover, the real wage rate $\tilde{w}$ is set high enough, then the economy tends to a warranted growth equilibrium with the rate of capital accumulation higher than the natural rate of growth G_n. However, the output of the economy will sooner or later be constrained by full employment. From then on, entrepreneurs' investment desires are no longer satisfied and capital accumulation is constrained by the available amount of saving, until the state of a restrained (high-level bastard à la Joan Robinson) Golden Age equilibrium is reached. Thus a sufficiently strong class force of workers will limit capital accumulation in the long run.
(6) When we extend the framework of analysis and let the real wage rate respond to the tightness in the labor market, the dynamic course of the economy depends on the degree to which workers can effectively make their power felt on real wages in the wake of the falling unemployment rate (as measured by v), and on the degree to which entrepreneurs' investment demand responds to the change in the (expected) real wage rate (as measured by $\eta_{\tilde{w}^e}$) in addition to the factors noted in (3) above.
(7) Specifically, in the case where the economy tends to accumulate at the rate above G_n (as in (5) above), the economy will exhibit a growth cycle around a Golden Age equilibrium (with a constant rate of unemployment, $1 - \bar{v}$) if pressure on real wages and/or entrepre-

neurs' response are sufficiently strong; or it will eventually be led to the restrained Golden Age equilibrium as discussed in (5) if these factors are small and they do not provide a sufficiently strong brake to curtail entrepreneurs' investment desires.

As summarized in the above paragraphs, class conflict over real wages has significant impact, either directly or through its interaction with entrepreneurial psychology and expectations, on the dynamic course of the capitalist economy. This aspect, however, has not been given due treatment, if not completely neglected, in the neo-Keynesian literature on economic growth and income distribution. In fact, the problem remains implicit in Joan Robinson's model (1962), while Kaldor and Kalecki attach too much importance to the entrepreneurial motivation in controlling the dynamics of the capitalist economy. By emphasizing the role of class conflict and thus bringing in an important Marxian perspective to the analysis, the present paper takes a first step in modifying the basic view on the motion of the capitalist economy as propounded by the neo-Keynesian authors.

There are several qualificatory remarks to be made about our model. First, we have assumed a simple single commodity economy with fixed coefficient technology. Furthermore, technical progress and, more specifically, the level of the natural rate of growth G_n have been treated only exogenously. Indeed this neglects the distinctive insight of Marx (1867: chs. 15, 25) in that the capitalist class can *to a certain extent* control the natural rate of growth G_n, through their influence on technology and social processes.[26] However, even for Marx the qualification of "to a certain extent" was a very important one and, indeed, herein lay, in his view, the major contradiction of capitalism. Thus, although it may not significantly alter the basic implications of our analysis here, modification of this simplified assumption will certainly give us richer understanding of the dynamics of the capitalist economy.

Second, we have assumed that the monetary authority controls nominal money supply in such a way that the real rate of interest is maintained constant. In fact, this implies that the monetary authority continuously increases the nominal money supply (but still offsets the "cost push" inflation going on at the rate of increase in money wage rates). This assumption rules out from our model any role that monetary factors might play in regulating the dynamic course of the economy. Alternatively, we may introduce a more active monetary policy (as done by Joan Robinson [1962] for the case where the economy comes to be overheated), and letting entrepreneurs' investment demand respond to changes in the real rate of interest.

Third, we have assumed that entrepreneurs being separated from ownership have no power to control the propensity to save out of gross profits, s_c. However, as has been argued strongly by Stephen Marglin (1975a, 1975b), it is perhaps more realistic to assume that in the modern capitalist economy entrepreneurs can at least to a certain extent control the savings propensity through retained earnings and other forms of institutional savings. This leads us, for one, to the empirical task of looking into the savings behavior of the economy more closely, and its result may entail a significant modification to our theoretical formulation.

Fourth, and most important, our theoretical discussion still lacks a complete theory of real wage determination. For, although explanation of money wage determination can appropriately be based upon the relative balance of class forces between capital and labor, the price policy parameter that links money wage rate to real wage rate, namely, the mark-up ratio γ, is left unexplained. We recall Kalecki's (1954) hint that the mark-up ratio depends on the strength of tensions between capitalists and workers as well as that among capitalists themselves. However, much remains in the state of a black box. Nor can we be satisfied, of course, with a cumstomarily determined level. We must also note how great a simplification has been achieved in the course of our mathematical analysis by using this assumption of constant mark-up ratio. Once we discard the latter, we can no longer separate, in general, the dynamics of the price system from those of the quantity system.

We will return to these important questions in our subsequent papers.

NOTES

This paper is an outgrowth of lectures given during the spring semester of 1975 at Harvard University and during the fall of 1975 at University of Tokyo. I am indebted to Professor Stephen Marglin (with whom I taught the course, and the content of whose lectures is published in a revised form [1976]) and many graduate students who participated in classroom discussions. The present version is a significantly revised version of the lectures. I have also benefited from discussions with Professor Masahiko Aoki who provided me with initial stimulation and from the seminars at Queen's University and University of Tokyo. I also acknowledge the financial support provided by Seimei-kai Foundation.

1. To construe the level of real wage as reflecting the state of class conflict between capital and labor expresses a Marxian standpoint. However, within the Marxian perspective, this is the class conflict only as it manifests itself in the sphere of exchange. See Rowthorn (1974).

2. Although Kalecki (1937, 1954) employs as Keynes the same Fisherian framework for the discussion of entrepreneurs' investment demand, Kalecki differs from Keynes in not emphasizing the subjective elements (long-term expectations and animal spirits) involved in the marginal efficiency of investment schedule discussed below. This, at first,

seems contradictory to Kalecki's emphasis on entrepreneurial evaluation of risk as the limitational factor of investment. However, evaluation of risk is linked primarily with the financial leverage position of the firm and is construed to be deduced objectively from it. (See Wellisz [1952–53]) for further discussion.) In an earlier paper, Ishikawa (1975), I have followed Kalecki more closely and studied the effect of financial leverage position of the firm on the long-run investment behavior and dynamic course of the economy. In the present paper, I am simplifying the analysis by omitting the financial aspect of the problem. However, as long as dividend payout ratio is assumed to be exogenously given and constant, there will be no major modification in the conclusion of the analysis even when risk element is included. Also for further discussion on the relation between Keynes's and Kalecki's formulations, see J. Robinson (1965: 96–97).

3. For rationales underlying the preservation of excess capacity in an imperfectly competitive economy, see Steindl (1952: ch. 2).

4. See Kaldor (1966). However, see a qualification made below in Section 7.

5. Albeit with qualifications, this assumption is commonly made in neo-Keynesian works, Kaldor (1959, 1963), Joan Robinson (1962: Essay 2), Asimakoplos (1970). Others include Okishio (1959, 1960) and Aoki (1975), which in a multi-sectoral circulating capital model, discuss the impact of workers' struggle for higher money wages on inflation (Okishio and Aoki) and also studies the dynamic stability property of the growth process (Aoki). There the assumption of constant mark-up ratio admits the separation of the dynamics of price adjustment from that of quantity adjustment and admits a great simplification of the analysis. The same simplification is present in our model.

6. We follow Aoki's (1975) formulation here. Incidentally, this assumption reflects the real world in that each year collective bargaining between corporate managers and union members takes place to revise the wage contract for the next year.

7. See J. Robinson (1962: 43–44). In her model, however, monetary policy is introduced to restrain investment when the economy becomes overheated.

8. Kalecki's formula stirred a controversy as to whether or not it was merely a tautology. Here I agree with the interpretation of J. Robinson (1965: 97–98) and hold against those of Kaldor (1956: Section III (b)) and Nuti (1970). We also note that even Kaldor must introduce some mechanism to complete the theory of income distribution that can be applied also to the case of underemployment (see criticism made by Atsumi [1960]).

9. This short-run property is clearly noted in Kalecki (1971a). See also J. Robinson (1942: 90 [1966 edition]), who also cites Kalecki's earlier discussion, and (1962: 42).

10. This is the meaning of "investment driven" character emphasized by Kaldor and commonly attributed to neo-Keynesian growth models. However, it is important to note that the "investment driven" character comes to the forefront because the real wage rate is already determined and is assumed to be constant.

11. See Marx (1894: ch. 15, section 1), Keynes (1936: ch. 23), and J. Robinson (1942: 71–72 [1966 edition]) and (1962: 73, 77–78).

12. In the familiar three-sector model with wage goods, investment goods, and luxury goods, the same supposition is expressed in the following manner. Namely, the entrepreneurs will produce the required amount of investment goods and luxury goods, but produce less of wage goods, and they let the workers with given money wages compete for the wage goods produced. See Kalecki (1971a). See also Marglin's (1976) characterization of the neo-Keynesian model.

13. The linearized system of (19) and (20) around (μ^{e*}, μ^*) is given by,

$$\begin{pmatrix} \dot{\mu}_t \\ \dot{\mu}_t^e \end{pmatrix} = \begin{pmatrix} 0 & -\eta_{\mu^e}^* G_n \\ \kappa & -\kappa \end{pmatrix} \begin{pmatrix} \mu_t - \mu^* \\ \mu_t^e - \mu^{e*} \end{pmatrix}$$

where $\eta_{\mu^e}^* = \eta_{\mu^e}(\mu^{e*})$. It is easy to see that this system is locally stable. Furthermore, we observe that, if $\kappa \geqq 4\eta_{\mu^e}^* G_n$, then the movement is monotonic, while, if $\kappa < 4\eta_{\mu^e}^* G_n$, the movement is oscillatory. In the latter case, further consideration becomes necessary, for the fact that μ_t^e overshoots μ^{e*} means that labor becomes underutilized again. Then a question arises as to whether or not the system returns to the old state of affairs with the share of profit, $\pi_o = \pi$ $(t \leqq t_o)$. However, for our purposes we need not go further into answering this question here.

14. We note that the locus representing $\dot{\pi}_t = 0$ (and below which $\dot{\pi}_t > 0$)

$$\mu = \frac{\mu^e}{\kappa\eta_{\mu^e}}(\kappa\eta_{\mu^e} + g(\mu^e) - G_n)$$

crosses the 45° line only once from above at the steady state equilibrium point (μ^{e*}, μ^*). Therefore, there must exist a time interval $[t_o, t_1)$ $(t_o < t_1 \leqq \infty)$ for which $\dot{\pi}_t > 0$.

15. This is seen when we note in (17) and (19)

$$\dot{\mu}^e_{t'} = \kappa\left(\frac{s_c\pi_o}{\beta G_n} - \mu^{e*}\right) < 0 \quad \text{where } \mu^{e*} = \mu^e_{t=t'} \ (t' < t_o)$$

$$\text{and } \dot{\mu}^e_t = \kappa\left(\frac{s_c\pi^*}{\beta G_n} - \mu^{e*}\right) = 0.$$

16. I say "in principle" because in reality complications arise due to non-shiftability of capital goods among different sectors.

17. Both in Marx (1865: section 14) and J. Robinson (1962: 70) (particularly in her discussion of the bastard Golden Age equilibrium), class struggle is present to resist the fall in real wage rate. Note that this mechanism is quite different from J. Robinson's discussion of "restrained" Golden Age equilibrium where investment is restrained not by the amount of savings forthcoming as we suppose here, but by financial control or by entrepreneurs' collective self-restraint (1962: 54–55). For a related discussion on Marx's and J. Robinson's analysis, see Harris (1975).

18. This is because the characteristic roots of the differential equations system (24) and (25) are $-\kappa$ and $-G_n$, which are both real and negative. In fact, equation (25) can be solved independently, and the expected rate of excess capacity variable does not have any active role to play in the system. However, both equations are presented to facilitate comparison with the Kaldor-Kaleckian solution.

19. Mathematically, equations (24) and (25) are replaced by $\dot{\mu}^e_t = (1 - \mu^e_t)$ and $\dot{\mu}_t = 0$. These imply that μ^e_t is adjusted to 1 in the long run. In Figure 6 (where alteration is made so that $G_c < \text{Min}[G_w, G_n]$) the economy is shown to move horizontally leftward after time $t = t_0$ along the lines $g = G_c$ (in the upper half) and $\mu = 1$ (in the lower half) until the expected rate of excess capacity converges to 1. During this time phase, entrepreneurs' investment desire is no longer fulfilled.

20. We shall hereafter assume that the elasticities $\eta_{\tilde{w}^e}$ and η_{μ^e} are constants (with $\eta_{\mu^e} < 1$). Moreover, as a standard of comparison, we assume that the equilibrium point (μ_1^{e*}, G_w^1) is a fixed point created by different values of $\eta_{\tilde{w}^e}$. This involves adjustment of the constant term in the investment function $g^d = g(\mu^e, \tilde{w}^e, \eta_{\tilde{w}^e}, \eta_{\mu^e}) = A{\mu^e}^{-\eta_{\mu^e}}{\tilde{w}^e}^{-\eta_{\tilde{w}^e}}$ such that $g(\mu_1^{e*}, \tilde{w}_1, \eta_{\tilde{w}^e}, \eta_{\mu^e}) = G_w^1$, or equivalently, $\log A = \log G_w^1 {\mu_1^{e*}}^{\eta_{\mu^e}} - \eta_{\tilde{w}^e} \cdot \log \tilde{w}_1$, where η_{μ^e} is given.

21. Assume that η_{μ^e} (<1) and $\eta_{\tilde{w}^e}$ to be given. Then from the equilibrium condition,

$$\mu^{e*} = \frac{s_c(1 - \tilde{w})}{g(\mu^e, \tilde{w}, \eta_{\tilde{w}^e}, \eta_{\mu^e})}$$

we obtain:

(i) $G_w^2 \geqq G_w^1$ implies $\mu_2^{e*} < \mu_1^{e*}$, and

(ii) $$\frac{\tilde{w}}{\mu^{e*}}\frac{d\mu^{e*}}{d\tilde{w}} = \frac{\eta_{\tilde{w}^e} - \dfrac{\tilde{w}}{1 - \tilde{w}}}{1 - \eta_{\mu^e}}$$

where the denominator is known to be positive.

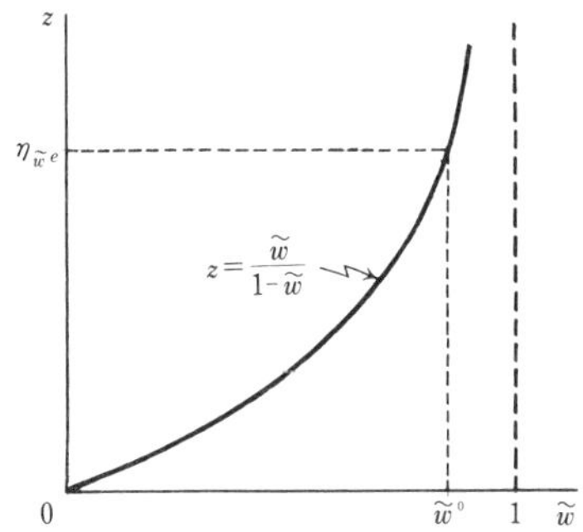

From property (ii) and from the figure given we observe that, for any given $\eta_{\tilde{w}^e}$, there exists a critical value of $\tilde{w}$, say $\tilde{w}^o$ defined by $\eta_{\tilde{w}^e} = \dfrac{\tilde{w}^o}{1 - \tilde{w}^o}$, such that

$$\frac{d\mu^{e*}}{d\tilde{w}} \gtreqless 0 \quad \text{as } \tilde{w} \lesseqgtr \tilde{w}^o.$$

It is then immediately seen that $\tilde{w}^o$ increases with $\eta_{\tilde{w}^e}$. Let us write $\tilde{w}^o = \tilde{w}^o(\eta_{\tilde{w}^e})$. We then observe:

(a) For any given $\eta_{\tilde{w}^e}$, if $\tilde{w}_1 < \tilde{w}_2 \leqq \tilde{w}^o(\eta_{\tilde{w}^e})$, then $\mu_2^{e*} > \mu_1^{e*}$, $G_w^2 < G_w^1$.
(b) For any given $\eta_{\tilde{w}^e}$, if $\tilde{w}_1 \leqq \tilde{w}^o(\eta_{\tilde{w}^e}) < \tilde{w}_2$, then $\mu_2^{e*} \gtreqless \mu_1^{e*}$.
(c) For any given $\eta_{\tilde{w}^e}$, if $\tilde{w}_1 > \tilde{w}^o(\eta_{\tilde{w}^e})$, then $\mu_2^{e*} < \mu_1^{e*}$.

Figure 7 is then obtained using these properties and noting that in our problem $\tilde{w}_1$ is given and fixed.

22. These figures are obtained by using (28) and examining how the employment rate (v) moves after $t = t_o$ for each possible (μ_2^{e*}, G_w^2). The broken curve in Figure 8 represents the set of possible equilibrium positions (μ_2^{e*}, G_w^2) such that $\dot{v}_t = 0$ at $t = t_o$ (so that $\dot{v}_t > 0$ above this locus and $\dot{v}_t < 0$ below this locus).

23. See also recent formulations of Marx's ideas by Goodwin (1969) and Eagly (1975) (although the latter is marred by mathematical ambiguities). Incidentally, these cyclical features accord with the postwar U.S. experience on profit-wage fluctuations as referred to by Boddy and Crotty (1974, 1975).

24. Recall that Keynes (1936: ch. 22) sought the primary cause of trade cycles in fluctuations of entrepreneurs' long-term expectations and their subjective attitudes toward them. We also note that Marx had a crude notion of investment function that responds to expected profitability of investment. See Marx (1867: 620–21).

25. Needless to say, the conditions also depend on the values of η_{μ^e} and the actual position of (μ_1^{e*}, G_w^1), which are here assumed to be given and fixed.

26. This feature is also present in J. Robinson. See (1962: 52).

References

Aoki, M. 1975. Income distribution and dual stability in a system of competitive monopolies. Economic Studies Quarterly 26. (in Japanese)

Asimakoplos, A. 1970. A Robinsonian growth model in one sector notation: An amendment. Australian Economic Papers 9 (Dec.): 171–76.

Atsumi, H. 1960. Mr. Kaldor's theory of income distribution, comment. Review of Economic Studies, 27.

Boddy, R., and J. Crotty. 1974. Class conflict, Keynesian policies, and the business cycle. Monthly Review (Oct.).

———. 1975. Class conflict and macro policy: The political business cycle. Review of Radical Political Economics 7 (Spring): 1–19.
Eagly, R. 1975. A macro model of the endogenous business cycle in Marxist analysis. Journal of Political Economy 80 (May/June): 525–39.
Goodwin, R. 1969. A growth cycle. In Socialism, Capitalism, and Economic Growth: Essays Presented to Maurice Dobb, ed. by C. Feinstein. Cambridge: Cambridge University Press. Reprinted in A Critique of Economic Theory, F. Hunt and J. Schwartz. Penguin (1972): 442–49.
Harris, D. 1975. The theory of economic growth: A critique and reformation. American Economic Review 65 (May): 329–37.
Ishikawa, T. 1975. A critical evaluation of the neo-Keynesian-Kaleckian economic growth models. Discussion Paper, University of Tokyo, (Nov.).
Kaldor, N. 1955–56. Alternative theories of distribution. Review of Economic Studies 23. Reprinted in his Essays on Value and Distribution. London: Gerald Duckworth, 1960.
———. 1957. A model of economic growth. Economic Journal 67. Reprinted in his Essays on Economic Stability and Growth. London: Gerald Duckworth, 1960.
———. 1959. Economic growth and the problem of inflation. Economica 26: 212–26 and 287–98. Reprinted in Essays on Economic Policy, vol. I. London: Gerald Duckworth, 1964.
———. 1963. Capital accumulation and economic growth. In The Theory of Capital, Proceedings of IEA Conference, ed. by Lutz and Hague. London: Macmillan.
———. 1966. Marginal productivity and macroeconomic theories of distribution. Review of Economic Studies 33: 309–19.
Kalecki, M. 1937. The principle of increasing risk. Economica 4. Reprinted in Essays in the Theory of Economic Fluctuations. New York: Farrar and Rinehart, 1939.
———. 1954. Theory of Economic Dynamics. London: Allen and Unwin.
———. 1971a. Class struggle and distribution of national income. Kyklos 24: 1–9.
———. 1971b. Selected Essays on the Dynamics of the Capitalist Economy. Cambridge: Cambridge University Press.
Keynes, J.M. 1936. The General Theory of Employment, Interest and Money. London: Macmillan.
Marglin, S. 1975a. What do bosses do? part II. Review of Radical Political Economics (Spring).
———. 1975b. Postscript to what do bosses do? Harvard Institute of Economic Research Discussion Paper 429 (Aug.).
———. 1976. Growth, distribution, and prices: An exposition of neo-classical, neo-Marxian and neo-Keynesian approaches (March).
Marx, K. 1867. Capital, vol. I. New York: International Publishers Edition, 1967.
———. 1894. Capital, vol. III. New York: International Publishers Edition, 1967.
———. 1865. Value, Price and Profit (published in London, 1898).
Nuti, D. 1970. Vulgar economy in the theory of income distribution. De Economist 118: 363–60. Reprinted in A Critique of Economic Theory, ed. by F. Hunt and J. Schwartz. Penguin (1972): 222–32.
Okishio, N. 1959. Inflation as expression of class conflict. Kokumin Keizai Zasshi. (in Japanese)
———. 1960. On wage-price spiral. Riron Keizaigaku (June). (in Japanese)
Robinson, J. 1942. An Essay on Marxian Economics. London: Macmillan (1966 edition).
———. 1962. Essays in the Theory of Economic Growth. London: Macmillan.
———. 1965. Kalecki and Keynes. In Collected Economic Papers, vol. III. Oxford: Basil Blackwell.
Rowthorn, B. 1974. Neo-classicism, neo-Ricardianism and Marxism. New Left Review 86 (July/Aug.): 63–87.
Steindl, J. 1952. Maturity and Stagnation in American Capitalism. Oxford: Basil Blackwell.
Wellisz, L. 1952–53. Entrepreneur's risk, lender's risk, and investment. Review of Economic Studies 20.

10. Wages, Work Intensity, and Unemployment

1. Introduction

International and intertemporal differences in labor productivity have been attributed traditionally to differences in technology, capital intensity, and the level of worker skills. Recent studies have stressed, however, that work intensity plays a major role in the determination of labor productivity. The endogeneity of work intensity has been stressed also as an explanation of involuntary unemployment.[1] But the endogeneity of work intensity can contribute to a theory of comparative economic performance only to the extent that the concept is grounded in a rigorous comparative static analysis of labor market behavior. This paper develops a model which recognizes that the level of work intensity reflects both the behavioral attributes of workers and the structural characteristics of production and exchange.

The model we develop shares with the earlier works of Calvo (1979) and Shapiro and Stiglitz (1984) a fundamental attribute of employer-employee contracts causing labor to fall outside the traditional Walrasian model. Namely, the employee, while receiving a specific wage, does not guarantee the delivery of a specific bundle of labor services. The dissatisfied employer can credibly threaten not legal suit, but rather *nonrenewal of contract*. Given these circumstances the profit-maximizing employer is normally willing to pay a wage higher than necessary simply to attract the number of labor hours desired. For the higher the wage paid, the greater the cost of job loss to the worker, and hence, the more likely that the worker will deliver satisfactory labor

Coauthored with Herbert Gintis, University of Massachusetts, Amherst. Originally published in *Journal of the Japanese and International Economies* 1 (1987): 195–228.

services. In such a framework, the labor market need not clear and the Walrasian analysis does not necessarily apply.

What we add to the earlier literature is the analysis of how the work intensity of workers is endogenously determined; heretofore determination of the level of work intensity has either been kept in a black box (as in Calvo, 1979; Bowles, 1985) or made exogenous in the form of a minimum performance standard (as in Shapiro and Stiglitz, 1984). Our analysis stresses the interaction of worker preferences, costs of job loss for workers, costs of work supervision and worker terminations for employers, and the level of social unemployment compensation as key to the determination of work intensity. Our enlarged model can sustain either full employment, voluntary unemployment, or involuntary unemployment equilibria. Our major results concern the comparative static properties of the labor market equilibrium with regard to both unemployment and work intensity when there are exogenous changes in these factors.

The organization of this paper is as follows. We demonstrate in Section 2 that the work intensity of an individual worker, under suitable conditions, responds positively to an increased threat of dismissal, an increase in the intensity of supervision, and a decline in the reservation utility. Section 3 then analyzes the equilibrium levels of wages, employment, rates of dismissal, and supervision intensity in a single firm, concluding that profits, output, and employment are negatively related to the reservation utility, while real unit labor costs, work intensity, labor productivity, and the wage rate are positively related to the reservation utility. The remainder of the paper shows that this result, suitably qualified, can be extended to a full labor market equilibrium framework. Sections 4 and 5 discuss the steady-state market equilibrium properties of the economy, first assuming a linear worker utility function, and then relaxing this assumption. In Section 5, we determine under what conditions steady-state equilibria fall under the categories of involuntary unemployment, voluntary unemployment, and full employment. Section 6 summarizes our major results. The Appendix proves that the firm equilibrium discussed in Section 3 is a true Nash equilibrium.

2. The Determinants of Work Intensity

The labor market we consider consists of a homogeneous workforce and is organized by a sequential renewal market, where each firm offers a contract consisting of uniform wage, denoted by w (measured in output units), and a conditional option for a renewal of employment in the next period. The criterion for renewal is such that a certain proportion, say f $(0 \leq f < 1)$, of workers who are regarded by the employer to have supplied the least work intensity (effort) are not renewed (i.e., dismissed).

We suppose that there exists a fundamental (ex ante) informational asymmetry between the workers and the firm with respect to the level of effort of each worker. Namely, while each worker's effort is perfectly known to the fellow workers in the firm, it is only imperfectly monitored and known to the firm. The inexactness involved here, denoted by m and specified more concretely later, can be decreased at a cost to the firm. Similarly, dismissal of workers may incur cost to the employer in the form of increased overhead costs and increased collective resistance by the workers. Thus the extent of monitoring (m) and dismissal (f) become matters of choice for the firm. These, together with wages (w), constitute the content of the contract offered to workers.[2]

In this section, we shall focus on the individual worker's response to the patterns of inducements and threats thus written into the contract. We shall show that if the rate of dismissal as chosen by the firm is positive, work intensity increases with the rate of dismissal and the intensity of monitoring, and decreases with the reservation utility.

We shall denote by i the work intensity of an individual worker, and by i_g the average work intensity of the firm's labor force. The probability of dismissal for an individual worker, to be denoted by d, and to be distinguished clearly from f, naturally depends on the rate of dismissal as determined by the firm, f, and on $(i - i_g)$, the extent to which the worker's intensity deviates from the group average. The latter is called the *emulation factor* and occupies a central place in the firm's work incentive inducement mechanism.[3] We shall write the relationship as

$$d = d(f, i - i_g) \tag{1}$$

with the assumed properties

$$f \geq 0, \quad d_1 > 0, \quad d_2 < 0, \quad d_{22} > 0 \tag{2a}$$

$$d(0, i - i_g) = 0 \quad \text{for any } i - i_g \tag{2b}$$

$$d(f, 0) = f \quad \text{for any } f > 0. \tag{2c}$$

The concrete form of the function $d(\cdot, \cdot)$ depends on the nature of the monitoring technology of the firm to be discussed below.[4] Assumption (2b) is a natural reflection of the fact that when the firm chooses not to fire any workers, workers do not have to worry at all about dismissals. Purely mathematically speaking, we are imposing the condition that the function d is discontinuous at $f = 0$. On the other hand, assumption (2c) implies that when the worker works just at the average intensity level, dismissal is supposed to occur randomly at the chosen rate f. We assume that there are sufficiently many workers so that the individual cannot affect the level of i_g. This means that the worker can affect the probability d only through the appropriate choice of his/her work intensity i. We will also show in the next section that under conditions of profit maximization, the employer always chooses f such that

$$0 \leq f < r, \tag{3}$$

where r is the rate of discount.

We shall adopt a discrete time framework, and suppose that a worker, once hired for a period, will receive the wage w at the end of the period, at which time the worker is either dismissed or rehired. Then in a stationary equilibrium the present value of utility for the employed worker is given by

$$V_e = \frac{u(w, i) + dV_u}{d + r} \tag{4}$$

where $u(w, i)$ represents the current period utility of the wage w and the work intensity i, V_e represents the present value of having a job, and V_u represents the present value of not having a job, both evaluated at the beginning of the period. V_u is assumed to be given by the market throughout the next section. (See [36] below for its determination.) We assume that the utility function $u(w, i)$ satisfies $u_w > 0$ and $u_{ii} \leq 0$ for all (w, i), and for any given w, $u_i < 0$ for a sufficiently large i.

Equation (4) can be rewritten as

$$rV_e = u(w, i) - d(V_e - V_u), \tag{4'}$$

meaning that the current rental "income" of the employed equals the current period utility from work minus the expected asset loss that the worker incurs due to possible dismissal. Clearly V_e must be at least as large as V_u, or equivalently current period utility $u(w, i)$ must be at least as great as the reservation utility rV_u, to induce an individual to work at all.

The worker must choose the level of work intensity i to maximize the present value V_e for given levels of w, f, r, V_u, and i_g. The nature of the solution depends on whether the rate of dismissal f is positive or zero. When f is zero, the emulation factor is irrelevant, and work intensity is chosen to maximize the worker's current period utility, given the wage level. We call this the voluntary intensity level (which may be zero). When f is positive, the work intensity is induced through the emulation mechanism and will exceed the voluntarily supplied level. In sum, the first-order condition for maximization of V_e is given by

$$\frac{d_2(f, i - i_g) \cdot \{u(w, i) - rV_u\}}{u_i(w, i)} = d(f, i - i_g) + r \qquad \text{for } f > 0 \tag{5a}$$

$$u_i \leq 0, \quad i \geq 0, \quad \text{and} \quad u_i(w, i) \cdot i = 0 \qquad \text{for } f = 0. \tag{5b}$$

(Note that when $f = 0$, maximization of V_e reduces to maximization of current utility $u[w, i]$.) The second-order condition is assumed to be satisfied by the specification of the utility function and by (2). In Section 5, we shall explicitly consider the case $f = 0$. For now, we assume that $f > 0$, so that (5a) holds. We shall suppose that a group effort equilibrium over identically situated workers is established as a symmetric Nash equilibrium, which is defined by the condition (5a) and

$$i = i_g \quad \text{(for every worker)}, \tag{6}$$

for given w, r, f, and rV_u. That these conditions, in fact, establish a symmetric Nash equilibrium is proved in the Appendix. Then the group equilibrium level of work intensity is determined implicitly as a unique solution to the equation

$$\frac{d_2(f, 0) \cdot \{u(w, i_g) - rV_u\}}{u_i(w, i_g)} = f + r. \tag{7}$$

We must now discuss more concretely the underlying monitoring technology of the firm, from which the dismissal probability function $d(\cdot, \cdot)$ is derived. We shall suppose that the measured work effort $\hat{\imath}$ equals the true work effort $\tilde{\imath}$ plus an error term which, for ease of exposition, we take to follow a symmetric triangular distribution with mean zero, and with maximum error $\pm m$. We may then take m as an expression of the level of resources (per worker) devoted by the firm to the monitoring activity.[5] If firms are to dismiss the workers whose observed effort $\hat{\imath}$ falls among the lowest $100f$ percent of the workforce, then the probability of a worker's being fired will be the conditional probability that his observed effort is less than or equal to the critical level, given the worker's true effort expended. Define.

$$G(x|i) \equiv \Pr\{\hat{\imath} < x | \tilde{\imath} = i\}.$$

Then $G(x|i)$ can be evaluated as

$$G(x|i) = \begin{cases} 0 & \text{for } x < i - m \\ \{x - (i - m)^2\}/2m^2 & \text{for } i - m \leq x < i \\ 1 - (i + m - x)^2/2m^2 & \text{for } i \leq x < i + m \\ 1 & \text{for } i + m \leq x. \end{cases} \tag{8}$$

This conditional probability distribution can be combined with a distribution function of the true effort input, whose density function we denote by $h(\tilde{\imath})$, to generate the probability distribution of observed effort input. In general, the density function of the observed work intensity, which we denote by $j(\hat{\imath})$, can be obtained as

$$j(\hat{\imath}) = \int_0^{\infty} h(\tilde{\imath})\hat{g}(\hat{\imath}|\tilde{\imath})\, d\tilde{\imath}.$$

where $\hat{g}(\tilde{\imath}|\tilde{\imath})$ is the density function associated with (8). The firm, having information on the shape of $j(\hat{\imath})$, chooses a critical level x_{crit} such that the workers whose observed effort $\hat{\imath}$ falls below x_{crit} are dismissed. Clearly x_{crit} must satisfy the relationship

$$\int_0^{x_{\text{crit}}} j(\hat{\imath})\, d\hat{\imath} = f. \tag{9}$$

The sole expectational equilibrium occurs when every worker provides the same level of work effort, i_g. This equilibrium can be characterized by the following conditions. First, since $h(\tilde{\imath})$ degenerates to a point mass at i_g, with large enough number of workers, (9) can safely be assumed to reduce to

$$G(x_{\text{crit}}|i_g) = f, \tag{10}$$

from which we can solve x_{crit} explicitly as

$$x_{\text{crit}} = \begin{cases} i_g - m + m\sqrt{2f} & \text{if } f < \frac{1}{2} \\ i_g + m - m\sqrt{2(1-f)} & \text{if } f \geq \frac{1}{2}. \end{cases} \tag{11}$$

We shall hereafter concentrate on the case $f < \frac{1}{2}$, the supposition being that large dismissal is too costly for the firm. (This condition can be defined rigorously in terms of the cost of dismissal function, $c(i_g)$, introduced later in the paper.) The probability of dismissal for a single worker is then given by

$$d = \begin{cases} (1/2m^2)\{i - i_g - m\sqrt{2f}\}^2 & \text{for } f > 0 \\ 0 & \text{for } f = 0. \end{cases} \tag{12}$$

In what follows we shall employ a shorthand expression,

$$\phi. = \sqrt{2f}. \tag{13}$$

It is easy to check that this function satisfies the curvature properties specified in (2a)–(2c) in the neighborhood of i_g.

With this concrete form of the emulation factor in hand, the expectational group effort equilibrium is easily verified (using [7]) to be defined by

$$\frac{u(w, i_g) - rV_{\text{u}}}{-u_i(w, i_g)} = ma(f), \tag{14}$$

where

$$a(f) \equiv \frac{f+r}{\phi}. \tag{15}$$

An alternative expression of (14) may be useful in interpreting its meaning. By substituting (14) into (4), and noting the fact that $d = f$ ex post, we obtain

$$V_{\rm e} - V_{\rm u} = (m/\phi)(-u_i(w, i)). \tag{16}$$

The term (m/ϕ) expresses the reciprocal of the marginal decrease in the individual dismissal probability, d, as a result of increasing the work intensity a little, evaluated at the symmetric group effort equilibrium. Hence workers determine their work intensity such that the marginal utility gain of working a little harder, defined by the marginal increase in the renewal probability (= marginal decrease in the dismissal probability) times the net benefit of having a job in this firm ($V_{\rm e} - V_{\rm u}$) equals the marginal current utility loss due to the same increased work intensity. Thus the positive wedge between $V_{\rm e}$ and $V_{\rm u}$ lies at the heart of inducing workers to work harder than they would voluntarily do. Although this essential property is common with the modes of Calvo (1979), Shapiro and Stiglitz (1984), and Bowles (1985), our present formulation goes beyond their models in specifying the manner by which the level of work intensity is endogenously determined.

Returning to (14) and applying the implicit function theorem, assuming that $u(w, i_g)$ is sufficiently regular, i_g can be solved as a unique function of w, f, m, and $rV_{\rm u}$; i.e.,

$$i_g = I(w, f, m, rV_{\rm u}). \tag{17}$$

This can be regarded as a "production function" of work intensity in the firm, to be distinguished from the technological production function introduced below (cf. [19]). Straightforward total differentiation of (14) gives

$$\begin{aligned} \partial i_g/\partial w &= -\{u_w + ma(f)u_{iw}\}/\Delta \\ \partial i_g/\partial f &= -ma'(f)u_i/\Delta \\ \partial i_g/\partial m &= -a(f)u_i/\Delta \\ \partial i_g/\partial(rV_{\rm u}) &= 1/\Delta, \end{aligned} \tag{18}$$

where

$$\Delta = u_i + ma(f)u_{ii}.$$

By noting that $u_{ii} \leq 0$, $r > f$ (cf. [3]), and that the group effort equilibrium occurs in the range $u_i < 0$, we observe that $\Delta < 0$. Since we also have

$$a'(f) = -(r-f)/\phi^3 < 0,$$

it follows immediately that:

Proposition 1. *If the rate of dismissal is positive, work intensity increases with the rate of dismissal and the intensity of monitoring, and decreases with the reservation utility.*

The relationship between the work intensity and the wage rate, in general, remains ambiguous, for u_{iw} may take any sign. However, we shall in the next section show that it is necessarily positive in the neighborhood of a firm equilibrium. It then verifies the efficiency wage argument (e.g., of Solow, 1979).

3. The Comparative Statics of the Firm

We next analyze the nature of the equilibrium wage, dismissal, and monitoring policies of the firm to see how they respond to changes in macroeconomic as well as firm organizational conditions. More specifically, we consider the effects of an increase in unemployment or external labor supply, a rise in the social unemployment compensation, and a rise in the cost of dismissal for the firm, caused by increased collective resistance by workers or increased overhead costs of hiring. In deriving specific comparative static results, we shall resort to the use of a linear approximation of the individual worker's utility function $u(w, i)$ around the firm equilibrium. The results are summarized in Propositions 2 and 3 below.

We suppose a simple production function of the form

$$Q = F(i_g L), \tag{19}$$

where L is the number of workers employed by the firm and i_g is the group equilibrium level of work intensity for each worker. The function F satisfies the usual well-behavedness properties:

$$F(0) = 0, \quad F(x) > 0, \quad F'(x) > 0, \quad F''(x) < 0 \qquad \text{for } x > 0.$$

We further suppose that the firm knows the work intensity response schedule (17).[6] We take the cost of dismissal (per worker fired) to be an increasing function of i_g on the grounds that the retaliation of workers to firings may be expected to be greater when the average work intensity is high (which is, in turn, based on the fundamental notion of fairness on the part of workers), and when a high level of intensity requires increased specific human capital, thus entailing higher training costs for new workers. We thus assume that the total cost of dismissal can be described by a multiplicative form[7]

$$C = c(i_g) \cdot f \cdot L \tag{20}$$

with

$$c(0) = 0, \quad c > 0, \quad c' > 0, \quad c'' \geq 0 \qquad \text{for } i_g > 0. \tag{21}$$

Finally, we assume that monitoring costs can be written as[8]

$$S = s(m)L \quad s, s'' > 0, \quad s' < 0, \quad \text{and} \quad s(\infty) = 0. \tag{22}$$

The firm will then maximize (normalizing the price of output to unity)

$$\pi = F(i_g L) - \{w + c(i_g)f + s(m)\}L \tag{23}$$

subject to (14), through the proper choice of wage, the size of employment, and the rate of dismissal. Since the constraint (14) is independent of L, the average labor cost per effective labor unit $e = (w + cf + s)/i_g$ is also independent of L. The optimization can be effected in two steps. First minimize e with respect to w, f, and m, and then determine the level L of employment. By straightforward differentiation, the first-order conditions for minimization of e are given by

$$I_w(e - c'(i_g)f) = 1 \tag{24}$$

$$c(i_g) = I_f / I_w \tag{25}$$

$$s'(m) = I_m / I_w \tag{26}$$

$$i_g = I(w, f, m, rV_{\mathrm{u}}). \tag{17}$$

The optimal L is then determined by maximizing (23), giving

$$F'(i_g L) = e. \tag{27}$$

Here I_w, I_f, and I_m represent the respective marginal work inducement effects of the wage, the dismissal rate, and the monitoring intensity previously discussed in (18). We have already seen that $I_m < 0$ and $I_f > 0$. It is then clear from (25) and (26) that I_w must be positive, and this confirms our statement made at the end of the last section.

Condition (24) expresses the optimal wage policy for a given rate of dismissal and the monitoring intensity: the optimal wage level is such that a dollar increase in wages just equals the increment in the marginal value product of labor $I_w \cdot F'(i_g L) = I_w \cdot e$ which it induces, net of the accompanying increase $c'(i_g)I_w \cdot f$ in the cost of dismissal. On the other hand, (25) expresses the familiar condition that the marginal rate of substitution between wages and the threat of dismissal, both seen as inputs to the production of work intensity, equals the ratio of the marginal factor costs $(c/1)$. Hence this condition can be viewed as the optimal dismissal policy for given levels of wages and the monitoring intensity. In a similar manner, condition (26) represents the optimal monitoring policy. Firm equilibrium is established if the chosen wage level, rate of dismissal, and monitoring intensity jointly satisfy these three optimal policies. Here we simply assume that such a firm equilibrium actually exists (See, however, note 18.)

For ease of exposition, we shall relegate the handling of a general utility function to a later section. For the present, we shall work with a linear approximation of the utility function presumed valid in the neighborhood of the equilibrium solution. Without loss of generality, we have

$$u(w, i) = w - bi, \quad b > 0. \tag{28}$$

We shall consider the effects on a firm equilibrium of an increase in the reservation utility, rV_u, on the one hand, and of a rise in the cost of dismissal, on the other. With respect to an increase in the reservation utility, we can show:

PROPOSITION 2. *Profits, output, employment, and the rate of dismissal are negatively related to the reservation utility, while monitoring intensity, real effective unit labor costs, work intensity, labor productivity, and the wage rate are positively related to the reservation utility.*

The proof is as follows. It is clear from the structure of the problem that the minimized value of the per effective unit labor cost $e = (w + cf + s)/i_g$ increases when the reservation utility rV_u increases. But then from (27) output Q and effective labor inputs $i_g L$ must decline. Also since $d\pi = -(i_g L) \cdot de$ holds around the equilibrium, profits must decrease. All these hold independent of any small adjustment in w, f, and m that the firm necessarily contemplates. This much is true whatever the shape of the utility function, as long as the second-order conditions are satisfied.

Given (28), the marginal work inducement of wage I_w becomes a constant, $1/b$, the system of equations (24), (25), (26), and (17) (or [16]) reduces to[9]

$$w - bi_g = \{c'(i_g) \cdot i_g - c(i_g)\}f - s(m) \tag{24'}$$

$$c(i_g) + bma'(f) = 0 \tag{25'}$$

$$s'(m) + ba(f) = 0 \tag{26'}$$

$$w - bi_g - rV_u = bma(f). \tag{14'}$$

We note first from (25′) that $a'(f)$ must be negative at the optimum. But since $a'(f) = -(r - f)/\phi^3$, the optimal dismissal rate must always be less than the discount rate. This justifies inequality (3), previously introduced as an assumption. Second, we observe from (25′) and (26′) that m and f can be solved as a function of i_g. Moreover,

$$dm/di_g = c'a'b/\Delta_1 \tag{29}$$

$$df/di_g = -c's''/\Delta_1 \tag{30}$$

where

$$\Delta_1 = bma''s'' - (a'b)^2. \tag{31}$$

By substituting these relationships into (14′), we can also express w as a function of i_g, given the level of rV_u. Moreover,

$$\partial w/\partial i_g = b[1 - \{a'c'(s' + s''m)/\Delta_1\}]. \tag{32}$$

Finally, from the entire system (24′), (25′), (26′), and (14′), we obtain

$$di_g/drV_u = \Delta_1/\Delta \tag{33}$$

with

$$\Delta = i_g\{c''f\Delta_1 - s''c'^2\} \tag{34}$$

being the determinant of the matrix associated with the totally differentiated system. Thus the nature of the movement of equilibrium depends critically on the signs of the expressions Δ_1 and Δ. These signs are determined from the second-order conditions. In fact, it is straightforward (yet arduous) to see $\Delta > 0$. By observing (34) this also implies $\Delta_1 > 0$. Also by using (14′) and (32) (together with the fact $s' + s''m > 0$) and noting that

$$dw/drV_u = 1 + (\partial w/\partial i_g)(di_g/drV_u) \tag{35}$$

the increase in wages exceeds that of the reservation utility. That the average labor productivity rises in the face of both a decreased effective labor input and an increased work intensity is obvious. This completes the proof of Proposition 2.

The fact that an increase in the reservation utility necessarily entails an increase in work intensity is surprising, and perhaps counter-intuitive. This property, to our knowledge, has not been described in the literature. Yet we have found it quite robust with respect to the specification of the model. Its substantive economic meaning lies in the fact that the firm finds it profitable both to reduce effective labor inputs and to substitute more work intensity per worker for a smaller number of workers, in reaction to the increase in per intensity labor costs that is induced by a rise in the reservation utility. Such a policy more than offsets the negative direct impact that the reservation utility has on work effort as we saw in Proposition 1.

Proposition 2 shows that, in general, the interests of the employer and the employees are unambiguously opposed concerning the movement of the reservation utility. Moreover, this fact is quite independent of the ways in which a change in the reservation utility is financed. It is often held, for instance, that employers oppose the social unemployment compensation due to their reluctance to bear the costs involved. Our result indicates that employers have an interest in minimizing the social wage even when they bear none of the costs of financing such payments.

Suppose next that in the neighborhood of equilibrium there occurs an additive shift in the cost of dismissal function: $c = c(i_g) + \beta$. It is then straightforward to verify (proof omitted) that:

PROPOSITION 3. *When the cost of dismissal function shifts upward, then profits, output, employment, and the rate of dismissal* (f) *decline, while the monitoring intensity* ($1/m$), *effective labor unit costs* (e), *wage* (w), *and the work intensity* (i_g) *all increase.*

Namely, the effect is qualitatively the same as that of an increase in the reservation utility. It is interesting to note that more powerful worker collectives, for instance, lead to higher wages (and lower profits), and at the same time, a higher work intensity and a higher labor productivity.[10] This feature may be viewed as providing groundwork for developing an alternative bargaining theory.

The unambiguous nature of our results summarized in Propositions 2 and 3 does depend on the special linear utility function (28). More generally, however, the above results can be interpreted as an evaluation of the first-order effect of the entire comparative static effects as the utility function is approximated by a linear function around the original firm equilibrium. Introduction of the second- and higher-order effects may either reinforce or offset the first-order effect.

4. The Steady-State Labor Market Equilibrium

We now bring together the supply and demand sides of our model, and discuss the character of the labor market equilibrium in the case of the linear utility function. We assume that the economy is composed of a fixed number of identical firms.[11] Without the loss of generality, we shall adopt the convention that the number of firms is equal to unity, so that the notation L for the level of employment in the representative firm can be used interchangeably to represent the total employment in the economy. We shall also suppose a fixed number N of workers. Closing the macro model requires identifying the mechanism by which the reservation utility rV_u is determined. A key consideration is the specification of the effect of the employment history of an individual worker on the probability of being rehired if unemployed. We shall assume, for the sake of simplicity, that the unemployed have equal probabilities of being rehired in any period.[12]

Let us suppose that an unemployed worker receives social compensation $\underline{w}$ at the end of the current period. Furthermore, let α $(0 \leq \alpha \leq 1)$ be the probability of being hired (or rehired) in any period, if unemployed in the beginning of that period. Then the basic equation governing the present value of the utility stream for the unemployed worker (at the beginning of the period) under a steady-state circumstance is given by

$$rV_u = (1-\alpha)\underline{w} + (1+r)\alpha V_e - \alpha V_u. \tag{36}$$

Thus the current rental "income" of the unemployed is the sum of an expected current flow income $(1-\alpha)\underline{w} + \alpha r V_e$ and an expected asset increase due to possibly being hired, $\alpha(V_e - V_u)$. This is the reservation utility for employed workers.

Equation (4), which exhibits the dependence of the present value of having a job upon the reservation utility, and equation (36), which exhibits the reverse dependence, together define a labor market equilibrium. How might this equilibrium be established? First, suppose workers and employers share an *anticipated* reservation utility $z_0 = rV_u$. Then as we have shown previously, under a linear utility function the levels of w, f, m, i_g, u, and L will be uniquely determined. In fact, Proposition 2 shows that they are all locally strictly monotonic functions of z_0. We shall express them as $w(z_0), f(z_0), m(z_0), ig(z_0)$, $u(z_0)$, and $L(z_0)$. In this case, a worker's optimized V_e must satisfy $rV_e = u(z_0) + \{f(z_0)/r\}(z_0 - rV_e)$, where $u(z_0) = w(z_0) - i_g(z_0)$. From this, the rental "income" of the employed is given by

$$rV_e = \frac{f(z_0)}{r+f(z_0)} z_0 + \frac{r}{r+f(z_0)} u(z_0) \equiv rV_e(z_0), \tag{37}$$

which is a weighted average of the current period utility from work and the reservation utility.

We now turn to the issue of the determinants of the probability of being rehired. Given our steady-state premises, and accepting dismissal as the sole form of job termination, the only source of new hiring consists of the replacement demand for dismissed workers. In this case, the probability of being rehired for a given anticipated reservation utility is determined as

$$\alpha = \min\left\{\frac{f(z_0)L(z_0)}{N-(1-f(z_0))L(z_0)}, 1\right\} \equiv \alpha(z_0), \tag{38}$$

where, since the number of firms is normalized to unity, L is to be construed as the general level of employment. Note also that the reserve pool of the unemployed is $N-(1-f)L$. $\alpha(z_0)=1$ is equivalent to $L(z_0)=N$. We shall write the value of z_0 such that $\alpha(z_0)=1$ as $\tilde{z}_0$. We already know that, under a linear utility function (28), $L(z_0)$ is less than, equal to, or greater than N according as z_0 is greater than, equal to, or less than $\tilde{z}_0$.

Returning to (36) with V_e and α now determined, we can determine the reservation utility, to be called ex post reservation utility, implicitly by

$$rV_u=(1-\alpha(z_0))\underline{w}+(1+r)\alpha(z_0)V_e(z_0)-\alpha(z_0)V_u. \tag{39}$$

By substituting (37) for $V_e(z_0)$, using $u(z_0)=z_0+bm(z_0)a(f[z_0])$ (which is derived from [14′]) into (39), and rearranging, we obtain the following explicit solution for rV_u:

$$rV_u=\frac{r(1-\alpha(z_0))}{r+\alpha(z_0)}\underline{w}+\frac{(1+r)\alpha(z_0)}{r+\alpha(z_0)}\left\{z_0+\frac{bm(z_0)}{\phi(z_0)}\right\}\equiv rV_u(z_0). \tag{40}$$

Thus the value of ex post reservation utility is obtained as a function of the level of the anticipated reservation utility. Clearly equilibrium is established if the ex post value equals the *anticipated value*, or

$$rV_u(z_0)=z_0\equiv rV_u^\circ. \tag{41}$$

Establishment of equilibrium is illustrated in Figure 1. In this figure, the horizontal axis represents the anticipated reservation utility z_0,

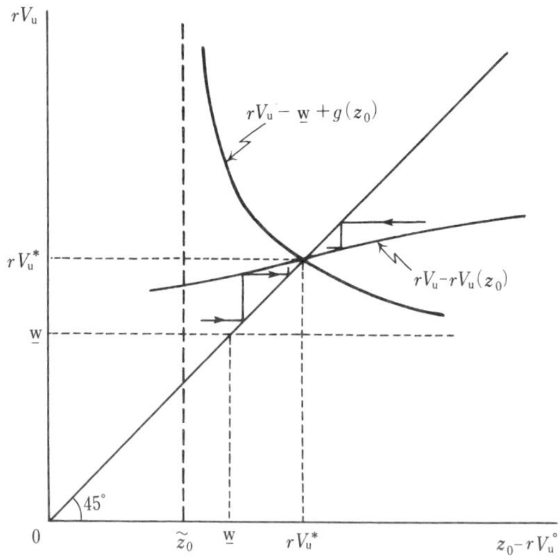

Figure 1. The steady-state macroeconomic equilibrium

while the vertical axis represents the ex post reservation utility rV_u. The level $\underline{\mathrm{w}}$ indicated along the horizontal axis represents the social unemployment compensation. Any steady-state equilibrium must lie along the 45° line emanating from the origin.

First, we rewrite (40) as

$$rV_\mathrm{u}(z_0) + \{A(z_0/r)\}\{rV_\mathrm{u}(z_0) - z_0\} = \underline{\mathrm{w}} + g(z_0), \tag{42}$$

where $A(z_0)$ and $g(z_0)$ are

$$A(z_0) \equiv (1+r)\alpha(z_0)/(1-\alpha(z_0)) \tag{43}$$

and

$$g(z_0) \equiv A(z_0)bm(z_0)/\phi(z_0). \tag{44}$$

Now within the domain $z_0 > \tilde{z}_0$, $g(z_0)$ can be rewritten as

$$g(z_0) = (1+r)\phi(z_0)m(z_0)\frac{bL(z_0)}{2(N - L(z_0))}, \tag{45}$$

where use has been made of the identities (13) and

$$\frac{\alpha(z_0)}{1-\alpha(z_0)} \equiv \frac{f(z_0)L(z_0)}{N - L(z_0)}. \tag{46}$$

But from Proposition 2 we observe that each multiplicative term in (45) is monotonically decreasing with respect to z_0, assuming the satisfaction of the second-order condition in the range $z_0 > \underline{\mathrm{w}}$. In the rest of our argument, we shall make this regularity assumption. Then clearly the curve representing $\underline{\mathrm{w}} + g(z_0)$ is downward sloping and stays above the horizontal line $rV_\mathrm{u} = \underline{\mathrm{w}}$ throughout the domain $z_0 > \tilde{z}_0$. Moreover, as z_0 approaches $\tilde{z}_0$ from the right, the curve becomes asymptotic to the vertical line $z_0 = \tilde{z}_0$. Hence this curve must cross the 45° line at a unique point, implying that a unique steady-state equilibrium exists in the range $rV_\mathrm{u} > \underline{\mathrm{w}}$. In Figure 1 this equilibrium occurs at the point $(rV_\mathrm{u}^*, rV_\mathrm{u}^*)$.

The graph of the function $rV_\mathrm{u} = rV_\mathrm{u}(z_0)$ is also depicted in the same figure. By rearranging (40) we can express rV_u as

$$rV_\mathrm{u}(z_0) = \frac{r(1-\alpha(z_0))}{r+\alpha(z_0)}\{\underline{\mathrm{w}} + g(z_0)\} + \frac{(1+r)\alpha(z_0)}{r+\alpha(z_0)}z_0,$$

which is a weighted average of $\underline{\mathrm{w}} + g(z_0)$ and z_0. Hence it lies between the $\underline{\mathrm{w}} + g(z_0)$ curve and the 45° line, and clearly passes through the equilibrium point $(rV_\mathrm{u}^*, rV_\mathrm{u}^*)$. A pseudodynamic process can then be defined by supposing, for instance, that the ex post reservation utility in this period becomes the anticipated reservation utility of the next period. Then we have a familiar cobweb process which would eventually bring the system to a steady-state equilibrium. Such a case is depicted in Figure 1. However, the process need not converge, as the rV_{u} locus may be negatively sloped with an absolute slope steeper than the 45° line, leading to an explosive cobweb.

The foregoing discussion can be summarized as follows:

PROPOSITION 4. *Under the assumptions that* (a) *new hiring is limited to replacement of dismissed workers and occurs randomly among the unemployed workers,* (b) *the utility function is linear, and* (c) *the second-order conditions for firm equilibrium are satisfied for the range* $rV_{\mathrm{u}} > \underline{\mathrm{w}}$, *there exists a unique steady-state involuntary unemployment equilibrium* $(w^*, f^*, m^*, i_g^*, L^*, \alpha^*, rV_{\mathrm{u}}^*)$ *satisfying the following set of equations:*

$$w^* - bi_g^* - rV_{\mathrm{u}}^* = bm^*a(f^*) \tag{47}$$

$$w^* - bi_g^* = \{c'(i_g^*)i_g^* - c(i_g^*)\}f^* - s(m^*) \tag{48}$$

$$c(i_g^*) + bm^*a'(f^*) = 0 \tag{49}$$

$$s'(m^*) + ba(f^*) = 0 \tag{50}$$

$$i_g^*F'(i_g^*L^*) = w^* + c(i_g^*)f^* + s(m^*) \tag{51}$$

$$\alpha^*\{N - (1 - f^*)L^*\} = f^*L^* \tag{52}$$

$$rV_{\mathrm{u}}^* = \underline{\mathrm{w}} + \alpha^*bm^*/\phi^*. \tag{53}$$

The first five equations (47)–(51) here specify the individual firm equilibrium for a given reservation utility, while the last two equations define the conditions for a steady-state labor market equilibrium. It is clear from (52) that full employment is equivalent to $f^* = 0$ or $\alpha^* = 1$. However, we know that f is strictly positive, given a linear utility function. We have also seen from Figure 1 that α never assumes the value unity. Hence full employment equilibrium is ruled out.

Furthermore, by substituting (47) into (37), we obtain

$$V_{\mathrm{e}}^* - V_{\mathrm{u}}^* = \frac{bm^*}{\phi^*}, \tag{54}$$

which is the fundamental microeconomic relationship (16) observed previously. Thus in equilibrium there is a positive wedge between the present value of having a job and the present value of not having a job. Of course, unemployed workers would be willing to take a job for a lower wage, but such a wage will not be offered by a rational enterprise. The unemployed are indeed involuntarily unemployed.[13] Conversely, the threat of dismissal entails a real punishment to workers.

We close this section by examining certain important comparative static properties of the market equilibrium associated with Proposition

4. First consider the effects of changes in two exogenous variables, the social unemployment compensation $\underline{w}$ and the total supply of workers N. It is immediately seen that either an increase in the compensation or a decrease in the supply of workers will cause the $\underline{w} + g(z_0)$ curve to shift upward (See Fig. 1.), leading to a rise in the equilibrium reservation utility. Applying Proposition 2, we have:

PROPOSITION 5. *When the total supply of workers declines, or social unemployment compensation increases, the equilibrium reservation utility rises. In response, the wage, the level of work intensity, and the extent of monitoring increase, while the rate of dismissal falls. In addition, total employment, total output, and total profit for firms all decline. Finally, the rate of unemployment increases in response to an increase in the social unemployment compensation.*

This proposition is of fundamental importance in understanding the role of unemployment in the capitalist economy. It confirms the rationality of the oft-noted tendency of employers to favor loose labor markets and to seek out additional sources of labor supply even when existing workers remain unemployed. The introduction of "Gast Arbeiter" in situations where domestic social circumstances permit, or tapping foreign workers through direct investment, are familiar examples (cf. Piore, 1979; Marglin, 1984). Moreover, it illustrates the limits of the Keynesian framework by showing the general impossibility of achieving full employment through policy correctives. The likely real world result of pushing a full employment policy too forcefully would be some combination of inflationary spiral, investment decline, and anti-Keynesian political backlash.

Consider next the case of an upward shift in the cost of dismissal function. This case is a little more complicated than the previous case, since it leads to a decline in the equilibrium reservation utility, quite the opposite of the effect of a rise in the social unemployment compensation. This fact is easily verified by the expression $g(z_0)$ in (45). For a given z_0, the value of $g(z_0)$ clearly decreases as the shift parameter β rises. Hence the effect of the individual experiment is always offset by changes in the market reservation utility. The question then is whether or not there exists a possibility that the latter effect overwhelms the former. The answer is no. In fact, we can show (again under the stated conditions of Proposition 4) that:

PROPOSITION 6. *When the cost of dismissal increases, the equilibrium reservation utility declines. The wage, the level of work intensity, and the extent of monitoring increase, while the rate of dismissal falls. In addition, total employment, total output, and total profit for firms all decline. The rate of unemployment increases.*

The proof proceeds in two steps. First, we note that in the new market equilibrium the value of the g function declines. This is immediately seen using Figure 1. Second, let us write the value of g as $g(z, \beta)$. It is defined by

$$g(z, \beta) = (1 + r)\phi(z, \beta)m(z, \beta)bL(z, \beta)/2(N - L(z, \beta)). \quad (55)$$

We already know that each of the component functions on the RHS, ϕ, m, L, is an increasing function of z and a decreasing function of β. Since $g(z, \beta)$ must decrease in the new equilibrium, we know at least that all three values, $\phi(z, \beta)$ (or equivalently $f[z, \beta]$), $m(z, \beta)$, and $L(z, \beta)$ cannot increase at the same time. There yet remains a possibility that one or two of the components increase in the new equilibrium, but we can show that such a possibility never actually occurs, and each of the three components must decline respectively (proof omitted).

5. Global Properties of the Labor Market Equilibrium

In the case of the linear utility function, the profit maximizing firm will necessarily choose a positive dismissal rate, and all steady-state equilibria are characterized by involuntary unemployment. This generalization no longer obtains in the case of a nonlinear utility function. We now examine the macro implications of our model in this more general case. We shall show in this section that zero dismissal steady-state equilibria are admissible. Such equilibria may take three possible forms:

(a) full employment with a market clearing wage;
(b) voluntary unemployment, with a wage rate taking the lower bound value set by the social unemployment compensation;
(c) involuntary unemployment with a wage rate determined by individual firms.

A necessary condition for the existence of such a zero dismissal equilibrium with a positive work intensity is that in the domain of a worker's current utility function $u(w, i)$ there be some wage above which the worker prefers a positive level of effort supply to a zero level; i.e., work is a utility rather than a disutility.[14] This is clearly implied by condition (5b), which defines individual workers' *voluntary intensity supply* when the employer sets $f = 0$. (For illustration of such a utility function see Fig. 2.) If, in addition, the cost of firing workers is sufficiently high (e.g., due to such factors as worker resistance, legal constraints, or high staffing costs), then firms may find it profitable to abide by whatever work intensity workers would voluntarily supply rather than using the threat of dismissal to induce work effort.

A plausible scenario within which zero dismissal equilibrium becomes a genuine possibility is constructed as follows. We assume that the preference structure of an individual worker satisfies the following properties:

(a) The marginal utility of wage is always positive, i.e., $u_w(w,i) > 0$ for all (w,i) in R^2_+.
(b) The indifference curves, $u(w,i) = \text{constant}$, are everywhere smooth, convex, and horizontally asymptotic to some $i = i_{\max}$. Thus $i_{\max}$ is the maximum work intensity that an individual can possibly sustain, whatever the wage level.
(c) Work is a disutility whenever the wage is zero. On the other hand, at a zero level of intensity, there exists a certain wage above which the slope of the indifference curve at $(w, 0)$ becomes negative. That is, at a sufficiently high wage level, a worker prefers a positive intensity to receiving the wage and not working at all.
(d) The locus of points $i = t(w)$ such that $u_i(w,i) = 0$ is monotonically increasing and concave. Moreover, it is strictly concave at least for a certain initial range of i. This, in turn, presupposes that $u_{iw}(w,i) > 0$ for all (w,i).[15]

These characteristics of the utility function assumed (called Assumption A) are illustrated in Figure 2, where the curve $i = t(w)$ represents the level of voluntary intensity for any given wage level. Given

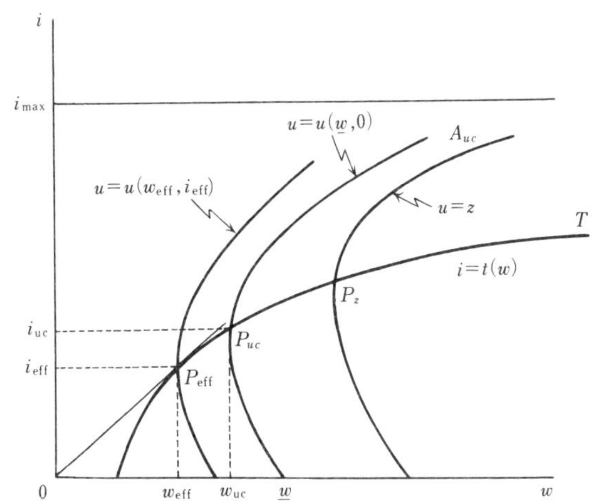

Figure 2. The general utility function

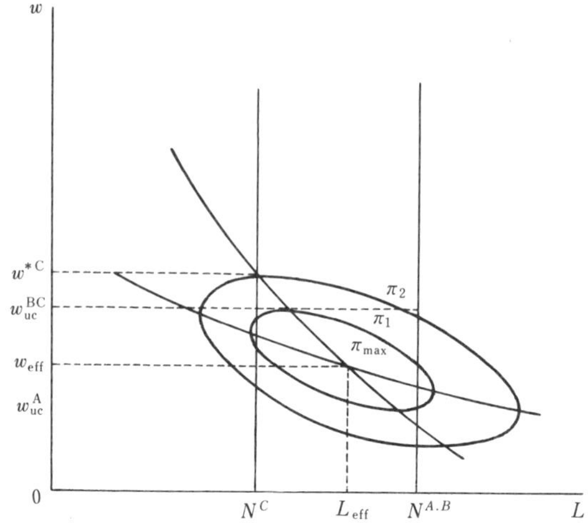

Figure 3. Alternative types of zero dismissal equilibrium

Assumption A, we note that there exists a unique point along the $i = t(w)$ locus below which the wage offered by the profit maximizing firm taking the zero dismissal policy never falls; nor does the work intensity fall below the level corresponding to this point. This is precisely the condition derived by Solow (1979). Let us call this point $P_{eff} = (w_{eff}, i_{eff})$, "eff" standing for the efficiency wage hypothesis. It is defined by the point of tangency between the locus $i = t(w)$ and a straight line emanating from the origin (See Fig. 2.), so that $t'(w) = wt(w)$.

Alternatively, this point is characterized in (L, w) space by the intersection of the optimal wage policy curve (under the constraint $f = 0$) representing the condition

$$t'(w)F'(t(w)L) = 1 \tag{56}$$

and the optimal employment policy curve (under the constraint $f = 0$) representing the condition

$$t(w)F'(t(w)L) = w. \tag{57}$$

This point is represented by the point (L_{eff}, w_{eff}), in Figure 3. In (L, w) space, the locus representing the optimal wage policy is always downward sloping, and furthermore, when it crosses the locus representing the optimal employment policy, the former always intersects the latter from below, thus ensuring the maximality of the extremum.[16] Because

$$dL/dw|_{\pi=\text{const}} = L(1 - F't')/(tF' - w), \tag{58}$$

it is easy to see that iso-profit curves form closed loops around the optimum $(L_{\text{eff}}, w_{\text{eff}})$. Since the number of firms is normalized to unity, this employment level L_{eff} becomes the notional demand for workers in the economy. As is clear from Figure 3, w_{eff} facilitates a lower bound for the wage level.

There is another lower bound for the wage level. It is given by the restriction that the current period utility from work $u(w, i)$ never falls below the reservation utility, which, in turn, is never less than the social unemployment compensation $\underline{w}$. Let us denote the point at which the indifference curve $u = u(\underline{w}, 0)$ intersects the curve $i = t(w)$ by $P_{\text{uc}}. = (w_{\text{uc}}, i_{\text{uc}})$. Since workers are willing to trade some wage for work (See Fig. 2.), we have $w_{\text{uc}} < \underline{w}$. Thus w_{uc} represents an additional lower bound for the wage level. We shall henceforth refer to the parametric value of reservation utility rV_{u} by z, and denote the point at which the indifference curve $u = z$ intersects the $i = t(w)$ curve by P_z. Note that P_z never lies to the left of P_{uc}.

Since w_{uc} reflects the social unemployment compensation while w_{eff} reflects the individual preference structure, the relative magnitude of the two lower bounds cannot be ascertained a priori. We shall first study the case $w_{\text{uc}} > w_{\text{eff}}$ and then discuss the opposite case. In what follows, we shall for the sake of both expositional ease and mathematical tractability introduce the following simplifying assumptions (called Assumption B): (i) the monitoring intensity m is exogenously fixed, and (ii) the cost of dismissal function $c(i_g)$ is a proportional function of i_g.

I. ALTERNATIVE TYPES OF LABOR MARKET EQUILIBRIUM UNDER $w_{\text{uc}} > w_{\text{eff}}$

In this case, the equilibrium must lie in the closed region bounded by the upper portion of the indifference curve $u = (\underline{w}, 0)$ and the $i = t(w)$ curve, i.e., the region $A_{\text{uc}} - P_{\text{uc}} - T$ in Figure 2. As Figure 3 illustrates, profits decrease as the wage increases in the domain $w \geq w_{\text{uc}}$. Hence if firms are to choose not to dismiss workers and if labor is abundant, firms will accept any bidding down of wages on the part of workers. On the other hand, if the same condition applies and labor is scarce, firms will bid up wages to acquire extra labor. In short, competitive forces operate along the $i = t(w)$ locus. These cases are represented in Figure 3 by the combination $(w_{\text{uc}}^{\text{B}}, N^{\text{B}})$, for the former, and $(w_{\text{uc}}^{\text{C}}, N^{\text{C}})$, for the latter, respectively.

But, in fact, firms are not confined to the $i = t(w)$ locus. They may increase profits by activating the threat of firing. The optimal wage and dismissal policies ([24], [25], [17]) under Assumption B reduce to

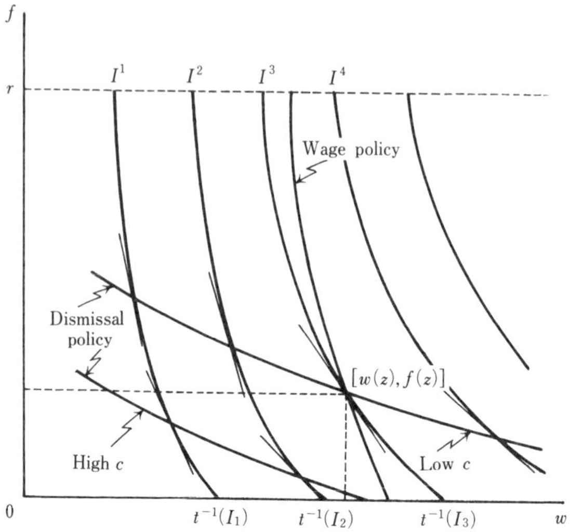

Figure 4. The firm equilibrium and its comparative statics with a general utility function

$$w/i_g = 1/I_w \tag{24''}$$

$$c \cdot i_g = I_f/I_w \tag{25''}$$

$$i_g = I(w, f, z). \tag{17''}$$

Here we note that the proportionality of the cost of dismissal function implies that the optimal wage policy curve (24″) is independent of the cost of dismissal function.

The isoquants of i_g for a given z in (w, f) space are illustrated in Figure 4. Because u_{iw} is assumed to be everywhere positive and u_i is negative in the region of our concern, the marginal work inducement effect of wage I_w and of dismissal I_f are both positive (cf. [18]). Thus the isoquants are negatively sloped, and once again, f takes r as its upper bound. The isoquant curvatures are, however, indeterminate. For ease of exposition, we shall assume these isoquants to be strictly convex to the origin in the range of consideration (Assumption C). The critical change from the case of the linear utility function is that for a certain range of intensities such that $0 \leq i_g < \sup\{t(w)\} \leq i_{\max}$, the isoquants have finite horizontal intercepts, e.g., $w_1 = t^{-1}(I_1)$, $w_2 = t^{-1}(I_2)$, $w_3 = t^{-1}(I_3)$. Although the shapes of the isoquants, in general, change as z varies, their horizontal intercepts, corresponding to voluntary intensity supplies, remain invariant.[17]

Consider now the optimal dismissal policy (25″) expressed geometrically by the tangency condition. Since the slope at tangency $c = c \cdot i_g$

as seen from the vertical axis becomes steeper as i_g increases, the locus of tangency points normally slopes downward, but need not intersect the horizontal axis. Given Assumption C, this tangency locus shifts uniformly downward as the cost of dismissal parameter c increases. For a sufficiently large c, then, the locus must intersect the horizontal axis. In Figure 4, we have illustrated these two possibilities: one with a value of c sufficiently low to maintain the tangency locus above the axis, and another sufficiently high to entail an intersection.

On the other hand, the slope of the optimal wage policy curve (24″) is given by

$$-dw/df|_{(24'')} = (I_f/I_w)\{(1 - \varepsilon_{f\cdot w})/\varepsilon_{w\cdot w}\} \tag{59}$$

where $\varepsilon_{f\cdot w}$ and $\varepsilon_{w\cdot w}$ are defined as the elasticity of the marginal work inducement effect of firing with respect to wage, and the elasticity of the marginal work inducement effect of wage with respect to itself, respectively. Formally, $\varepsilon_{f\cdot w} = w \cdot I_{fw}/I_f$ and $\varepsilon_{w\cdot w} = -w \cdot I_{w\cdot w}/I_w$. Although I_{fw} and I_{ww} can, in general, have any sign, we expect I_{fw} to be positive under normal circumstances, reflecting the complementarity of inputs, and I_{ww} to be nonpositive, reflecting nonincreasing returns. Hence $\varepsilon_{f\cdot w}$ and $\varepsilon_{w\cdot w}$ are both expected to be nonnegative.

By comparing (59) with the slope of the isoquants I_f/I_w, viewed from the vertical axis, we see that

$$\varepsilon_{f\cdot w} + \varepsilon_{w\cdot w} < 1 \quad (\text{for all } w, f, \text{and } z) \tag{60}$$

provides one sufficient (but by no means a necessary) condition under which the optimal wage policy curve always crosses the isoquants from above, thus intersecting the optimal dismissal policy curve necessarily from above, which is required for a stable firm equilibrium. We shall suppose that a stable equilibrium exists (Assumption D).[18] The intersection, however, may occur either along the horizontal axis, implying zero dismissal, or in the interior region, implying positive dismissal. In the former case, either of the two cases discussed previously, namely, $(w_{\text{uc}}^{\text{B}}, N^{\text{B}})$ or $(w_{\text{uc}}^{\text{C}}, N^{\text{C}})$ in Figure 4, holds as a firm equilibrium, while in the latter case, the firm equilibrium is similar to that under a linear utility function. The macroeconomic properties of this case can be summarized as:

PROPOSITION 7. *Under Assumptions* A, B, C, *and* D, *and when* $w_{\text{uc}} > w_{\text{eff}}$, *three types of steady-state labor market equilibrium are possible:*

(Ia) *An involuntary unemployment equilibrium with a positive rate of dismissal and* $u(w, i_g) > rV_{\text{u}} > u(\underline{w}, 0)$.

(Ib) *A full employment equilibrium with zero dismissal and* $w > w_{\text{uc}}$.

(Ic) *A voluntary unemployment equilibrium with zero dismissal and* $w = w_{uc}$.

Case (Ia) obtains when the reservation utility level z is such that the firm wage and dismissal policy curves, as discussed above, intersect at an interior point, and the macroeconomic equilibrium condition $\alpha(z) = f(z)L(z)/\{N - (1 - f(z))L(z)\}$ holds. The analysis of this case, in particular the way by which z adjusts to establish the macro equilibrium, directly parallels our discussion in the previous section and will not be repeated here. As we have already seen, this case more likely occurs under a relatively low c.

Case (Ib) obtains when the reservation utility z is such that the firm wage and dismissal policy curves intersect along the horizontal axis ($f = 0$), $z = u(w, t[w])$, and the optimal employment corresponds to full employment. In this situation, firms would prefer to ration scarce labor, but in a market context are forced into competitive wage bidding for extra workers when they discover that they cannot realize the optimal policies $(w_{\text{eff}}, L_{\text{eff}})$. Case (Ic) obtains when the reservation utility z is such that the firm wage and dismissal policy curves intersect along $f = 0$ (just as in the previous case), $z = u(\underline{w}, 0) = u(w_{uc}, t(w_{uc}))$, and the optimal employment corresponding to w_{uc} (as implied by (57)) is strictly less than N. Because workers are not dismissed, the unemployed will never be hired. But they are just as well off as the employed. Cases (Ib) and (Ic) more likely occur under a relatively high c. As already noted, between these two cases, case (Ib) more likely occurs with a relatively small N.

II. ALTERNATIVE TYPES OF LABOR MARKET EQUILIBRIUM $w_{\text{eff}} \geq w_{uc}$

In this case the only modification necessary to Proposition 7 is that case (Ic) of voluntary unemployment be replaced by an involuntary unemployment equilibrium of the Solow type. The firm equilibrium corresponding to this case has already been represented in Figure 3 by the combination (w_{uc}^{A}, N^{A}). Thus no workers are fired, but there are a certain number of workers who are hired permanently, and who enjoy a higher utility than those who are unemployed. This result obtains because firms benefit from the control over wages and employment even without dismissal of workers. We thus have:

PROPOSITION 8. *Under Assumptions* A, B, C, *and* D, *and when* $w_{\text{eff}} \geq w_{uc}$, *three types of steady-state labor market equilibrium are achievable:*

(IIa) *An involuntary unemployment equilibrium with a positive rate of dismissal and* $u(w, i_g) > rV_u > u(\underline{w}, 0)$.

(IIb) *A full employment equilibrium with zero dismissal and* $w > w_{\text{eff}}$.

(IIc) *An involuntary unemployment equilibrium with no dismissal and* $w = w_{\text{eff}}$.

Case (IIc) can be regarded as a limiting case of (IIa). We have thus succeeded in generalizing the Solow-type involuntary unemployment equilibrium. While the Solow-type world is completely stationary, the (IIa) world is compatible with constant replenishing of unemployed workers. It is a mobile world.

6. Concluding Remarks

The first and most immediate application of our analysis, given its comparative static framework, lies in cross-country and intertemporal comparisons of the natural rates of unemployment. Why are some economies more prone to relatively high rates of unemployment than others? Our model suggests that the answer may be rooted, at least in part, in the character of the employment relationship.

We have isolated and emphasized the individual worker's-wage–work-intensity trade-off (as described by the utility function), the cost of dismissal for the firm, and the level of social unemployment compensation as well as the availability of external labor supply as key to this relationship. We have shown (Proposition 4) that when the worker's utility function is linear there necessarily exists a unique and positive natural rate of unemployment with a steady inflow and outflow of workers into the unemployment pool. Moreover, a higher social unemployment compensation and/or a higher cost of dismissal for the firm leads to a higher natural rate of unemployment (Propositions 5 and 6).

A more general form of individual utility function invokes exactly the same kind of analytical complication and ambiguity in results as the literature on optimal income taxation. Yet under what we believe to be a plausible specification (which accommodates Solow-type efficiency wage argument) we have shown that, economywide, the labor market admits types of steady-state equilibrium other than the above case, including full employment Walrasian equilibrium with a voluntary work intensity supply, and voluntary or involuntary unemployment with a stationary unemployment pool (with no dismissals) (Propositions 7 and 8). This last case is identical with the Solow-type efficiency wage hypothesis.

Even in such a general setting, the same factors that we have isolated above play the important role. We have seen that, given the nature of the utility function, the level of social unemployment compensation, and the size of labor supply, relatively low firing costs more likely lead to a regime whereby firms activate the dismissal mechanism to induce work effort over the level supplied voluntarily by workers, thus entailing involuntary unemployment. On the other hand, sufficiently high firing costs lead to a regime whereby firms abide by the voluntarily supplied work intensity. Full employment equilibrium then arises when, in addition, labor is relatively in short supply, while otherwise either voluntary or involuntary unemployment occurs.

These factors doubtless vary widely across time and space. The wage–work-intensity trade-off, and in particular, the range over which the utility of work intensity is nonnegative, clearly depends upon the cultural, social, and historical environment shaping the workers' attitudes, as well as the material factors (e.g., physical working conditions, labor management practices) underlying employer-employee relations. The cost to the firm of dismissing and replacing workers, in turn, depends on such factors as the strength of worker solidarity, the extent of legal protection of job security, and the level of firm-specific human capital (the last of which remains implicit in the model). For instance, it is often pointed out that the legal protection of job security is more precarious for American workers than for their European and Japanese counterparts.[19] This circumstance renders the threat of firing more powerful, and ceteris paribus, makes the involuntary unemployment regime emerge more easily in the United States than other countries. Careful empirical analysis along the lines suggested by our inquiry would be worth pursuing.

Second, our analysis also has specific implications on cross-country and intertemporal differences in labor productivity. We have shown that even those countries having exactly the same technology and capital/labor ratio may differ widely in work intensity and thus in labor productivity. Differences in work intensity again arise due to different combinations of factors that govern the employment relationship. More specifically, given the world of a linear wage–work-intensity trade-off of workers, countries with a higher cost of dismissal for the firm, a higher social unemployment compensation, and a more restricted opportunity for tapping external labor supply, ceteris paribus, realize a higher work intensity as well as labor productivity (Propositions 5 and 6). That a stronger worker solidarity (again ceteris paribus) results in a higher work intensity and a higher labor productivity may sound paradoxical to many readers. Yet the explanation lies in the fact that a higher firing cost induces the firm to increase the wage as a major means for extracting work effort, and moreover, the firm always finds it optimal to do so to such an extent that the work intensity rises in net.

In fact, we may alternatively regard this feature as a foundation for a new (and seemingly more compelling) bargaining theory of wage determination. These results also invite interesting empirical study.

Third and finally, we must note an important limitation of our analysis. Our model is still very rudimentary as a macroeconomic theory, for it assumes the operation of Say's law. What impacts do different levels of work intensity, employment, and profits have on the demand side of the economy, in particular on the investment demand of firms? In order to answer such a question, extension of the model to incorporate the product and financial markets clearly becomes necessary. Such tasks are left for future study.

Appendix

In this appendix we shall show that the solution $i = i_g$ satisfying (15) indeed constitutes a Nash equilibrium. This is done by verifying that the $j(\hat{\imath})$ function does indeed reduce to the triangular distribution around i_g even when an infinitesimal mass of workers deviate from i_g. Suppose a proportion p $(0 < p < 1)$ of workers in the firm provide intensity i_g and the rest provide $i_g - e$, where we assume $0 < e < m$. Then by observing the basic relation

$$\begin{aligned}\Pr\{\hat{\imath} \le x\} &= \Pr\{\tilde{\imath} = i_g\}\Pr\{\hat{\imath} \le x|\tilde{\imath} = i_g\}\\ &\quad + \Pr\{\tilde{\imath} = i_g - e\}\Pr\{\hat{\imath} \le x|\tilde{\imath} = i_g - e\}\\ &= pG(x|i_g\} + (1-p)G(x|i_g - e\},\end{aligned}$$

we obtain the density function $j(x; e)$ of observed work effort as

$$j(x; e) = p(dG(x|i_g)/dx) + (1-p)(dG(x|i_g - e)/dx).$$

Let us define the intervals $I_1, I_2, \ldots, I_7$ as

$$\begin{aligned}I_1 &= \{x|x < i_g - e - m\}\\ I_2 &= \{x|i_g - e - m \le x < i_g - m\}\\ I_3 &= \{x|i_g - m \le x < i_g - e\}\\ I_4 &= \{x|i_g - e \le x < i_g\}\\ I_5 &= \{x|i_g \le x < i_g - e + m\}\\ I_6 &= \{x|i_g - e + m \le x < i_g + m\}\\ I_7 &= \{x|i_g + m \le x\}.\end{aligned}$$

Then by using expression (8), we can easily calculate $j(x; e)$ as

$$j(x;e) = \begin{cases} 0 & \text{for } I_1 \\ \{(1-p)/m^2\}\{x-(i_g-e-m)\} & \text{for } I_2 \\ \{1/m^2\}\{(1-p)(x-(i_g-e-m))+p(x-(i_g-m))\} & \text{for } I_3 \\ \{1/m^2\}\{p(x-(i_g-m))+(1-p)(i_g-e+m-x)\} & \text{for } I_4 \\ \{1/m^2\}\{p(i_g+m-x)+(1-p)(i_g-e+m-x)\} & \text{for } I_5 \\ \{p/m^2\}\{i_g+m-x) & \text{for } I_6 \\ 0 & \text{for } I_7. \end{cases}$$

The graph of this function is piecewise linear with slopes $(1-p)/m^2$ in I_2, $1/m^2$ in I_3, $(2p-1)/m^2$ in I_4, $-1/m^2$ in I_5, p/m^2 in I_6, and 0 otherwise. Thus it has three upward segments and two downward segments.

Suppose now that all workers supply intensity i_g. A single worker of mass $1-p$ deviating from this level by a small amount will then choose $e(p)$ to maximize the present value V_e of employment, subject to the distribution $j(x;e)$. It is clear that $j(x;e)$ in this case tends to the triangular distribution with mean i_g and base $\pm m$ as p approaches unity. Thus $e(p)$ will tend to zero as p approaches unity, and the deviator's work intensity will approach the level i_g. This completes the proof.

NOTES

We thank Masahiko Aoki, Samuel Bowles, Clive Bull, Harvey Leibenstein, Stephen Marglin, Masahiro Okuno, Bob Rowthorn, Robert Solow, Lester Thurow, and Martin Weitzman, and two anonymous referees for helpful comments in the preparation of this paper. An earlier version of the paper was presented in seminars at New York University, October 1983, and at the National Bureau of Economic Research Summer Labor Workshop (organized by Richard Freeman) in 1984, and we would also like to thank the participants for stimulating discussion. One of the authors is grateful to the American Council of Learned Societies for providing a liberal fellowship, and the Massachusetts Institute of Technology for providing the superb research environment during 1982–84 that made the research contained in this paper possible.

1. That endogeneity of work intensity matters in the pursuit of full employment policy was discussed in a classic article on the political business cycle by Kalecki (1943), and its theme was extended and applied to the U.S. economy by Boddy and Crotty (1975). However, these studies lacked microeconomic theoretical explanations. Recent studies by Calvo (1979), Solow (1979, 1980), Malcomson (1981), Akerlof (1982), Gintis and Bowles (1982), Miyazaki (1984), Shapiro and Stiglitz (1984), Yellen (1984), and Okuno-Fujiwara (1987), besides our current work, are all attempts to provide theoretical foundations for the relationship between work intensity and unemployment. These works also relate to the quantity constraint models of Clower, Barro-Grossman, Benassy, and Malinvaud, in particular, the "classical unemployment" regime as it is called by Malinvaud (1977), in that the level of wages, left exogenous in the quantity constraint models, is set optimally by firms upon consideration of work intensity incentives. Negishi's (1979: ch. 7) kinked demand curve approach, which tried to remedy this exogeneity problem, contains an efficiency wage argument similar to Solow's as a supplementary argument.

2. We may alternatively view dismissal as formally the same as imposing a fine upon the worker rather than firing him/her. Similarly, nonrenewal of contract can be thought of as the norm, and rehiring the worker may be considered the same as giving a bonus.

However, it would be interesting to investigate the implications of various other and more explicit types of bonus systems. Miyazaki (1984) analyzes the case where the wage rate depends on the average work intensity of the group (i.e., a group piece rate system), and further discusses the macroeconomic equilibrium. To a certain extent, Miyazaki's analysis and our analysis here are complementary to each other. Okuno (1984) discusses in detail the work inducement effect of the bonus system. Other incentive wage schemes that rely on seniority schemes, if not outright bonding (the difficulty of which has already been discussed by Becker and Stigler (1974)), have been suggested also as a solution to the work incentive problems. See Lazear (1979), and see also the discussions by Yellen (1984), Carmichael (1985), and Shapiro and Stiglitz (1985). Determining the circumstances in which each of various incentive schemes will become the preferred means requires careful theoretical as well as empirical analysis, and is beyond the scope of the present paper. Furthermore we omit discussion of the normative properties of the present type of employment arrangement, which are discussed in detail by Shapiro and Stiglitz (1984) and Okuno-Fujiwara (1987).

3. The latter, the *emulation factor*, is analyzed in Ishikawa (1981). There are two possible types of emulation, one "spontaneous" and the other "induced." Spontaneous emulation arises when the social or cultural environment is such that workers intrinsically desire to outperform their peers, and is similar to Akerlof's (1980) " reputation" effect or "social customs" effect, except that in the case of the emulation effect the social norm is endogenously determined. The induced emulation discussed in this paper, on the other hand, is a response to the firm's incentive structures. Akerlof's (1976) "rat race" example, where the payment scheme is so structured that workers of high ability are induced to work sufficiently hard as to avoid being classified with the less able, is similar to induced emulation based upon a bonus payment system. Induced emulation based upon a promotional hierarchy is discussed by Malcomson (1981) and Lazear and Rosen (1981) (though the latter is in a slightly different context of skill acquisition). See also Akerlof (1982), who discusses some implications for involuntary unemployment. One of the examples he gives can be interpreted as providing a clear theoretical ground for Solow's efficiency wage hypothesis discussed below.

4. To assume that the firm announces an explicit dismissal and monitoring policy (and to be written into the contract) at the start of the production period is reasonable only in a pure comparative static analysis. While this is acceptable for our purposes, in a short-run dynamic context, it is more appropriate that this be replaced by a more realistic assumption that workers respond to an anticipated rate of dismissal, based, for instance, on the ex post relationship between the rates of dismissal and monitoring and the group work intensity that they observe from experience. See (29) and (30). An important point for us to observe is that even if the workers should decide their individual work intensity with respect to such a schedule, it is optimal for the firm to maintain the very policies that generated the relationships (29) and (30) in the first place. To see this, one only needs to reformulate the unit efficiency cost minimization problem as a calculus of variations problem in the functional space of w, f, and m (using the ordinary differential equations [29], [30], and [14′] differentiated with respect to i_g) and observe that the optimization degenerates to a flat schedule whose values are determined by (24′), (25′) and (26′). It implies that firms cannot gain anything by exploiting different schedules.

5. Note that our monitoring technology is different from the sampling mechanism customarily used in the literature. It is assumed here that emulation among workers operates in full when every worker is monitored and the workers with lowest observed intensities are identified. Of course, there may be room for sampling to economize on the monitoring cost in exchange for making emulation among workers less keen, and yet make the mechanism more profitable in net for the firm. Such a comparison of different monitoring technologies is certainly an interesting question; yet that discussion is beyond the scope of the current paper.

6. The assumption that the firm knows the worker response schedule conforms to the general methodological position that the firm has perfect knowledge of its production function. One might object that if differences in observed work effort represent only observational errors, then actually to expend monitoring resources may appear irrational.

This objection is not valid, since profits are in general higher with monitoring than without. The following analogy is instructive. Suppose all automobile drivers are equally likely to violate traffic rules. Nevertheless, the greater the number of police officers assigned to patrol intersections, the fewer the number of offenses that will be committed. It may be *unjust* to punish those who happen to be caught, but it is in no way irrational from the viewpoint of reducing the volume of offenses.

7. It is a straightforward extension to treat c as a function of i_g and f and let $C = c(i_g, f)L$, so long as the second partial derivative of c with respect to i_g is nonnegative. Also for more background discussion and references concerning the relationship between the work intensity and training costs, see Gintis (1976).

8. The assumptions imposed on $s(m)$ can be justified as follows. Let the per worker monitoring cost be an increasing strictly convex function of the monitoring intensity $(1/m)$, i.e., $S = \sigma(1/m)$ with $\sigma' > 0, \sigma'' > 0$. Thus we have identically $s(m) = \sigma(1/m)$. But then $s'(m) = -\sigma'/m^2 < 0$ and $s''(m) = \sigma''/m^4 + 2\sigma'/m^3 > 0$, which is equivalent to (22). We also note that $s'(m) + s''(m) \cdot m = \sigma''/m^3 + \sigma'/m^2 > 0$. This property will be used in our comparative static analysis below.

In reality there exists a possibility that a certain portion of monitoring resources are lumpy in nature, leading to increasing returns to scale. This will destroy the proportional nature of the cost function in (23), and, hence, the two-step optimization procedure for the firm. We would expect substitution of more supervision for dismissal as its direct effect.

9. Comparison of (24′) and (14′) reveals that the existence of a firm equilibrium under the linear utility function requires that $c''(i)$ be strictly positive (so that $c' \cdot i_g - c > 0$). We have already argued that this condition is realistic. However, in the case of a general utility function, $c'' = 0$ is permissible (cf. Section 5).

10. This result is similar in spirit to Freeman and Medoff (1984). One important proviso to Proposition 3 is that if the shift in the cost of dismissal function also involves changes in the slope, i.e., the sensitivity of cost with respect to the realized level of work intensity, as in the case of a proportional shift in the function, then there occurs a mitigating effect in the opposite direction that at least partially offsets the above effects. Then the net effect becomes ambiguous. However, changes in the slope of the function are more appropriately construed as changes in the notion of fairness among workers, rather than changes that directly increase the cost. Hence we confine ourselves to the case of an additive shift.

11. Alternatively, we may introduce free entry and exit of firms and an explicit financial sector regulating the condition of entry. Calvo's (1979) zero profit condition represents a simple example of this alternative.

12. The presence of voluntary quits as another basis for separation, for instance, would bid employers to consider the basis of previous separation for each worker when they engage in new hiring. But even within our framework that dismissal is the sole cause of separation from the firm, it may be reasonable to take the probability of being hired and the workers' preferences as affected by the duration of unemployment. We shall here ignore these subtleties.

13. The similarity of our result to the conclusions of Calvo (1979), Malcomson (1981), and Shapiro and Stiglitz (1984) is also clear. But these works do not yet seem to have succeeded in bringing out fully the implications of the employment relationship on macroeconomic equilibrium. Thus in Calvo's model, the act of dismissal by employers remains as a black box. For Shapiro and Stiglitz, a totally exogenous "separation (quit)" takes the place of dismissal in explaining the flow (replacement) demand of labor in a steady state (cf. Eq. [52]). Thus the existence and magnitude of unemployment in their model hinge critically on a factor outside the logic of the model. For Malcomson, the involuntary unemployment equilibrium depends on the differentiation of the labor force into superior and inferior workers—a factor of questionable importance in dealing with macroeconomic phenomena. We believe that our model has a clear advantage in explaining the problem at hand.

14. See Akerlof (1982), who argues that, in general, workers involved in an unconstrained choice optimize work intensity according to principles of fairness and reciproc-

ity. What is considered "fair" and "reciprocal" may, of course, depend upon the wage rate and the reservation utility. But it will be critically dependent on social, cultural, and organizational factors as well.

15. It may be argued that a rise in wages might above a certain level "spoil" the workers. In such a case, the locus $i = t(w)$ will be inverted u-shaped. Such a feature only widens the range of possible unemployment equilibria; it poses no new problems but complicates the characterization of the global equilibrium. Hence, we shall assume that $u_{iw} > 0$.

16. The reciprocal of the slope of the optimal wage policy curve is $dL/dw|_{(56)} = (-t''F'/tt'F'') - (t'L/t) < 0$ while the reciprocal of the slope of the optimal employment policy curve is $dL/dw|_{(57)} = \{(1 - t'F')/t^2F''\} - (t'L/t)$. The sign of the latter expression is, in general, indeterminate. However, at the point of intersection of the two curves (where $1 - t'F' = 0$), the absolute slope of the optimal employment policy curve is smaller than that of the optimal wage policy curve.

17. In the case of a linear utility function, the isoquants were vertically parallel to each other so that only relabeling of the level of i_g was necessary in the face of variation in z. However, this is no longer true in the general case.

18. There exists a firm equilibrium for a general case in which the simplifying Assumptions B, C, and D do not hold.

19. It is often argued, for instance, that job security is more precarious (at least until very recently) for American workers than for their European and Japanese counterparts. See Summers (1976), comments by the *Harvard Law Review* (1980), and Stieber and Blackburn (1983). This circumstance would, ceteris paribus, render the threat of dismissal focused in this paper relatively more powerful in the United States than elsewhere. Actually Bowles et al. (1983) and Schor (1983) are emerging examples of the empirical studies illustrating the relevance (in explaining the changes in productivity growth) of the cost of job loss in the context of the United States.

REFERENCES

Akerlof, G. 1976. The economics of caste and of the rat race and other woeful tales. Quarterly Journal of Economics. 90: 599–617.

———. 1980. A theory of social custom, of which unemployment may be one consequence. Quarterly Journal of Economics. 94: 749–75.

———. 1982. Labor contracts as partial gift exchange. Quarterly Journal of Economics. 97: 543–69.

Becker, G.S., and G.J. Stigler. 1974. Law enforcement, malfeasance, and compensation of enforcers. Journal of Legal Studies 3: 1–18.

Boddy, R., and J. Crotty. 1975. Class conflict and macro-policy: The political business cycle. Review of Radical Political Economics. 7: 1–19.

Bowles, S. 1985. The production process in a competitive economy: Walrasian, neo-Hobbesian, and Marxian models. American Economic Review. 75: 16–36.

Bowles, S., D. Gordon, and T. Weisskopf. 1983. Hearts and minds: A social model of U.S. productivity growth. Brookings Papers on Economic Activities 381–405.

Calvo, G. 1979. Quasi-Walrasian theories of unemployment. American Economic Review. 69 (Papers and Proceedings): 102–7.

Carmichael, L. 1985. Can unemployment be involuntary?: Comment. American Economic Review. 75: 1213–14.

Freeman, R.B., and J.L. Medoff. 1984. What Do Unions Do? New York: Basic Books.

Gintis, H. 1976. The nature of labor exchange and the theory of capitalist production. Review of Radical Political Economics. 8: 36–54.

Gintis, H., and S. Bowles. 1982. The welfare state and long-term economic growth: Marxian, neoclassical, and Keynesian approaches. American Economic Review. 72 (Papers and Proceedings): 341–45.

Harvard Law Review. 1980. Protecting at will employees against wrongful discharge: The duty to terminate only in good faith, 93: 1816–44.

Ishikawa, T. 1981. Rōdō iyoku no kettei yōin to shiteno 'emulation' kōka ni tsuite (The emulation effect as a determinant of work motivation). Keizaigaku Ronshū 47: 2–15. (In Japanese)

Kalecki. M. 1943. Political aspects of full employment. Political Quarterly 14: 322–30.

Lazear, E. 1979. Why is there mandatory retirement? Journal of Political Economy 87: 1261–84.

Lazear, E., and S. Rosen. 1981. Rank-order tournaments as optimum labor contracts. Journal of Political Economy. 89: 841–64.

Malcomson, J. 1981. Unemployment and the efficiency wage hypothesis. Economic Journal. 91: 848–66.

Malinvaud, E. 1977. The Theory of Unemployment Reconsidered. Oxford: Blackwell.

Marglin, S.A. 1984. Growth, Distribution and Prices. Cambridge, Mass.: Harvard University Press.

Miyazaki, H. 1984. Work norms and involuntary unemployment. Quarterly Journal of Economics. 99: 297–311.

Negishi, T. 1979. Microeconomic Foundations of Keynesian Macroeconomics. Amsterdam: North-Holland.

Okuno, M. 1984. Corporate loyalty and bonus payments: An analysis of work incentives in Japan. In Economic Analysis of the Japanese Firm, ed. by M. Aoki. Amsterdam: North-Holland.

Okuno-Fujiwara, M. 1987. Monitoring cost, agency relationship, and equilibrium modes of labor contract. Journal of Japanese and International Economics 1(2): 147–67.

Piore, M. 1979. Birds of Passage: Migrant Labor in Industrial Societies. New York: Cambridge University Press.

Schor, J. 1983. Social wages and the business cycle: Measuring the cost of job loss. In Money and Macro Policy, ed. by M. Jarsulec. Boston: Kluwer-Nijhoff.

Shapiro, C., and Stiglitz, J. 1984 Equilibrium unemployment as a worker discipline device. American Economic Review. 74: 433–44.

———. 1985. Can unemployment be involuntary?: Reply. American Economic Review. 75: 1215–17.

Solow, R. 1979. Alternative approaches to macroeconomic theory: A partial review. Canadian Journal of Economics 12: 339–54.

———. 1980. On theories of unemployment. American Economic Review. 70: 1–11.

Stieber, J., and J. Blackburn, eds. 1983. Protecting Unorganized Employees against Unjust Discharge. School of Industrial Relations, Michigan State University.

Summers, C. 1976. Individual protection against unjust dismissal: Time for a statute. Virginia Law Review 62: 481–532.

Yellen, J. 1984. Efficiency wage models of unemployment. American Economic Review. 74 (Papers and Proceedings): 200–205.

11. Interindustry and Firm Size Differences in Job Satisfaction among Japanese Workers

1. Introduction

It is often pointed out that despite the recent rise in the levels of income and wealth the greater part of Japanese households do not feel much comfort and richness in actual living. No doubt long working hours, long commuting time, heavy congestion, and exorbitant rise of land prices in the major metropolitan areas go a long way in explaining such impoverishment.

Another important determinant of the richness of living, however, is the richness of the quality of work life. This is because work is not only a means to acquire goods and services necessary for living but is also a field of activity in which people exhibit their ability and responsibility, thereby contributing to society and in which they simultaneously further their ability itself. Are Japanese employers responding positively to such expectations on the part of workers? Does the degree of fulfilment of such expectations differ greatly among individuals depending on which employer one works for and which type of job one holds?

This paper looks on such a feature as a problem of distribution of job satisfaction among individuals and investigates the factors that determine the current state of distribution using micro survey data on individual attitudes and consciousness.[1] The dataset for the present study is workers' responses to the Survey on the Accumulation of Assets and on Worker Life in Major Metropolitan Areas conducted by the Ministry of Labour in November, 1990.[2] The purpose of this survey is to investigate the effect on workers' asset formation and work

Originally published in *Labour Market and Economic Performance: Europe, Japan and the USA*, edited by Toshiaki Tachibanaki, pp. 183–215 (Basingstoke: Macmillan Press, 1994).

attitudes of the widened gap in wealth distribution that arose on account of the acute rise in land and stock prices after 1985. It asks the level, purpose as well as the (historical) source of workers' wealth holding and at the same time raises various questions on worker attitude toward work as well as on the concept of fairness with respect to income and wealth distribution. Among the responses to these questionnaires, this paper focuses on those concerning individual workers' evaluation of job satisfaction.

Related to the present study is a long-standing empirical investigation on the relationship between organizational setups and incentive mechanisms of firms and the extent of worker commitment toward jobs. Such investigations have traditionally belonged to the fields of industrial sociology and psychology, on the one hand, and of labor management and control, on the other.[3] These studies have usually been carried out in the context of within or across specific organizations. Since the advent of concern over work motivation as an important determinant of labor productivity and macroeconomic unemployment, however, there is a growing trend for such studies to be intermeshed with mainstream economic analysis.

Among the existing literature, the most recent and perhaps methodologically the most relevant study to the present one is that of Lincoln and Kalleberg (1990).[4] They have chosen the city of Atsugi (on the outskirts of Tokyo) as the study site and conducted a sample survey on manufacturing establishments and the workers therein. From the establishments is collected the information on detailed organizational characteristics and from workers is collected the information on individual attributes, occupational and job characteristics, hierarchical positions, the nature of social bonds with fellow workers, and both pecuniary and nonpecuniary job rewards, and the responses to the queries on the extent of work commitment and job satisfaction. The authors then related these responses to the foregoing explanatory variables.

Lincoln and Kalleberg's main conclusion is that the high work commitment of the workers observed (which confirms earlier investigations carried out in Japan) is a contrived one in the sense that it is derived from the operation of a wide-ranging inducement apparatus set up inside Japanese firms (which is against the "culturalist" view). While the high commitment of workers is certainly a major success for Japanese employers, it simultaneously entails a large gap between the expectations and the reality on the part of workers, which is why they have been observed to express relatively low job satisfaction.[5]

The present study partly complements Lincoln and Kalleberg's detailed work in that it has a much larger sample frame, covering the entire (nonagricultural) industrial as well as occupational spectrum and covering three major metropolitan areas of Japan. It is thus particularly suitable to obtaining a bird's-eye view of the distribution of job satisfaction among Japanese workers and of factors that tend to associate with job satisfaction.

The organization of this chapter is as follows. Section 2 summarizes the general nature of the data. Section 3 spells out the observed characteristics of job satisfaction on various dimensions and discusses the basic conceptual framework within which different job satisfaction scores may appear. Section 4 presents a model and the estimation result of the ordered probit analysis as applied to workers' evaluation of whether or not due reward is paid for their effort. Section 5 discusses the result of a similar ordered probit analysis as applied to the workers' evaluation of the extent of challenging and stimulating experiences on the job. Section 6 concludes by summarizing the main findings, discussing the general implications and noting the qualifications of the present analysis.

2. Characteristics of the Data

The data comes from the population of regularly employed married household heads who are employed in privately owned establishments with 30 or more regular employees in three major metropolitan areas (Tokyo, Nagoya, and Osaka). The survey chose persons randomly: 10 persons each from 1,200 establishments that were in themselves selected randomly on the basis of the 1986 Establishment Census. The questionnaire form was delivered to each sampled individual via the establishment, and the response was mailed back directly to the sender from the individual. Responses were thus collected from 5,600 individuals, the response rate being 46.3 percent. Because of the condition that a worker must be a married household head to be included in the sample, responses by female persons were limited to only 1.4 percent of the total samples. Hence, this paper restricts the analysis to responses by male individuals only, and furthermore, to those made by individuals aged 25 and above. It appears that the second condition enables the analysis to focus on people who have largely completed the search and job-matching processes.

Table 1 shows the mean attributes of the respondents as classified by each age group. It also shows the distribution of annual labor earnings as well as that of net worth (which includes the market value of golf club memberships). Reflecting the recent acute rise in the land price in these metropolitan areas, there indeed is an immense difference between the dispersion of earnings and that of net worth as measured by the ratio of respective mean values of the top and the bottom

Table 1. Mean Attributes of the Sample[a]

Age group	25–34	35–44	45–54	55–	Total
Schooling (years)	14.9	14.2	13.1	12.6	13.9
Duration of service (years)	7.8	15.9	23.3	20.5	16.8
Occupation					
Profess./technical	25.8	22.2	17.9	19.3	21.4
Managerial	8.4	25.5	36.1	37.8	26.0
Skilled/production operatives	3.0	3.9	5.8	4.9	4.4
Clerical, sales, and others	62.8	48.4	40.2	38.0	48.2
Firm size (%)					
Large (1,000 and more employees)	55.9	55.0	52.1	32.2	52.0
Medium (100–999 employees)	33.8	35.0	35.5	48.3	36.3
Small (less than 100 employees)	10.3	10.0	12.4	19.5	11.7
Industry (%)					
Construction	9.6	11.4	9.2	10.7	10.3
Manufacturing (incl. mining)	23.7	24.0	30.4	23.6	25.8
Utility	2.9	2.4	2.8	2.3	2.6
Transportation and communications	7.5	10.3	16.0	12.7	11.7
Wholesale and retail	23.4	25.2	21.0	15.0	22.5
Finance and insurance	8.5	8.4	5.7	3.4	7.1
Real estate	2.2	1.2	0.9	3.2	1.5
Service	22.1	17.0	14.0	29.0	18.5
Employed earnings[b] (¥10,000/year)					
Bottom quartile	355	451	507	329	418
Median	460	625	730	600	600
Top quartile	705	964	1,083	1,076	983
Net worth (¥10,000)					
Bottom quartile	−31	413	1,099	1,514	265
Median	500	2,900	4,600	5,900	3,000
Top quartile	5,247	8,565	12,854	15,280	10,488
Sample size	1,203	2,096	1,641	559	5,549

NOTES:

[a]Mean figures are calculated by excluding missing values.

[b]The composition of the Census of Wages (Ministry of Labour, surveyed in June, 1990) samples for the corresponding population of workers, i.e., male regular workers aged 25 and above who are employed in privately owned establishments with 30 or more regular employees in three major metropolitan areas (Tokyo, Nagoya, and Osaka) is as follows:

Schooling = 13.1 years

Duration of service = 13.8 years

Production workers' ratio (= Production workers in mining, construction, and manufacturing industries to workers in all industries) = 20.0%

Firm size: Large firms = 43.8%, Medium firms = 19.1%, Small firms = 38.1%

Industry: Construction = 5.6%, Manufacturing (incl. mining) = 40.1%, Utility = 1.0%, Transportation and communications = 13.6%, Wholesale and retail = 18.1%, Finance and insurance = 4.8%, Real estate = 1.3%, Service = 15.7%.

quartiles of the distribution (2.4 for the former and 39.6 for the latter for the age groups combined).[6]

As the accompanying note to Table 1 shows, however, there exist certain sampling biases in this survey. The manufacturing industry is underrepresented as compared with nonmanufacturing industries, and even within the manufacturing industry blue-collar workers seem to be rather heavily underrepresented as compared with white-collar workers. Similarly small-sized firms are underrepresented vis-à-vis medium- and large-sized firms. Subsequent analysis shows that such sampling biases indeed call for cautious qualifications when overall evaluation of the distribution of job satisfaction is made.

3. Worker Consciousness of Job Worth and Indices of Job Satisfaction

The study begins by looking at the workers' views on the meaning they attach to the job (hereinafter termed job worth). The survey asks the respondent which of the following three alternative views is the closest to his own:

(a) Job worth derives from intrinsic interest in the job, so that the levels of earnings and assets are irrelevant;

(b) Job worth does not derive solely from earnings and assets, yet in order for meaningfulness to be felt the job must assure earnings and assets that would at least enable the job holder to own a house;

(c) Job worth depends squarely on the levels of earnings and assets that can be acquired from the job.

It is to be stressed that this is not a question about the respondent's current state of affairs but about his idea in general. Table 2 summarizes the responses for each age group.

As seen from Table 2, the view that some moderate amounts of earnings and assets are to be secured by the job is supported by the greater part of the population. Yet at the same time, each of the polar views that either intrinsic interest or pecuniary reward alone is important is taken by about 10 percent and that adherence to intrinsic interest in the job shows a notable increase among older people (i.e., aged

Table 2. Workers' Views on Job Worth (%)

Content of job worth	Age 25–34	Age 35–44	Age 45–54	Age 55–
Intrinsic interest in the job	8.7	8.4	9.8	15.7
Moderate amount of earnings and assets	80.6	81.0	79.7	70.8
Earnings and assets alone	10.7	10.6	10.4	13.5
Total	100.0	100.0	100.0	100.0

Note: Percentage ratios are calculated by excluding missing values.

55 and over). Between the young (aged 25–34) and the medium age (aged 35–44 and 45–54) groups there seems to be little difference in the concept about job worth.

The increased evaluation of intrinsic job interest among the older people may be explained, first, by a life-cycle effect of decreased monetary needs as they complete the process of child rearing and of paying back housing mortgages, and second, by a particular cohort effect that they passed through a period of dire economic severity during and immediately after World War II. It is difficult, however, to distinguish these two effects in the data.

On the other hand, it is worth noting that the young generation, reared in the age of material affluence and often suspected of having discontinuity in ideas and values (as the popular word "new human beings" connotes), is not different from the age groups 35–44 and 45–54 in terms of what they look for in the job.[7]

About the respondent's current state of job satisfaction the survey asks whether or not

A. due reward for effort is attained in terms of pay and promotion,
B. the job allows one to exhibit one's own ability fully,
C. the job involves new challenges and is stimulating,
D. the job involves a broad realm of responsibility.

For each item, the respondent chooses one of five categories: "satisfied," "somewhat satisfied," "neither satisfied nor dissatisfied," "somewhat dissatisfied," and "dissatisfied." Note that A not only refers to current pay but also refers to past history and future prospects on promotion within the firm. In effect, it asks whether the respondent's past and current effort has been fairly rewarded. Its content may largely be construed as pecuniary. B, C, and D, on the other hand, clearly refer to nonpecuniary attributes of the job.

Figure 1 shows for each questionnaire item the proportions of those workers in the sample as grouped by age whose response was either "satisfied" or "somewhat satisfied," and Figure 2 shows the same proportions for those whose response was either "dissatisfied" or "somewhat dissatisfied." (Hereinafter, the categories "satisfied" and "somewhat satisfied" are frequently aggregated and are simply termed "satisfied," and similarly for the categories "dissatisfied" and "somewhat dissatisfied," termed "dissatisfied."

Figures 1 and 2 may give the overall impression that the job satisfaction level of Japanese workers is on the whole high, especially with regard to nonpecuniary dimensions. However, the previously noted sampling bias in the distribution of respondents and the analysis below (Sections 4 and 5) jointly show that the bars of Figure 1 are overstated,

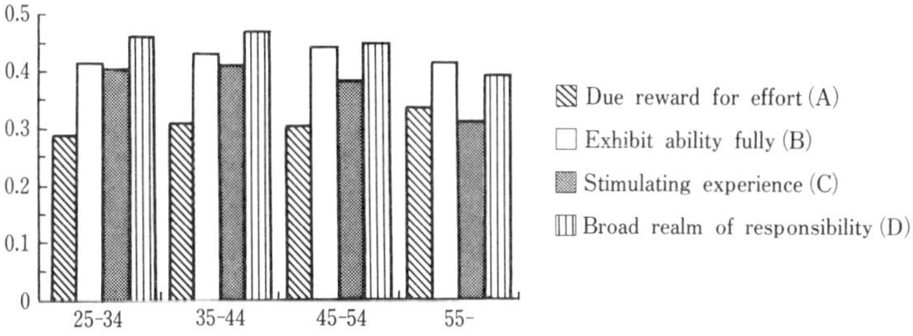

Figure 1. Satisfaction about job

NOTE: The height of each bar represents the proportion of individuals who responded "satisfied" or "somewhat satisfied."

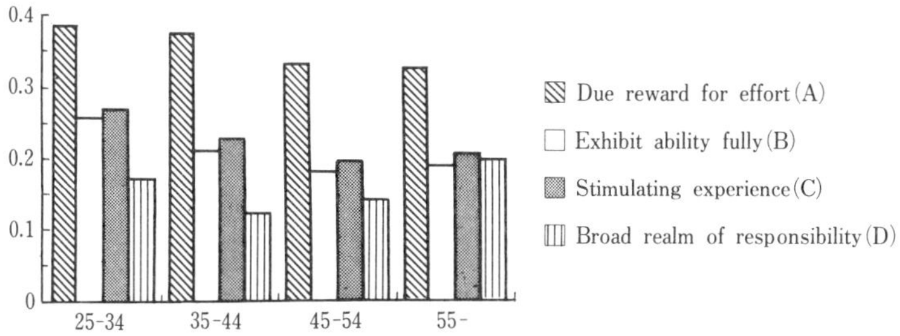

Figure 2. Dissatisfaction about job

NOTE: The height of each bar represents the proportion of individuals who responded "dissatisfied"or "somewhat dissatisfied".

while those of Figure 2 are understated. Hence it would be quite misleading to accept these absolute numbers at their face value.

Comparison of Figures 1 and 2 shows that, for each age group, the item for which the frequency of satisfaction exhibits the highest score is D (broadness of responsibility) while that exhibiting the lowest score is A (due reward for effort). B (exhibit ability fully) and C (stimulating) hold intermediate positions, and yet for each age group B gets a slightly higher frequency score than C. The frequency of workers expressing dissatisfaction on each of the four items also gradually declines with age, but for age 55 and over the tendency reverses itself, if not sharply. In particular, a significant rise occurs in the proportion of people who express dissatisfaction over D (broadness of responsibility). It is not difficult to imagine that mandatory retirement and other personnel practices that affect the older people's workplace rather drastically are the cause of such a reversal.

What, then, determines the workers' responses to the questions? What sort of correlations are present among the responses to four questions within each individual? In particular, does dissatisfaction on pecuniary rewards (A) tend to be compensated for by satisfaction on nonpecuniary rewards B, C, D (thus facilitating the "equalizing difference" argument) or do both tend to be assortative?

The first question will for now (pending the discussion in the concluding section) be answered as follows. Items A, B, C, and D all contain elements that depend on individuals' inherent framework of values and subjective valuation. Evaluation of "due reward for effort" obviously depends on what one regards as the proper concept of "effort" and then on what one considers a "fair reward." The judgment also seems likely to depend on one's observation of the "effort" expended by other workers in the local reference group.[8] Evaluation of whether or not the job allows one to "exhibit ability fully" depends much on how exactly one understands one's own ability, including one's potential. Evaluation of whether the job is "stimulating" or not is naturally influenced by one's perception of the gap between one's already achieved ability and one's potential ability. It is a well-established proposition in psychology that tasks that are far removed from an individual's potential ability are more painful than pleasant stimulation, while tasks that contribute little to developing one's potential ability are hopelessly boring.[9] Finally, evaluation of the "broadness of responsibility" depends much on how one sets out the appropriate context of responsibility for oneself.

The proposition that individuals' responses to items A, B, C, and D are intermediated by their respective frameworks of evaluation seems to be attested to by the fact that despite the existence of large differences in the shape of the distribution of hierarchical ranks (note that rank is clearly an important objective element influencing the amount of pecuniary as well as nonpecuniary rewards) between age groups (as seen in Fig. 3), the frequencies of satisfaction and dissatisfaction on all items as shown in Figures 1 and 2 do not differ much between age groups.

On the other hand, even if each individual has his/her own framework of reference it does not necessarily mean that it is distributed completely randomly over individuals. It is perhaps appropriate to construe as follows. Based on the levels of past learning and experience, individuals form certain expectations as to what constitutes a fair achievement level on each of the four items A, B, C, and D. "Effort" is then interpreted in a widest sense including not only highly motivated and attentive direct productive effort but also conscious deferral of leisure and accumulation of knowledge as well as affective capacity either in school or on the job. The fair achievement level thus com-

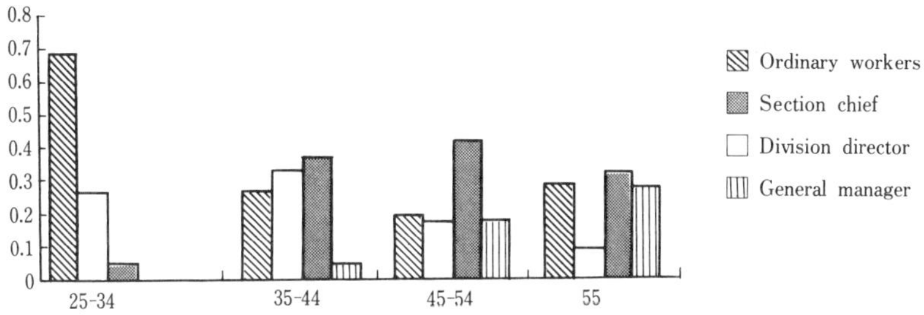

Figure 3. Distribution of hierarchical ranks among respondents

Table 3. Correlation among Various Job Satisfaction Indices[a]

	A	B	C	D
A	1.0	0.392	0.333	0.335[b]
B	(0.542)	1.0	0.536	0.472
C	(0.484)	(0.702)	1.0	0.487
D	(0.470)[b]	(0.627)	(0.635)	1.0

NOTES:
[a]The definition of job satisfaction indices is as follows:
A = Due reward for effort.
B = Exhibit ability fully.
C = Involves new challenge and stimulation.
D = Involves broad realm of responsibility.
[b]The measure of association in the upper-right box is the square root of Cramer's mean squared quotient. The figures in parentheses in the lower-left box are the ordinary correlation coefficients by regarding the satisfaction indices as continuous variables.

monly depends on an individual's level of schooling and occupational history, and one may safely suppose the existence of a relatively stable structure of evaluation among individuals.

Simultaneous to conceiving the fair achievement levels, individuals evaluate the achievement levels realized by their current job. And depending on the magnitude of the gap between the fair and realized levels, they form a judgment in terms of five category levels, "satisfied" through "dissatisfied." In sum, when the gap becomes sufficiently large, they express "dissatisfaction."

Turning to the second question, the categorical responses to each job satisfaction item have been assigned numerical values of 5 for "satisfied," 4 for "somewhat satisfied," 3 for "neither satisfied nor dissatisfied," 2 for "somewhat dissatisfied," and 1 for "dissatisfied." The extent of correlation among different items is then calculated using these numerical values. The figures in the upper-right corner of Table 3 give the square root of Cramer's mean squared quotient (i.e., a measure of association for discrete variables), while the figures in parentheses in the lower-left corner give the usual correlation coefficient (taking the numerical indices to be continuous variables). In terms of the squared root of mean square quotient, the correlations between A index and B, C, and D indices are around 0.3–0.4, while those among B, C, and D indices are around 0.5.[10]

The relatively high correlations among B, C, and D indices are naturally expected, for the amount and quality of information handled and the extent and realm of decision making normally go together in shaping up the objective job environment that commonly underlies the psychological mappings of B, C, and D indices. The positive correlations between A and B, C, D indices, on the other hand, provide *prima facie* evidence that pecuniary and nonpecuniary job rewards do not stand in a compensatory relationship. That is, those who are satisfied (dissatisfied) with the quality of the job are more likely to be simultaneously satisfied (dissatisfied) with pecuniary rewards than the reverse.

4. Determinants of Satisfaction with Respect to Due Rewards for Effort

Suppose that a fair level of reward as conceived by individuals in the light of their past and current experience can, for each age group, be expressed by a common linear function of education, duration of service (tenure in the firm), occupation, and commuting time. As the level of past effort is not directly measurable, education and duration of service are taken to be its proxy variables. They measure the cumulated time devoted to acquiring the general background knowledge and affective capacities and those that are specific to the firm. Furthermore, for some occupational types, past efforts to acquire abilities specific to the job are taken into consideration. Professional and technical jobs, management jobs, and skilled worker and production operative jobs are considered to belong to such categories. The length of commuting time is also regarded as one, if not major, dimension of effort. A statistical error term is further introduced to take account of any other influence that may not be directly measured by the above variables. Differences in the individuals' framework of values clearly constitute one of such influences.

On the other hand, the realized level of reward as perceived by a worker depends on education, duration of service, and occupational type. It is further influenced by the size of firm and industrial difference. The possibility that asset holding affects the worker's perception is also considered. Another possibility to examine is the influence of hierarchical ranks acting independently of the preceding variables.

Other nonmeasured influences are stacked in a separate statistical error term.

By following the framework of analysis discussed in the previous section, an individual's job satisfaction is supposed to depend on the magnitude of the gap between the realized level of reward and what is conceived as a fair level of reward. This gap, to be called the satisfaction score and denoted by y, is then expressed for individual i in each age group by

$$\begin{aligned} y_i = {} & b_0 + b_1 \text{ educ}_i + b_2 \text{ tenure}_i + b_3 \text{ sptech}_i + b_4 \text{ manage}_i + b_5 \text{ prod}_i \\ & + b_6 \text{ commtime}_i + b_7 \text{ net worth}_i + b_8 \text{ large}_i + b_9 \text{ small} \\ & + b_{10} \text{ manuf} + b_{11} \text{ util}_i + b_{12} \text{ transcom}_i + b_{13} \text{ wholret}_i \\ & + b_{14} \text{ finins}_i + b_{15} \text{ realest}_i + b_{16} \text{ service}_i + u_i \end{aligned} \tag{1}$$

In some parts of estimation, an additional term, b_{17} rank$_i$, is included. The explanatory variables are defined as follows:

educ = years of schooling, tenure = duration of service
sptech = dummy for professional and technical jobs
manage = dummy for managerial jobs
prod = dummy for skilled worker or production operative jobs
commtime = commuting time (1 for less than 30 minutes, . . . , 5 for more than 2 hours)
net worth = real and net financial wealth held in ¥10 million (the market value of golf club memberships included)
large = dummy for large firms with 1,000 or more employees
small = dummy for small firms with less than 100 employees
manuf = dummy for manufacturing (including mining) industry
util = dummy for utility industry
transcom = dummy for transportation and communications industry
wholret = dummy for wholesale and retail industry
finins = dummy for financial and insurance industry
realest = dummy for real estate industry
service = dummy for service industry
rank = hierarchical rank in the employed firm (1 for an ordinary worker, 2 for a section chief (*kakari-chō*) and equivalent, 3 for a director (*kachō*) and equivalent, and 4 for a general manager (*buchō*) and equivalent)

Dummy variables take the value 1 if the respondent belongs to the category in question, and take the value 0 otherwise.

The statistical error term u_i is defined as the difference between the two error terms defined earlier. The normalization assumption is that u_i takes 0 as its mean, and 1 for its variance. (This gives the scaling factor for the measurement of the satisfaction score discussed above.) It is further supposed that u_i is distributed normally.

Given the foregoing assumptions, the degree of satisfaction on each item can be analyzed in terms of an ordered probit model. Suppose that within each age group there are four threshold values $0, a_1, a_2, a_3$ $(0 < a_1 < a_2 < a_3)$ with respect to the satisfaction score y_i such that

⟨*domain of y*⟩	⟨*the response*⟩
$y_i < 0$	→ "dissatisfied"
$0 \leqq_i < a_1$	→ "somewhat dissatisfied"
$a_1 \leqq y_i < a_2$	→ "neither satisfied nor dissatisfied"
$a_2 \leqq y_i a_3$	→ "somewhat satisfied"
$a_3 \leqq y_i$	→ "satisfied"

The coefficients $b_0, \ldots, b_{16}$ (and b_{17}) and the unknown threshold values a_1, a_2, a_3 are then simultaneously estimated by the maximum likelihood method.[11] The coefficients b_j $(j = 1, 2, \ldots, 16, 17)$ express the size of the contribution of each factor on the satisfaction score. Among these coefficients b_1 through b_3 indicate the net contribution to satisfaction, which is defined as each factor's contribution to the realized level of reward net of its contribution to the fair level of reward.

When (1) is estimated for each age group and the results are contrasted with the result of a pooled estimation (whereby all age groups are pooled together), it is shown that the null hypothesis that the vector of coefficients $(b_0, \ldots, b_{16}, a_1, a_2, a_3)$ is the same for all age groups is not rejected (in terms of the likelihood ratio test).[12] Therefore, only the result of the pooled estimation will be discussed in the sequel. The estimation result is shown in Table 4.

It is perhaps easier to understand the implications of this result by looking at Figures 4 and 5. Figure 4 presents two curves. First, the upward sloping curve shows the relationship between the estimated deterministic part of the satisfaction score, hereinafter to be called xb-score, and the predicted probability value that an individual's response is either "somewhat satisfied" or "satisfied," i.e.,

$$Pr\{y_i \geqq \hat{a}_2\} = Pr\{u_i \geqq \hat{a}_2 - x_i\hat{b}\}$$
$$= 1 - F(\hat{a}_2 - x_i\hat{b})$$

where ˆ indicates the estimated value, $x_i\hat{b}$ is a vector notation for the deterministic part of the RHS of (1), and $F(\ )$ is the cumulative density

Table 4. Ordered Probit Regression Results on Pooled Data

	All ages (25–)	
	(1)	(2)
const.	1.100	1.013
	(0.150)	(0.151)
educ	−0.00151	−0.00169
	(0.00820)	(0.00838)
tenure	−0.00367	−0.0128
	(0.00224)	(0.00244)
sptech	−0.107	−0.130
	(0.0473)	(0.0474)
manage	0.364	0.199
	(0.0444)	(0.0478)
prod	−0.175	−0.0804
	(0.108)	(0.109)
commtime	−0.0332	−0.0358
	(0.0214)	(0.0214)
net worth	0.0222	0.0165
	(0.00399)	(0.00404)
large	0.357	0.438
	(0.0420)	(0.0429)
small	−0.203	−0.254
	(0.0647)	(0.0650)
manuf	−0.0915	−0.0442
	(0.0649)	(0.0652)
util	0.332	0.448
	(0.120)	(0.121)
transcom	−0.0107	0.0542
	(0.0795)	(0.0799)
wholret	−0.0925	−0.0824
	(0.0663)	(0.0664)
finins	0.389	0.403
	(0.0832)	(0.0834)
realest	−0.105	−0.139
	(0.155)	(0.155)
service	0.0502	0.0656
	(0.0702)	(0.0704)
rank	–	0.214
	–	(0.0229)
A1	0.885	0.895
	(0.0268)	(0.0271)
A2	1.738	1.760
	(0.0322)	(0.0326)
A3	3.133	3.177
	(0.0481)	(0.0488)
Diff. FS	0.560	0.692
	(0.0643)	(0.0660)
Diff. MF	0.481	0.447
	(0.0724)	(0.0726)
Num. of obs.	3,595	3,595
Log likelihood	−4,994.8	−4,950.7

NOTE: Dependent variable = satisfaction index A on due reward for effort.

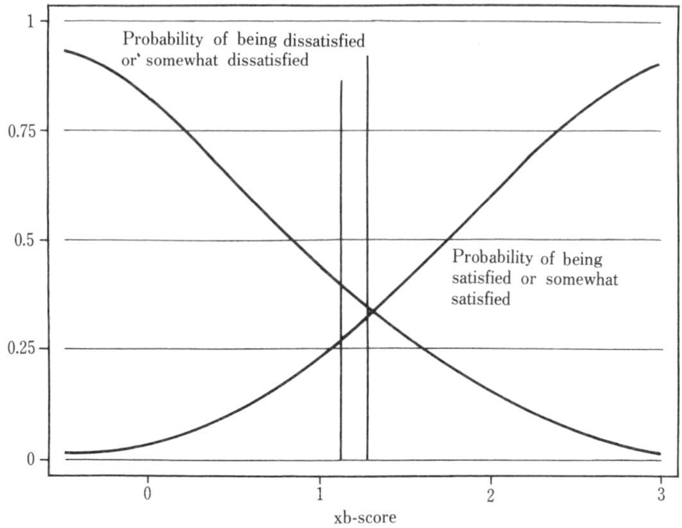

Figure 4. The relationship between xb-score and the probability of satisfaction with respect to due rewards for effort

function of a standard normal variable. Second, the downward sloping curve shows the relationship between the xb-score defined previously and the predicted probability value that the individual's response is either "somewhat dissatisfied" or "dissatisfied," i.e.,

$$\begin{aligned} Pr\{y_i < \hat{a}_1\} &= Pr\{u_i < \hat{a}_1 - x_i\hat{b}\} \\ &= F(\hat{a}_1 - x_i\hat{b}). \end{aligned}$$

Quite obviously from the specification (1), the higher is the xb-score on the horizontal axis, the higher is the probability of being satisfied and the lower is the probability of being dissatisfied. The predicted probability value along each curve can be reinterpreted, via the law of large numbers, as the proportion of workers having the same xb-score which responds as such. Among the two vertical lines, the right-hand one expresses the mean value of xb-score in the sample. The probability levels implied by the intersection points of this line with the two curves conceptually correspond to the bar graphs of Figures 1 and 2 (except that the former represents the mean values over four age groups).[13] The vertical line on the left-hand side will be explained later.

The horizontal bar chart of Figure 5, on the other hand, shows the estimated impact of a unit change in some selected variables on the xb-score. The horizontal axis represents a change in the xb-score. By

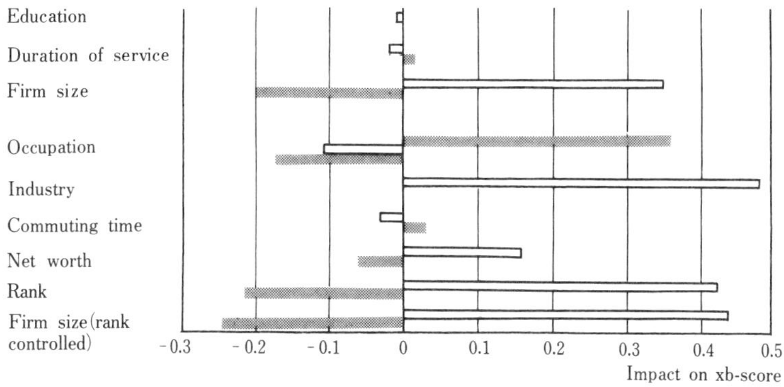

Figure 5. Determinants of job satisfaction with respect to due rewards for effort

NOTES: The standard of comparison and the unit change of each factor chosen to evaluate the impact on xb-score are as follows:

Factor	Upper bar (black)	Standard of comparison	Lower bar (white)
(1) Education	Junior high school graduate	High school graduate	College graduate
(2) Duration of service	5 years	10 years	15 years
(3) Firm size	Small (–99 employees)	Medium (100–999 employees)	Large (1000– employees)
(4) Occupation	Skilled worker/ produc. operat. (blue-collar)	White-collar (clerical, (sales and others)	Prof./technic. (white) managerial (grey)
(5) Industry	Manufacturing	Wholesale and retail	Finance and insurance
(6) Commuting time	–0.5 hour	0.5–1 hour	1–1.5 hours
(7) Net worth	Mean of bottom quartile (¥2.65 million)	Median (¥30 million)	Mean of top quartile (¥104.88 million)
(8) Rank	Ordinary worker	Section chief	General manager
(9) Firm size, rank controlled	Small	Medium	Large

The bars for (1)–(7) are drawn on the basis of estimated coefficients for equation (1) while the bars (8)–(9) are drawn on the basis of those for equation (1) with the addition of the rank variable.

looking at these bars simultaneously with Figure 4, prediction can be made as to how large a change in the probability of being satisfied or that of being dissatisfied the specified change in the explanatory variables would generate. Because of the non-linearity involved, the magnitude of the probability changes, in general, depends on where on the horizontal axis one measures from. Table 5 illustrates the numerical impact in question as measured from the calculated mean xb-score of the sample.

From Figure 5, the following characteristics are observed. First, the effects of schooling and duration of service are negligibly small. This

Table 5. The Relationship between the Deviation in xb-Score from Its Sample Mean and the Changes in the Probabilities of Satisfaction and Dissatisfaction (%)

Δxb-Score	−0.8	−0.6	−0.4	−0.2	+0.2	+0.4	+0.6	+0.8
Δ Probability of satisfaction	−21.7	−17.6	−12.8	−6.7	+7.8	+15.6	+23.3	+31.1
Δ Probability of dissatisfaction	+31.1	+23.3	+15.6	+7.8	−6.7	−12.8	−17.6	−21.7

SOURCE: Figure 4.

holds in spite of their importance as determinants of earnings and hierarchical ranks.[14] The most plausible interpretation of this result seems to be that an increase in schooling or duration of service not only raises the actual rewards but also raises the conceptual level of fair rewards. It is therefore consistent with the assumption that schooling and duration of service are proxies for individuals' past effort.

Second, the effects of commuting time and net worth are in the expected direction. Their quantitative significance, however, is relatively small. The coefficient of commuting time is not even statistically significant. The coefficient of net worth is statistically strongly significant (at the 1-percent level), yet the difference in xb-score generated by the top and bottom quartiles of the distribution of net worth (which may be identified as the haves and have-nots, respectively) is 0.23, amounting to relatively little in its effect on satisfaction (See Table 5.). One caveat is that the nonresponse rate on the net worth figure amounts to about a third of the total sample, which calls for a further examination to ascertain if such a magnitude of missing values might not generate a downward bias in the estimation of the net worth effect.

The estimated net worth coefficient provides an answer, if not a conclusive one, to the suspicion raised frequently recently that the widened gap in the distribution of wealth might be badly affecting the work motivation of Japanese workers. The answer from this study does not buttress this suspicion, at least as long as the wealth gap stands at the current level. Yet it does impart a warning that a further worsening in the distribution of wealth would possibly lead to deterioration of job satisfaction which, in view of the notion of job worth held by the great majority of workers, would lead to a decline in work motivation.

Third, among occupational types there are rather sizeable differences in the degree of job satisfaction concerning rewards for effort between managerial and blue-collar (skilled worker and production operatives) jobs and between managerial and professional or technical jobs. In terms of xb-score, the former amounts to 0.54 while the latter amounts to 0.47. The blue-collar and professional/technical workers indeed have relatively strong dissatisfaction about rewards for effort when compared with white-collar workers in general.[15]

Fourth, among the industrial categories there exists little difference between the manufacturing and the wholesale/retail sectors, yet there is a sizeable difference between these two industries and the finance/insurance sector. In terms of xb-score, the latter amounts to 0.48. (The estimated difference in the two coefficients $b_{14} - b_{10}$ together with its standard error is shown as "Diff. MF" near the bottom of Table 4.) Between the manufacturing and finance/insurance sectors there exists around 24–36 percent difference in annual wage earnings throughout age groups after controlling for schooling, duration of service, occupational types, and firm size, and such an earnings differential clearly lies in the background for such a big differential in satisfaction. (Further discussion is made in the concluding part of the paper.)

Fifth, concerning hierarchical ranks, there exists a large difference between a general manager and an ordinary worker. The xb-score differs by as much as 0.64. The fact that satisfaction is high among high-ranking workers and is low among low-ranking workers is not necessarily obvious, however. For, if each rank is paid what workers in that rank regard as fair and if promotion occurs in ways workers regard as fair, then a significant part of the difference in question must disappear. What would still remain is the dissatisfaction with respect to the scarcity of the opportunity for promotion and/or the hierarchical structure itself. It seems, therefore, that differences in satisfaction among different ranks reflect complaints that exist around the operation of personnel management inside firms.

Sixth, and finally, there appears to be a large difference among firms of different sizes in their capacity to generate job satisfaction.[16] Between large firms (with 1,000 or more employees) and small firms (with less than 100 employees) the xb-score differs by 0.56 (i.e., see "Diff. FS" ($= b_8 - b_9$) recorded near the bottom of Table 4). In Figure 5, there is another bar placed at the bottom, which represents the effect of firm size, this time controlling for the rank of the individual (thus corresponding to the estimates of column [2] of Table 4). This implies that, comparing among workers with the same rank, there is 0.64 difference in terms of xb-score between large and small firms. The gap of 0.08 that occurs depending on whether or not the rank is controlled arises mainly from the fact that the probability of assuming a higher position is larger in small firms than in large firms.[17]

Viewed from the opposite angle, even if small firms are more likely to promote individuals, the effect in reducing the job satisfaction differential between large and small firms is at most 13 percent (= 0.08/0.64). Naturally the existence of large wage-*cum*-nonwage benefit differentials between large and small firms lies at the heart of the matter.

It has been remarked earlier that there exists a significant underrepresentation of the manufacturing industry, blue-collar workers, and small firms in the current sample. Although by no means a fully justifiable procedure, a rough adjustment of the mean xb-score was made on the basis of column (1) estimates, using the mean schooling and duration of service figures and the industrial, firm size, and white-collar/blue-collar composition figures of the 1990 Census of Wages data. The result is shown as the left-hand side vertical line in Figure 4. Adjusted figures show that individuals who are not satisfied with respect to the fairness of reward are indeed much larger in proportion than those who are satisfied.

5. Determinants of Job Satisfaction with Respect to Nonpecuniary Qualities

What about the satisfaction indices B (exhibit ability fully), C (stimulating), and D (broadness of responsibility)? As shown in Section 3, there exist relatively high correlations among these indices. In fact, the ordered probit analyses for the respective indices (conducted separately for each age group) have arrived at qualitatively very similar results. This implies that the explanatory variables at hand have quite analogous effects on each of the three nonpecuniary dimensions of job satisfaction.[18] In the following, the nonpecuniary attributes of the job will be represented by index C, namely whether or not the job provides challenge and stimulating experiences.

Basically, the same model as in the case of satisfaction on due rewards for effort is employed. The only modification is that of excluding the variables "commtime" and "net worth" as they seem irrelevant to the question of challenge and stimulating experience on the job. The results of estimation are given in Table 6.

Figures 6 and 7 are depicted for each age group on the basis of estimated coefficients in Table 6. Considering the two vertical lines in Figure 6, the right-hand one shows the unadjusted mean of the xb-score, while the left-hand one shows its adjusted mean explained previously. The size of adjustment is largest among the age group 25–34.

The impact of each factor on the xb-score is summarized by Figure 7 (prepared analogously to Figure 5), this time drawn for each age group. It is apparent that certain features differ significantly among age groups.[19]

First, while the net impact of schooling and duration of service on satisfaction is negligible (just as in the case of satisfaction on due rewards), there is a single exception to the rule, i.e., the effect of schooling for age group 25–34, which is positive and statistically significant. Between high school and college graduates, the xb-score differs as much as 0.27. Note also that the rank variable is not statistically significant for this age group. These results imply that, in the life stage during which promotion is not yet a major concern, schooling differentials play a leading role in allocating individuals to jobs with rich learning opportunities that, in turn, facilitate the major source of challenge and stimulation.

Second, observing among different industries, the advantage of the finance/insurance industry over the manufacturing industry, noted previously in the case of satisfaction on due rewards, still holds for the young age group (aged 25–34) as the xb-score differential reaches 0.6 (See "Diff. MF" coefficient at the bottom of Table 6.). The advantage of the finance/insurance industry, however, declines monotonically with age. For the age group 45–54, it effectively disappears, and for the age group 55 and above the tendency is the reverse: it is now the manufacturing industry that has the advantage (0.34 in xb-score, although not statistically significant).[20] It is to be remarked that these features also hold for B and D indices. This result indicates that the finance/insurance industry, while maintaining comparative advantage in terms of rewards for effort, does not succeed in maintaining comparative advantage in the long run over the intrinsic quality of the job. Alternatively speaking, some form of a compensating relationship in the lifetime between pecuniary and nonpecuniary rewards is operating among a certain subset of industries.

The foregoing discussion has dealt with characteristics that are specific to age. Another point that is characteristic of nonpecuniary qualities of the job (vis-à-vis pecuniary rewards) is the place occupied by professional/technical workers. It has already been noted that these jobs are positioned close to blue-collar workers in terms of satisfaction on pecuniary rewards, yet with respect to the existence of challenging and stimulating experience they are positioned close to managerial jobs. The advantage of professional/technical jobs over blue-collar jobs in terms of xb-score amounts to 0.35–0.4 for the age groups up to 45–54, and then jumps to 0.68 for the age group 55 and above, far surpassing that of managerial jobs. Therefore, more than any other type of job, workers with this type of job continue to receive stimulating experience even when they become older.

Concerning the impact of firm size, a similar feature to the case of

Table 6. Ordered Probit Regression Results on Data for Each Age Group

	Age 25–34		Age 35–44		Age 45–54		Age 55–	
	(1)	(2)	(1)	(2)	(1)	(2)	(1)	(2)
const.	−0.165	−0.178	1.256	1.185	1.149	1.0182	1.126	1.0606
	(0.354)	(0.354)	(0.214)	(0.214)	(0.205)	(0.206)	(0.279)	(0.282)
educ	0.0681	0.0659	0.00141	−0.0183	0.0116	−0.0157	0.00939	−0.000098
	(0.0197)	(0.0198)	(0.0112)	(0.0116)	(0.0111)	(0.0118)	(0.0176)	(0.0185)
tenure	−0.000477	−0.00299	−0.00338	−0.0107	−0.00403	−0.00968	−0.00349	−0.00440
	(0.00957)	(0.00998)	(0.00453)	(0.00466)	(0.00364)	(0.00374)	(0.00391)	(0.00395)
sptech	0.215	0.213	0.166	0.157	0.214	0.202	0.575	0.533
	(0.0784)	(0.0784)	(0.0622)	(0.0623)	(0.0781)	(0.0783)	(0.138)	(0.140)
manage	0.236	0.212	0.309	0.176	0.272	0.102	0.292	0.196
	(0.115)	(0.119)	(0.0587)	(0.0619)	(0.0634)	(0.0681)	(0.110)	(0.125)
prod	−0.196	−0.198	−0.188	−0.107	−0.148	−0.0106	−0.0980	−0.0709
	(0.202)	(0.202)	(0.131)	(0.132)	(0.127)	(0.129)	(0.257)	(0.258)
large	0.294	0.302	0.230	0.285	0.353	0.425	0.162	0.179
	(0.0754)	(0.0759)	(0.0552)	(0.0558)	(0.0639)	(0.0649)	(0.119)	(0.120)
small	−0.104	−0.109	−0.151	−0.177	−0.0543	−0.129	−0.0144	−0.0127
	(0.113)	(0.113)	(0.0844)	(0.0846)	(0.0909)	(0.0918)	(0.130)	(0.130)
manuf	0.200	0.203	0.176	0.207	0.214	0.290	0.172	0.209
	(0.119)	(0.119)	(0.0853)	(0.0856)	(0.102)	(0.103)	(0.182)	(0.183)
util	0.256	0.267	0.208	0.311	0.183	0.321	0.138	0.207
	(0.206)	(0.207)	(0.167)	(0.168)	(0.184)	(0.185)	(0.343)	(0.346)
transcom	0.111	0.117	−0.172	−0.111	−0.0790	0.0443	−0.121	−0.0864
	(0.155)	(0.155)	(0.103)	(0.103)	(0.113)	(0.115)	(0.200)	(0.201)
wholret	0.423	0.417	0.101	0.0901	0.318	0.354	0.232	0.253
	(0.122)	(0.122)	(0.0851)	(0.0852)	(0.106)	(0.106)	(0.189)	(0.189)
finins	0.801	0.790	0.400	0.376	0.253	0.327	−0.171	−0.130
	(0.150)	(0.150)	(0.109)	(0.109)	(0.144)	(0.145)	(0.297)	(0.298)

Table 6 – continued

realest	0.374	0.346	−0.216	−0.249	0.643	0.763	0.065	0.0739
	(0.230)	(0.233)	(0.223)	(0.224)	(0.301)	(0.302)	(0.293)	(0.293)
service	0.105	0.0998	0.0321	0.0121	0.349	0.409	−0.00248	0.0244
	(0.124)	(0.124)	(0.0912)	(0.0914)	(0.115)	(0.116)	(0.172)	(0.173)
rank	–	0.0496	–	0.218	–	0.235	–	0.0832
	–	(0.0560)	–	(0.0314)	–	(0.0342)	–	(0.0508)
A1	0.682	0.683	0.790	0.802	0.835	0.851	0.690	0.692
	(0.0445)	(0.0445)	(0.0389)	(0.0395)	(0.0502)	(0.0511)	(0.0738)	(0.0740)
A2	1.552	1.553	1.734	1.758	1.992	2.027	1.981	1.986
	(0.0550)	(0.0550)	(0.0459)	(0.0466)	(0.0587)	(0.0599)	(0.0936)	(0.0939)
A3	2.900	2.902	3.124	3.165	3.386	3.444	3.178	3.187
	(0.0751)	(0.0751)	(0.0605)	(0.0614)	(0.0751)	(0.0767)	(0.123)	(0.123)
Diff. FS	0.398	0.411	0.381	0.462	0.407	0.554	0.177	0.192
	(0.116)	(0.116)	(0.0847)	(0.0856)	(0.0939)	(0.0965)	(0.145)	(0.145)
Diff. MF	0.601	0.586	0.224	0.170	0.0387	0.0374	−0.343	−0.339
	(0.128)	(0.129)	(0.0969)	(0.0974)	(0.125)	(0.125)	(0.278)	(0.278)
Num. of obs.	1181	1181	2067	2067	1593	1593	522	522
Log likelihood	−1653.1	−1652.7	−2813.6	−2789.4	−2052.7	−2029.1	−680.6	−679.3

NOTE: Dependent variable = satisfaction index C on stimulating experience.

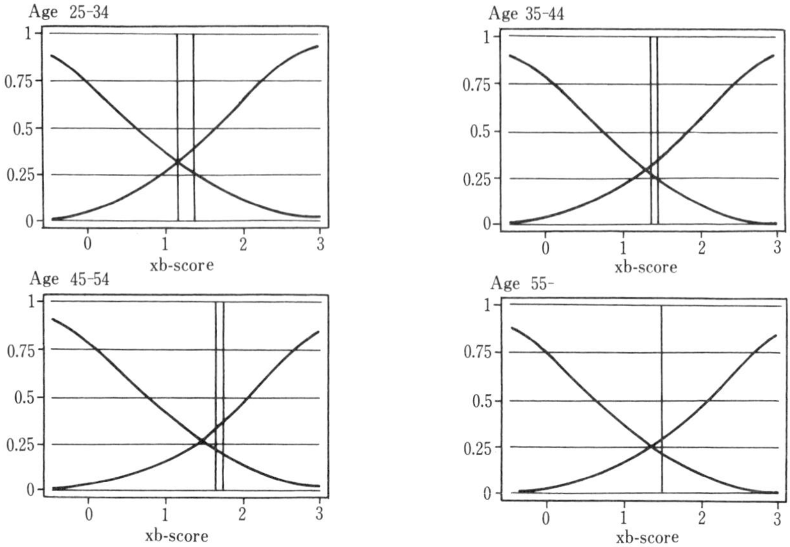

Figure 6. The relationship between xb-score and the probability of satisfaction with respect to the existence of stimulating experience on the job

NOTE: In each figure, the upward-sloping curve represents the probability of being satisfied or somewhat satisfied, while the downward-sloping curve represents the probability of being dissatisfied or somewhat dissatisfied.
SOURCE: Table 6.

pecuniary rewards is observed, except that its effect diminishes for the age group 55 and above. There is a sizeable difference (0.3–0.4 in terms of xb-score) between large and small firms in their capacity to generate satisfaction about stimulating experience among workers and, moreover, such a difference does not diminish much even if the relative ease of being promoted in small firms is taken into account.

6. Concluding Remarks

This study has analyzed the determinants of job satisfaction among Japanese workers by using micro survey data on worker attitudes collected in three major metropolitan areas of Japan. More specifically, the paper has examined how workers' job satisfaction relates to such factors as education, job tenure in the firm, industry, occupation, firm size, and wealth holding.

Job satisfaction has been considered in two dimensions; first, how the worker's effort is rewarded in terms of pay and promotion, and second, how stimulating an experience the job provides. The former may bc regarded as largely, though not exclusively, pecuniary, while the latter concerns an intrinsic or a nonpecuniary quality of the job. In fact, the latter is taken to represent two other nonpecuniary qualities of the job explored in the survey, whether or not the job allows the worker fully to exhibit his/her ability and whether or not the job allows the holder to exercise a broad realm of responsibility. The major findings of the paper are as follows.

First, on both pecuniary and nonpecuniary dimensions the difference in firm size has notable impact on the degree of satisfaction. The advantage of large firms does not diminish even if the tendency (confirmed within the data) for workers in small firms to be promoted more easily than their counterparts in large firms is taken into consideration.

Second, as compared with ordinary white-collar (clerical, sales, and service) jobs, blue-collar jobs are clearly at a disadvantage on both dimensions of job satisfaction. Against the same standard, professional/technical jobs have an advantage with respect to nonpecuniary qualities (whose extent increases as workers become older) but are at a disadvantage with respect to (satisfaction with) pecuniary rewards. This appears to be one of the very few cases in the data for which something close to the principle of equalizing difference is operating.

Third, industrywise, there exists a significant difference in the degree of satisfaction concerning pecuniary rewards between the manufacturing and wholesale/retail industries, on the one hand, and the finance/insurance industry, on the other. Yet, with respect to the capacity of providing stimulating experience (and other nonpecuniary qualities) the relative advantage of the finance/insurance industry declines quickly with age, and it may even turn into a disadvantage for workers in the older age group.

Fourth, even though the levels of education and firm job-tenure certainly enhance wage earnings and the chances of getting to a higher rank, they have virtually no effect at all on workers' job satisfaction in both dimensions. (The single exception is the effect of education on young workers' feeling of stimulating experience on the job.) Such discrepancy in the results may be explained by the simultaneous rise in the levels of rewards (in both dimensions) that workers consider as fair and those that they actually receive.

Fifth, there exists a statistically significant wealth effect on the degree of satisfaction concerning pecuniary rewards, yet quantitatively its effect is a relatively mild one. Therefore, the acute rise in the skewness of wealth distribution that Japan experienced recently has yet to affect the work motivation of individuals seriously, in particular, the young workers who do not own land in the urban area. The present result does facilitate a conclusion, however, to the effect that a further worsening in the dispersion of wealth distribution might possibly adversely

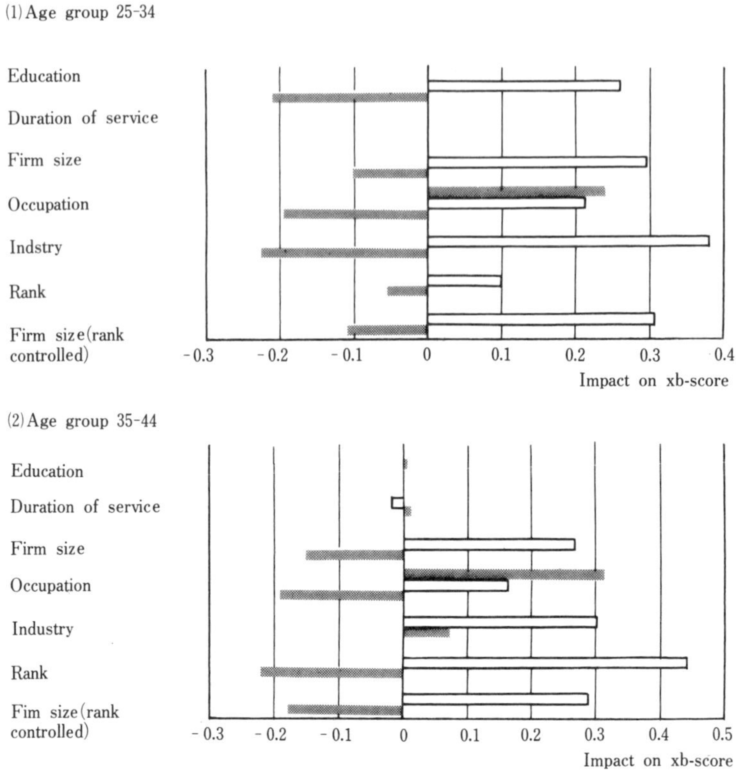

Figure 7. Determinants of job satisfaction with respect to the existence of stimulating experience on the job

NOTE: The standard of comparison and the unit change in each explanatory factor is identical with that of Figure 5. The commuting time and net worth variables have been excluded from the set of explanatory variables.

affect the motivation of workers as a whole by increasing the number of workers who feel that they are not paid a fair reward.

So much for the findings. Overall, one may be inclined to point out a paradox. The paradox is that workers in the manufacturing sector (blue-collar workers, in particular, but not limited to them), which boasts of internationally renowned productivity and quality of products, exhibit relatively low scores in terms of job satisfaction, or to be more precise, high incidence of worker dissatisfaction about the job on both pecuniary and nonpecuniary grounds. The manufacturing sector in Japan is also associated with an intricate network of small subsidiary firms, and the smallness of firm size is shown to be an additional factor contributing to the incidence of worker dissatisfaction.

(3) Age group 45–54

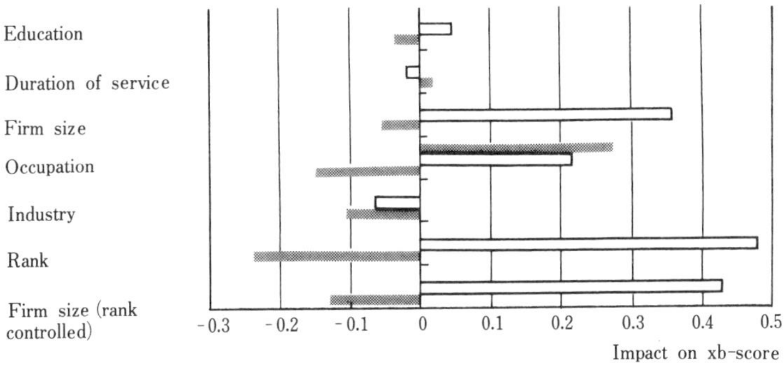

(4) Age group 55–

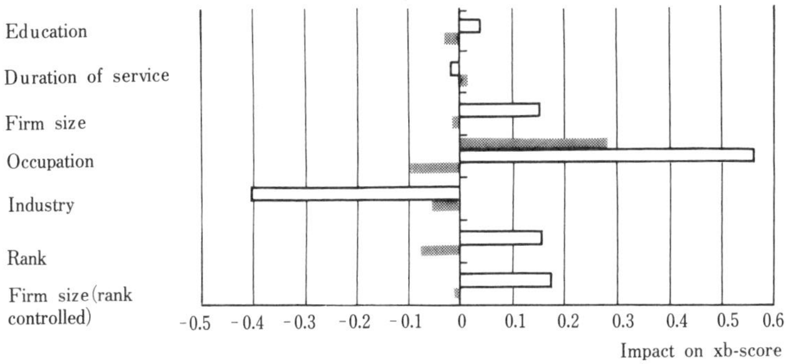

It is perhaps not far-fetched to relate such high incidence of dissatisfaction to the existence of the dualistic division in the labor market that is most heavily enmeshed in the manufacturing industry.

A parallel study by the author based on the micro dataset of the Census of Wages and employing the methodology of switching regressions (as applied by Dickens and Lang, 1985) has delineated the existence of a clear dualistic wage structure in the overall Japanese labor market. One component, the primary sector, is represented by an earnings equation with high rates of return to both education and experience (both internal and external) and is generally associated with high wages, while the other component, the secondary sector, is represented by an earnings equation with almost no returns to education and external experience but with a moderate rate of return on internal experience and yet is generally characterized by low wages and relatively long working hours. The moderate rate of return on internal experience is not much of a blessing for secondary sector workers, for either voluntarily or involuntarily they tend to move among firms frequently, thereby losing the opportunity to reap any benefit. Incidence of the secondary sector turned out to be particularly high in the manufacturing industry, and especially among the blue-collar jobs. As the secondary sector job is associated with little learning opportunities, such workers may also naturally feel discontent with respect to the nonpecuniary qualities of the job.[21]

One general implication of this study concerning worker welfare, and more specifically for enriching the lifelong quality of work life for Japanese workers, might be to raise the specialty content of the job.[22] It would be particularly helpful to older workers. In terms of practice, however, it may not be so simple, for it would certainly require a major reappraisal and restructuring of the personnel management system. More specifically, examination of possible tradeoffs that such a modification in job content would entail, e.g., deteriorating breadth of knowledge held by workers, must be made. In any case, in an increasingly aging society like Japan, such a reappraisal would certainly be a welcome move on the part of workers, and it might even facilitate a profitable source of organizational innovation for employers.

This study concludes by pointing out two qualifications of the present analysis. The first concerns the limitation of the data. Because of the sampling design, attitudes of workers employed in very small firms (with less than 30 employees) are not considered, and because of the smallness of the samples female workers have been excluded from the analysis. Yet as far as the excluded female samples are concerned, they tend to exhibit a higher incidence of job dissatisfaction than male counterparts, which accords well with the popular expectation. It is also unfortunate that the survey lacks data on working hours. One of the main dependent variables, rewards for effort, could have been analyzed much further had there been information on working hours.

The second qualification pertains to the basic methodology adopted in the analysis. The point is that there may be an alternative interpretation to the respondents' answer of "neither satisfied nor dissatisfied" concerning job satisfaction indices. A fairly large proportion of workers actually chose that answer. The interpretation adopted in this study has been that the size of the gap between the fair and the realized levels of reward for an individual with that particular answer lies in between the range generating satisfaction and the range registering complaint. It is based on the presumption that all individuals have a considered opinion and evaluation of their jobs when they are given a questionnaire. Without such preparation, however, individuals may simply refuse or avoid answering the question that delves deeply into their identity by taking the choice "neither satisfied nor dissatisfied." Although the estimation results (Tables 4 and 6) indicate consistency of the data with the present interpretation (cf. the meaningfulness of the boundary coefficients), it does not necessarily mean that the alternative interpretation is foreclosed by the data.

The distinction of well-considered responses from those that are not certainly requires a more refined design of the questionnaire form. A more refined survey should also contain questions on the possible concrete sources of job satisfaction (like the ones collected by Lincoln and Kalleberg), the lack of which has led the present study to rest at a rather superficial level of relating job satisfaction to the observable environment of employment.

Notes

I would like to thank Kuramitsu Muramatsu, Motohiro Morishima, and Mari Sako as well as other participants of the conference for helpful discussions, and Paul Ryan, Atsushi Seike, and Hiroshi Yoshikawa for valuable comments and criticism on earlier versions of the paper. I would also like to thank Yoshie Ohta and her staff at the Ministry of Labour for not only permitting me to use the data but also conducting a special inquiry to improve a portion of it. Finally, I would like to acknowledge the financial support provided by the Tokyo Center for Economic Research under its project entitled The Problem of Human Resources and Their Future Perspectives in Japan.

1. Discussion of the distribution of such subjective scores as whether or not "expectation" is "fulfilled" obviously faces, in principle, the difficulty known as interpersonal utility comparisons. Yet as long as individual differences in preferences are random and are statistically independent of the observable individual attributes and characteristics of the workplace that are chosen as the explanatory variables of the present analysis, it can be examined whether or not there exists stable dependence of "satisfaction" on the variables just listed. This constitutes the major presumption of the analysis below.

2. For an overall discussion of the findings from the survey, see Ministry of Labour (1991a).

3. The classic works in the fields of industrial sociology, industrial psychology, and labor management and control include Blauner (1964), Whyte (1995), and Edwards (1979), respectively.

4. Lincoln and Kalleberg (1990). This includes a useful survey of the existing literature on work commitment and job satisfaction in Japan (See pp. 53–62.). I am indebted to Mari Sako for informing me of the existence of this work.

5. Another major purpose of Lincoln and Kalleberg's study not mentioned in the text is comparison of work attitudes between Japanese workers and American workers, for which they have conducted a similar survey in the city of Indianapolis. Interested readers are also referred to this portion of their study.

6. Respondents were frequently found to err about knowledge of the size of the firm they worked in. (This became apparent when several individuals who belonged to the same establishment answered differently about firm size.) After weeding out all the questionable responses, the author requested the Ministry of Labour to investigate the correct size of the firm; they then kindly tracked down all the names of the establishments to which questionable samples belonged and obtained the correct figures of firm size by using their own records of establishments. Corrected firm size figures are employed throughout the analysis reported in this paper.

Another difficulty with the data was that missing values appeared frequently concerning the value of real wealth holding. In cases where information on the date and method of acquisition (either through new purchase or through inheritance) is obtained, the missing values are estimated by assigning the mean value of the real assets having similar physical attributes in the respective area (Tokyo, Nagoya, or Osaka).

Finally, nonresponses with respect to the ownership of golf club memberships were identified as zero holding.

7. This aspect on job worth seems quite independent of the frequently discussed changes in the importance that workers attach to family or individual leisure life as compared with life at work or life in an organization. Across age cohorts, young workers are observed to show relatively more concern on the former. This aspect of changes in worker consciousness is surveyed and discussed in Ieuji (1986: 6–14) and Ministry of Labour (1991b). Also Muramatsu (1992), in a survey on white-collar workers in the automobile and automobile parts industries in the Nagoya area, notes the simultaneous existence of the tendency for the value orientation toward family life to increase among the young workers and the tendency for the feeling of the necessity of job worth (i.e., meaningfulness of the job) to remain constant across the age groups, which seems to support the hypothesis that the two facets of valuation are independent (See Muramatsu, 1992: 60–61.).

8. The author is indebted to a comment by Paul Ryan with regard to the ambiguity of the meaning of "effort" used in an earlier version of the paper.

9. See Scitovsky (1992: 34–35), in particular the discussion on the Wundt curve.

10. The Mantel–Haenszel chi-square statistics obtained indicate that the null hypothesis that there exists a linear relationship between any two of B, C, and D indices is rejected by a wide margin. Hence, there is no reason to suppose that these indices are substantively identical. On the other hand, it will later be stated (see note 18 below) that the model in this paper is not powerful enough to be able to delineate the causes of different responses to each of these indices.

11. For a more detailed explanation about the estimation method, see Maddala (1983: 46–49).

12. In fact, in terms of the likelihood ratio test, the null hypothesis that all the coefficients are identical among four different age groups was not rejected, with the chi-square test statistic equalling 42.22 with 60 degrees of freedom.

13. When compared with Figures 1 and 2, the calculated value of the satisfaction probability tends to be underestimated. This discrepancy results from the exclusion of those samples with missing values on net worth in the regression procedure. The excluded samples amounted to 1,831 in the total sample size of 5,519.

14. For annual wage earnings the rates of return on schooling and job tenure in the firm are estimated as follows. The explanatory variables in the log-earnings equations are identical with those in equation (1), with controls on firm size, occupation, and industry:

Age group	25–34	35–44	45–54	55–
Schooling (%)	4.6	2.9	3.2	3.7
Job tenure (%)	3.4	0.9	0.8	1.6

All of these coefficients are statistically significant at the 1-percent level.

The next figures represent the estimated coefficients on the same set of variables when an ordered probit model is applied to the individual's position in the hierarchy (with the numerical assignment of 4 for a general manager, 3 for a division director, 2 for a section chief, and 1 for an ordinary worker) whereby firm-size dummies are included as the other explanatory variables:

Age group	25–34	35–44	45–54	55–
Schooling	0.152	0.177	0.208	0.181
Job tenure	0.131	0.0476	0.0335	0.0112

These figures express the impact of each variable on the xb-score, just as in the main text. The effect of job tenure is thus found monotonically to decline with age, while that of schooling is found to stand still. All the coefficients are statistically significant at the 1-percent level.

15. The estimated coefficients of occupational dummies in the log earnings functions reported in note 14 above are as follows:

Age group	25–35	35–44	45–54	55–
Professional/Technical	−0.0220	0.0265	0.000505	0.165
	(0.0207)	(0.0162)	(0.0231)	(0.0624)
Managerial	0.0358	0.140	0.133	0.262
	(0.0308)	(0.0150)	(0.0186)	(0.0523)
Skilled/Production	0.0249	−0.112	−0.112	0.0582
	(0.0786)	(0.037)	(0.0424)	(0.132)

The figures in parentheses are standard errors. The base of the occupational dummies is taken to be a white-collar occupation other than the three categories listed above.

16. A statistically significant positive effect of plant size on worker job satisfaction (as well as on workers' feeling of commitment toward work) has also been found (See Lincoln and Kalleberg, 1990: 228, Table 8.1.).

17. In fact, the coefficients of firm size dummies in the ordered probit equations described in note 14 above are:

Age group	25–34	35–44	45–54	55–
Large firms	−0.394	−0.342	−0.336	−0.273
Small firms	0.182	0.118	0.422	−0.0106

where the base of firm size is taken to be the medium-sized firm with 100–999 regular employees. The coefficients for large firms are all statistically significant at the 1-percent level, whereas for small firms only the estimate for the age group 45–54 is statistically significant at the 1-percent level.

18. This also highlights the limitation of the present data. Had it contained information on objective job characteristics, such as that collected by Lincoln and Kalleberg, differences in the responses to the three items of nonpecuniary attributes could have been analyzed further.

19. In fact, the likelihood ratio test similar to the one described in note 12 above conducted on B, C, and D indices, respectively, has shown that, in each case, the null hypothesis of identical coefficients among different age groups is rejected at the 1-percent significance level.

20. One possible explanation for the reversal of the coefficient in the finance industry may be that workers there tend to move to subsidiary or related firms from their late 40s so that few workers in high-ranking positions remain in the sample for the age group 55 and above. As a matter of fact, the sample counts of this particular group of workers turned out to be only 19, which no doubt explains the statistical weakness of the estimate. Yet the composition of these 19 samples in terms of the hierarchical position occupied turned out to be 7 general managers, 1 division director, 1 section chief and 9 ordinary workers, and 1 unknown. Therefore, the above conjecture does not seem to hold.

21. The switching regression results referred to in the text are reported in Ishikawa and Dejima (1993). For the pioneering contribution applying this methodology in the context of a U.S. study, see Dickens and Lang (1985: 792–805).

22. See the proposal made in Seike (1992).

References

Blauner, R. 1964. Alienation and Freedom: The Factory Worker and His Industry. Chicago: University of Chicago Press.

Dickens, W., and K. Lang. 1985. A test of dual labor market theory. American Economic Review 75 (Sept.).

Edwards, R. 1979. Contested Terrain: The Transformation of thc Workplace in the Twentieth Century. New York: Basic Books.

Ieuji, Y. 1986. Jakunensō no kinrō ishiki no henka to kigyō keiei (Changes in the Work Consciousness of the Young and Firm Management). Rōdō Tōkei Chōsa Geppō 38 (June): 6–14.

Ishikawa. T., and T. Dejima. 1993. Measuring the extent and nature of duality in the Japanese labour market. Paper presented at the International Workshop Europe, Japan and the United States: Technological Progress and Financial Structure (Turin, 1–3 April). The Japanese version appeared in T. Ishikawa, ed., Nihon no Shotoku to Tomi no Bunpai (Distribution of Income and Wealth in Japan). Tokyo: University of Tokyo Press, 1994.

Lincoln, J.R., and A.L. Kalleberg. 1990. Culture, Control and Commitment: A Study of Work Organization and Work Attitudes in the United States and Japan. Cambridge: Cambridge University Press.

Maddala, G.S. 1983. Limited-Dependent and Qualitative Variables in Econometrics. Cambridge: Cambridge University Press.

Ministry of Labour. 1991a. Shisan Kakusa to Kinrōsha Seikatsu ni kansuru Kenkyūkai Hōkokusho (The Report of the Research Group on Wealth Dispersion and Worker Life) (Aug.).

———. 1991b. Gendai Wakamono no Shokugyō Ishiki: Shokugyō Ishiki no Henka ni Taiō suru tameni (Occupational Consciousness of the Contemporary Young) (Sept.).

Muramatsu, K. 1992. White collar no hatarakigai to nōryoku shugi (Job Meaningfulness for White-Collar Workers and Meritocracy), Nanzan Keizai Kenkyū 7 (Oct.): 60–61.

Scitovsky, J. 1992. The Joyless Economy: The Psychology of Human Satisfaction. 2nd ed. New York: Oxford University Press.

Seike, A. 1992. Kōreisha no Rōdō Keizaigaku (The Labor Economics of the Elderly). Tokyo: Tōyō Keizai.

Whyte, W.F. 1955. Money and Motivation: An Analysis of Incentives in Industry. New York: Harper & Row.

Index